My Little Monster

7

Robico

CONTENTS

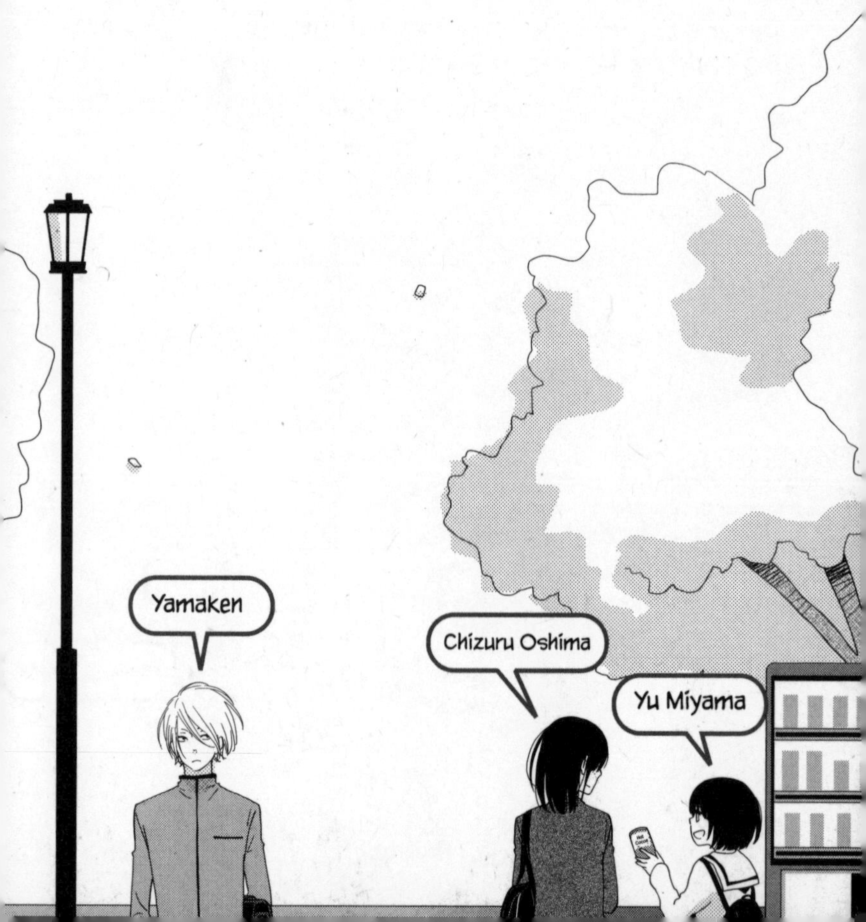

Yamaken
Chizuru Oshima
Yu Miyama

STORY

When Shizuku Mizutani does a favor for problem child Haru Yoshida, who sits next to her in school, he develops a huge crush on her. Attracted to his innocence, she eventually falls for him, too, but when she asks him out, he inexplicably turns her down. Shizuku temporarily locks away her romantic feelings. Then she starts to change by facing people more assertively, and she tells Haru again that she likes him. Her confession goes right over his head this time, but when Haru visits her house on Valentine's Day, which also happens to be her birthday, Shizuku's love for him grows, and she boldly confesses her feelings for him one more time. It should have gotten through to him this time, but...?

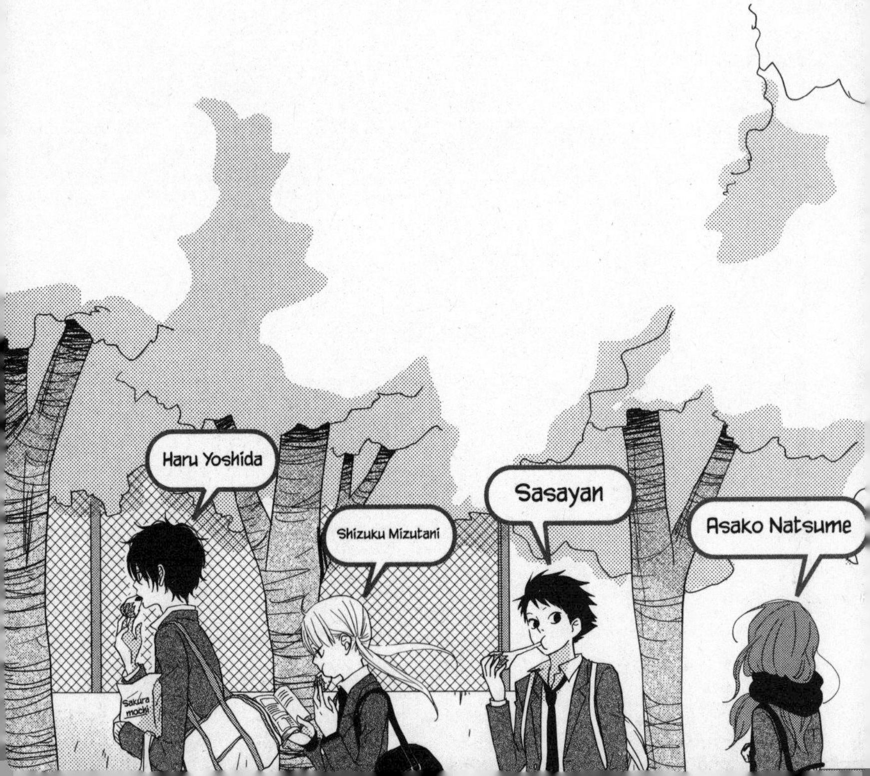
Asako Natsume
Sasayan
Shizuku Mizutani
Haru Yoshida
Sakura mochi

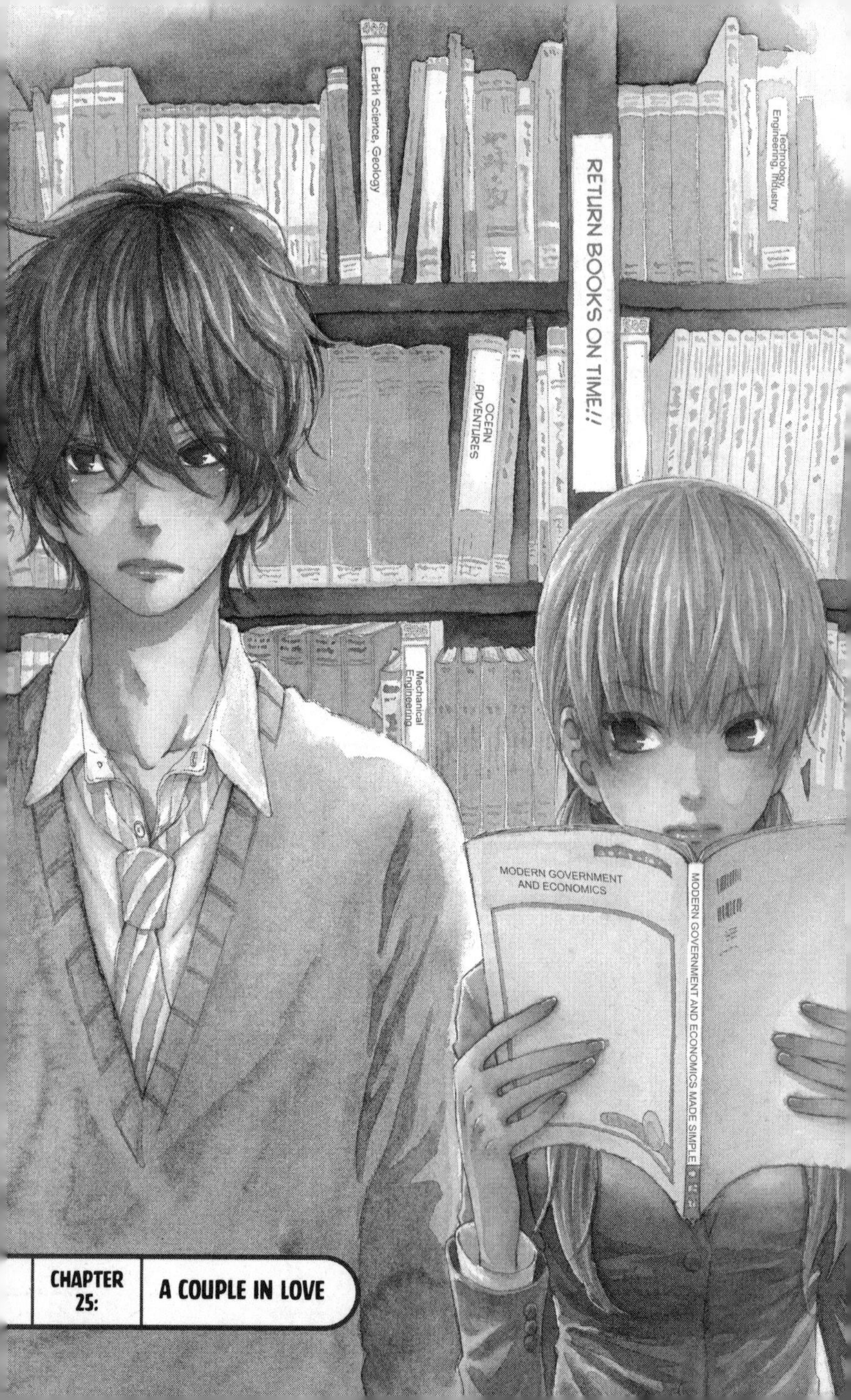
Earth Science, Geology
RETURN BOOKS ON TIME!!
Technology, Engineering, Industry
OCEAN ADVENTURES
Mechanical Engineering
MODERN GOVERNMENT AND ECONOMICS
MODERN GOVERNMENT AND ECONOMICS MADE SIMPLE
CHAPTER 25:
A COUPLE IN LOVE

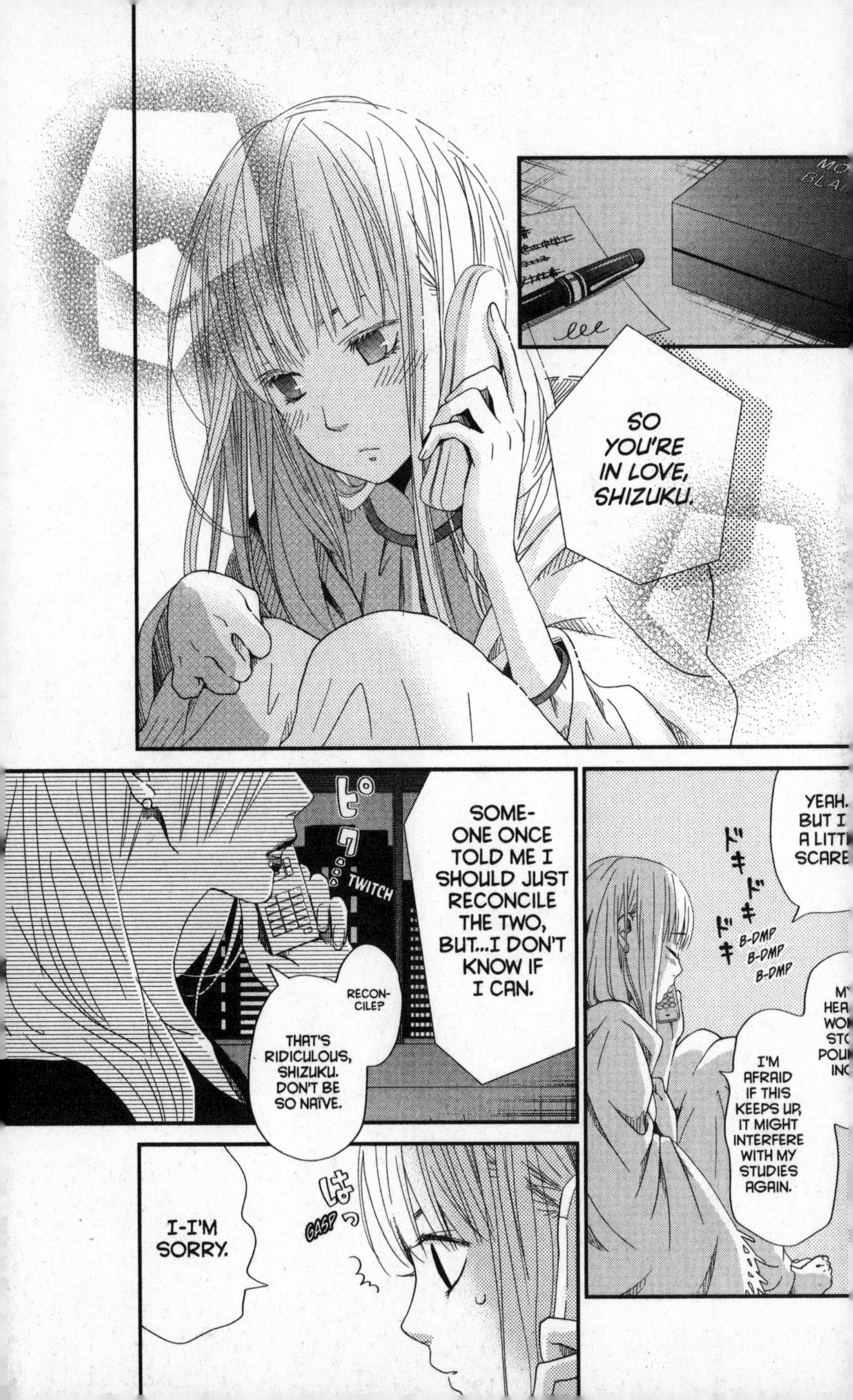
SO YOU'RE IN LOVE, SHIZUKU.
YEAH. BUT I A LITT SCARE
ドキドキドキ
B-DMP B-DMP B-DMP
I'M AFRAID IF THIS KEEPS UP, IT MIGHT INTERFERE WITH MY STUDIES AGAIN.
SOME-ONE ONCE TOLD ME I SHOULD JUST RECONCILE THE TWO, BUT...I DON'T KNOW IF I CAN.
ピク
TWITCH
RECON-CILE?
THAT'S RIDICULOUS, SHIZUKU. DON'T BE SO NAÏVE.
はっ
GASP
I-I'M SORRY.

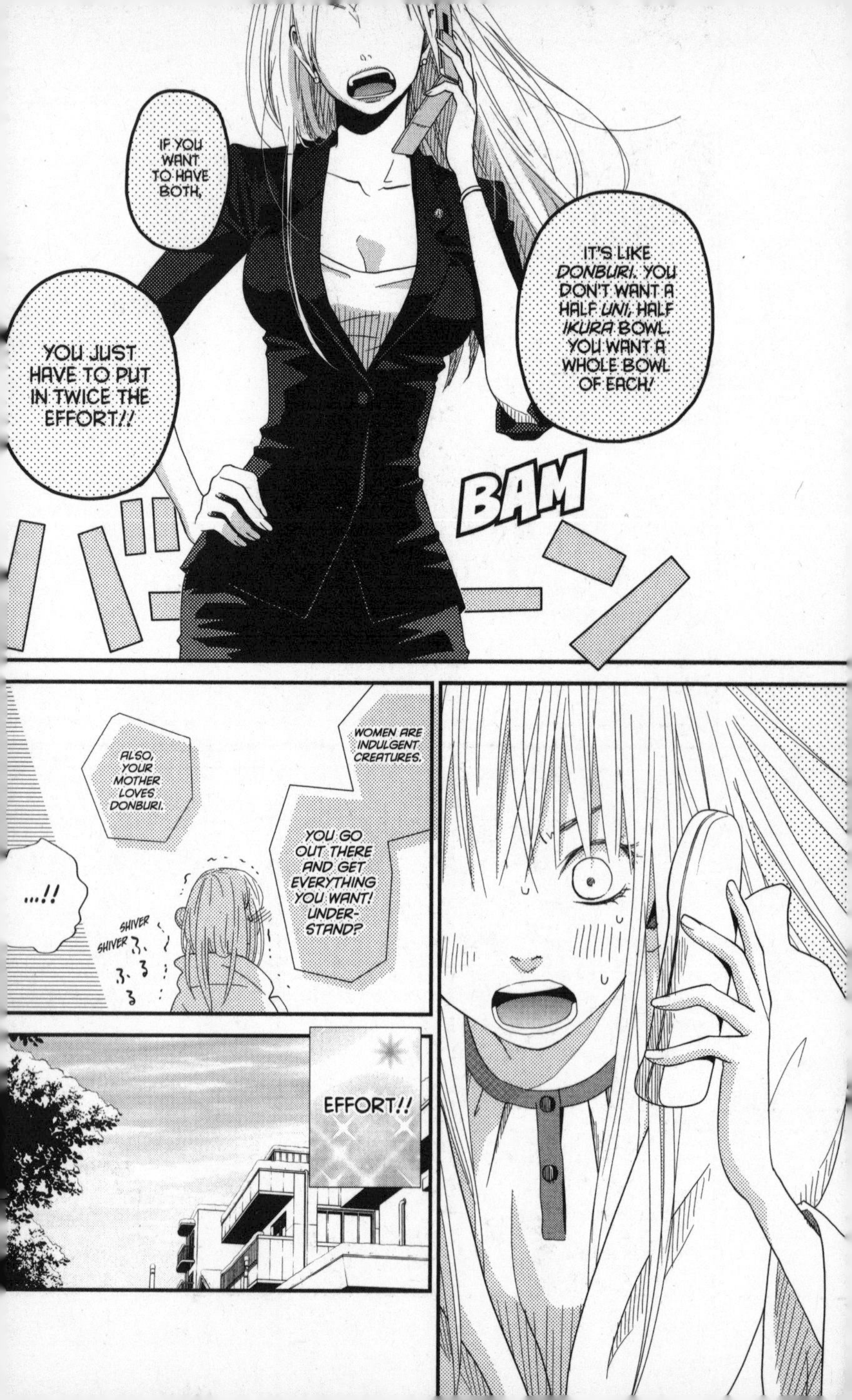
IT'S LIKE *DONBURI*. YOU DON'T WANT A HALF *UNI*, HALF *IKURA* BOWL. YOU WANT A WHOLE BOWL OF EACH!
IF YOU WANT TO HAVE BOTH,
YOU JUST HAVE TO PUT IN TWICE THE EFFORT!!
BAM
WOMEN ARE INDULGENT CREATURES.
ALSO, YOUR MOTHER LOVES DONBURI.
YOU GO OUT THERE AND GET EVERYTHING YOU WANT! UNDER-STAND?
SHIVER SHIVER
...!!
EFFORT!!

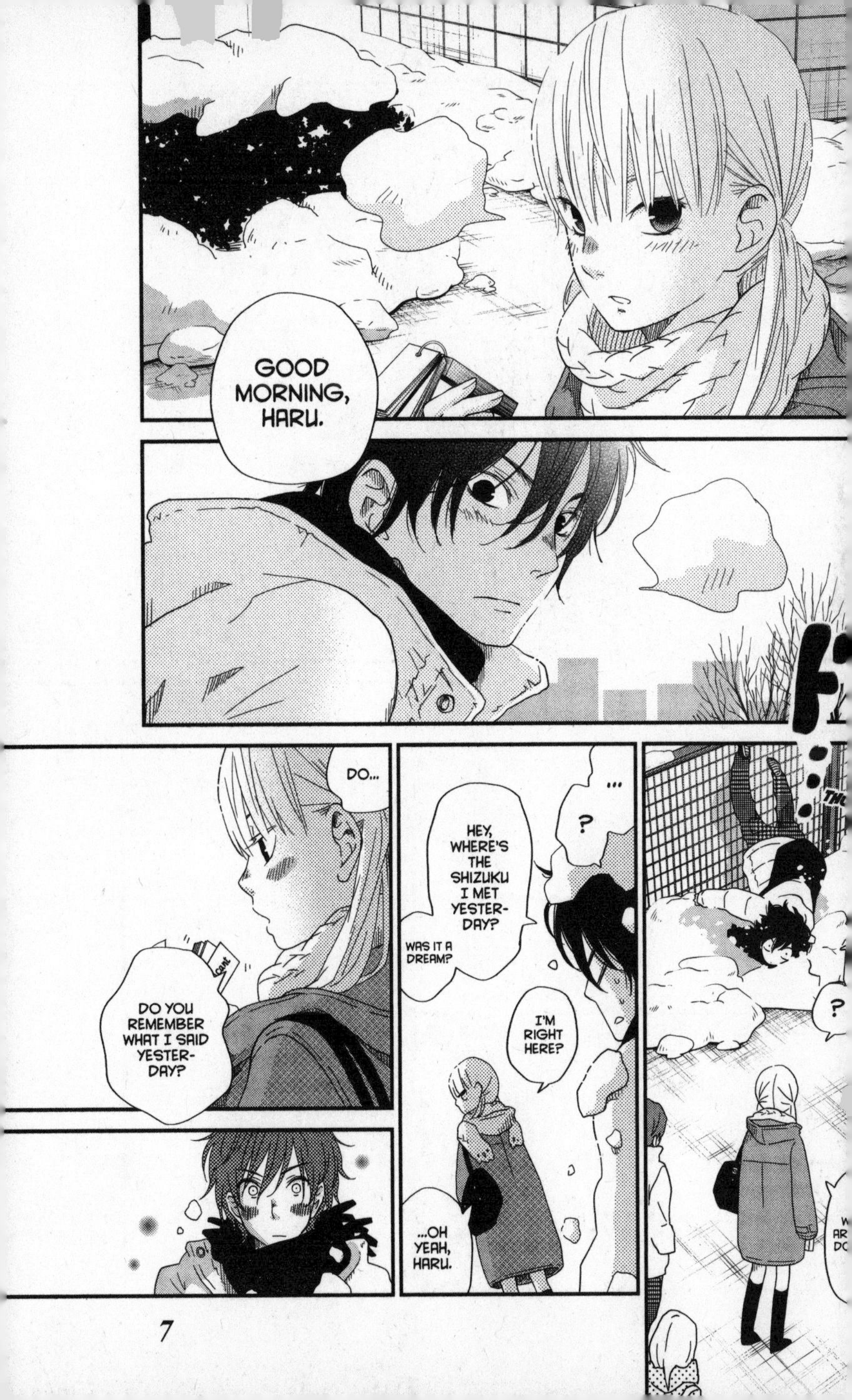
GOOD MORNING, HARU.
?
...
?
HEY, WHERE'S THE SHIZUKU I MET YESTER-DAY?
WAS IT A DREAM?
I'M RIGHT HERE?
...OH YEAH, HARU.
DO...
DO YOU REMEMBER WHAT I SAID YESTER-DAY?

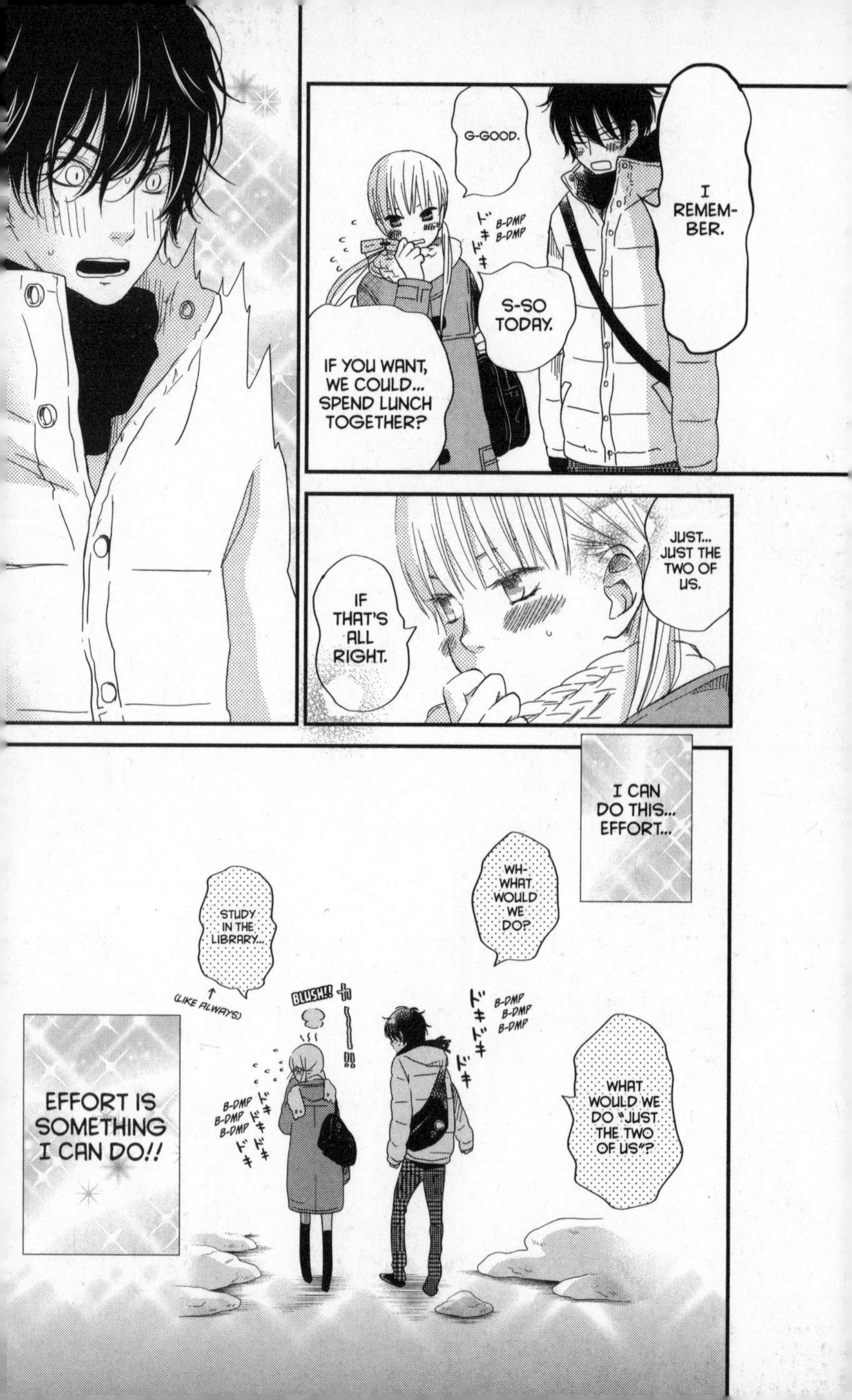
I REMEMBER.
G-GOOD.
ドキドキ
B-DMP B-DMP
S-SO TODAY.
IF YOU WANT, WE COULD... SPEND LUNCH TOGETHER?
JUST... JUST THE TWO OF US.
IF THAT'S ALL RIGHT.
I CAN DO THIS... EFFORT...
WH-WHAT WOULD WE DO?
ドキドキドキ
B-DMP B-DMP B-DMP
WHAT WOULD WE DO "JUST THE TWO OF US"?
STUDY IN THE LIBRARY...
(LIKE ALWAYS)
BLUSH!!
B-DMP B-DMP B-DMP
EFFORT IS SOMETHING I CAN DO!!

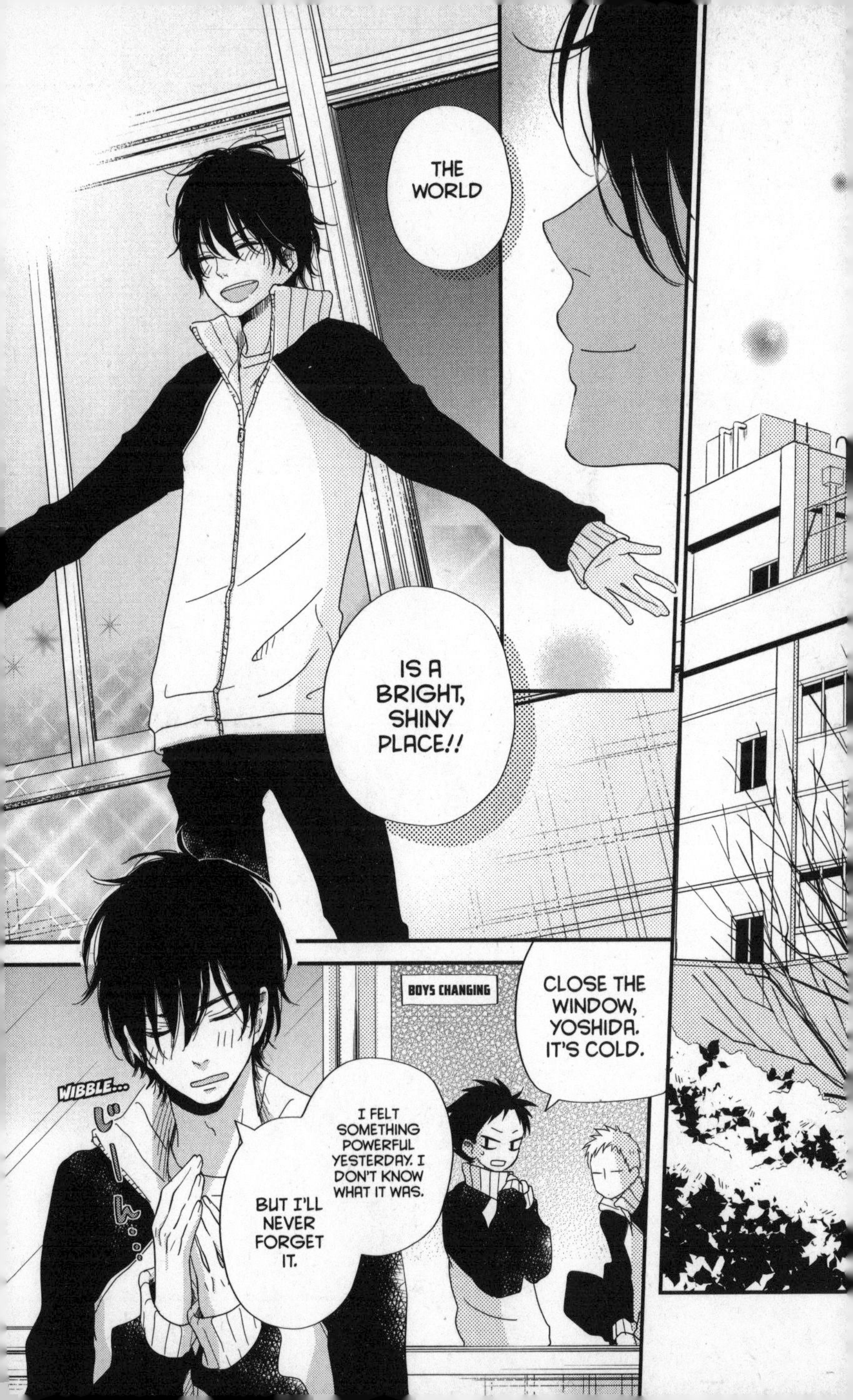
THE WORLD
IS A BRIGHT, SHINY PLACE!!
BOYS CHANGING
CLOSE THE WINDOW, YOSHIDA. IT'S COLD.
I FELT SOMETHING POWERFUL YESTERDAY. I DON'T KNOW WHAT IT WAS.
BUT I'LL NEVER FORGET IT.
WIBBLE...
じーん…

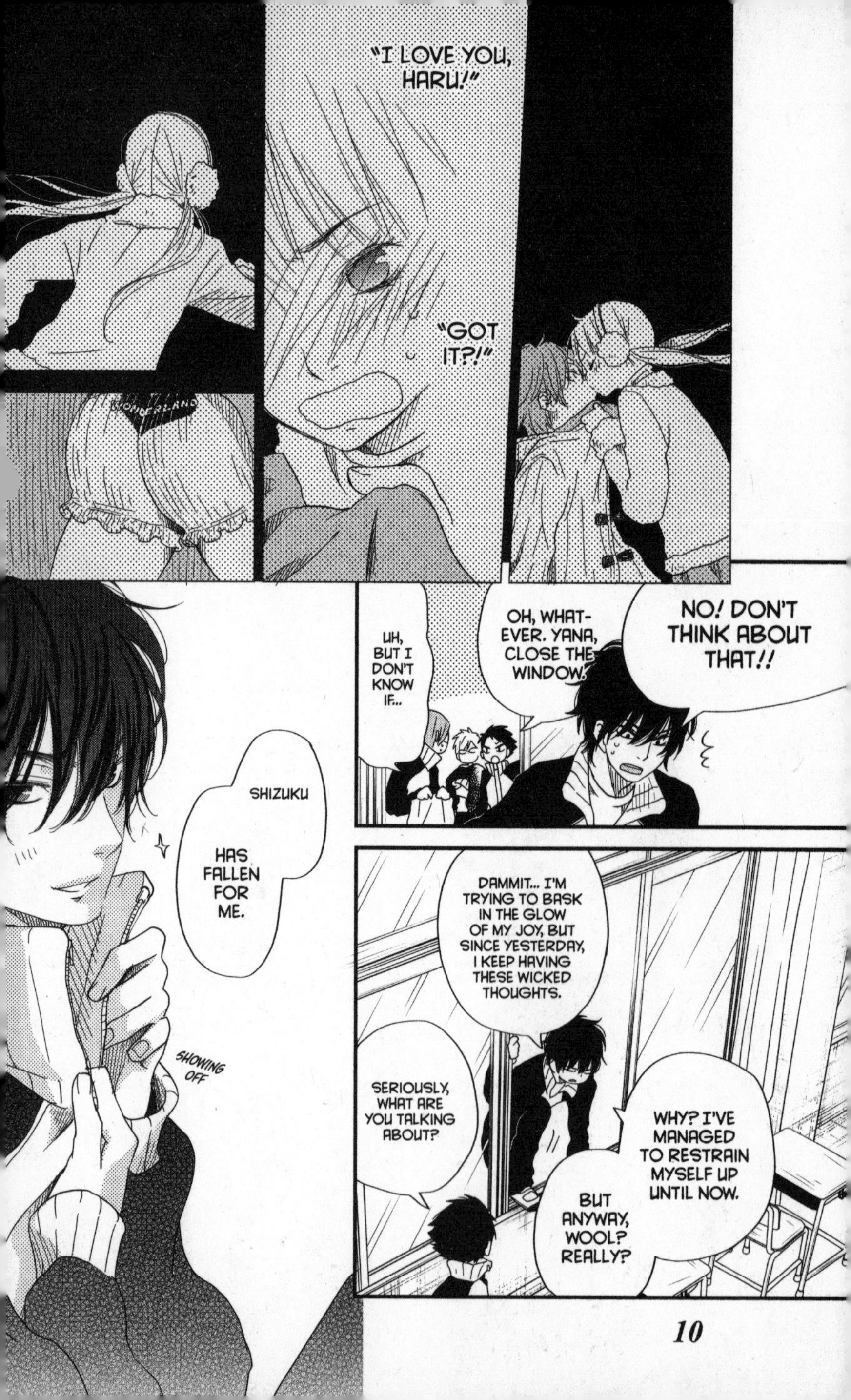
"I LOVE YOU, HARU!"
"GOT IT?!"
NO! DON'T THINK ABOUT THAT!!
OH, WHATEVER. YANA, CLOSE THE WINDOW.
UH, BUT I DON'T KNOW IF...
DAMMIT... I'M TRYING TO BASK IN THE GLOW OF MY JOY, BUT SINCE YESTERDAY, I KEEP HAVING THESE WICKED THOUGHTS.
WHY? I'VE MANAGED TO RESTRAIN MYSELF UP UNTIL NOW.
BUT ANYWAY, WOOL? REALLY?
SERIOUSLY, WHAT ARE YOU TALKING ABOUT?
SHIZUKU
HAS FALLEN FOR ME.
SHOWING OFF

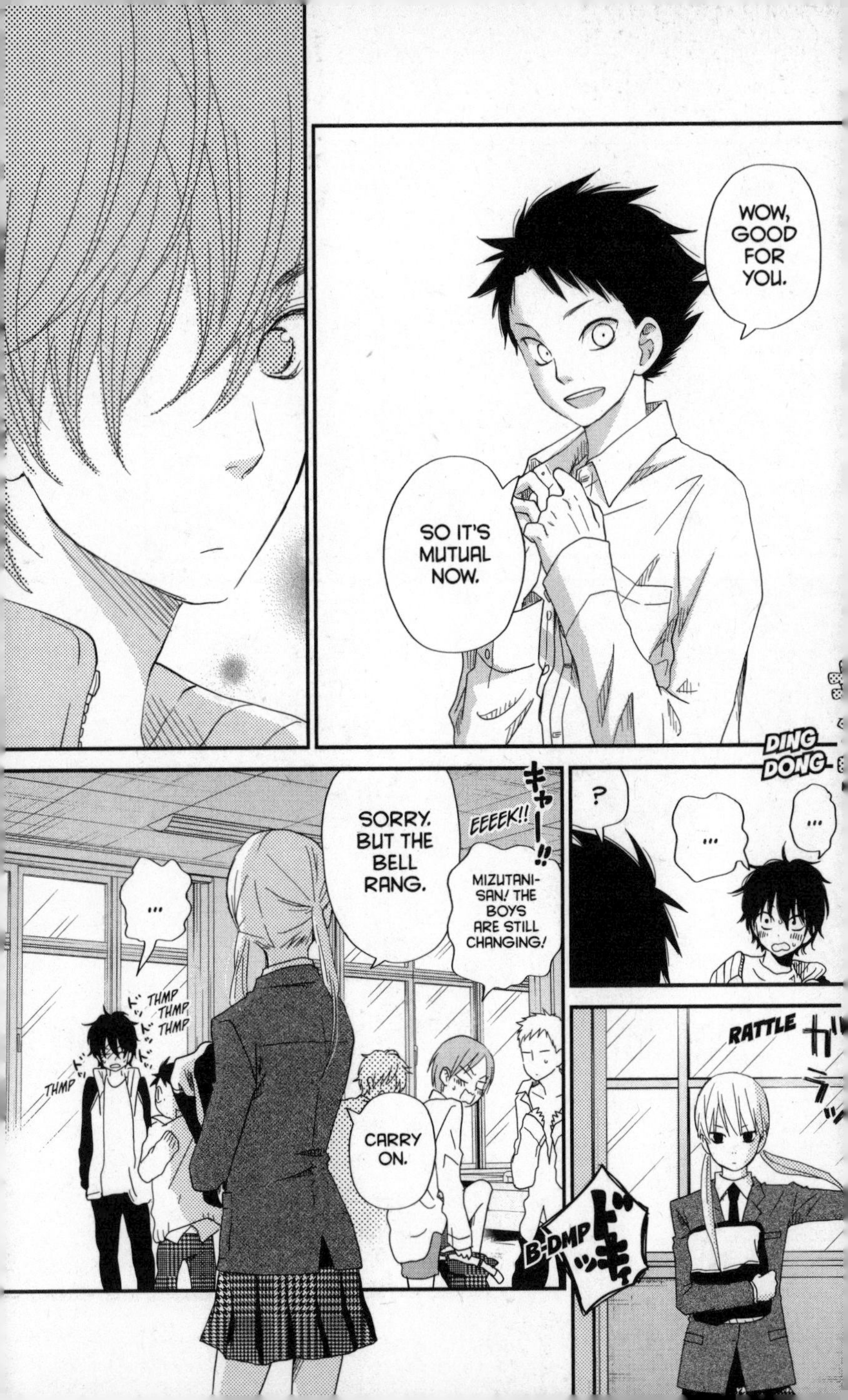

WOW, GOOD FOR YOU.
SO IT'S MUTUAL NOW.
DING DONG
?
...
...
RATTLE
B-DMP
EEEEK!!
MIZUTANI-SAN! THE BOYS ARE STILL CHANGING!
SORRY. BUT THE BELL RANG.
...
THMP THMP THMP
THMP
CARRY ON.

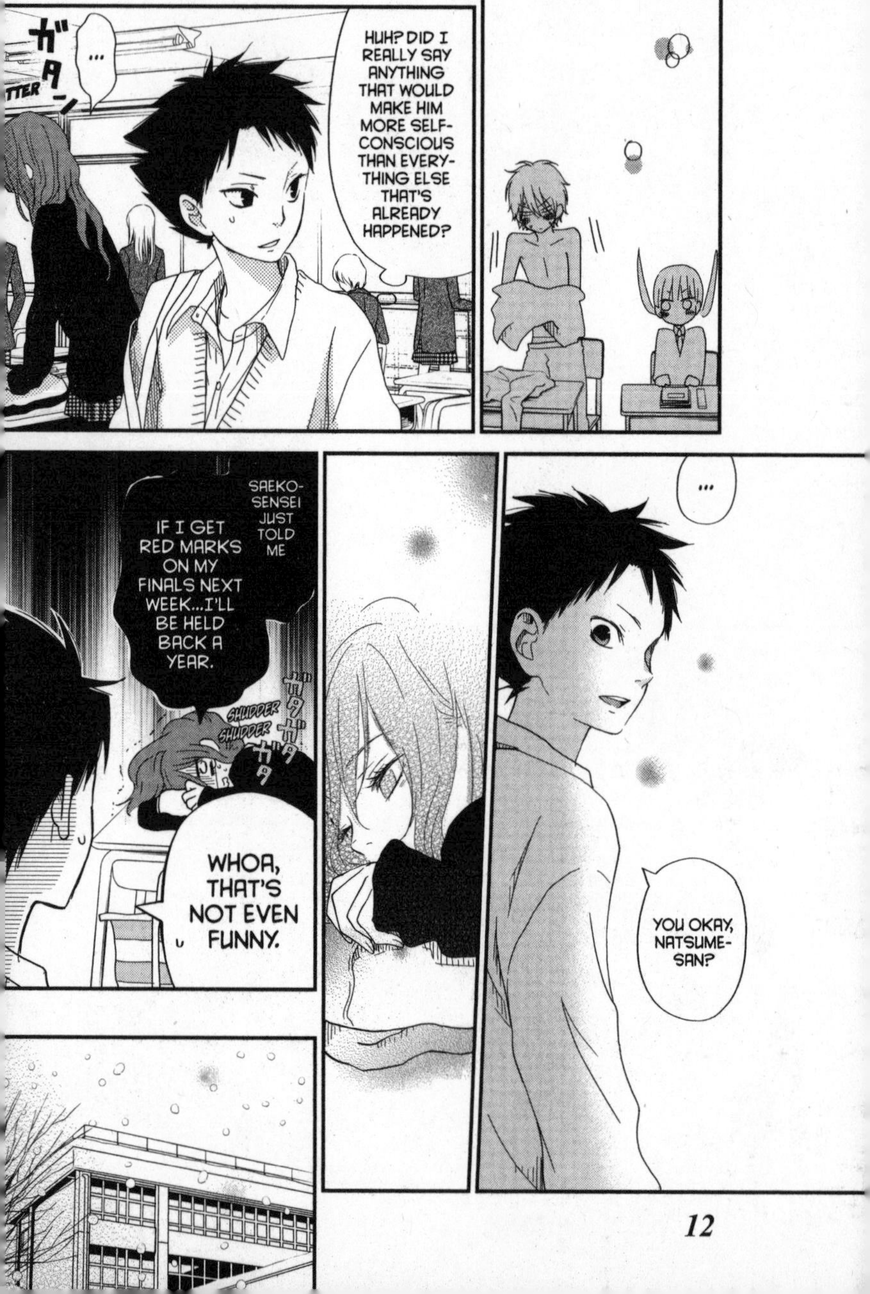

HUH? DID I REALLY SAY ANYTHING THAT WOULD MAKE HIM MORE SELF-CONSCIOUS THAN EVERYTHING ELSE THAT'S ALREADY HAPPENED?
...
...
YOU OKAY, NATSUME-SAN?
SAEKO-SENSEI JUST TOLD ME
IF I GET RED MARKS ON MY FINALS NEXT WEEK...I'LL BE HELD BACK A YEAR.
SHUDDER
SHUDDER
WHOA, THAT'S NOT EVEN FUNNY.

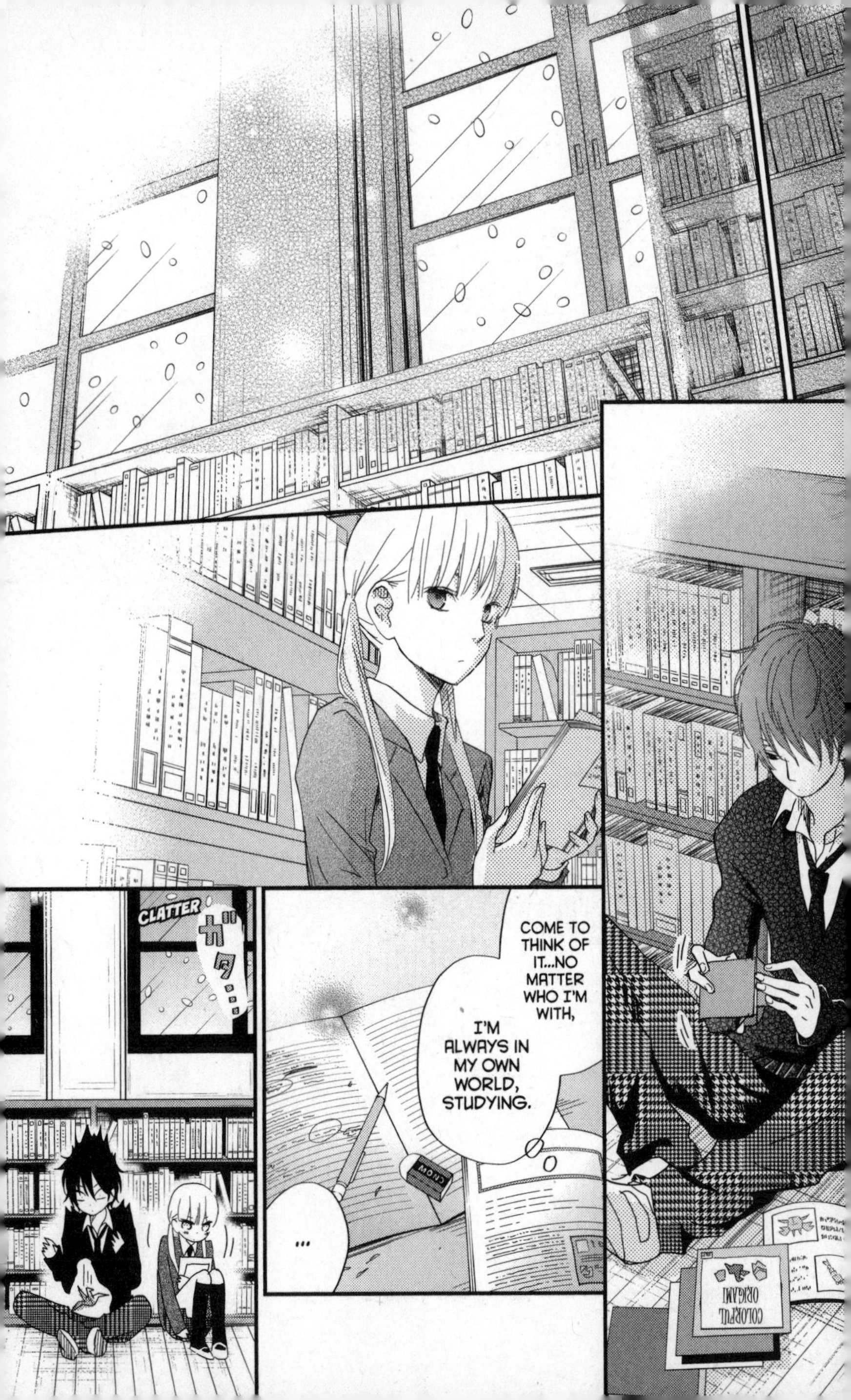
COLORFUL ORIGAMI
COME TO THINK OF IT...NO MATTER WHO I'M WITH,
I'M ALWAYS IN MY OWN WORLD, STUDYING.
...
CLATTER
ガタ…

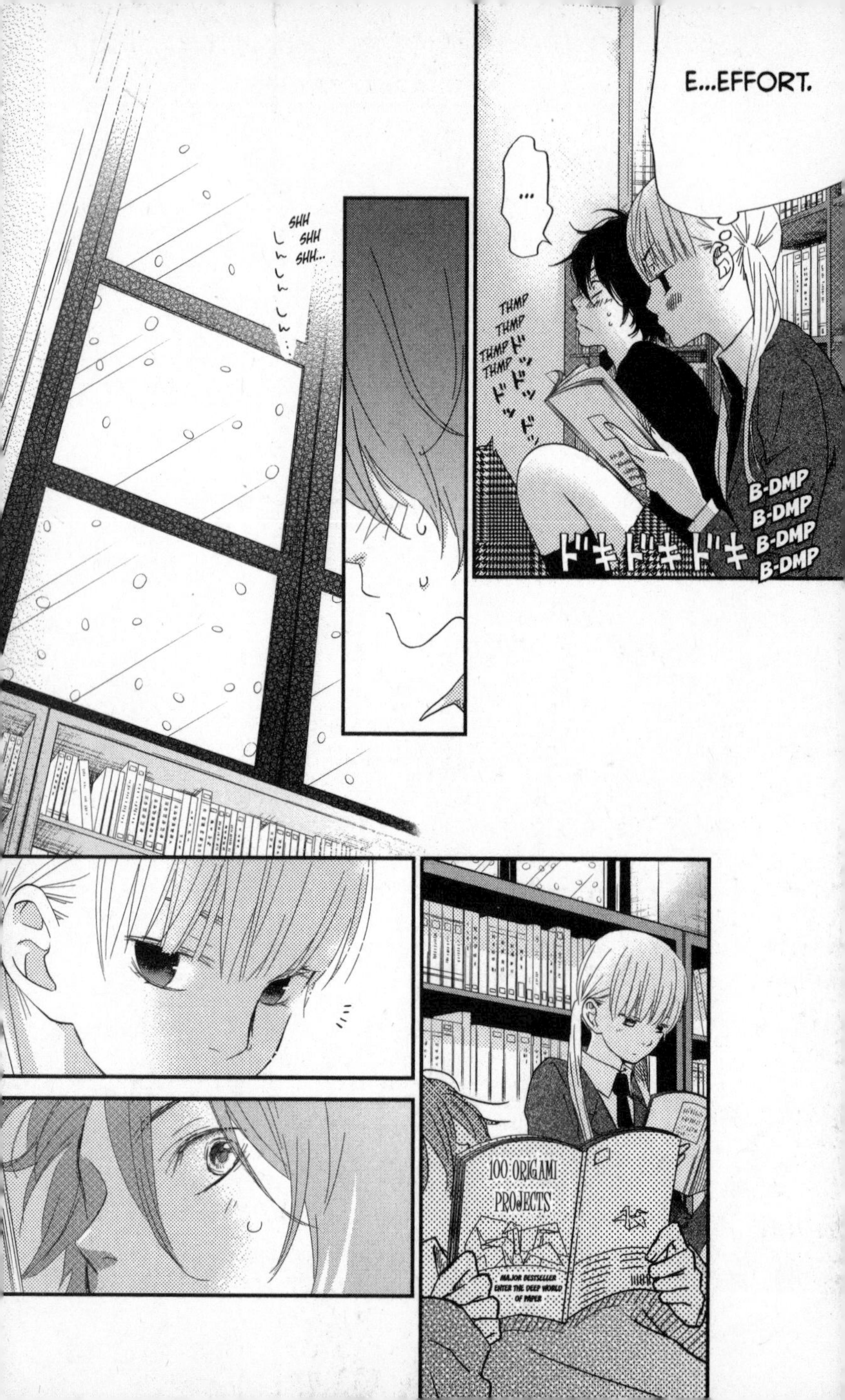
E...EFFORT.
...
THMP THMP THMP THMP
ドッドッドッドッ
ドキドキドキ
B-DMP B-DMP B-DMP B-DMP
SHH SHH SHH...
しんしんしん...
100 ORIGAMI PROJECTS
MAJOR BESTSELLER
ENTER THE DEEP WORLD OF PAPER

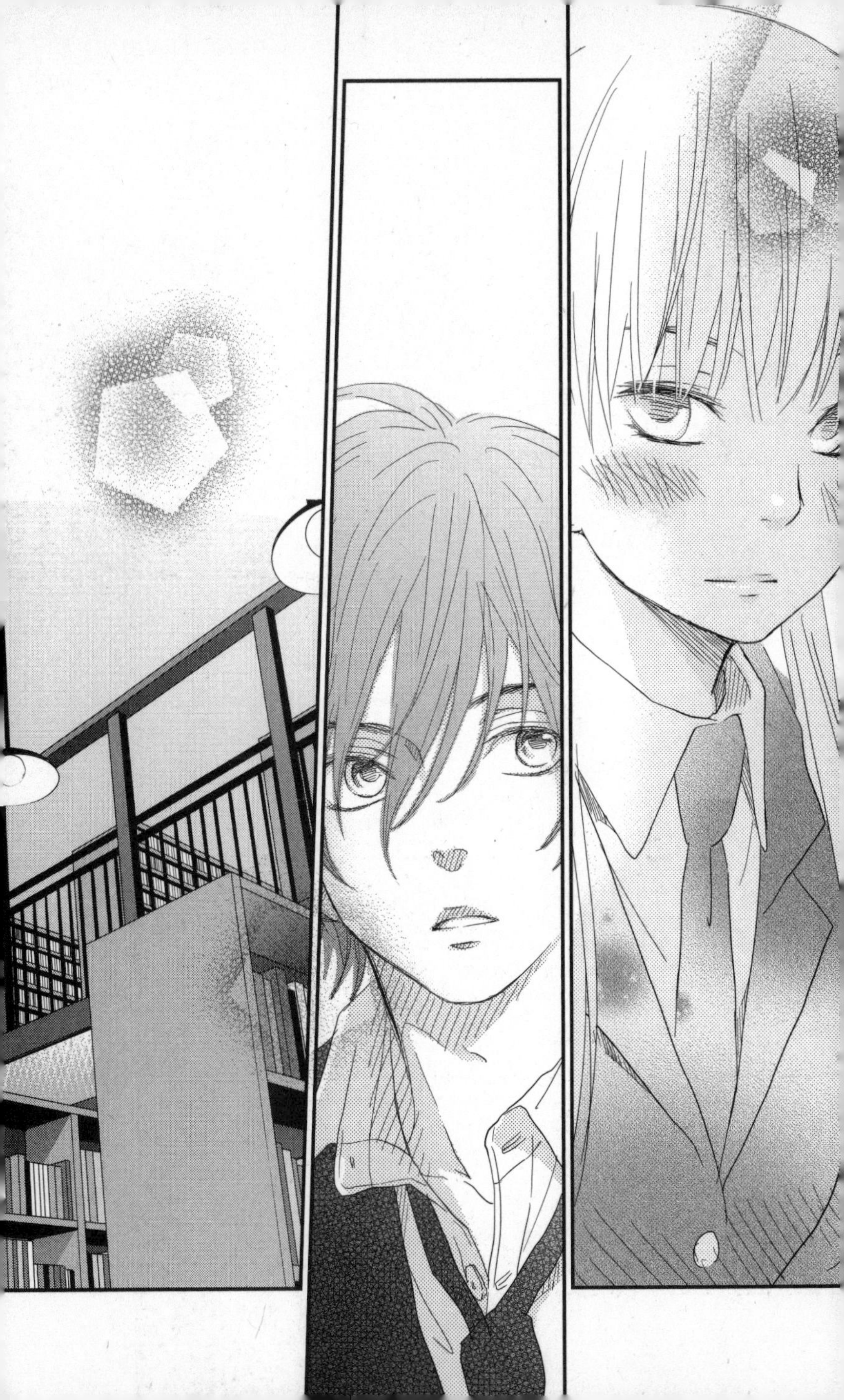

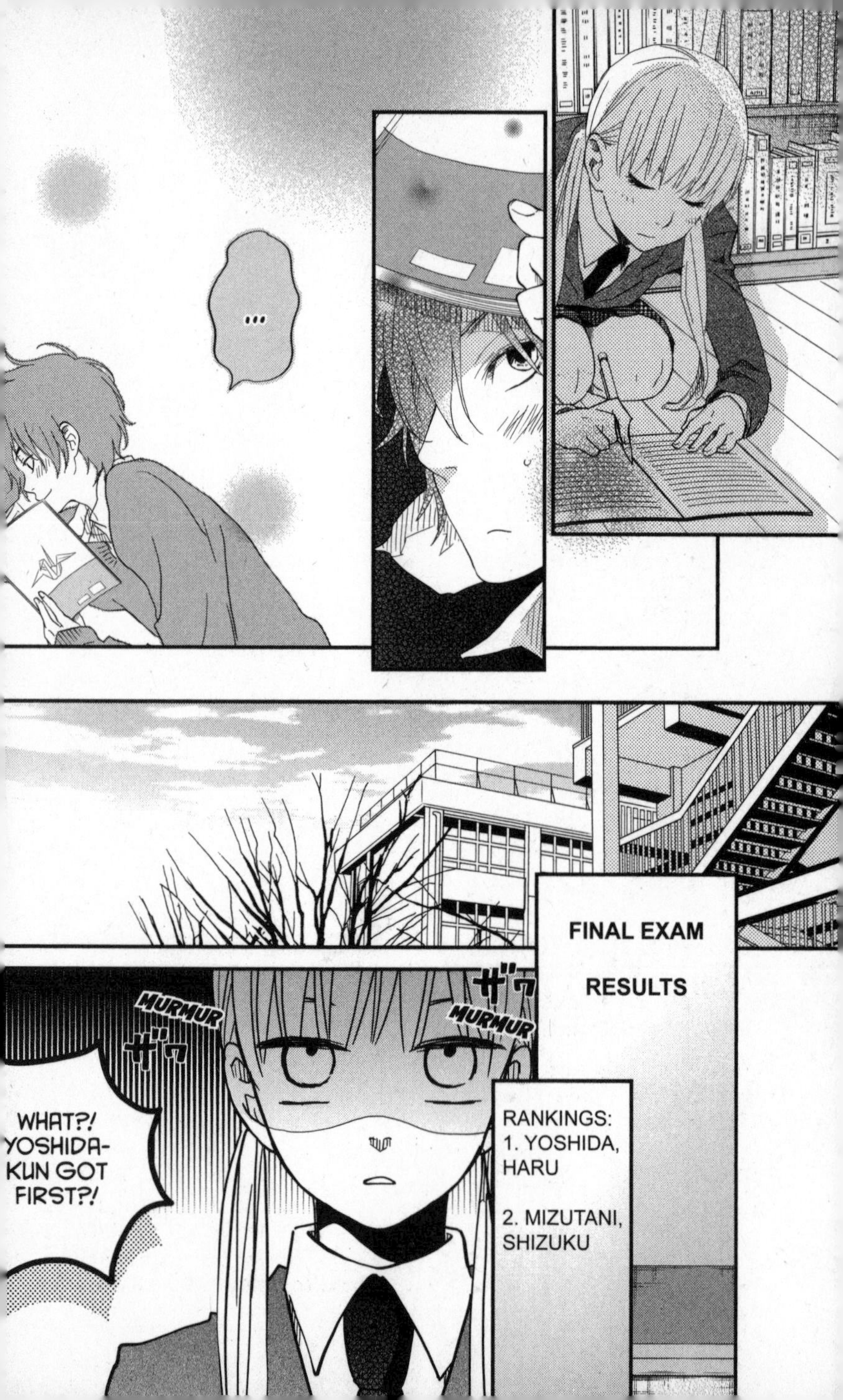
...
FINAL EXAM RESULTS
ザワ
MURMUR
RANKINGS:
1. YOSHIDA, HARU
2. MIZUTANI, SHIZUKU
MURMUR
ザワ
WHAT?! YOSHIDA-KUN GOT FIRST?!

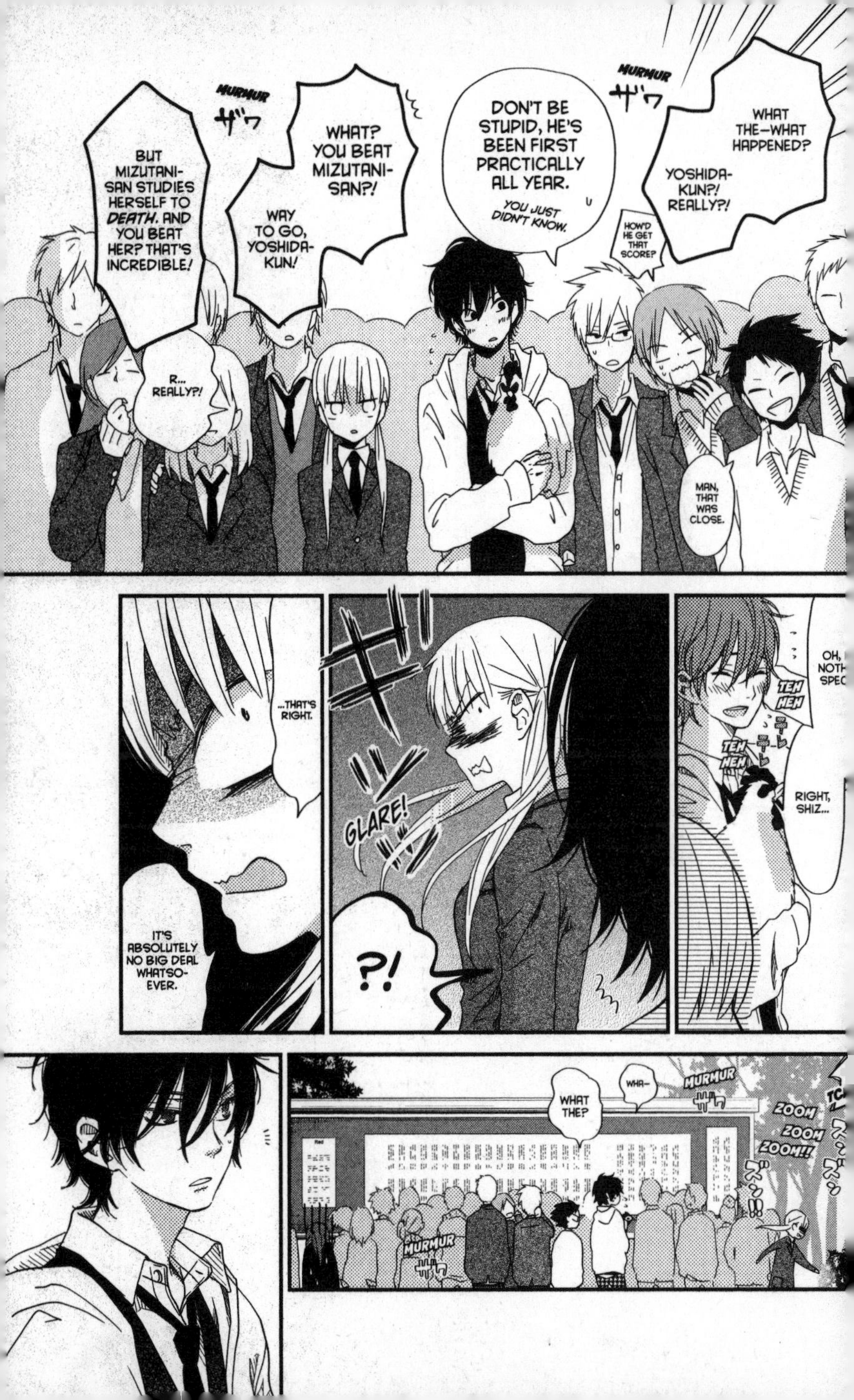
WHAT THE—WHAT HAPPENED?
YOSHIDA-KUN?! REALLY?!
MURMUR
ザワ
HOW'D HE GET THAT SCORE?
DON'T BE STUPID, HE'S BEEN FIRST PRACTICALLY ALL YEAR.
YOU JUST DIDN'T KNOW.
WHAT? YOU BEAT MIZUTANI-SAN?!
WAY TO GO, YOSHIDA-KUN!
MURMUR
ザワ
BUT MIZUTANI-SAN STUDIES HERSELF TO DEATH. AND YOU BEAT HER? THAT'S INCREDIBLE!
R... REALLY?!
MAN, THAT WAS CLOSE.
TEH HEH
TEH HEH
RIGHT, SHIZ...
GLARE!
?!
...THAT'S RIGHT.
IT'S ABSOLUTELY NO BIG DEAL WHATSO-EVER.
ZOOM ZOOM ZOOM!!
MURMUR
ザワ
WHA—
WHAT THE?
MURMUR
ザワ

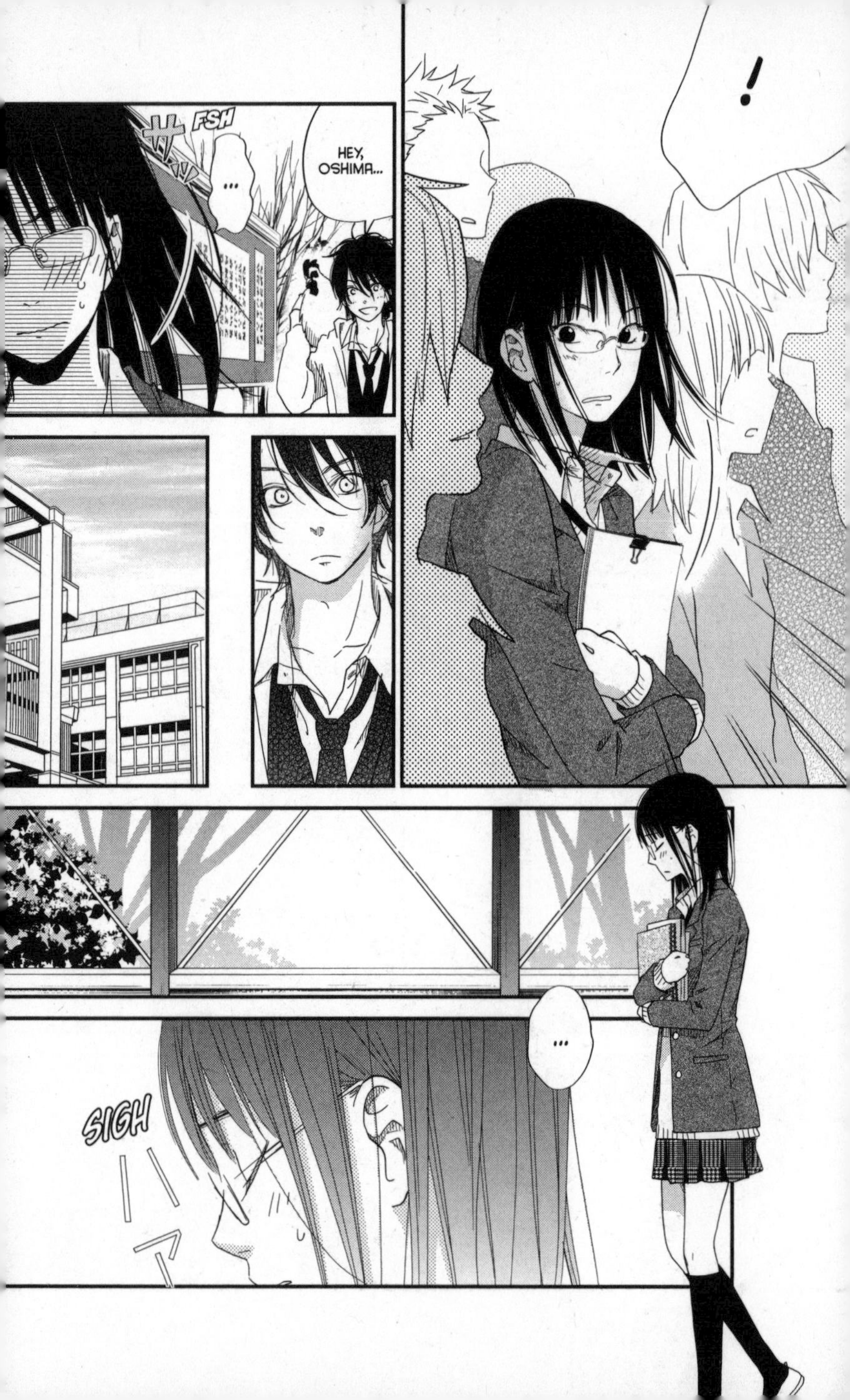
!
HEY, OSHIMA...
FSH
...
...
SIGH

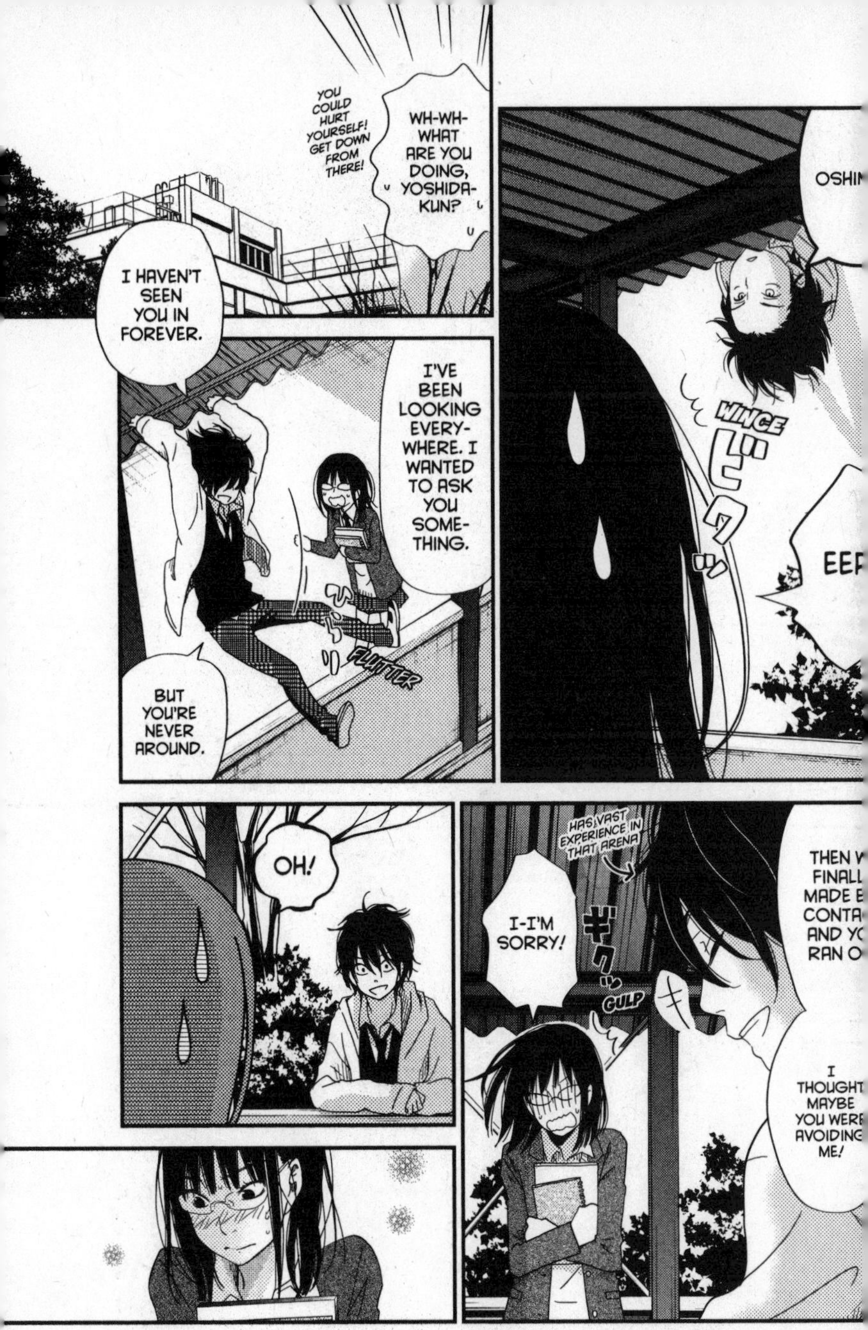
OSHIM
WINCE
EEP
WH-WH-WHAT ARE YOU DOING, YOSHIDA-KUN?
YOU COULD HURT YOURSELF! GET DOWN FROM THERE!
I HAVEN'T SEEN YOU IN FOREVER.
I'VE BEEN LOOKING EVERY-WHERE. I WANTED TO ASK YOU SOME-THING.
FLUTTER
BUT YOU'RE NEVER AROUND.
THEN W
FINALL
MADE E
CONTA
AND YO
RAN O
I THOUGHT MAYBE YOU WERE AVOIDING ME!
HAS VAST EXPERIENCE IN THAT ARENA
GULP
I-I'M SORRY!
OH!

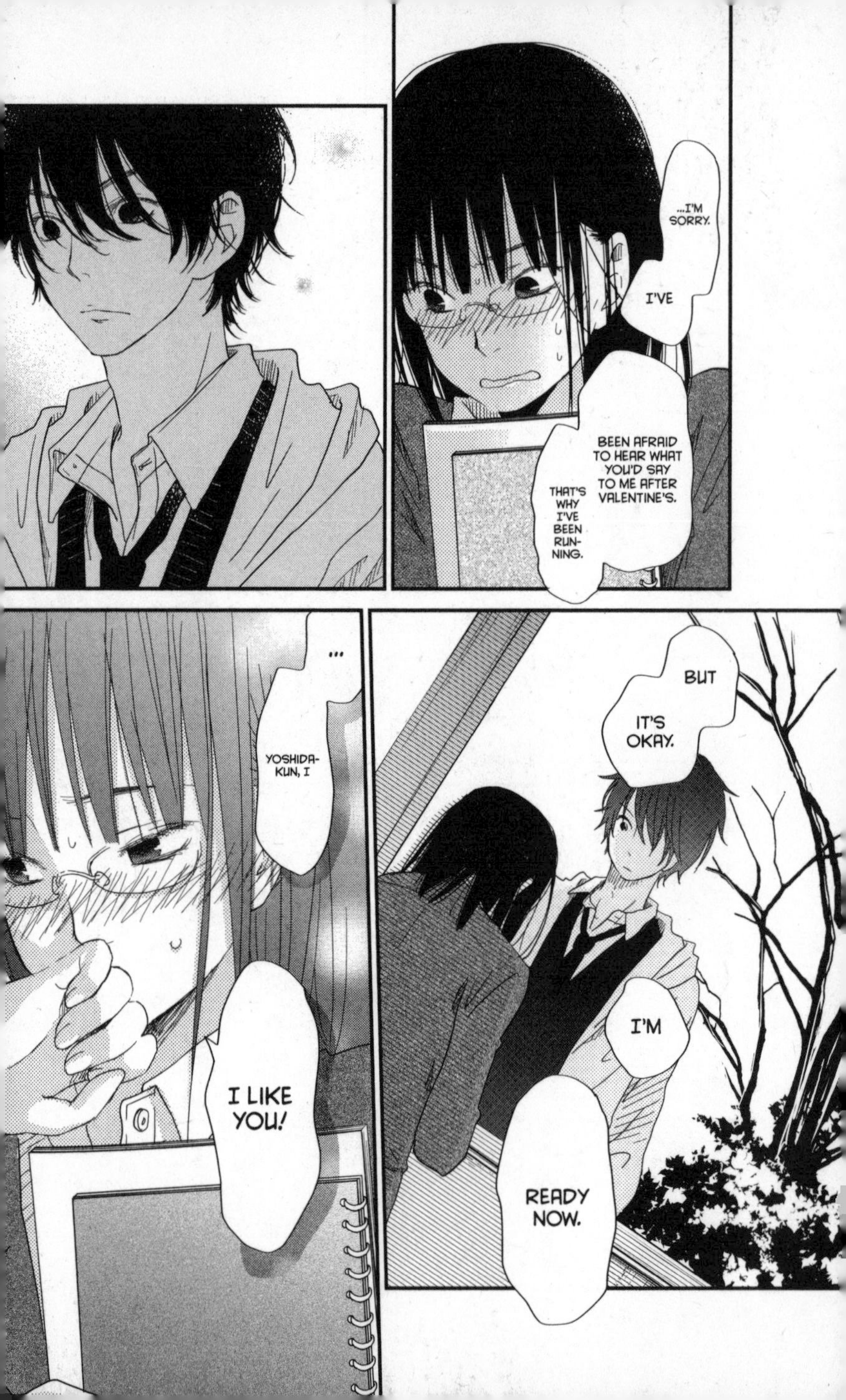
...I'M SORRY.
I'VE
BEEN AFRAID TO HEAR WHAT YOU'D SAY TO ME AFTER VALENTINE'S.
THAT'S WHY I'VE BEEN RUN-NING.
BUT
IT'S OKAY.
I'M
READY NOW.
...
YOSHIDA-KUN, I
I LIKE YOU!

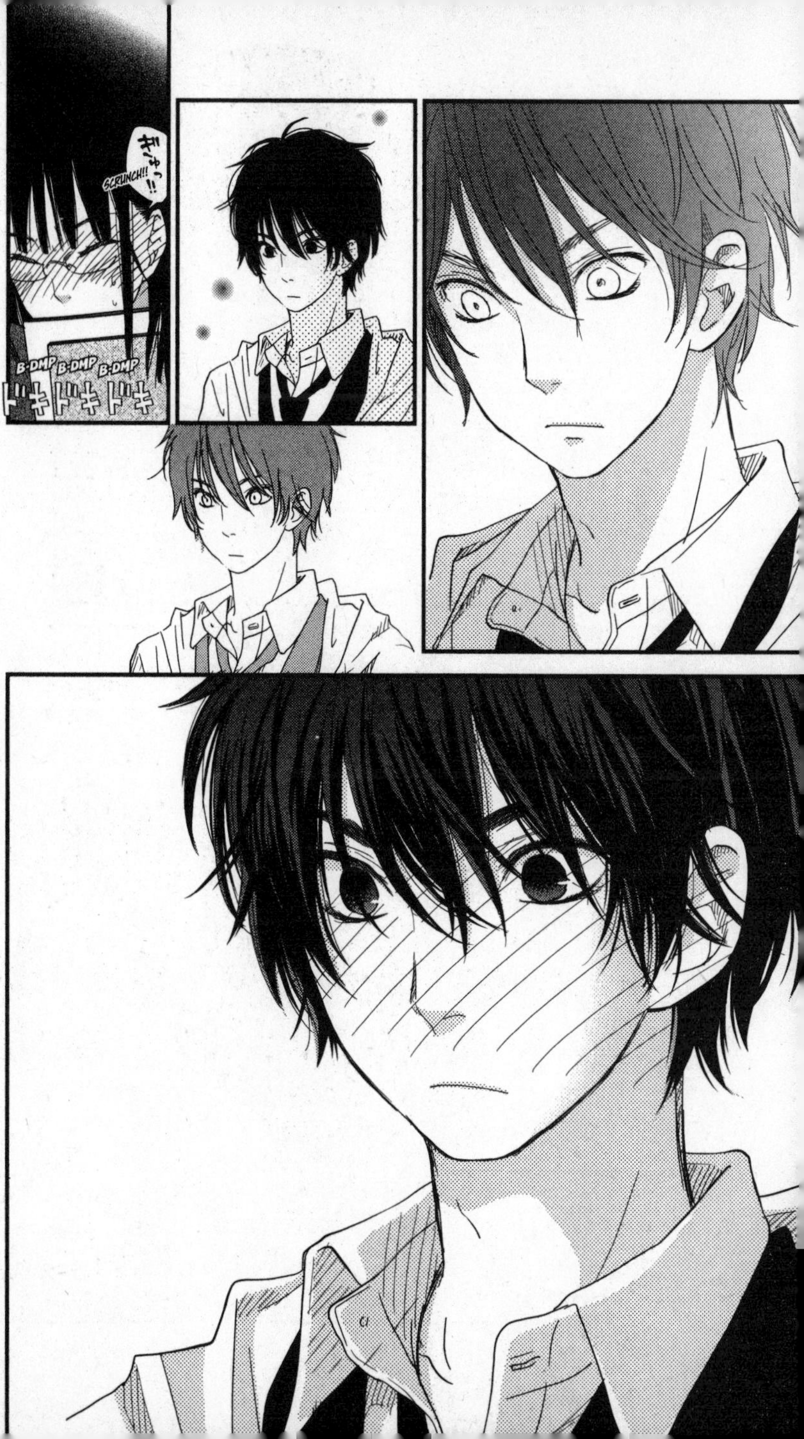
ぎゅっ!!
SCRUNCH!!
ドキドキドキ
B-DMP B-DMP B-DMP

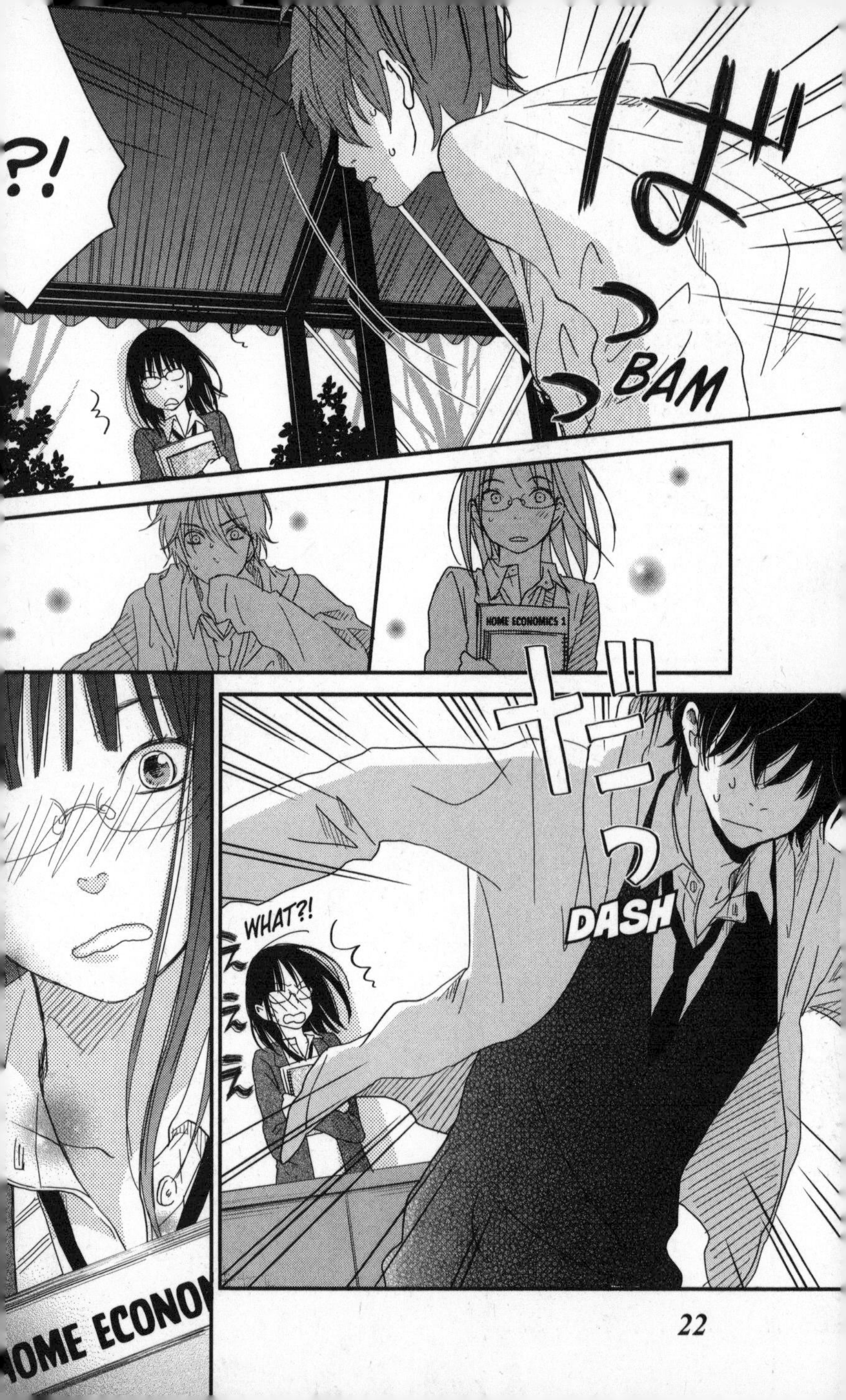

ばっ
BAM
?!
HOME ECONOMICS 1
ガダッ
DASH
WHAT?!
HOME ECONO

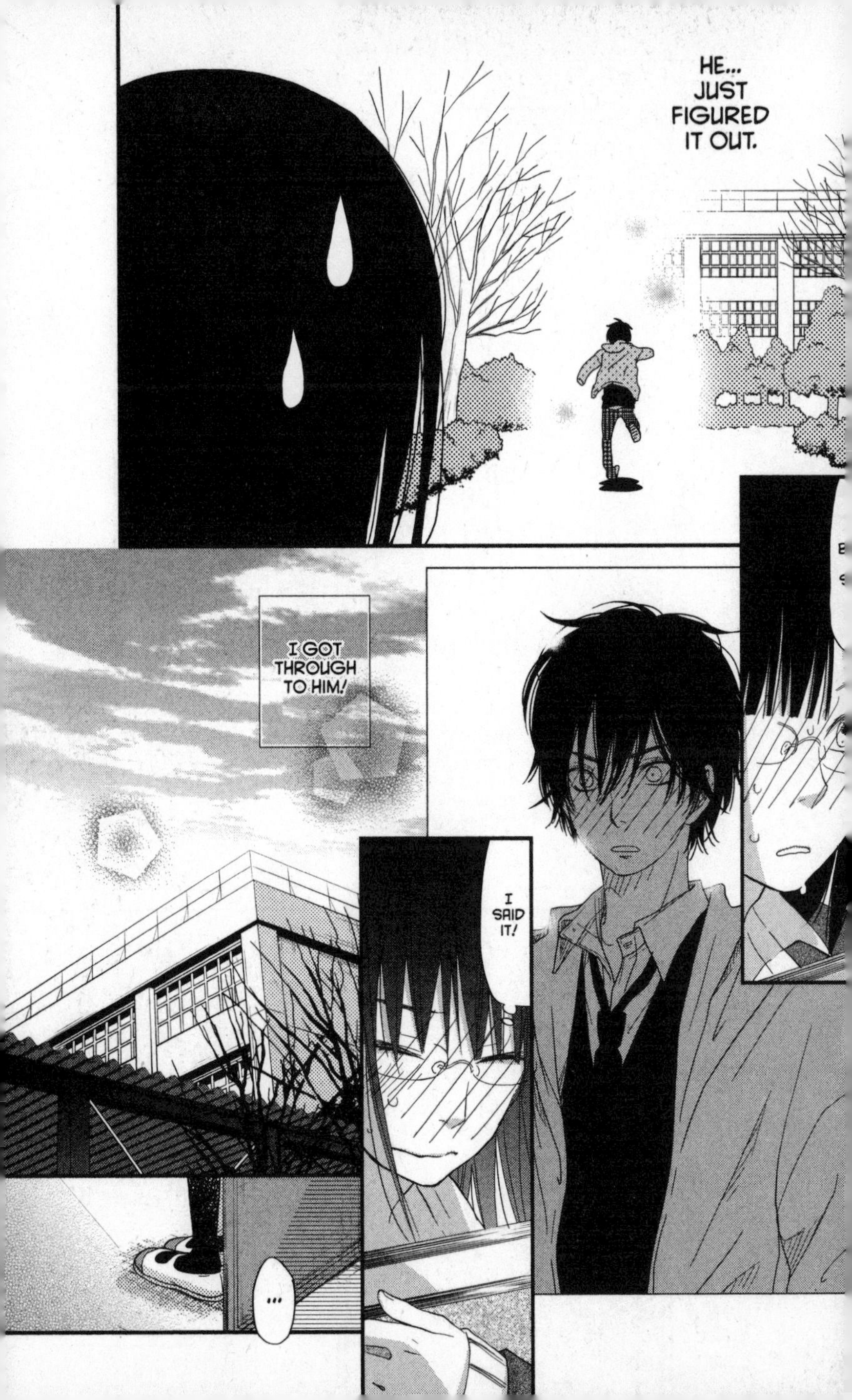
HE... JUST FIGURED IT OUT.
I GOT THROUGH TO HIM!
I SAID IT!
...

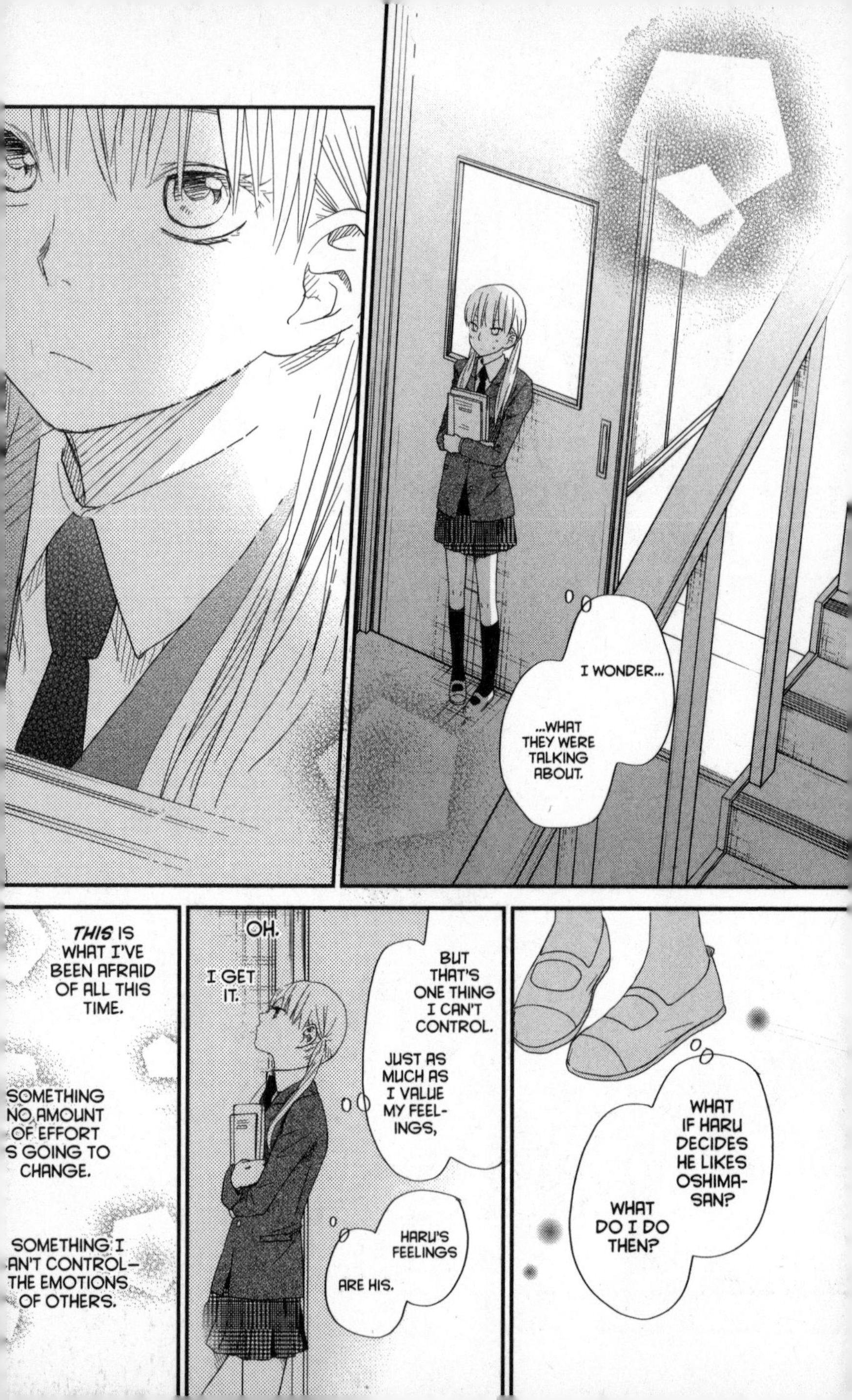
I WONDER...
...WHAT THEY WERE TALKING ABOUT.
WHAT IF HARU DECIDES HE LIKES OSHIMA-SAN?
WHAT DO I DO THEN?
BUT THAT'S ONE THING I CAN'T CONTROL.
JUST AS MUCH AS I VALUE MY FEELINGS,
HARU'S FEELINGS
ARE HIS.
OH.
I GET IT.
THIS IS WHAT I'VE BEEN AFRAID OF ALL THIS TIME.
SOMETHING NO AMOUNT OF EFFORT S GOING TO CHANGE.
SOMETHING I AN'T CONTROL— THE EMOTIONS OF OTHERS.

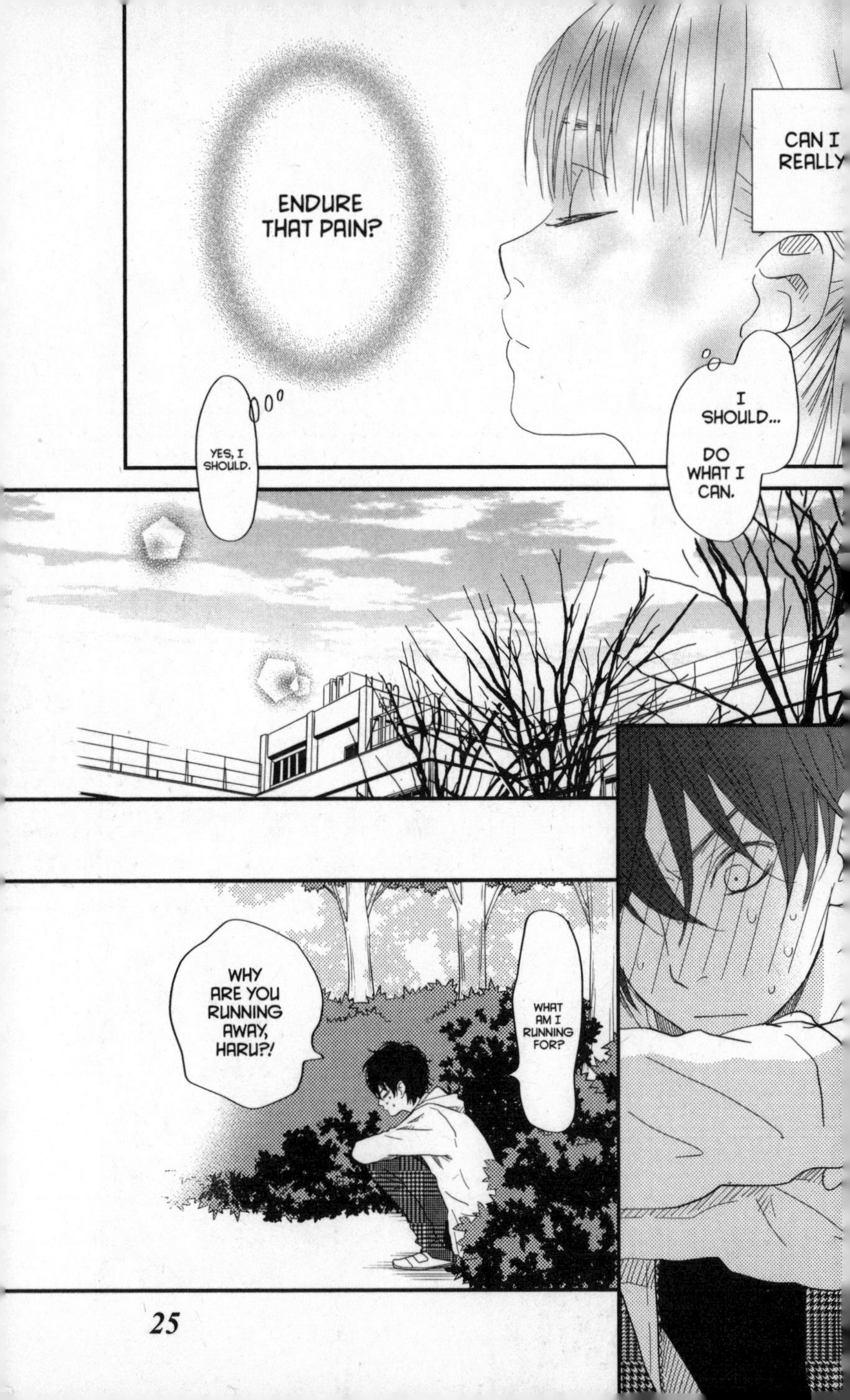
CAN I REALLY
ENDURE THAT PAIN?
I SHOULD...
DO WHAT I CAN.
YES, I SHOULD.
WHAT AM I RUNNING FOR?
WHY ARE YOU RUNNING AWAY, HARU?!

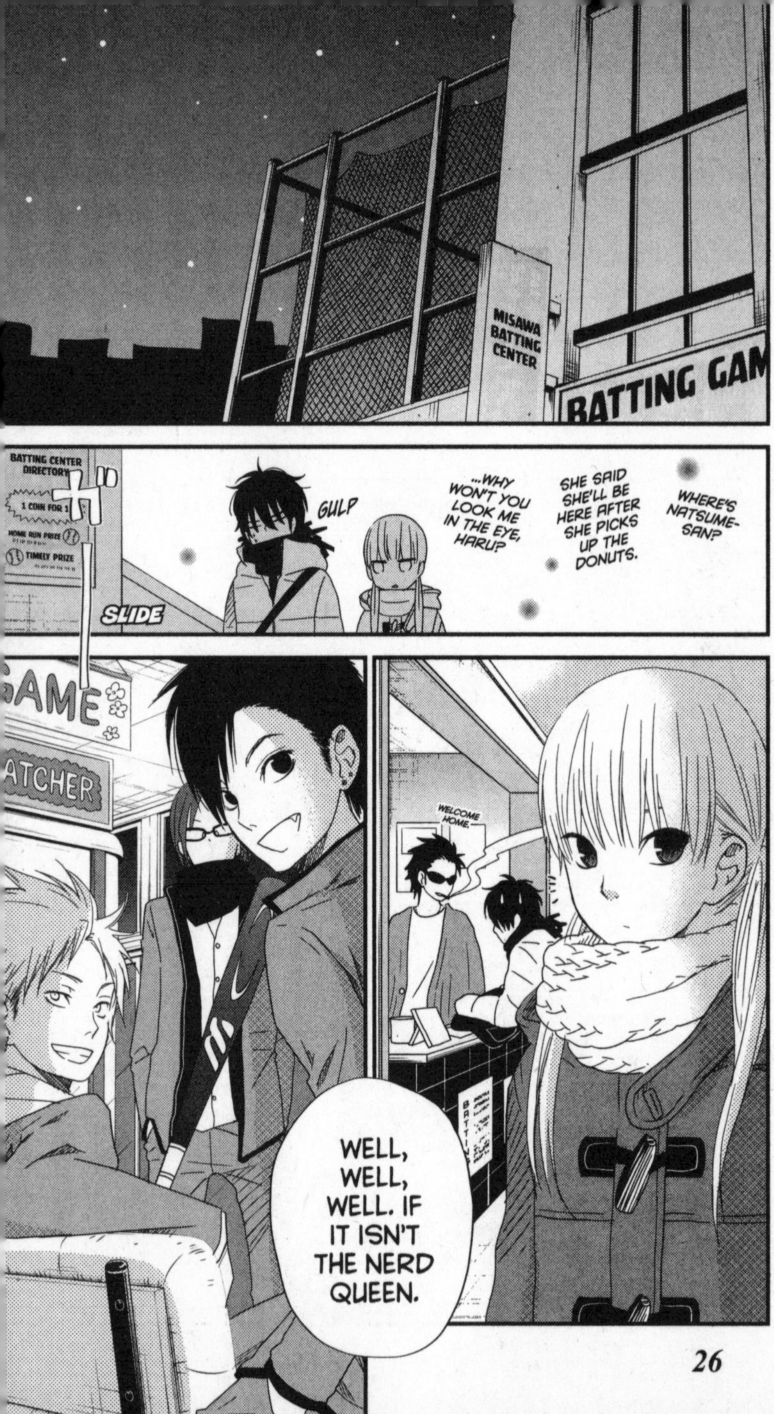

MISAWA BATTING CENTER
BATTING GAM
WHERE'S NATSUME-SAN?
SHE SAID SHE'LL BE HERE AFTER SHE PICKS UP THE DONUTS.
...WHY WON'T YOU LOOK ME IN THE EYE, HARU?
GULP
BATTING CENTER DIRECTORY
1 COIN FOR 1
HOME RUN PRIZE
TIMELY PRIZE
SLIDE
WELCOME HOME.
GAME
ATCHER
WELL, WELL, WELL. IF IT ISN'T THE NERD QUEEN.

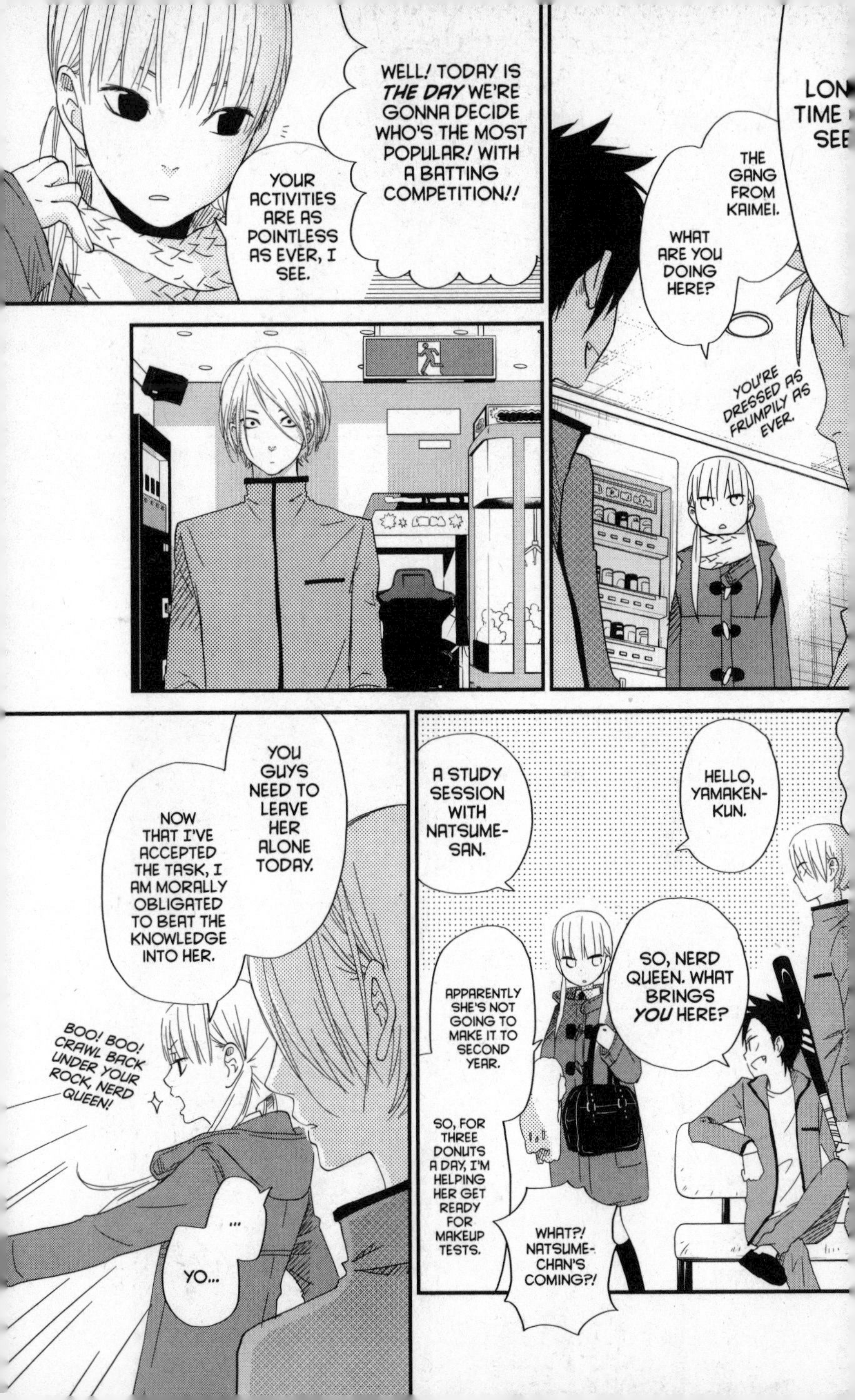
LON TIME SEE
THE GANG FROM KAIMEI.
WHAT ARE YOU DOING HERE?
YOU'RE DRESSED AS FRUMPILY AS EVER.
WELL! TODAY IS *THE DAY* WE'RE GONNA DECIDE WHO'S THE MOST POPULAR! WITH A BATTING COMPETITION!!
YOUR ACTIVITIES ARE AS POINTLESS AS EVER, I SEE.
HELLO, YAMAKEN-KUN.
SO, NERD QUEEN. WHAT BRINGS *YOU* HERE?
A STUDY SESSION WITH NATSUME-SAN.
APPARENTLY SHE'S NOT GOING TO MAKE IT TO SECOND YEAR.
SO, FOR THREE DONUTS A DAY, I'M HELPING HER GET READY FOR MAKEUP TESTS.
WHAT?! NATSUME-CHAN'S COMING?!
YOU GUYS NEED TO LEAVE HER ALONE TODAY.
NOW THAT I'VE ACCEPTED THE TASK, I AM MORALLY OBLIGATED TO BEAT THE KNOWLEDGE INTO HER.
BOO! BOO! CRAWL BACK UNDER YOUR ROCK, NERD QUEEN!
...
YO...

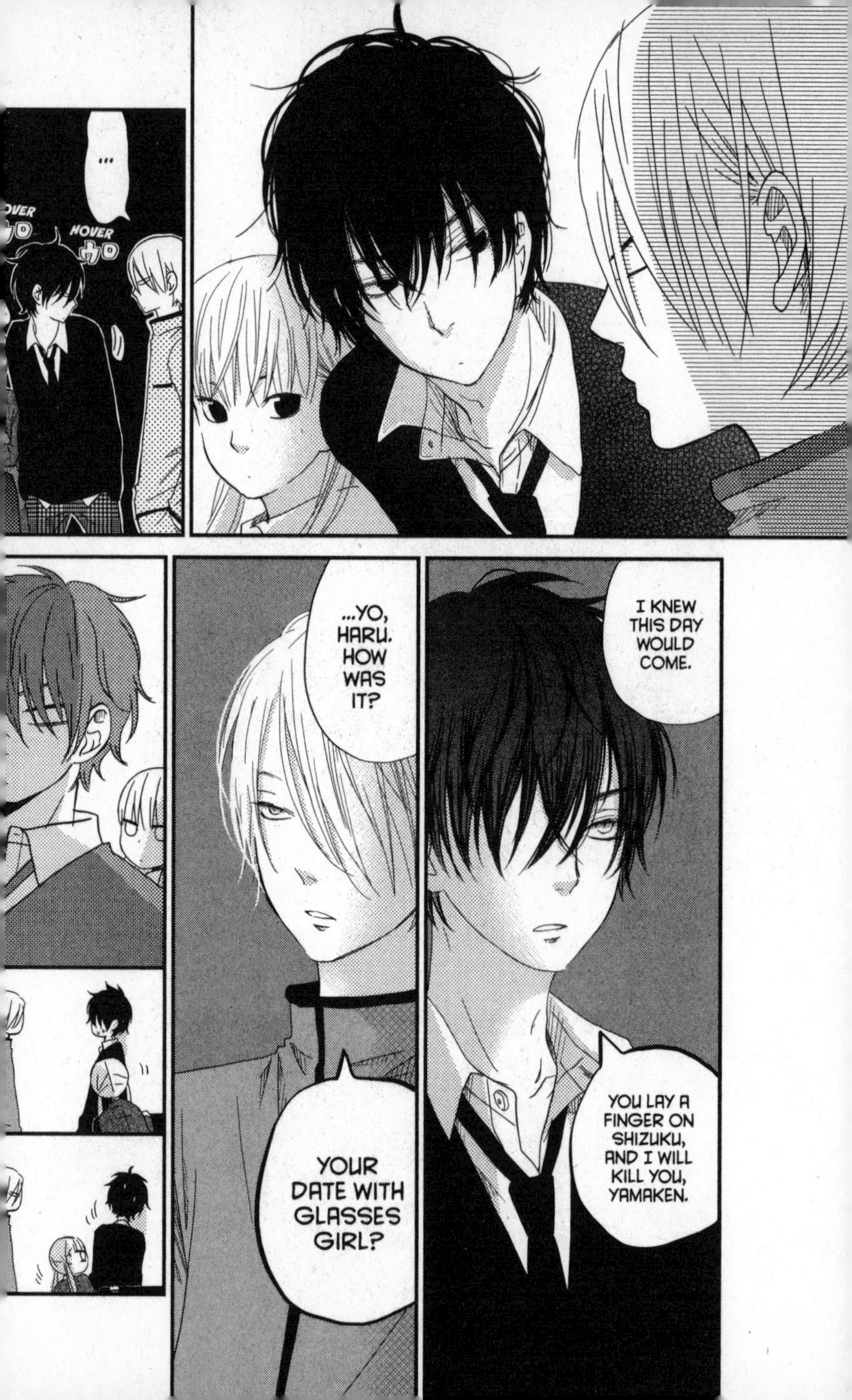
...
HOVER
HOVER
I KNEW THIS DAY WOULD COME.
YOU LAY A FINGER ON SHIZUKU, AND I WILL KILL YOU, YAMAKEN.
...YO, HARU. HOW WAS IT?
YOUR DATE WITH GLASSES GIRL?

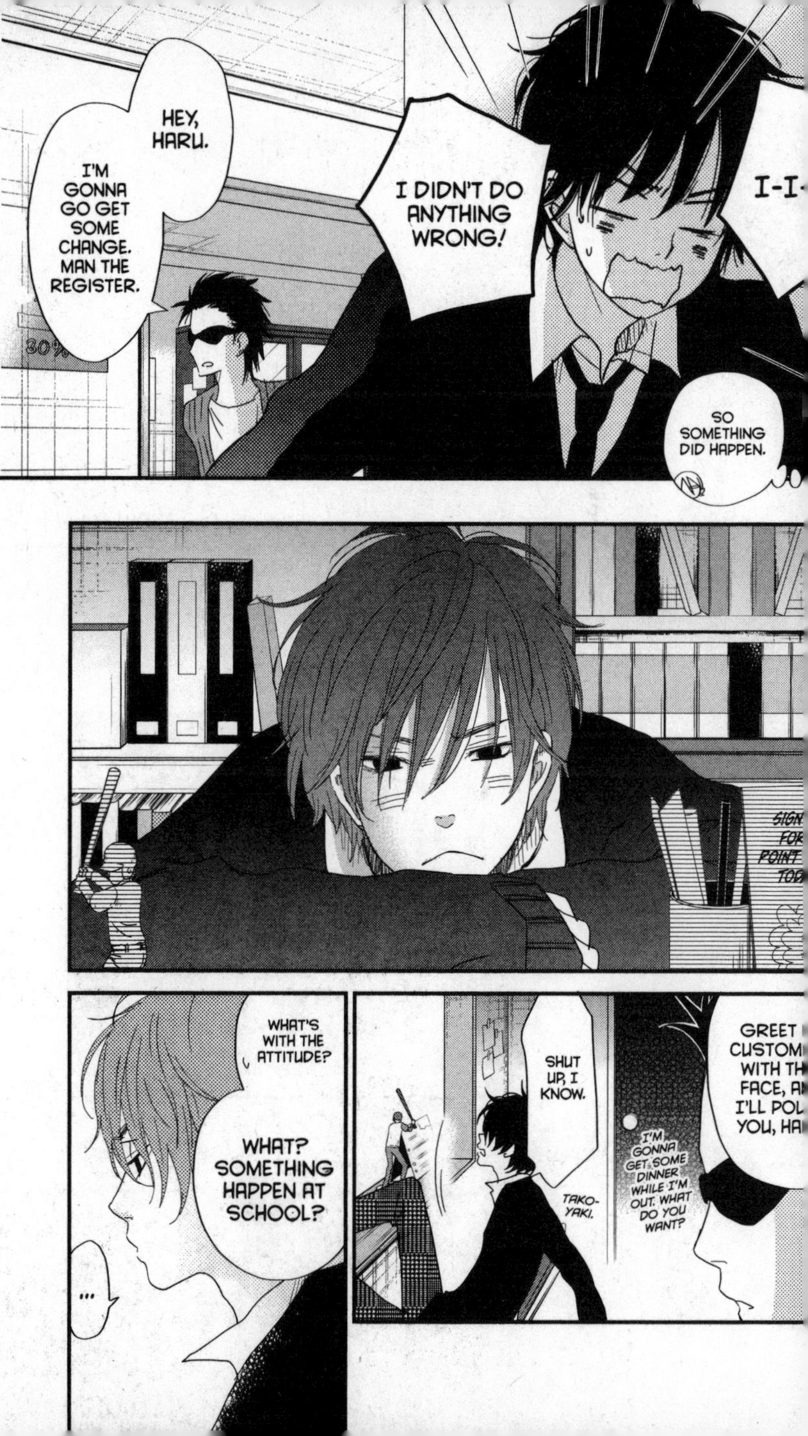
I-I-
I DIDN'T DO ANYTHING WRONG!
SO SOMETHING DID HAPPEN.
HEY, HARU.
I'M GONNA GO GET SOME CHANGE. MAN THE REGISTER.
30%
GREET CUSTOM WITH TH FACE, AI I'LL POL YOU, HA
SHUT UP, I KNOW.
I'M GONNA GET SOME DINNER WHILE I'M OUT. WHAT DO YOU WANT?
TAKO-YAKI.
WHAT'S WITH THE ATTITUDE?
WHAT? SOMETHING HAPPEN AT SCHOOL?
...

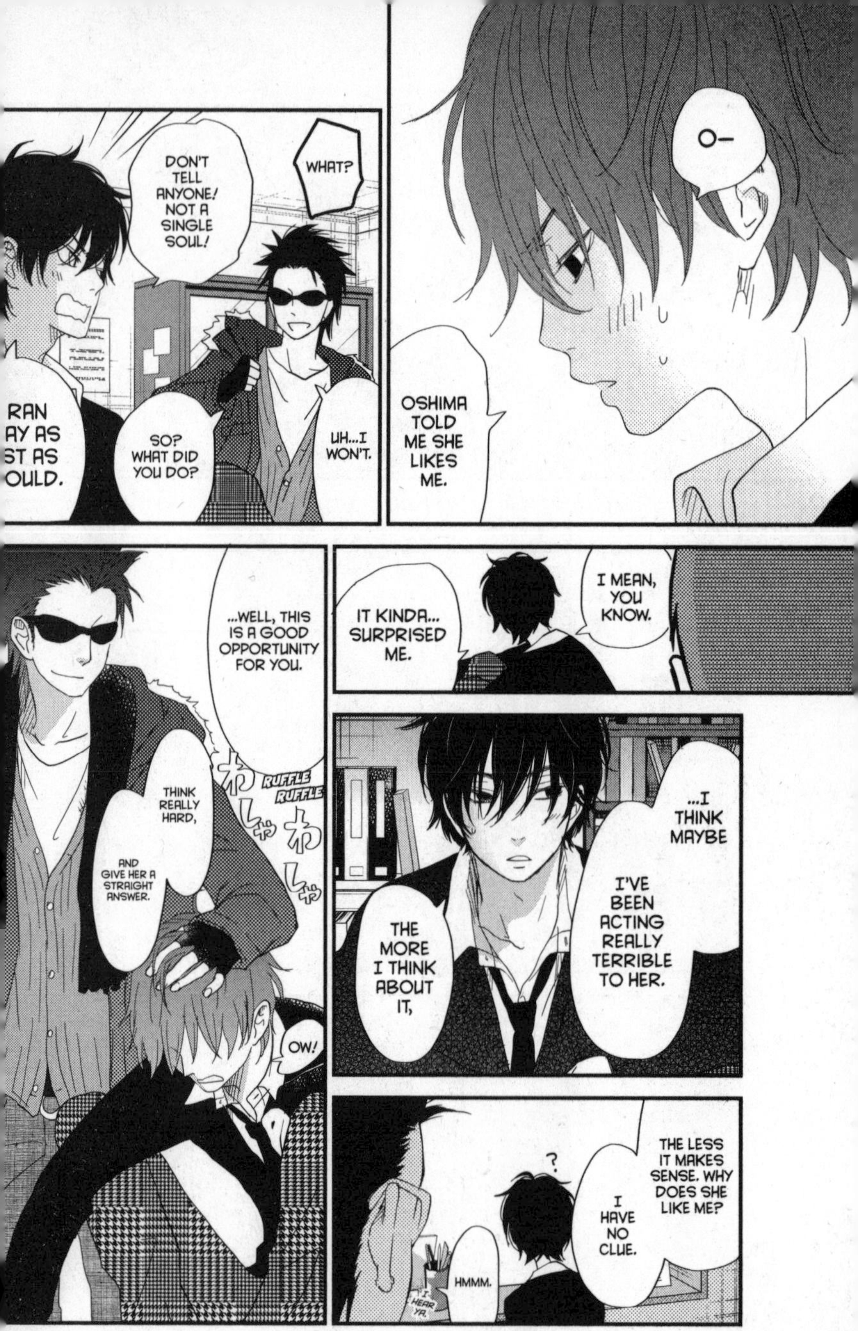
O–
OSHIMA TOLD ME SHE LIKES ME.
WHAT?
DON'T TELL ANYONE! NOT A SINGLE SOUL!
UH...I WON'T.
SO? WHAT DID YOU DO?
RAN AY AS ST AS OULD.
I MEAN, YOU KNOW.
IT KINDA... SURPRISED ME.
...I THINK MAYBE
I'VE BEEN ACTING REALLY TERRIBLE TO HER.
THE MORE I THINK ABOUT IT,
THE LESS IT MAKES SENSE. WHY DOES SHE LIKE ME?
?
I HAVE NO CLUE.
HMMM.
I HEAR YA.
...WELL, THIS IS A GOOD OPPORTUNITY FOR YOU.
わしゃ わしゃ
RUFFLE RUFFLE
THINK REALLY HARD,
AND GIVE HER A STRAIGHT ANSWER.
OW!

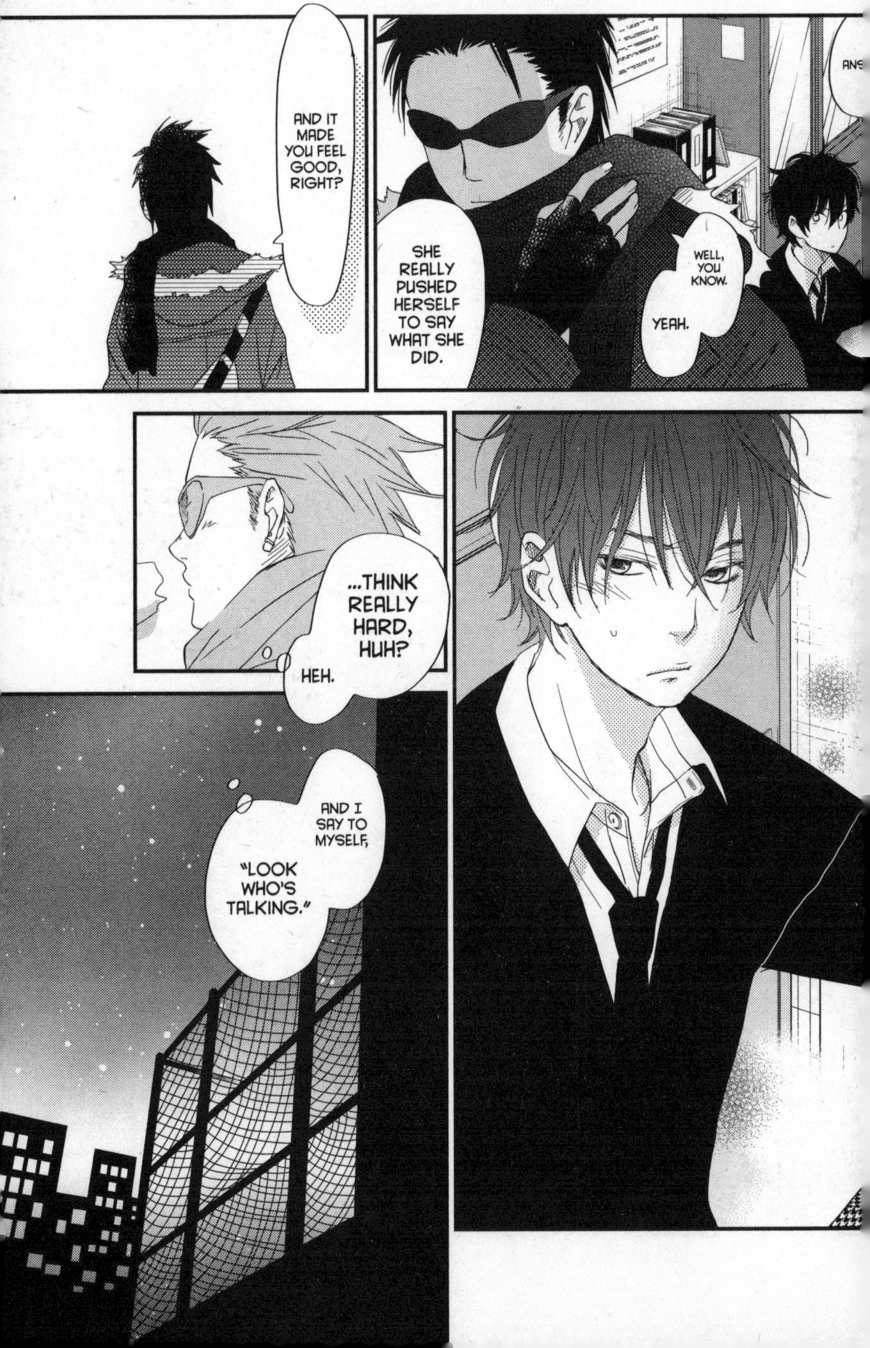
WELL, YOU KNOW.
YEAH.
SHE REALLY PUSHED HERSELF TO SAY WHAT SHE DID.
AND IT MADE YOU FEEL GOOD, RIGHT?
...THINK REALLY HARD, HUH?
HEH.
AND I SAY TO MYSELF, "LOOK WHO'S TALKING."

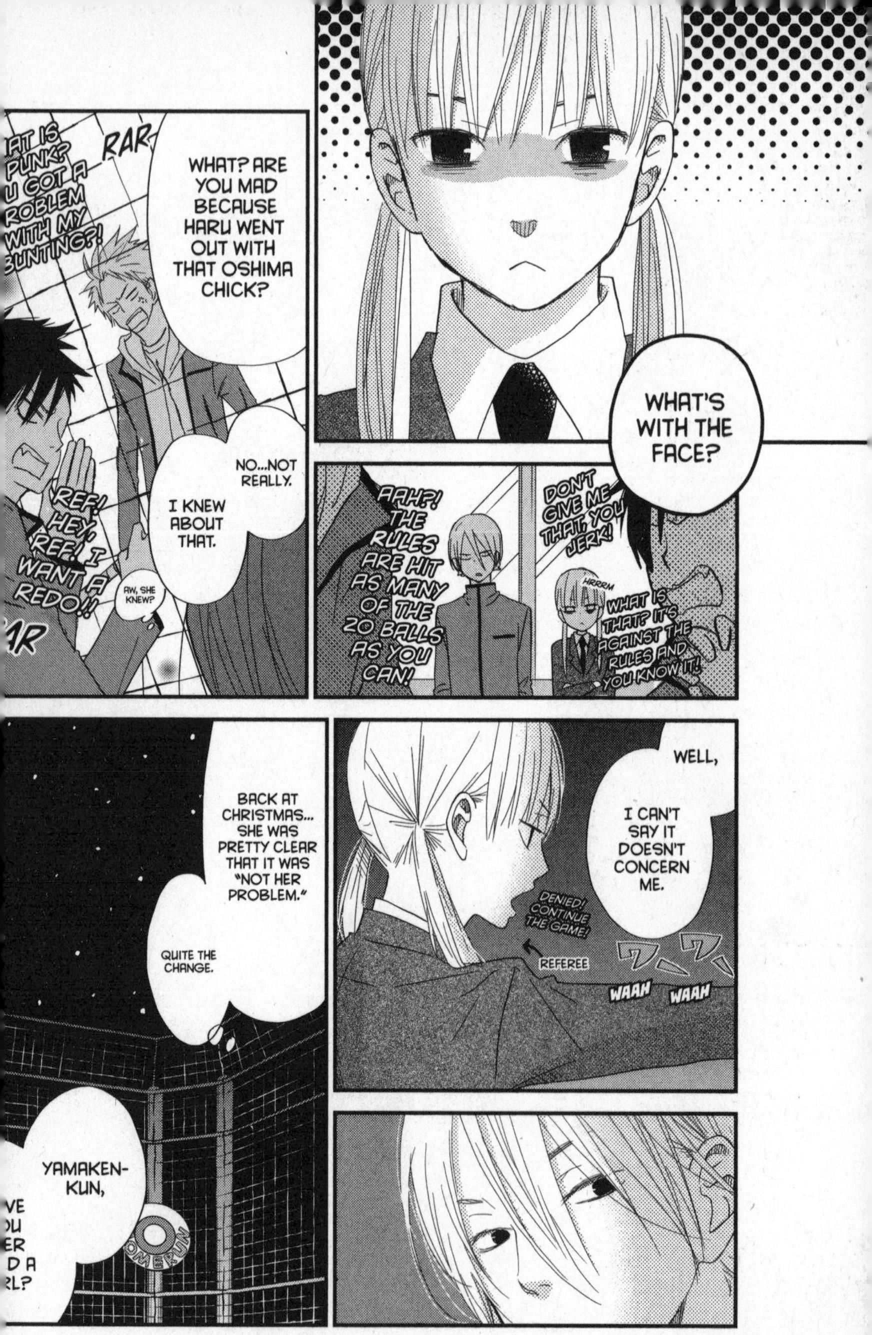
WHAT'S WITH THE FACE?
DON'T GIVE ME THAT, YOU JERK!
AAH?! THE RULES ARE HIT AS MANY OF THE 20 BALLS AS YOU CAN!
HRRRM
WHAT IS THAT? IT'S AGAINST THE RULES AND YOU KNOW IT!
WHAT? ARE YOU MAD BECAUSE HARU WENT OUT WITH THAT OSHIMA CHICK?
RAR
AT IS PUNK? U GOT A ROBLEM WITH MY BUNTING?!
NO...NOT REALLY.
I KNEW ABOUT THAT.
REF! HEY, REF! I WANT A REDO!!
AW, SHE KNEW?
AR
WELL,
I CAN'T SAY IT DOESN'T CONCERN ME.
DENIED! CONTINUE THE GAME!
REFEREE
WAAH
WAAH
BACK AT CHRISTMAS... SHE WAS PRETTY CLEAR THAT IT WAS "NOT HER PROBLEM."
QUITE THE CHANGE.
YAMAKEN-KUN,
VE OU ER D A RL?
OME RUN

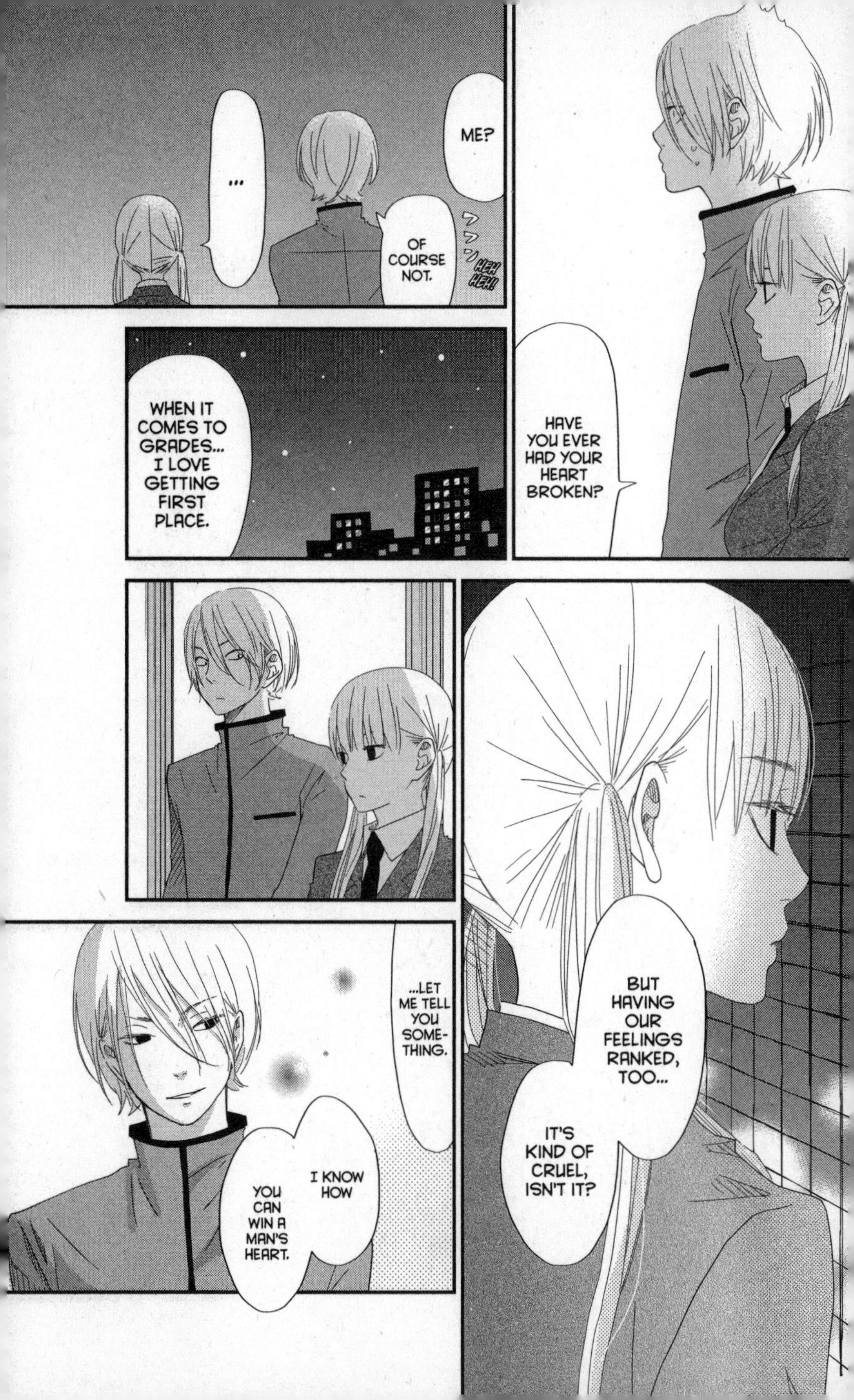
HAVE YOU EVER HAD YOUR HEART BROKEN?
ME?
OF COURSE NOT.
HEH HEH!!
...
WHEN IT COMES TO GRADES... I LOVE GETTING FIRST PLACE.
BUT HAVING OUR FEELINGS RANKED, TOO...
IT'S KIND OF CRUEL, ISN'T IT?
...LET ME TELL YOU SOME-THING.
I KNOW HOW
YOU CAN WIN A MAN'S HEART.

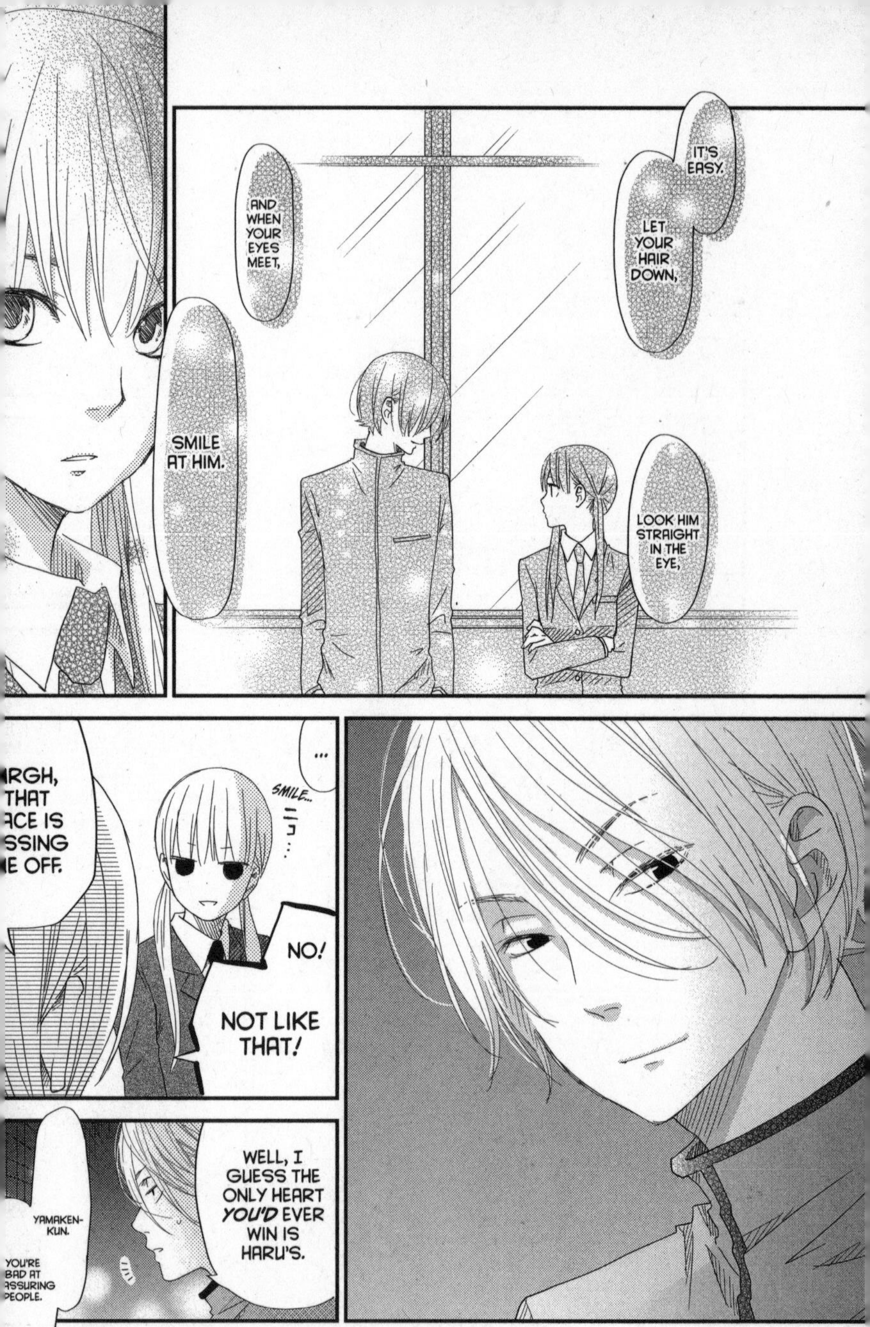

IT'S EASY.
LET YOUR HAIR DOWN,
LOOK HIM STRAIGHT IN THE EYE,
AND WHEN YOUR EYES MEET,
SMILE AT HIM.
...
SMILE...
ニコ...
RGH, THAT ACE IS SSING E OFF.
NO!
NOT LIKE THAT!
WELL, I GUESS THE ONLY HEART *YOU'D* EVER WIN IS HARU'S.
YAMAKEN-KUN.
YOU'RE BAD AT ASSURING PEOPLE.
!!

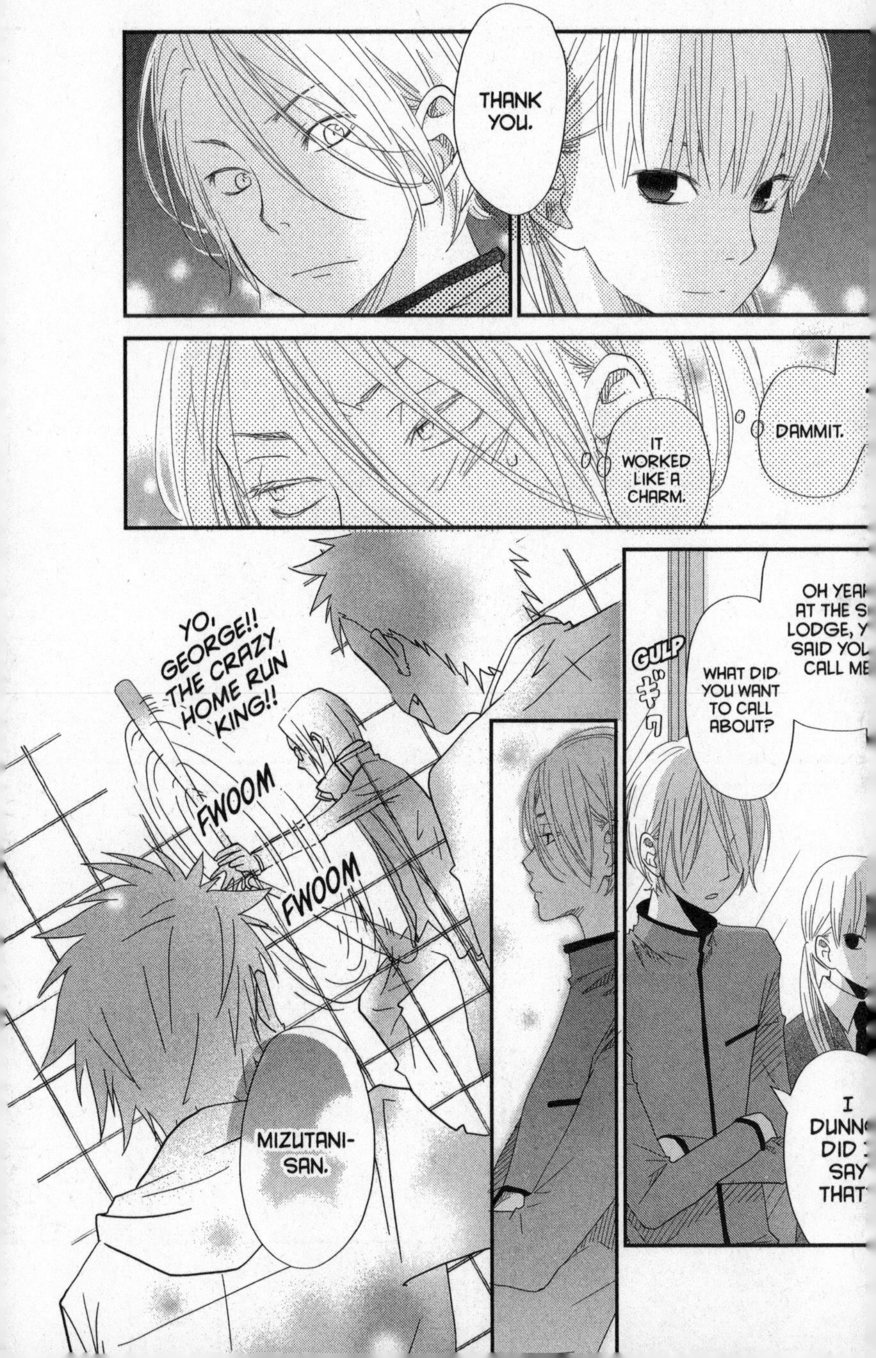
THANK YOU.
DAMMIT.
IT WORKED LIKE A CHARM.
OH YEA AT THE S LODGE, Y SAID YOU CALL ME
GULP
WHAT DID YOU WANT TO CALL ABOUT?
I DUNN DID SAY THAT
YO, GEORGE!! THE CRAZY HOME RUN KING!!
FWOOM
FWOOM
MIZUTANI-SAN.

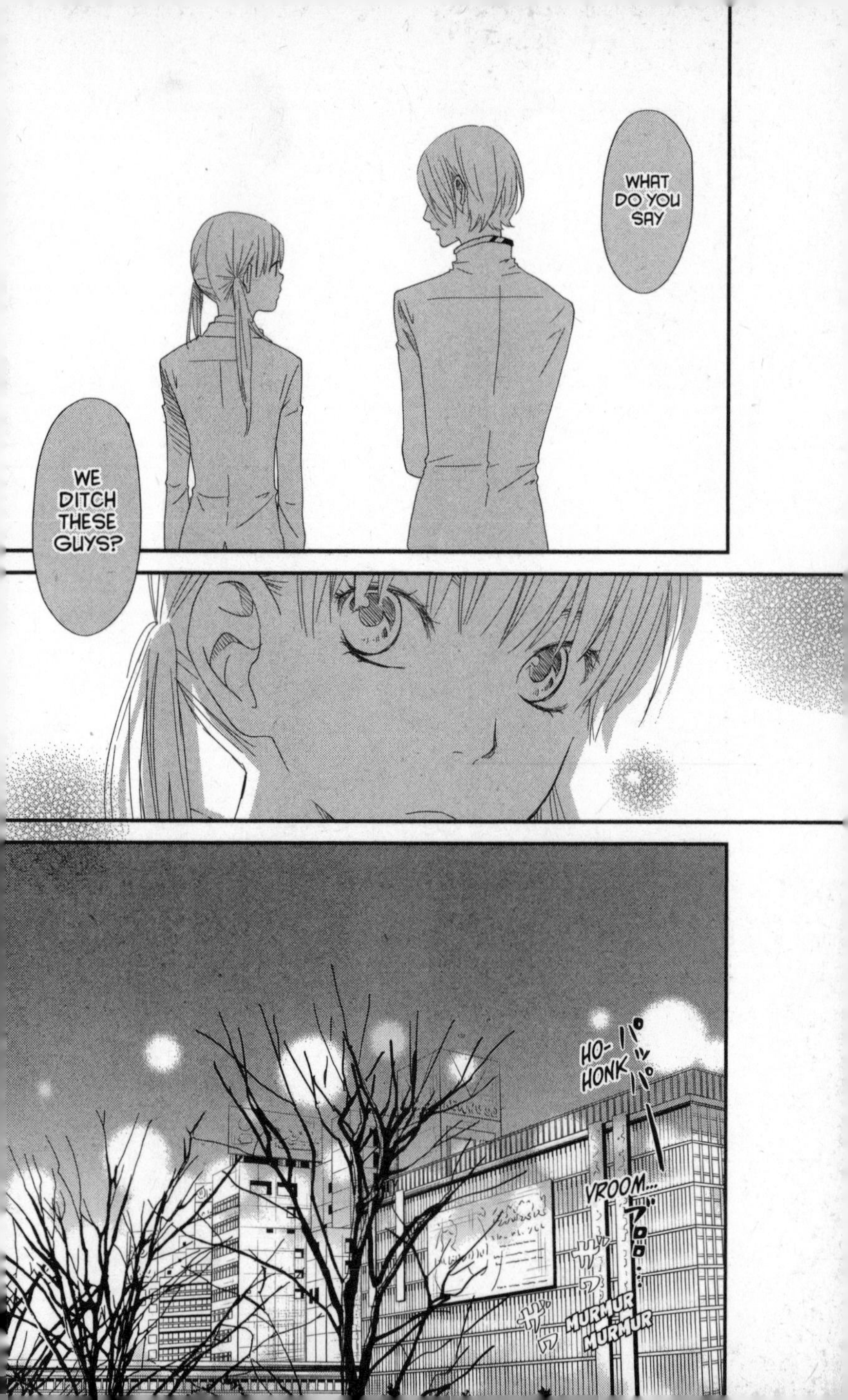
WHAT DO YOU SAY
WE DITCH THESE GUYS?
HO-HONK
パッパー
VROOM...
ブロロ…
ザワ ザワ
MURMUR MURMUR

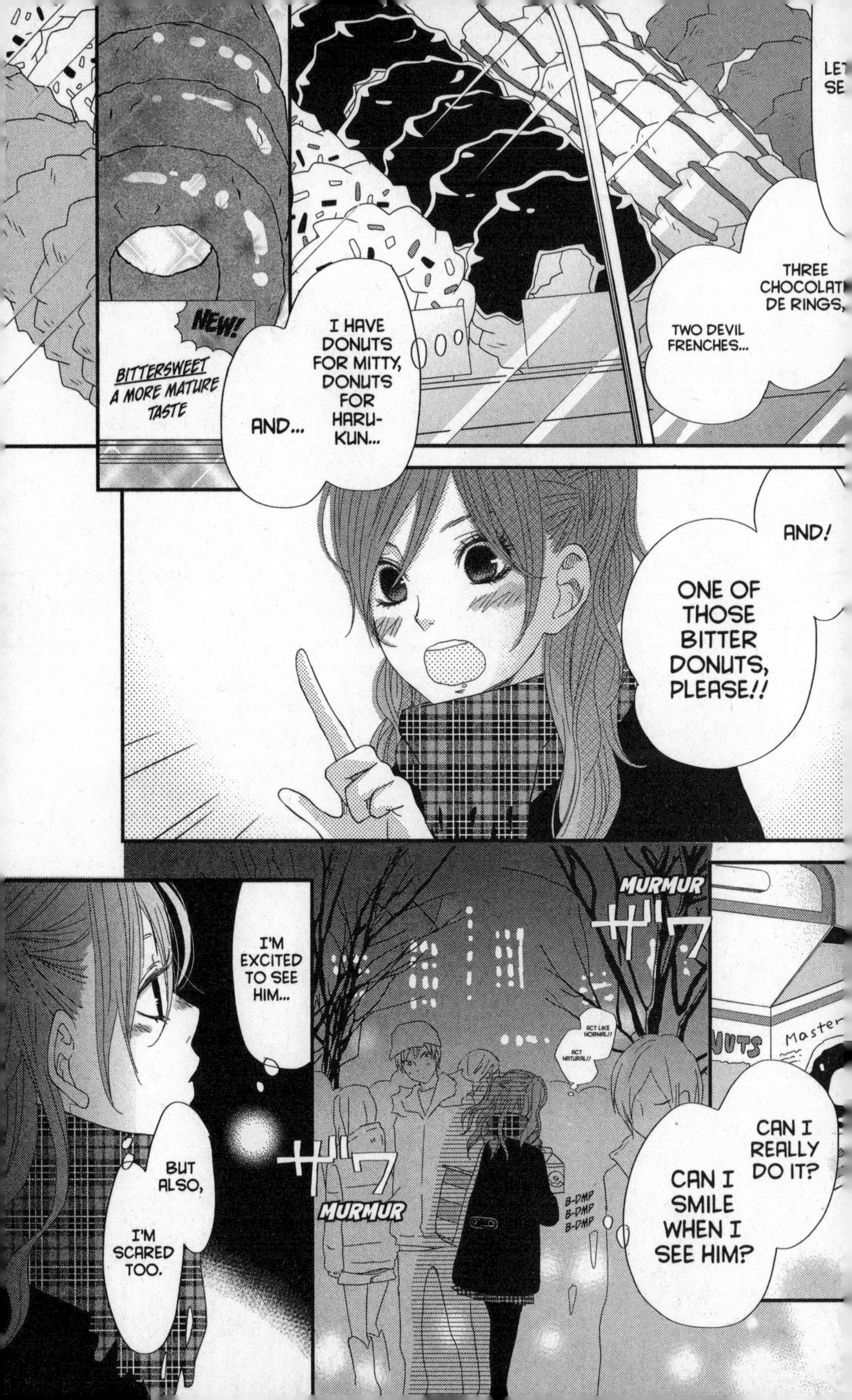
LET SE
THREE CHOCOLAT DE RINGS,
TWO DEVIL FRENCHES...
I HAVE DONUTS FOR MITTY, DONUTS FOR HARU-KUN...
AND...
NEW!
BITTERSWEET A MORE MATURE TASTE
AND!
ONE OF THOSE BITTER DONUTS, PLEASE!!
MURMUR
ザワ
NUTS
Master
CAN I REALLY DO IT?
CAN I SMILE WHEN I SEE HIM?
ACT LIKE NORMAL!!
ACT NATURAL!!
B-DMP B-DMP B-DMP
ザワ
MURMUR
I'M EXCITED TO SEE HIM...
BUT ALSO,
I'M SCARED TOO.

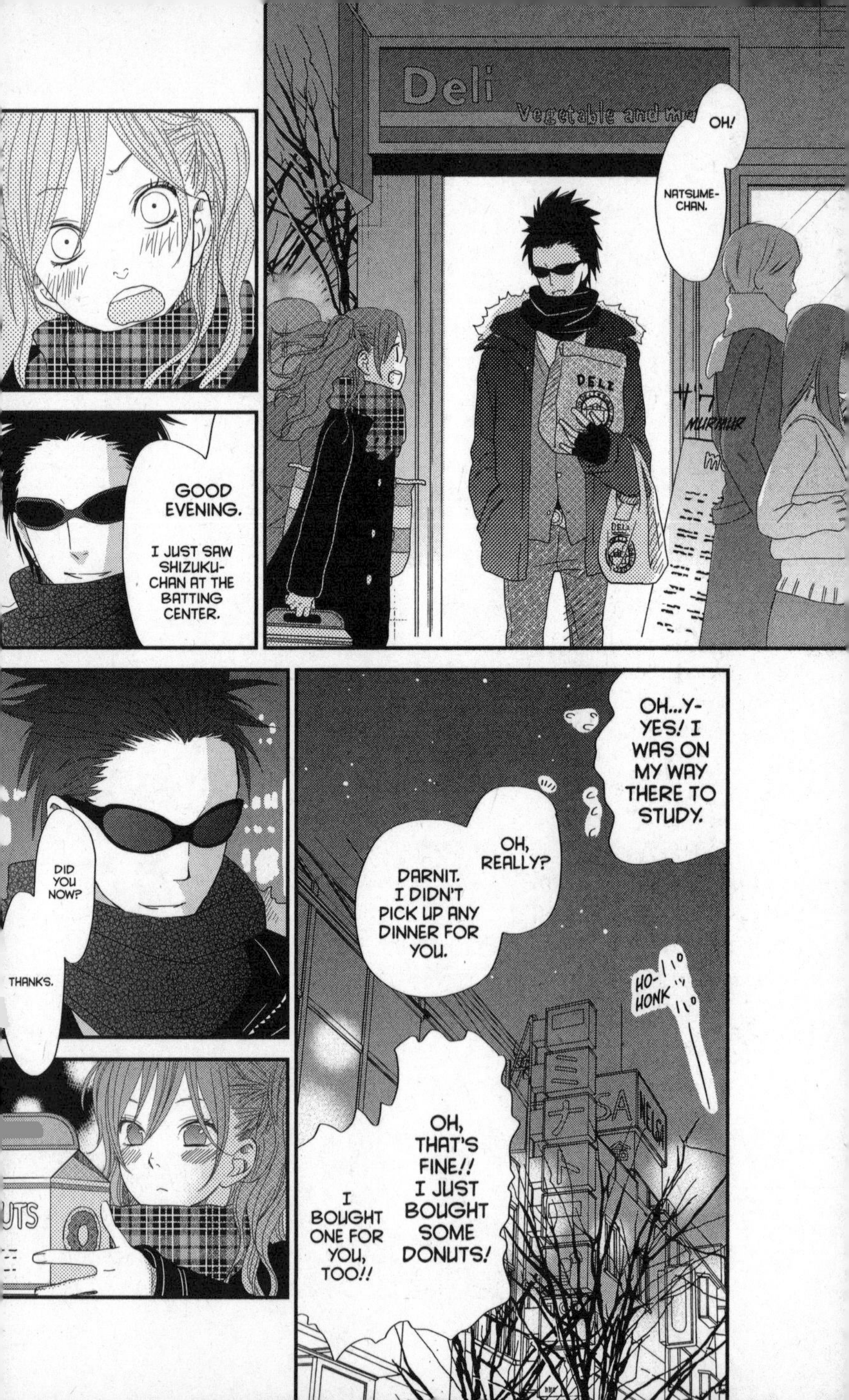
Deli
OH!
NATSUME-CHAN.
MURMUR
GOOD EVENING.
I JUST SAW SHIZUKU-CHAN AT THE BATTING CENTER.
OH...Y-YES! I WAS ON MY WAY THERE TO STUDY.
OH, REALLY?
DARNIT. I DIDN'T PICK UP ANY DINNER FOR YOU.
HO-HONK
OH, THAT'S FINE!! I JUST BOUGHT SOME DONUTS!
I BOUGHT ONE FOR YOU, TOO!!
DID YOU NOW?
THANKS.

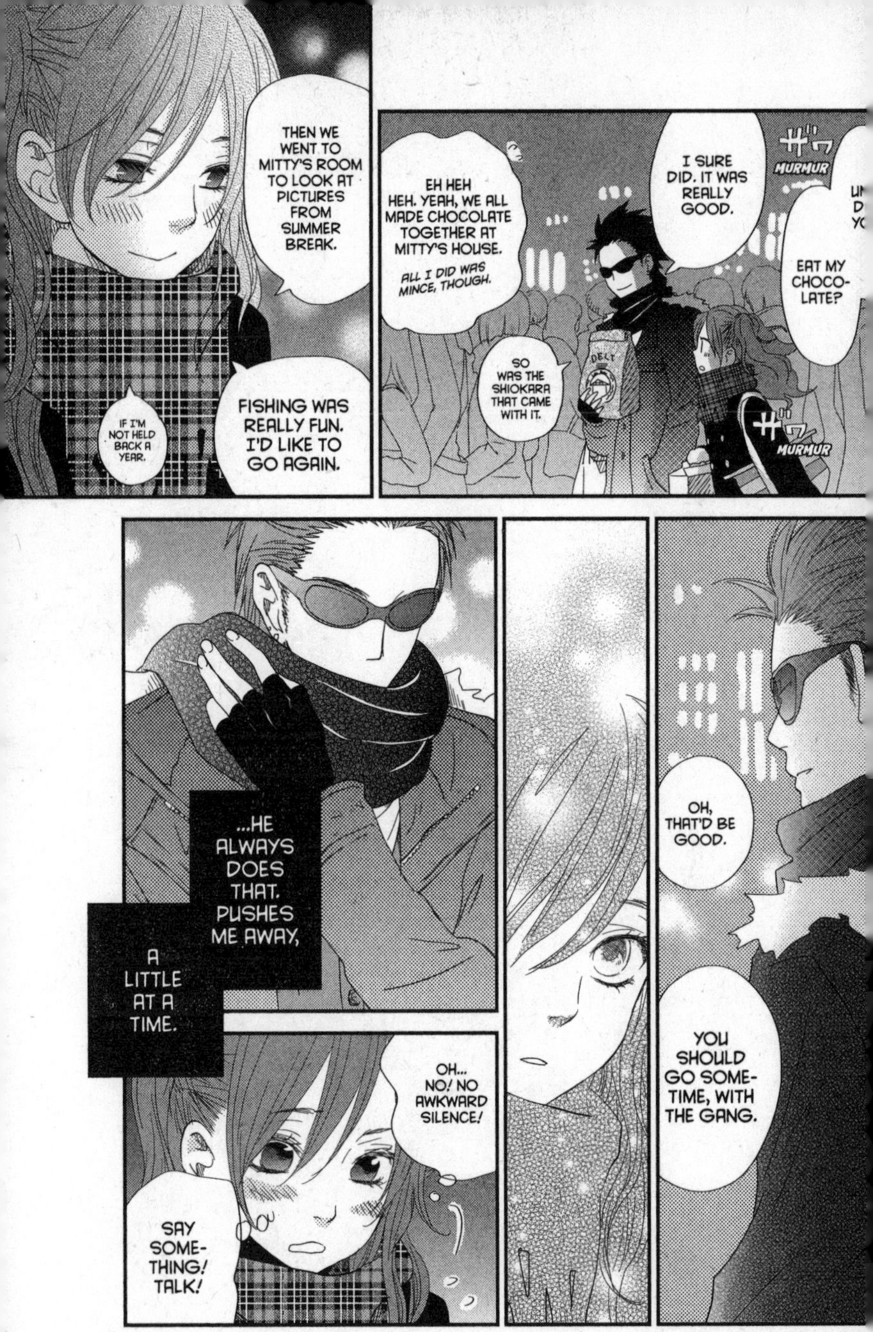
EAT MY CHOCOLATE?
MURMUR
I SURE DID. IT WAS REALLY GOOD.
EH HEH HEH. YEAH, WE ALL MADE CHOCOLATE TOGETHER AT MITTY'S HOUSE.
ALL I DID WAS MINCE, THOUGH.
SO WAS THE SHIOKARA THAT CAME WITH IT.
MURMUR
THEN WE WENT TO MITTY'S ROOM TO LOOK AT PICTURES FROM SUMMER BREAK.
FISHING WAS REALLY FUN. I'D LIKE TO GO AGAIN.
IF I'M NOT HELD BACK A YEAR.
OH, THAT'D BE GOOD.
YOU SHOULD GO SOMETIME, WITH THE GANG.
...HE ALWAYS DOES THAT. PUSHES ME AWAY,
A LITTLE AT A TIME.
OH... NO! NO AWKWARD SILENCE!
SAY SOMETHING! TALK!

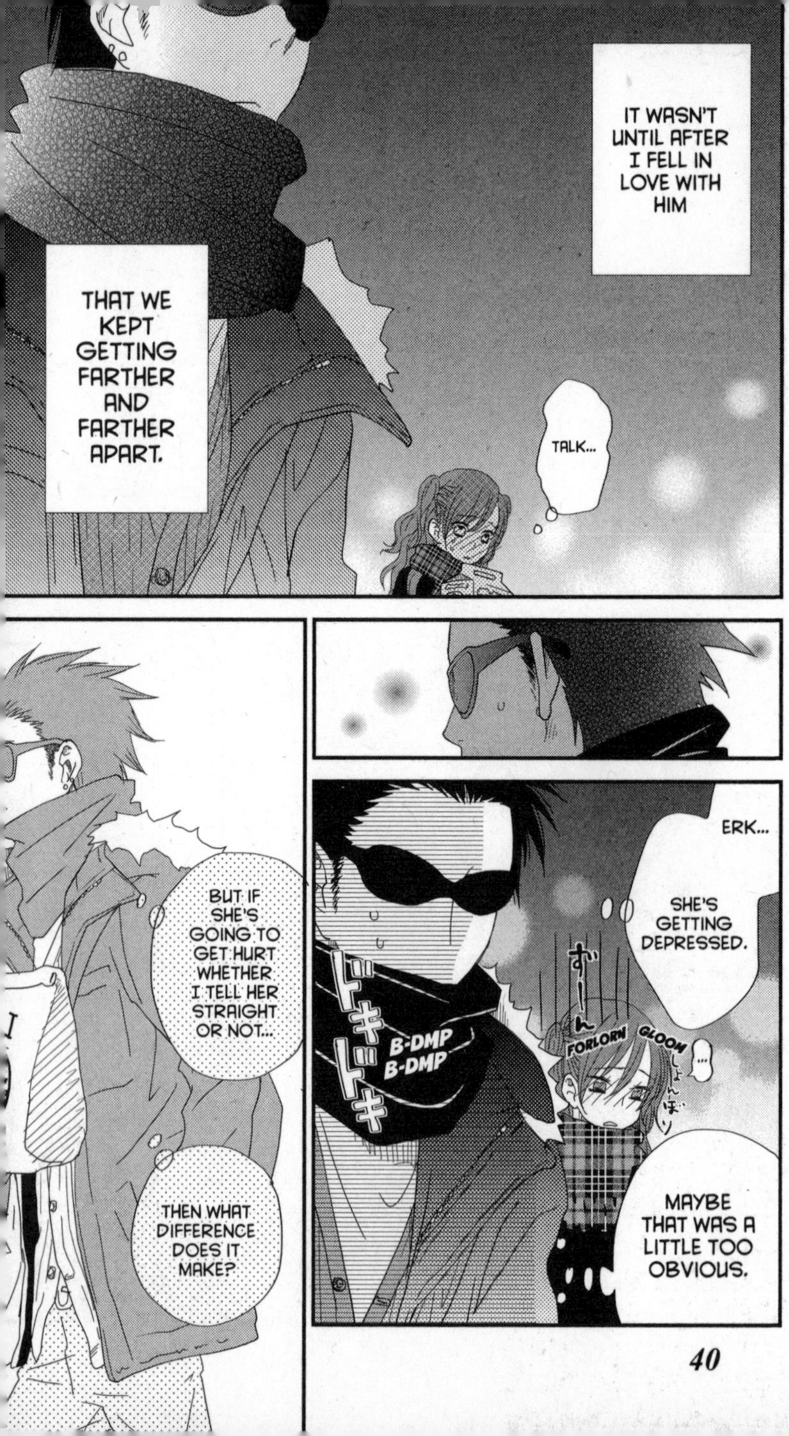
IT WASN'T UNTIL AFTER I FELL IN LOVE WITH HIM
TALK...
THAT WE KEPT GETTING FARTHER AND FARTHER APART.
ERK...
SHE'S GETTING DEPRESSED.
ドキドキ
B-DMP B-DMP
ずーん
FORLORN
しょんぼり
GLOOM
...
MAYBE THAT WAS A LITTLE TOO OBVIOUS.
BUT IF SHE'S GOING TO GET HURT WHETHER I TELL HER STRAIGHT OR NOT...
THEN WHAT DIFFERENCE DOES IT MAKE?

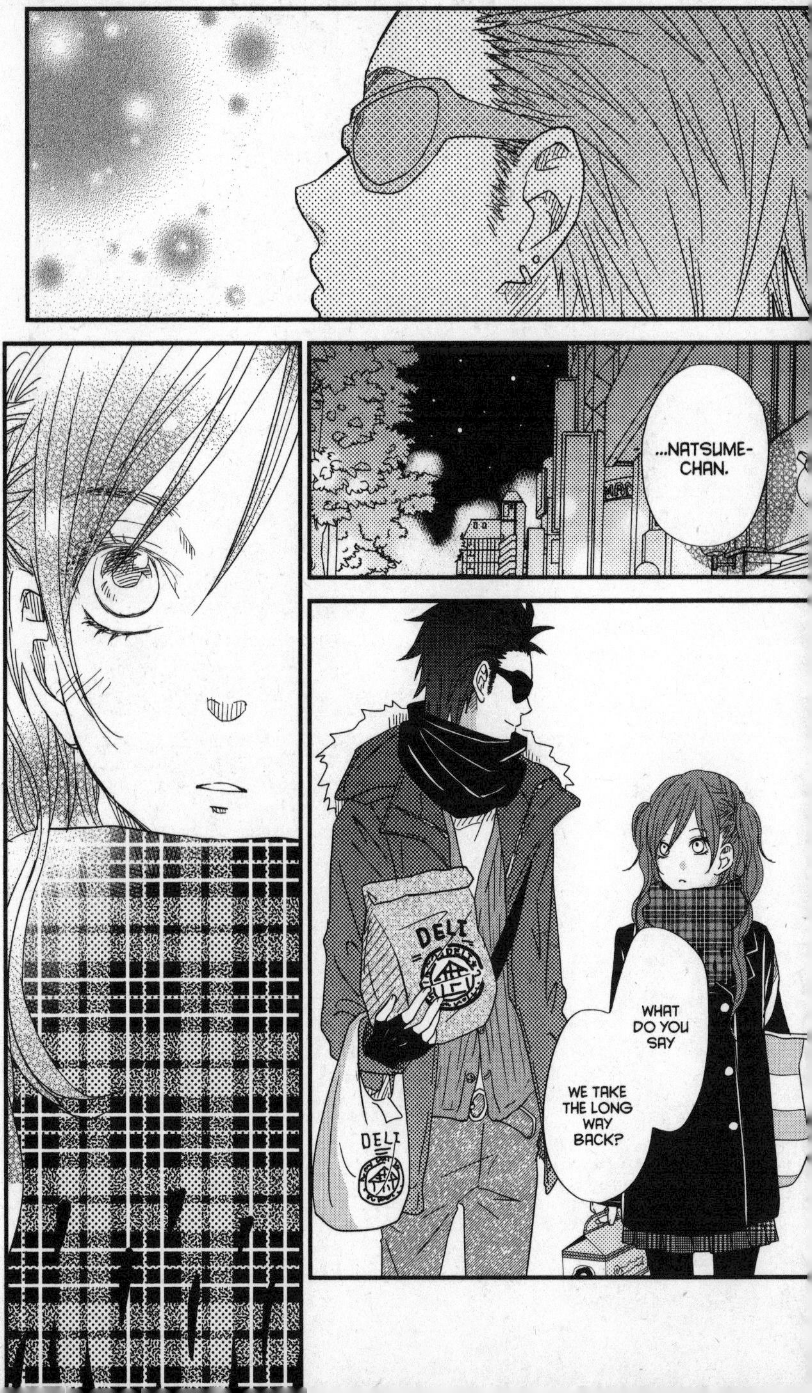
...NATSUME-CHAN.
WHAT DO YOU SAY
WE TAKE THE LONG WAY BACK?
DELI
DELI

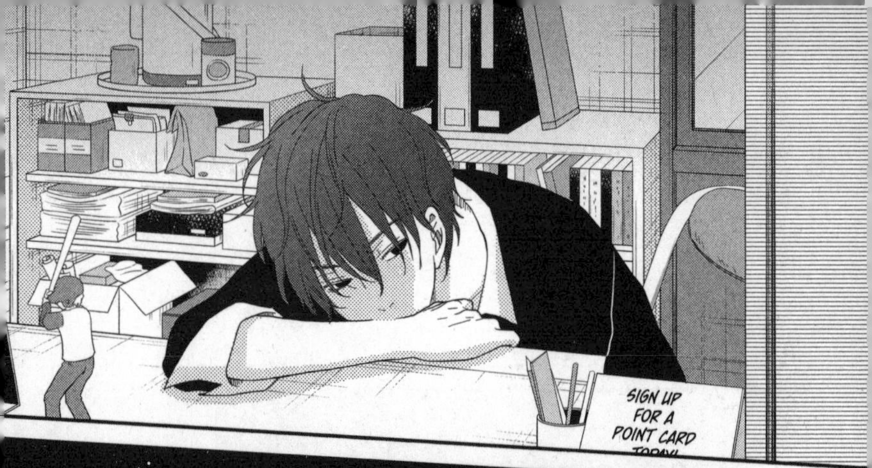
SIGN UP
FOR A
POINT CARD

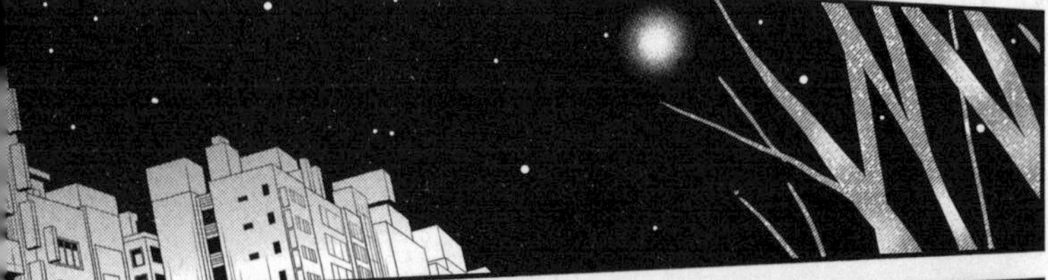

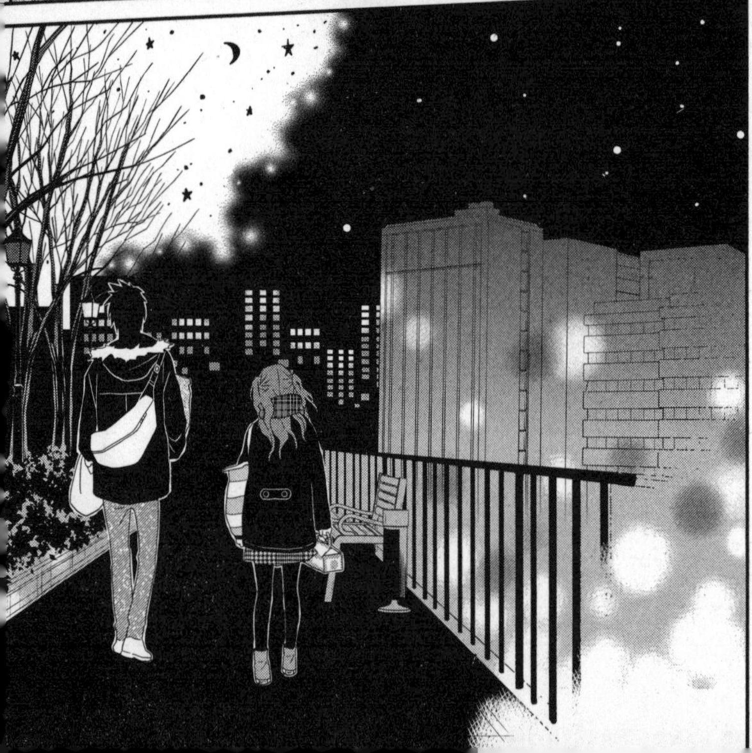

IN THE LIBRARY

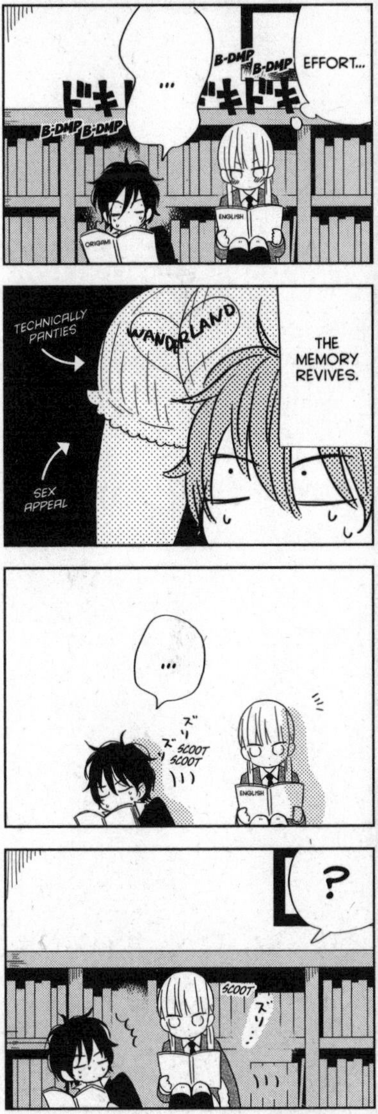
EFFORT...
B-DMP
B-DMP
ドキドキ
...
B-DMP
B-DMP
ENGLISH
ORIGAMI
THE MEMORY REVIVES.
WANDERLAND
TECHNICALLY PANTIES
SEX APPEAL
...
ズリ
ズリ
SCOOT
SCOOT
ENGLISH
?
SCOOT
ズリ...

OH YEAH, WE DID DO THAT

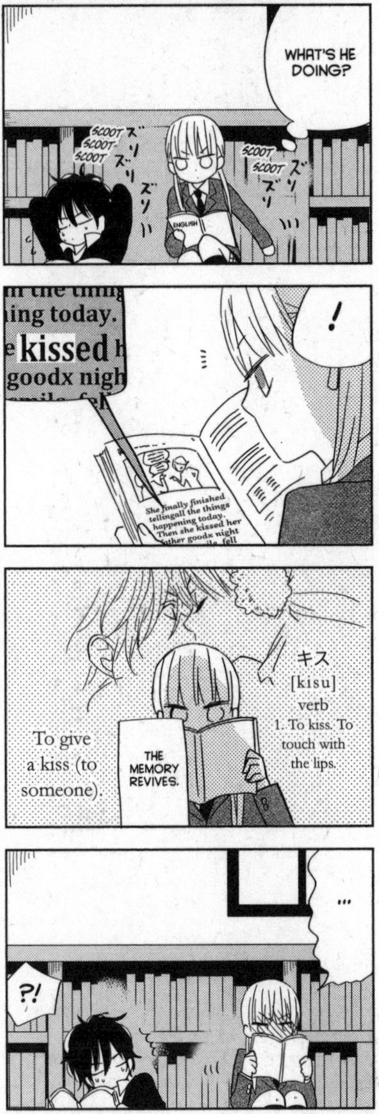
WHAT'S HE DOING?
SCOOT
SCOOT
ズリ
ズリ
SCOOT
SCOOT
SCOOT
ズリ
ズリ
ズリ
ENGLISH
!
ing today.
kissed
goodx nigh
She finally finished tellingall the things happening today. Then she kissed her father goodx night
キス
[kisu]
verb
1. To kiss. To touch with the lips.
To give a kiss (to someone).
THE MEMORY REVIVES.
...
?!

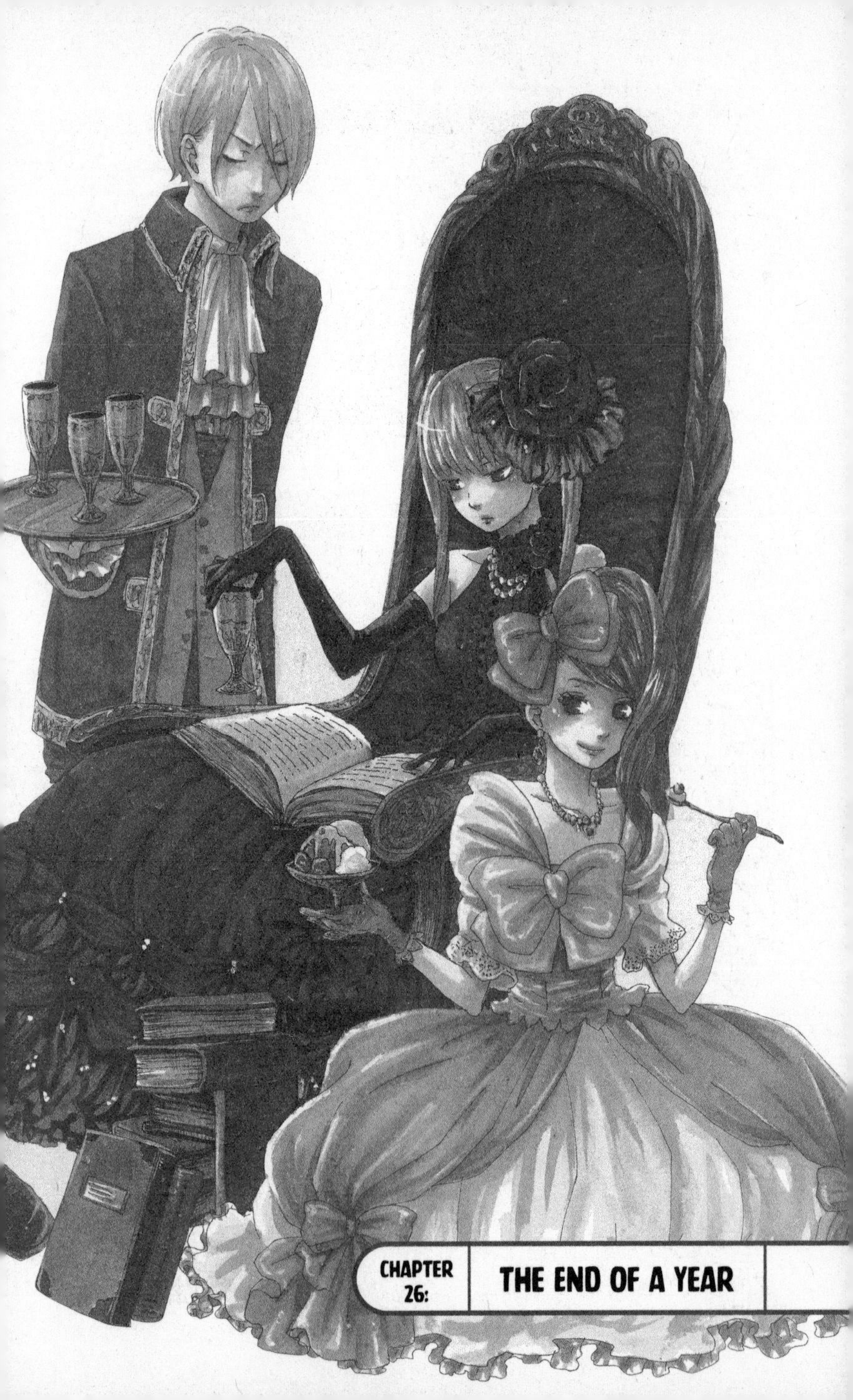

CHAPTER 26: THE END OF A YEAR

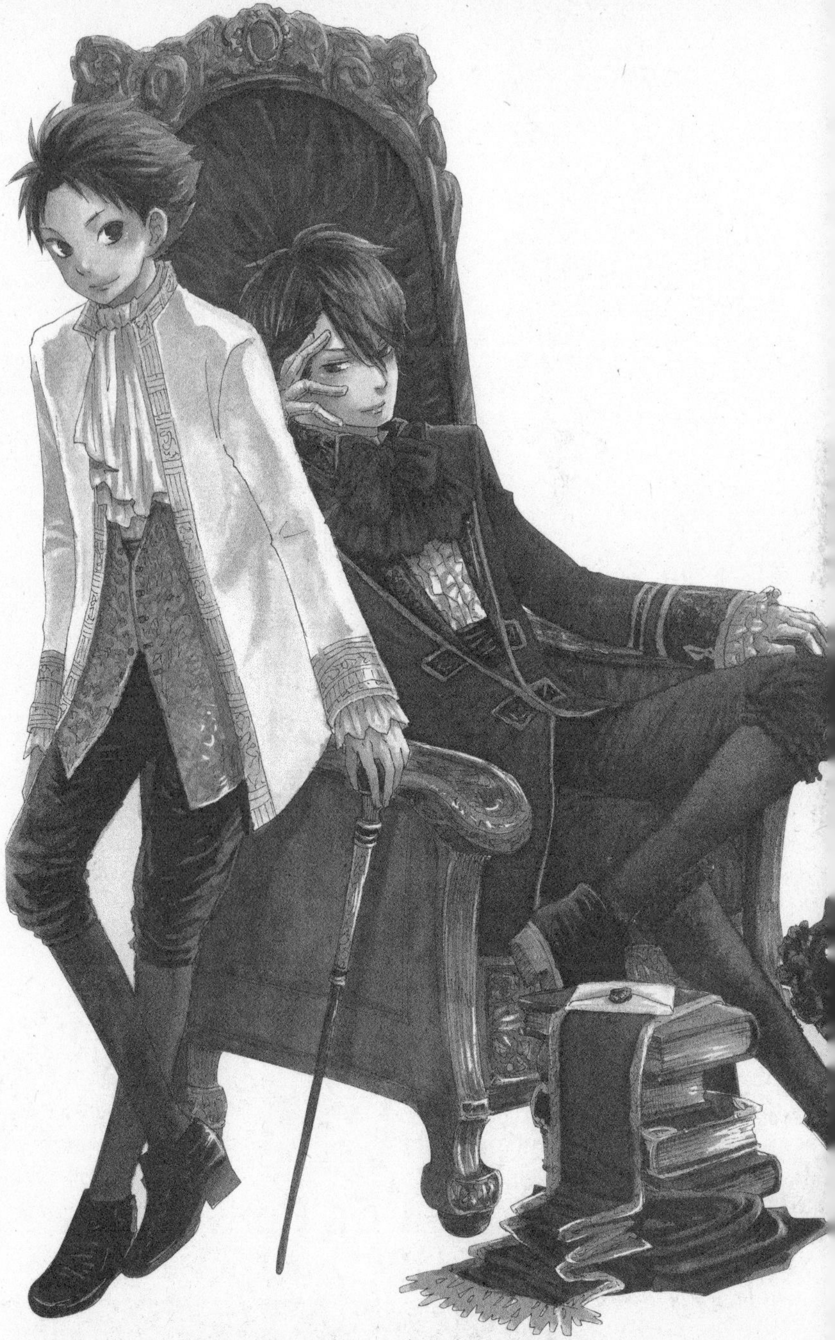

High School 1st Year: Summer, in the mountains with Haru and everyone.

Photo Album

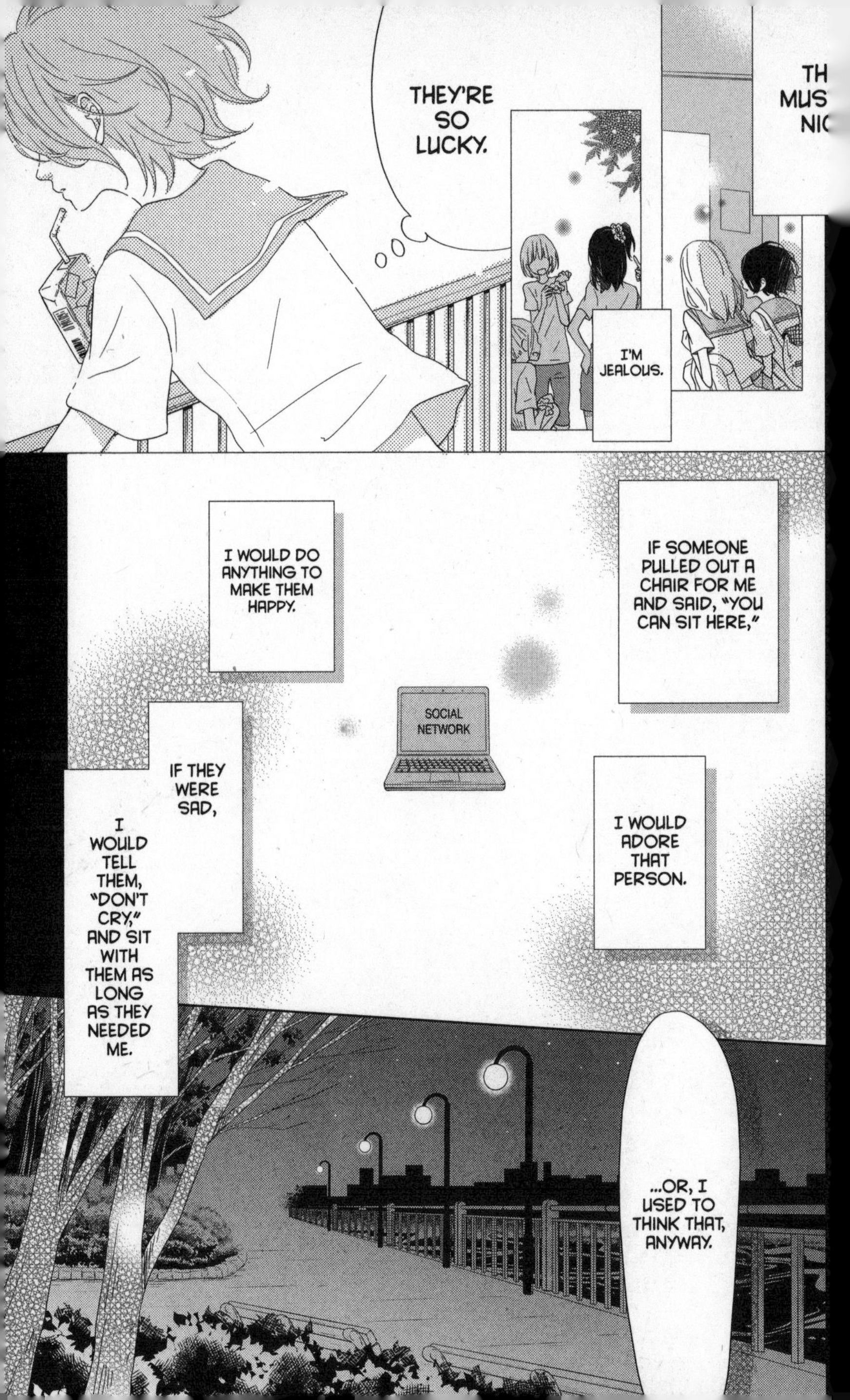

TH
MUS
NI
I'M JEALOUS.
THEY'RE SO LUCKY.
IF SOMEONE PULLED OUT A CHAIR FOR ME AND SAID, "YOU CAN SIT HERE,"
I WOULD ADORE THAT PERSON.
I WOULD DO ANYTHING TO MAKE THEM HAPPY.
SOCIAL NETWORK
IF THEY WERE SAD,
I WOULD TELL THEM, "DON'T CRY," AND SIT WITH THEM AS LONG AS THEY NEEDED ME.
...OR, I USED TO THINK THAT, ANYWAY.

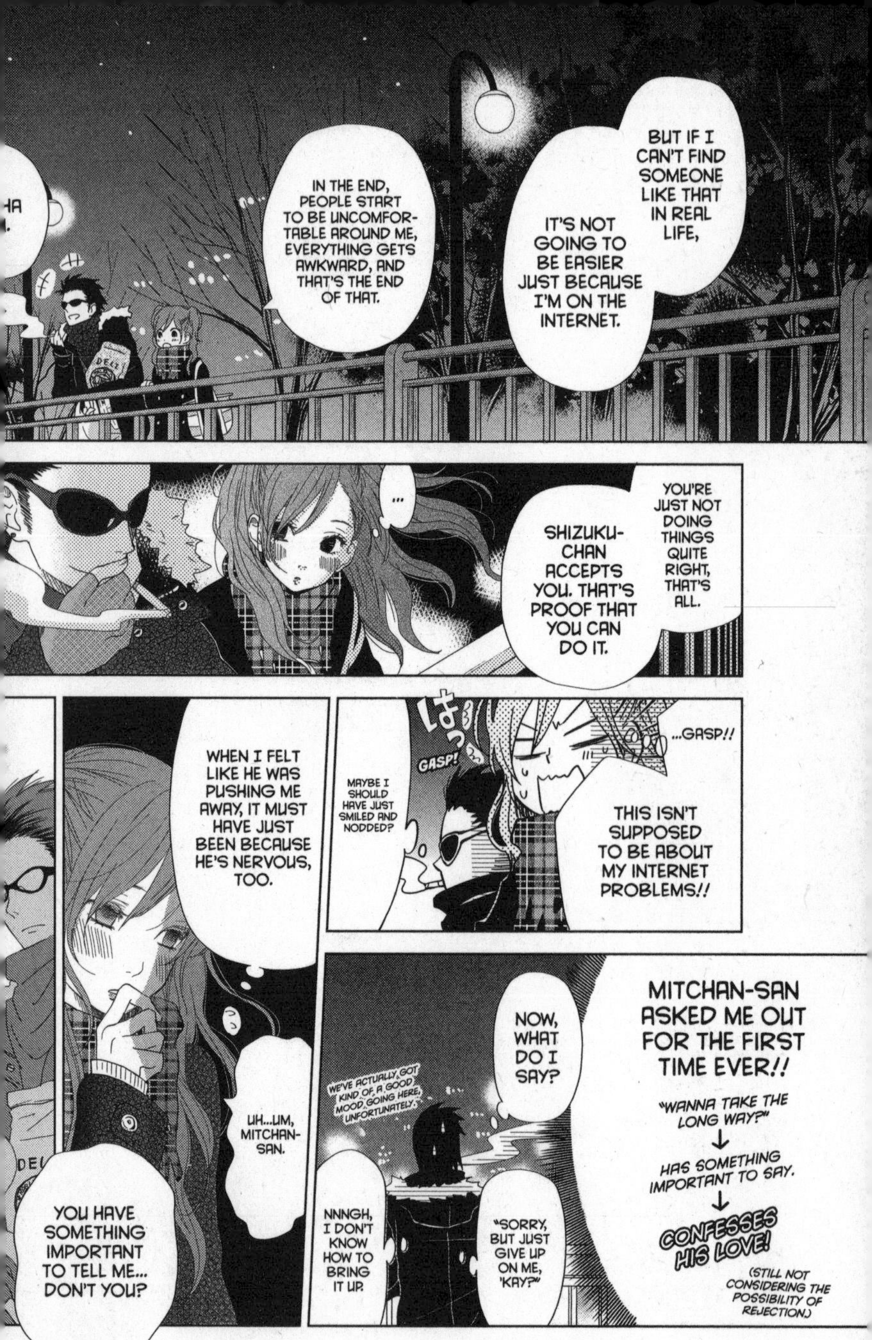
BUT IF I CAN'T FIND SOMEONE LIKE THAT IN REAL LIFE,
IT'S NOT GOING TO BE EASIER JUST BECAUSE I'M ON THE INTERNET.
IN THE END, PEOPLE START TO BE UNCOMFORTABLE AROUND ME, EVERYTHING GETS AWKWARD, AND THAT'S THE END OF THAT.
YOU'RE JUST NOT DOING THINGS QUITE RIGHT, THAT'S ALL.
SHIZUKU-CHAN ACCEPTS YOU. THAT'S PROOF THAT YOU CAN DO IT.
...
...GASP!!
はっ
GASP!
THIS ISN'T SUPPOSED TO BE ABOUT MY INTERNET PROBLEMS!!
MAYBE I SHOULD HAVE JUST SMILED AND NODDED?
MITCHAN-SAN ASKED ME OUT FOR THE FIRST TIME EVER!!
"WANNA TAKE THE LONG WAY?"
↓
HAS SOMETHING IMPORTANT TO SAY.
↓
CONFESSES HIS LOVE!
(STILL NOT CONSIDERING THE POSSIBILITY OF REJECTION.)
NOW, WHAT DO I SAY?
WE'VE ACTUALLY GOT KIND OF A GOOD MOOD GOING HERE, UNFORTUNATELY.
"SORRY, BUT JUST GIVE UP ON ME, 'KAY?"
NNNGH, I DON'T KNOW HOW TO BRING IT UP.
WHEN I FELT LIKE HE WAS PUSHING ME AWAY, IT MUST HAVE JUST BEEN BECAUSE HE'S NERVOUS, TOO.
UH...UM, MITCHAN-SAN.
YOU HAVE SOMETHING IMPORTANT TO TELL ME... DON'T YOU?

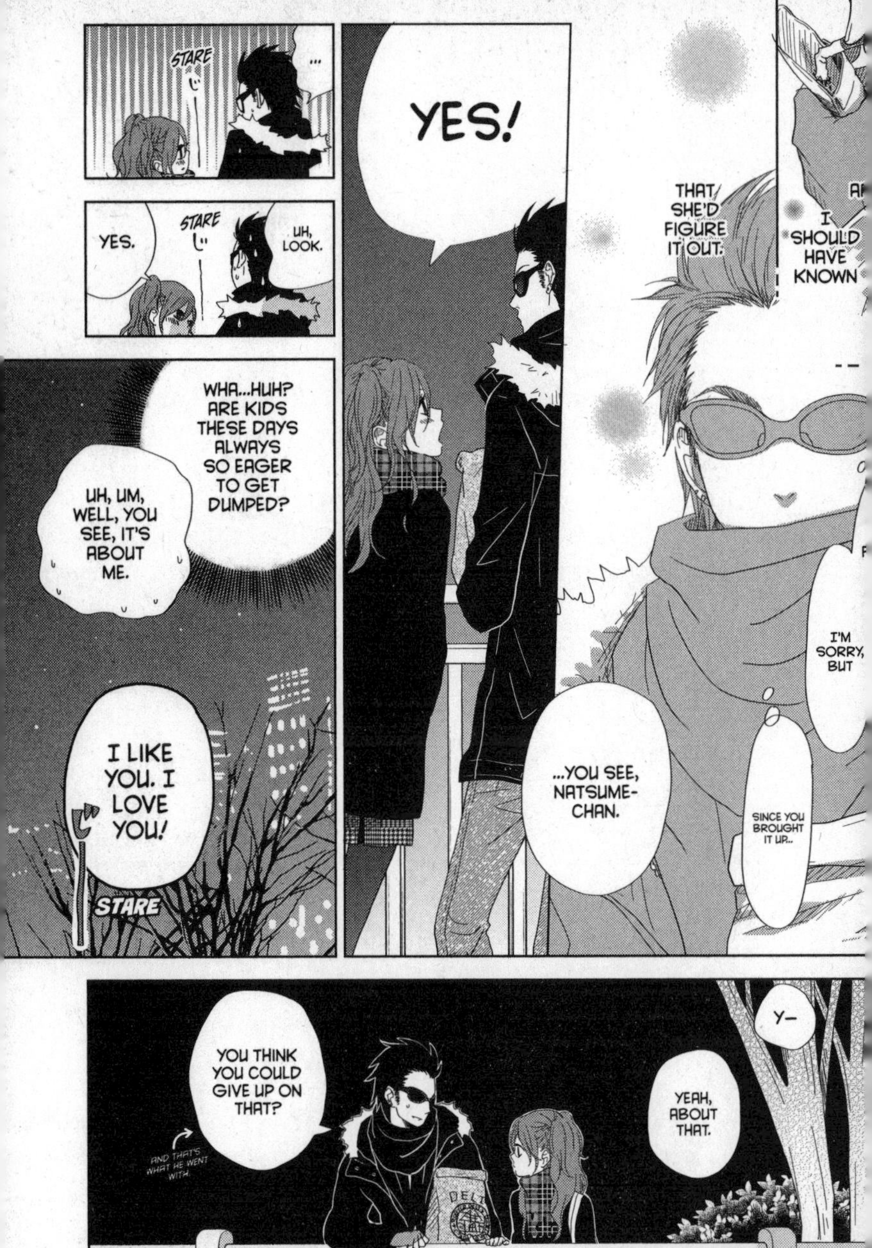
I SHOULD HAVE KNOWN
THAT SHE'D FIGURE IT OUT.
I'M SORRY, BUT
SINCE YOU BROUGHT IT UP...
...YOU SEE, NATSUME-CHAN.
YES!
...
STARE
UH, LOOK.
STARE
YES.
WHA...HUH? ARE KIDS THESE DAYS ALWAYS SO EAGER TO GET DUMPED?
UH, UM, WELL, YOU SEE, IT'S ABOUT ME.
I LIKE YOU. I LOVE YOU!
STARE
Y—
YEAH, ABOUT THAT.
YOU THINK YOU COULD GIVE UP ON THAT?
AND THAT'S WHAT HE WENT WITH.

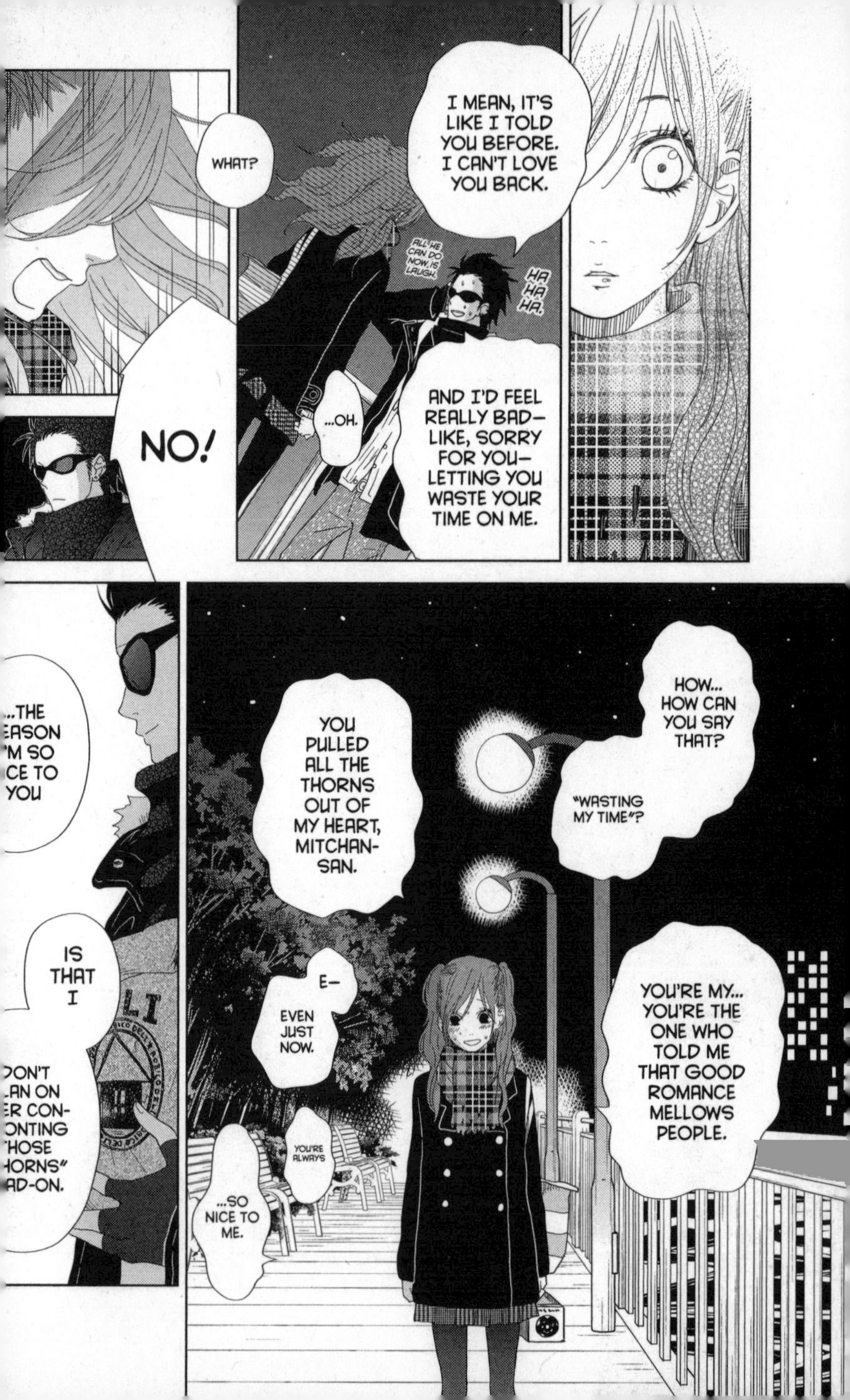
I MEAN, IT'S LIKE I TOLD YOU BEFORE. I CAN'T LOVE YOU BACK.
HA HA HA.
ALL HE CAN DO NOW, IS LAUGH.
AND I'D FEEL REALLY BAD— LIKE, SORRY FOR YOU— LETTING YOU WASTE YOUR TIME ON ME.
...OH.
WHAT?
NO!
HOW... HOW CAN YOU SAY THAT?
"WASTING MY TIME"?
YOU PULLED ALL THE THORNS OUT OF MY HEART, MITCHAN-SAN.
YOU'RE MY... YOU'RE THE ONE WHO TOLD ME THAT GOOD ROMANCE MELLOWS PEOPLE.
E—
EVEN JUST NOW.
YOU'RE ALWAYS
...SO NICE TO ME.
...THE EASON 'M SO CE TO YOU
IS THAT I
DON'T LAN ON ER CON- ONTING THOSE HORNS" AD-ON.

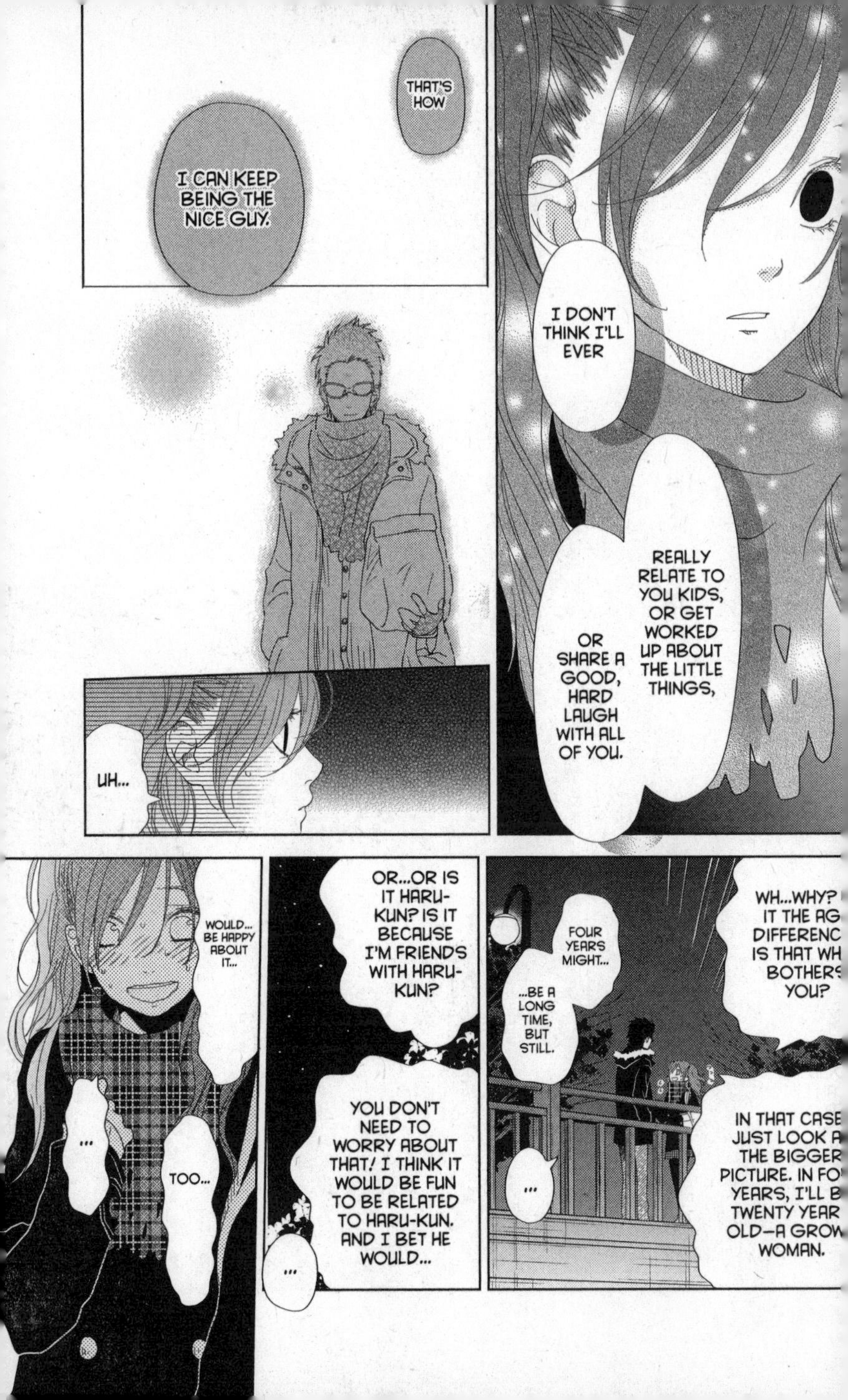
I DON'T THINK I'LL EVER
REALLY RELATE TO YOU KIDS, OR GET WORKED UP ABOUT THE LITTLE THINGS,
OR SHARE A GOOD, HARD LAUGH WITH ALL OF YOU.
THAT'S HOW
I CAN KEEP BEING THE NICE GUY.
UH...
WH...WHY? I IT THE AG DIFFERENC IS THAT WH BOTHERS YOU?
FOUR YEARS MIGHT...
...BE A LONG TIME, BUT STILL.
IN THAT CASE JUST LOOK A THE BIGGER PICTURE. IN FO YEARS, I'LL B TWENTY YEAR OLD—A GROW WOMAN.
...
OR...OR IS IT HARU-KUN? IS IT BECAUSE I'M FRIENDS WITH HARU-KUN?
YOU DON'T NEED TO WORRY ABOUT THAT! I THINK IT WOULD BE FUN TO BE RELATED TO HARU-KUN. AND I BET HE WOULD...
...
WOULD... BE HAPPY ABOUT IT...
TOO...
...

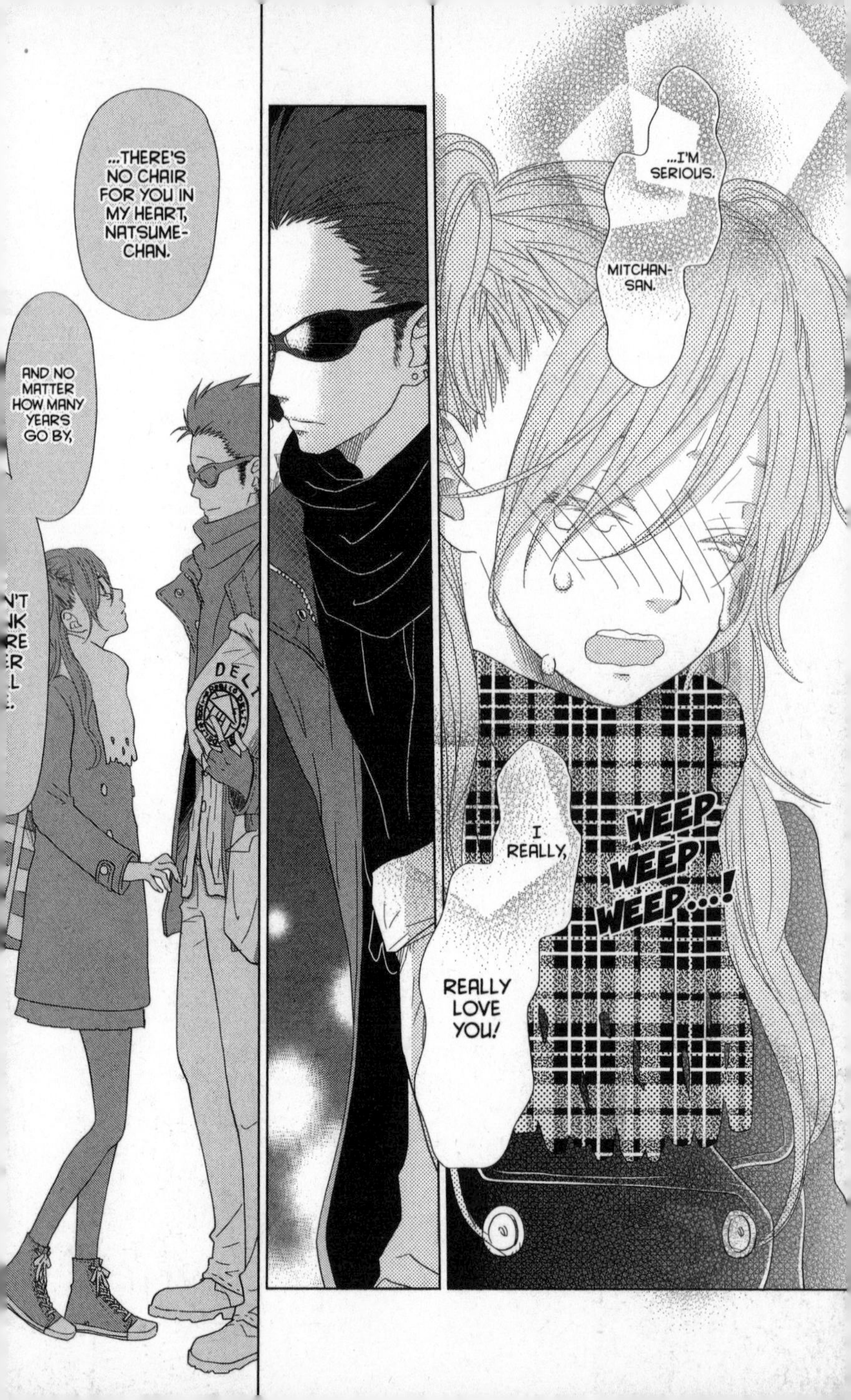
...I'M SERIOUS.
MITCHAN-SAN.
WEEP WEEP WEEP...!
I REALLY,
REALLY LOVE YOU!
...THERE'S NO CHAIR FOR YOU IN MY HEART, NATSUME-CHAN.
AND NO MATTER HOW MANY YEARS GO BY,

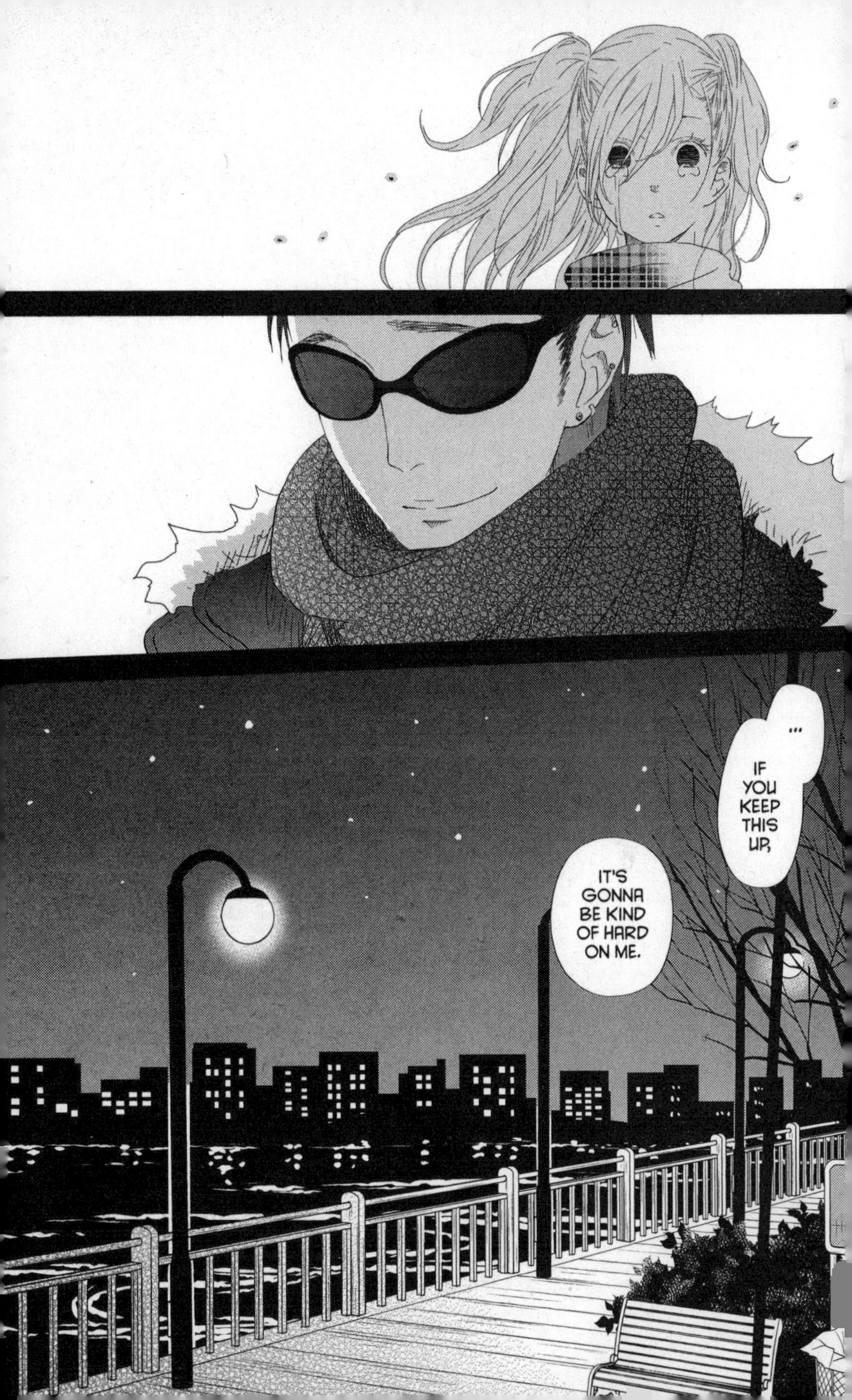
...
IF YOU KEEP THIS UP,
IT'S GONNA BE KIND OF HARD ON ME.

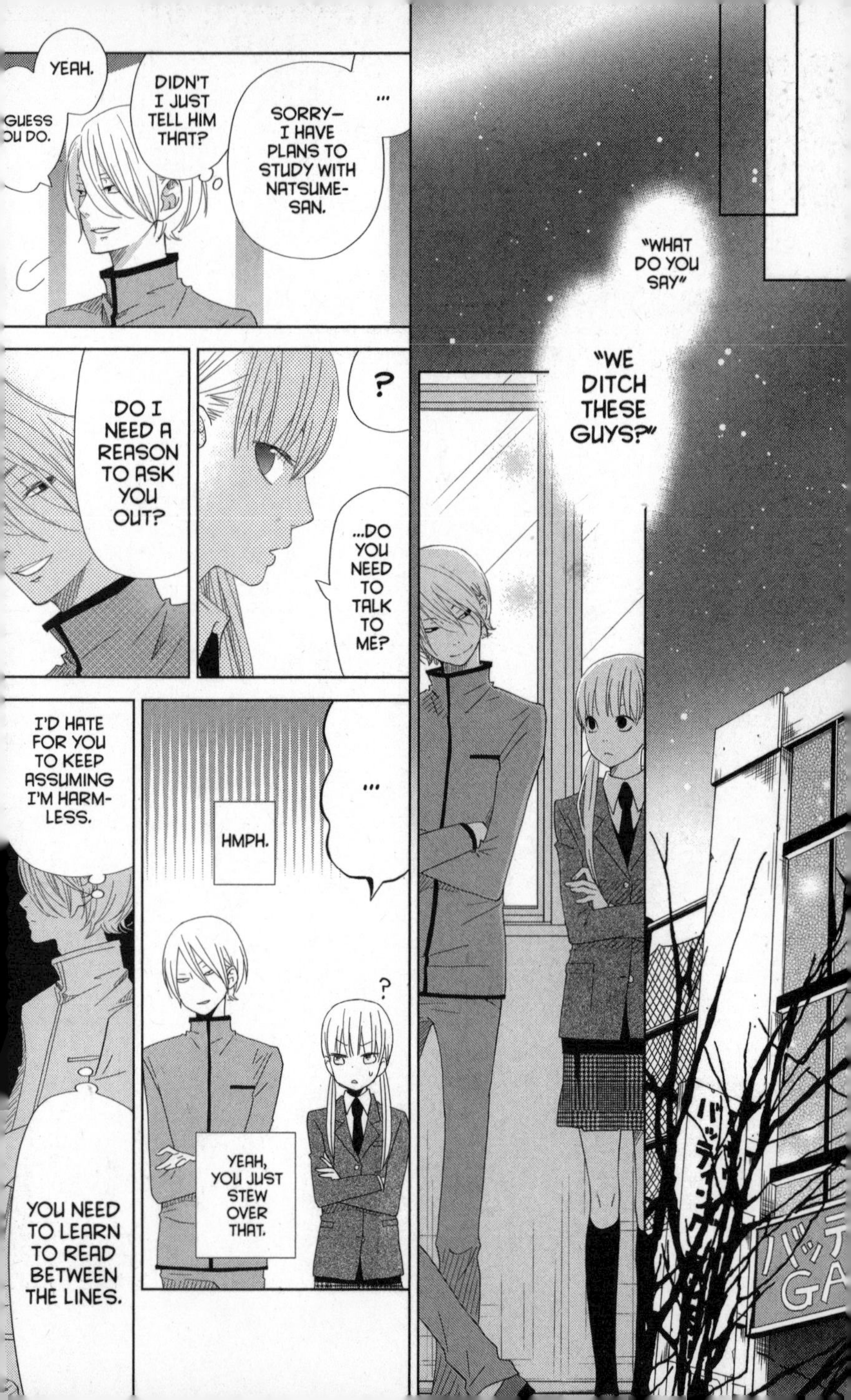
"WHAT DO YOU SAY"
"WE DITCH THESE GUYS?"
...
SORRY— I HAVE PLANS TO STUDY WITH NATSUME-SAN.
DIDN'T I JUST TELL HIM THAT?
YEAH.
GUESS YOU DO.
?
...DO YOU NEED TO TALK TO ME?
DO I NEED A REASON TO ASK YOU OUT?
...
HMPH.
YEAH, YOU JUST STEW OVER THAT.
I'D HATE FOR YOU TO KEEP ASSUMING I'M HARMLESS.
YOU NEED TO LEARN TO READ BETWEEN THE LINES.

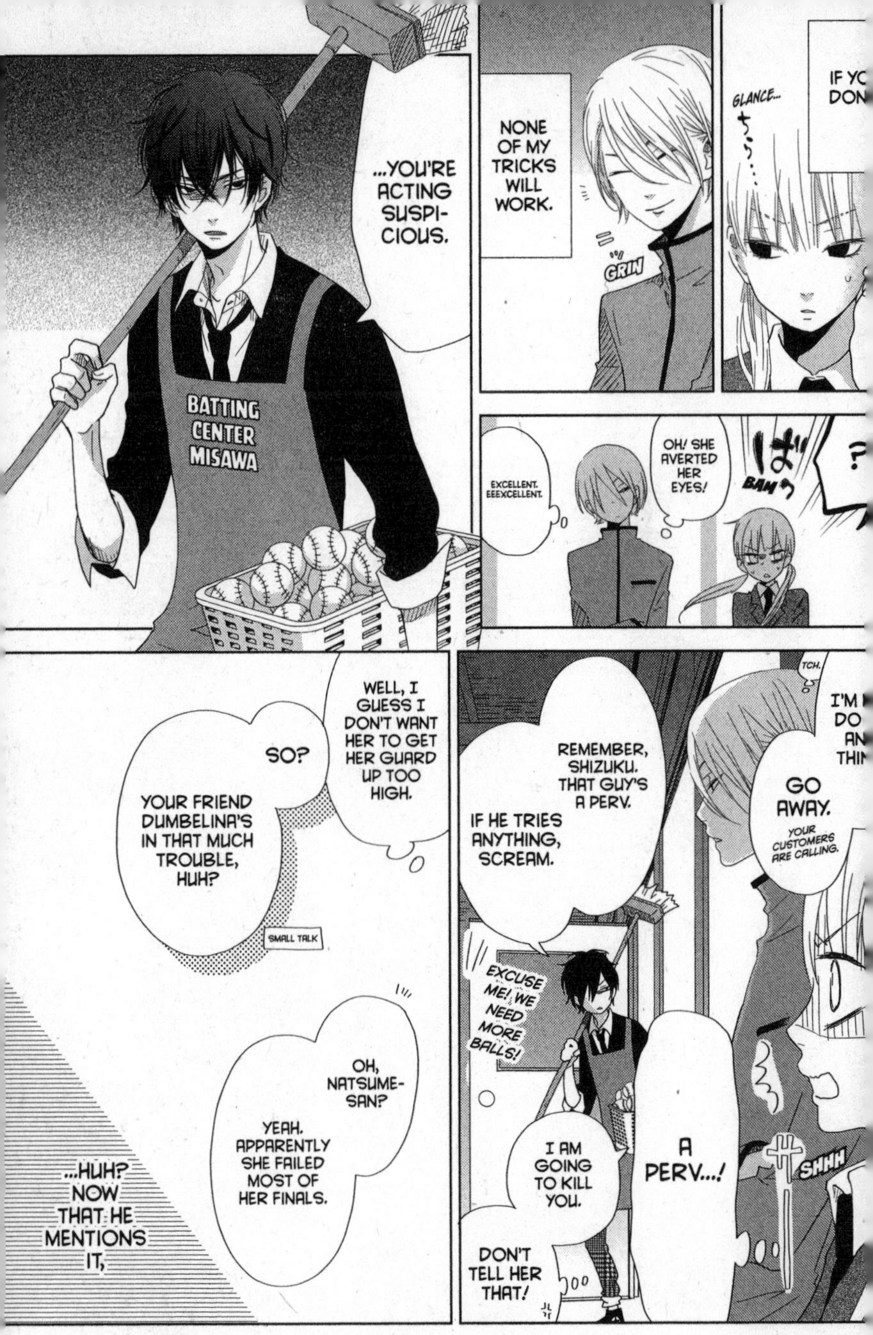
IF YO
DON
GLANCE...
ちら...
NONE OF MY TRICKS WILL WORK.
GRIN
?
ば
BAM
OH! SHE AVERTED HER EYES!
EXCELLENT. EEEXCELLENT.
...YOU'RE ACTING SUSPICIOUS.
BATTING CENTER MISAWA
TCH.
I'M
DO
AN
THIN
GO AWAY.
YOUR CUSTOMERS ARE CALLING.
REMEMBER, SHIZUKU. THAT GUY'S A PERV.
IF HE TRIES ANYTHING, SCREAM.
EXCUSE ME! WE NEED MORE BALLS!
A PERV...!
SHHH
I AM GOING TO KILL YOU.
DON'T TELL HER THAT!
WELL, I GUESS I DON'T WANT HER TO GET HER GUARD UP TOO HIGH.
SO?
YOUR FRIEND DUMBELINA'S IN THAT MUCH TROUBLE, HUH?
SMALL TALK
OH, NATSUME-SAN?
YEAH. APPARENTLY SHE FAILED MOST OF HER FINALS.
...HUH? NOW THAT HE MENTIONS IT,

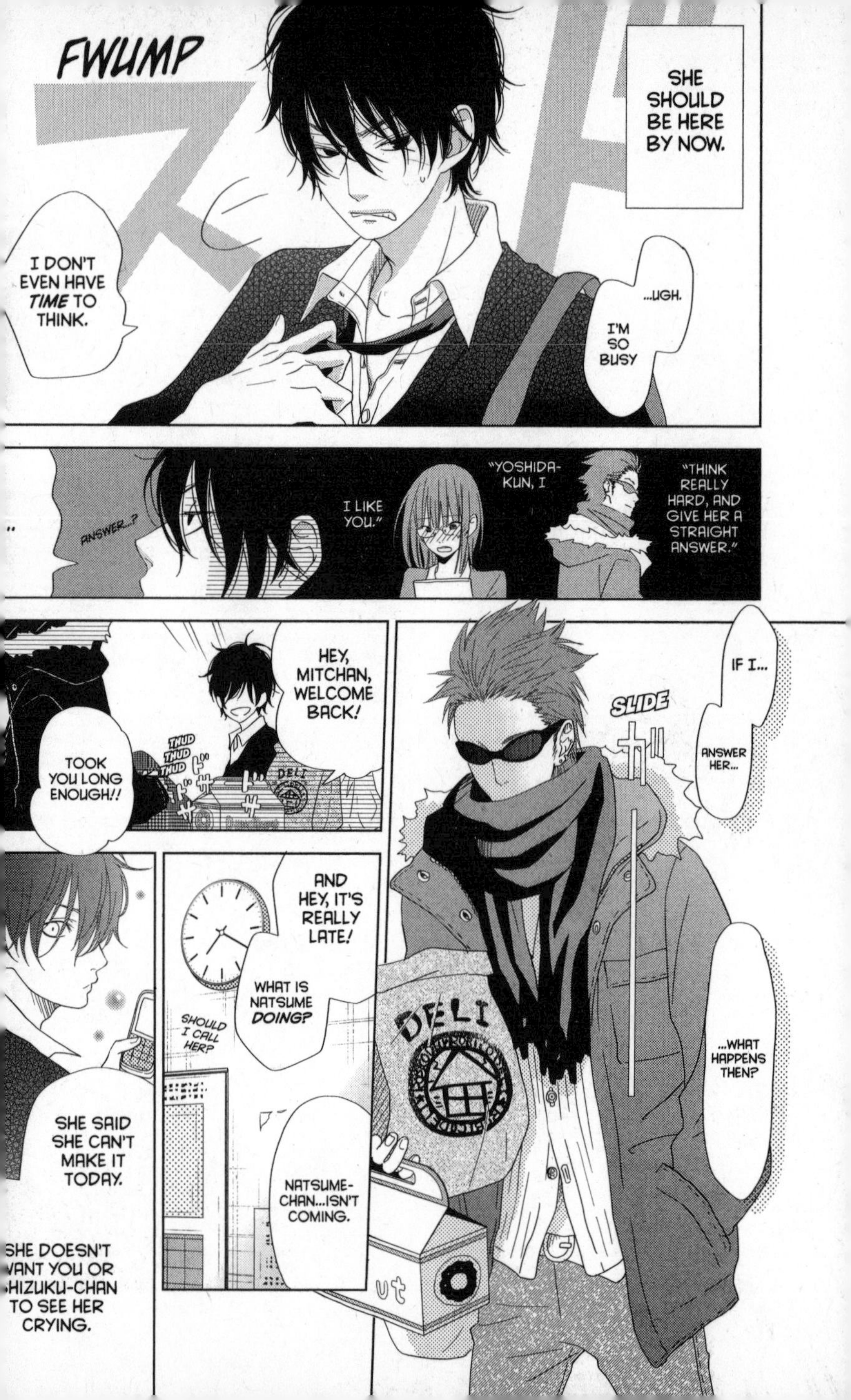
SHE SHOULD BE HERE BY NOW.
FWUMP
...UGH.
I'M SO BUSY
I DON'T EVEN HAVE TIME TO THINK.
"THINK REALLY HARD, AND GIVE HER A STRAIGHT ANSWER."
"YOSHIDA-KUN, I
I LIKE YOU."
ANSWER...?
IF I...
SLIDE
ANSWER HER...
...WHAT HAPPENS THEN?
HEY, MITCHAN, WELCOME BACK!
THUD THUD THUD
TOOK YOU LONG ENOUGH!!
DELI
AND HEY, IT'S REALLY LATE!
WHAT IS NATSUME DOING?
SHOULD I CALL HER?
NATSUME-CHAN...ISN'T COMING.
SHE SAID SHE CAN'T MAKE IT TODAY.
HE DOESN'T VANT YOU OR HIZUKU-CHAN TO SEE HER CRYING.

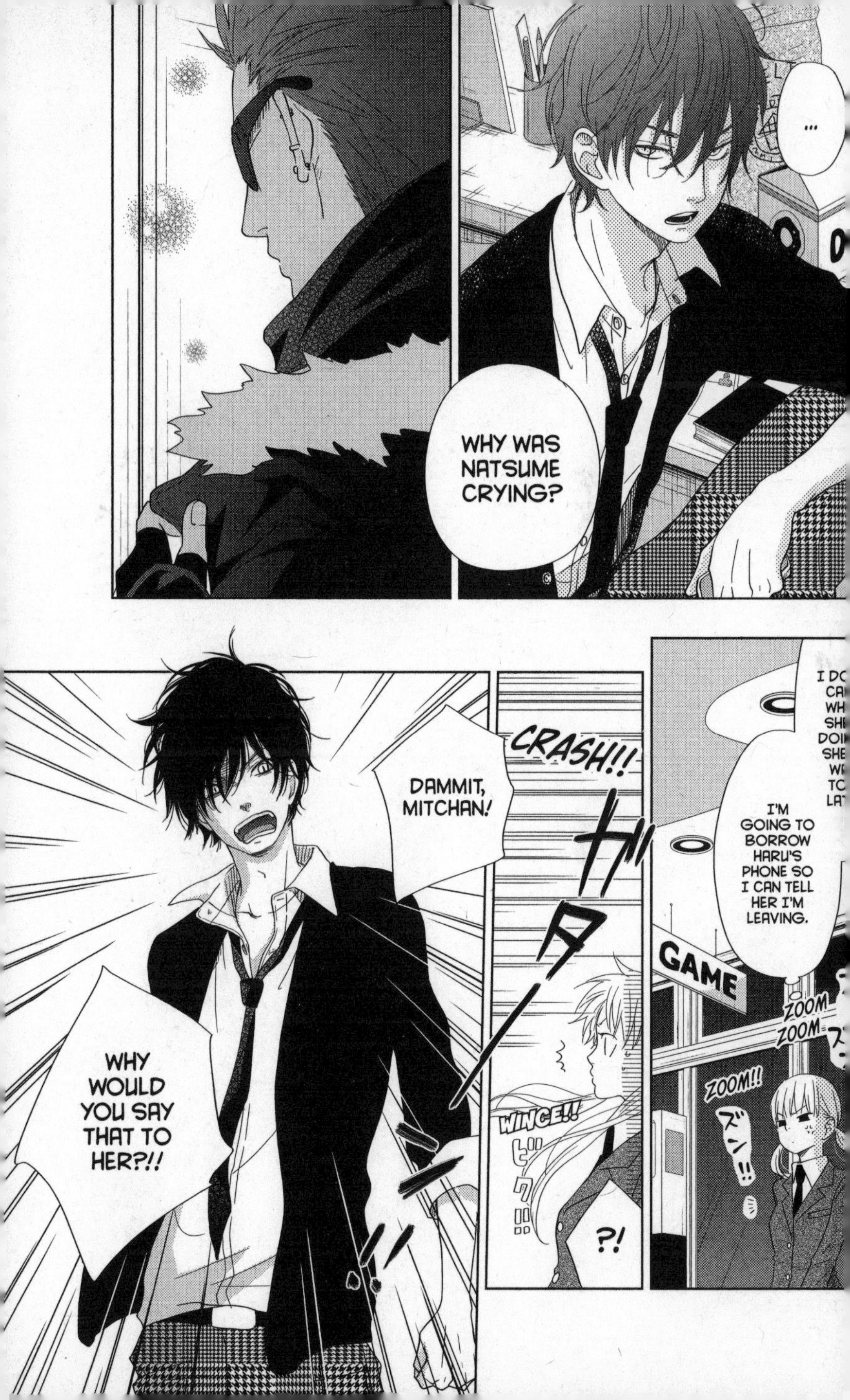
...
WHY WAS NATSUME CRYING?
I'M GOING TO BORROW HARU'S PHONE SO I CAN TELL HER I'M LEAVING.
GAME
ZOOM ZOOM
ZOOM!!
CRASH!!
WINCE!!
?!
DAMMIT, MITCHAN!
WHY WOULD YOU SAY THAT TO HER?!!

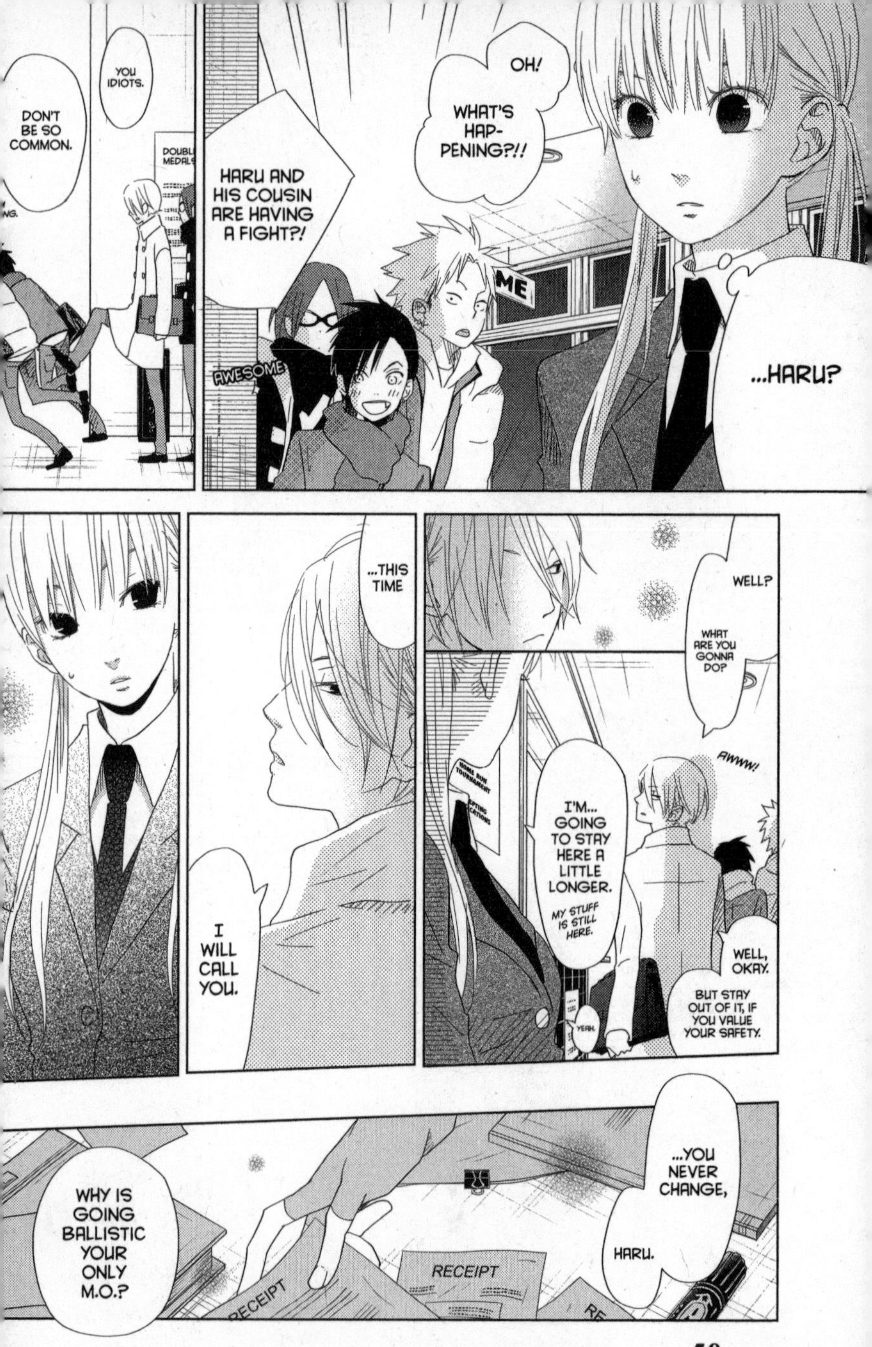
OH!
WHAT'S HAP-PENING?!!
HARU AND HIS COUSIN ARE HAVING A FIGHT?!
AWESOME
...HARU?
YOU IDIOTS.
DON'T BE SO COMMON.
WELL?
WHAT ARE YOU GONNA DO?
AWWW!
WELL, OKAY.
BUT STAY OUT OF IT, IF YOU VALUE YOUR SAFETY.
I'M... GOING TO STAY HERE A LITTLE LONGER.
MY STUFF IS STILL HERE.
YEAH.
...THIS TIME
I WILL CALL YOU.
...YOU NEVER CHANGE,
HARU.
WHY IS GOING BALLISTIC YOUR ONLY M.O.?
RECEIPT
RECEIPT

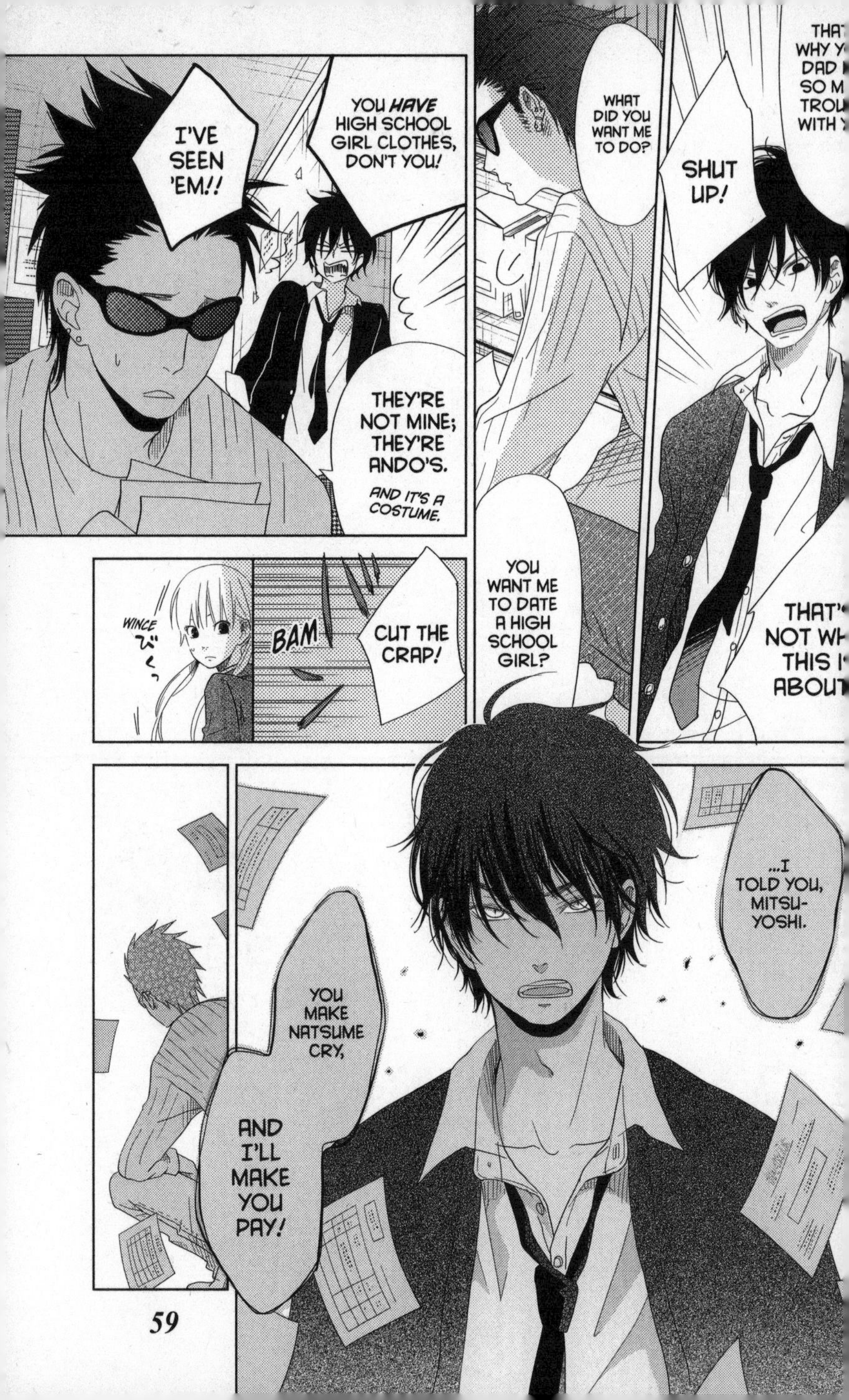
THA'
WHY Y
DAD
SO M
TROU
WITH Y
WHAT DID YOU WANT ME TO DO?
SHUT UP!
YOU WANT ME TO DATE A HIGH SCHOOL GIRL?
THAT'
NOT WH
THIS I
ABOUT
YOU *HAVE* HIGH SCHOOL GIRL CLOTHES, DON'T YOU!
I'VE SEEN 'EM!!
THEY'RE NOT MINE; THEY'RE ANDO'S.
AND IT'S A COSTUME.
CUT THE CRAP!
BAM
WINCE
びくっ
...I TOLD YOU, MITSU-YOSHI.
YOU MAKE NATSUME CRY,
AND I'LL MAKE YOU PAY!

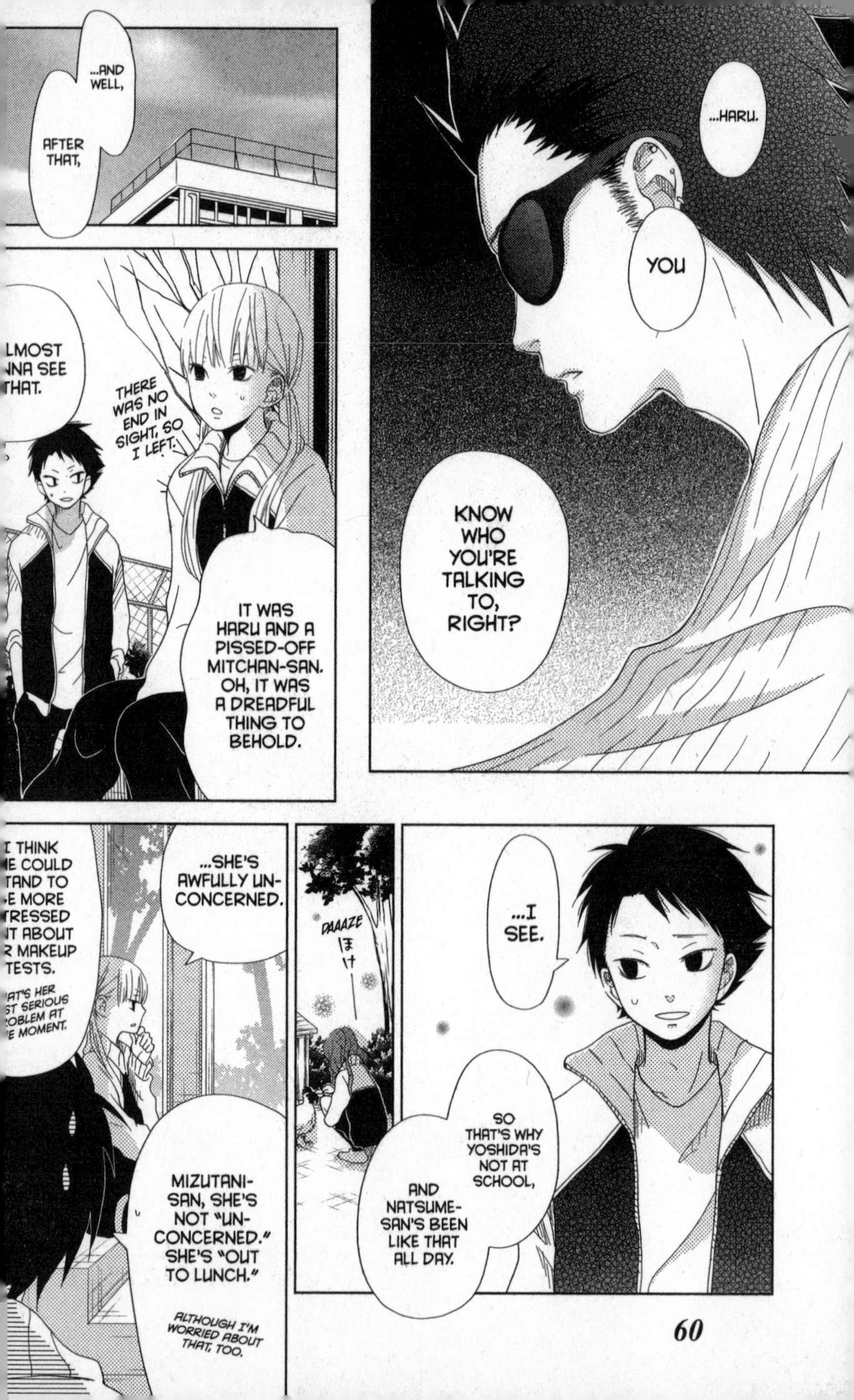
...HARU.
YOU
KNOW WHO YOU'RE TALKING TO, RIGHT?
...AND WELL,
AFTER THAT,
LMOST NNA SEE THAT.
THERE WAS NO END IN SIGHT, SO I LEFT.
IT WAS HARU AND A PISSED-OFF MITCHAN-SAN. OH, IT WAS A DREADFUL THING TO BEHOLD.
...I SEE.
SO THAT'S WHY YOSHIDA'S NOT AT SCHOOL,
AND NATSUME-SAN'S BEEN LIKE THAT ALL DAY.
DAAAZE
ほけー
...SHE'S AWFULLY UN-CONCERNED.
I THINK E COULD TAND TO E MORE TRESSED IT ABOUT R MAKEUP TESTS.
AT'S HER ST SERIOUS OBLEM AT E MOMENT.
MIZUTANI-SAN, SHE'S NOT "UN-CONCERNED." SHE'S "OUT TO LUNCH."
ALTHOUGH I'M WORRIED ABOUT THAT, TOO.

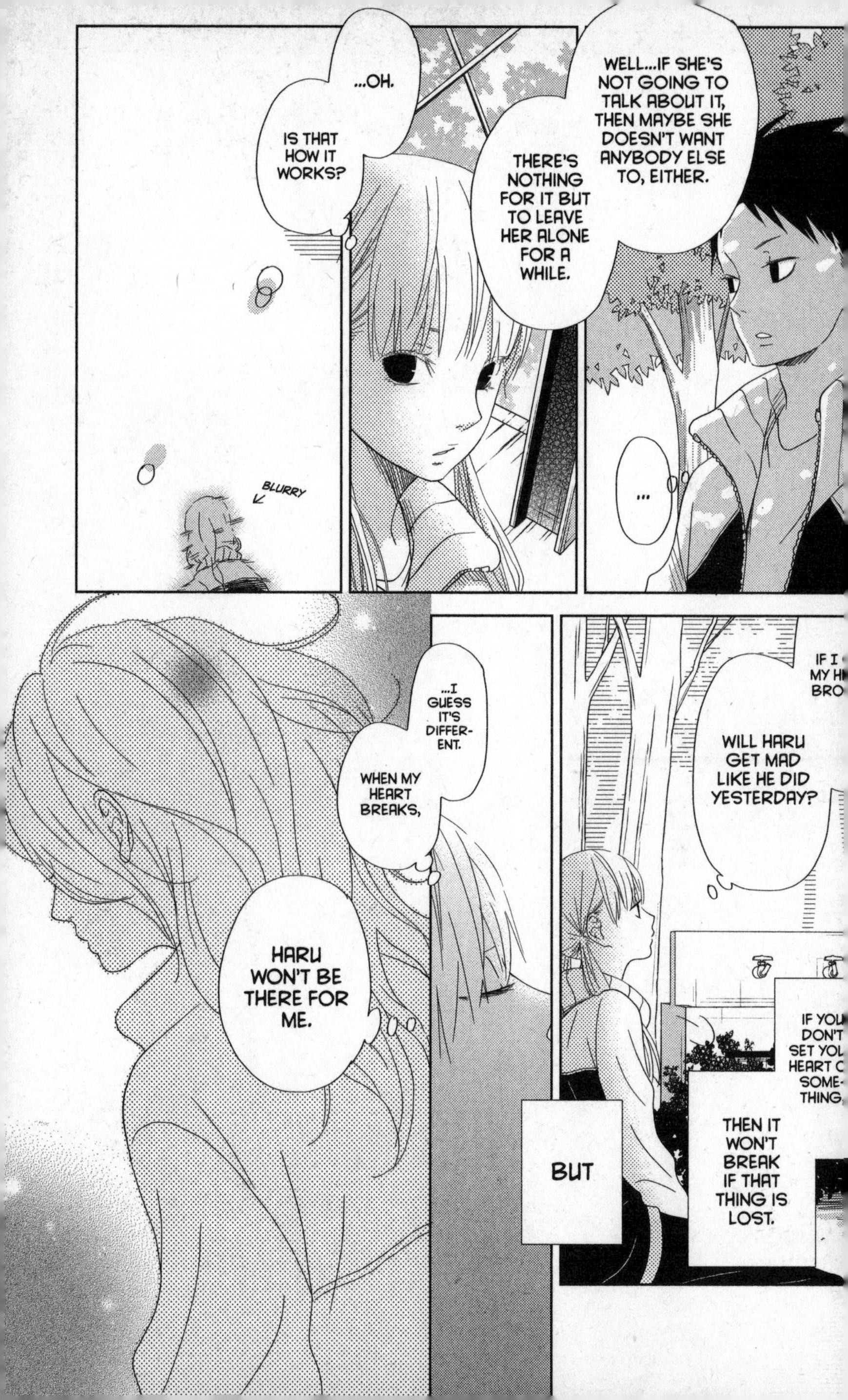
WELL...IF SHE'S NOT GOING TO TALK ABOUT IT, THEN MAYBE SHE DOESN'T WANT ANYBODY ELSE TO, EITHER.
THERE'S NOTHING FOR IT BUT TO LEAVE HER ALONE FOR A WHILE.
...
...OH.
IS THAT HOW IT WORKS?
BLURRY
WILL HARU GET MAD LIKE HE DID YESTERDAY?
THEN IT WON'T BREAK IF THAT THING IS LOST.
BUT
...I GUESS IT'S DIFFERENT.
WHEN MY HEART BREAKS,
HARU WON'T BE THERE FOR ME.

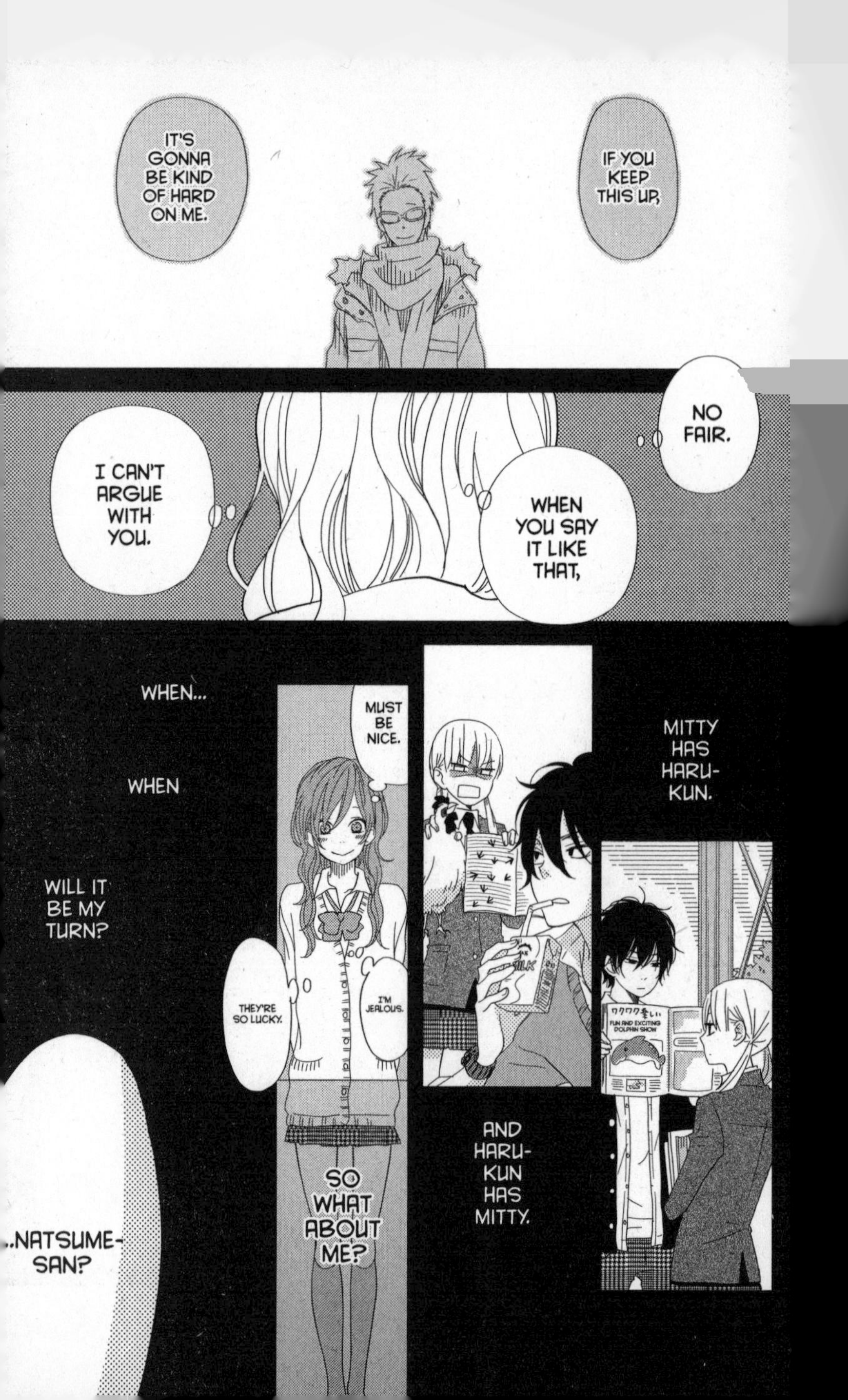
IF YOU KEEP THIS UP,
IT'S GONNA BE KIND OF HARD ON ME.
NO FAIR.
WHEN YOU SAY IT LIKE THAT,
I CAN'T ARGUE WITH YOU.
MITTY HAS HARU-KUN.
FUN AND EXCITING DOLPHIN SHOW
AND HARU-KUN HAS MITTY.
MUST BE NICE.
I'M JEALOUS.
THEY'RE SO LUCKY.
SO WHAT ABOUT ME?
WHEN...
WHEN
WILL IT BE MY TURN?
..NATSUME-SAN?

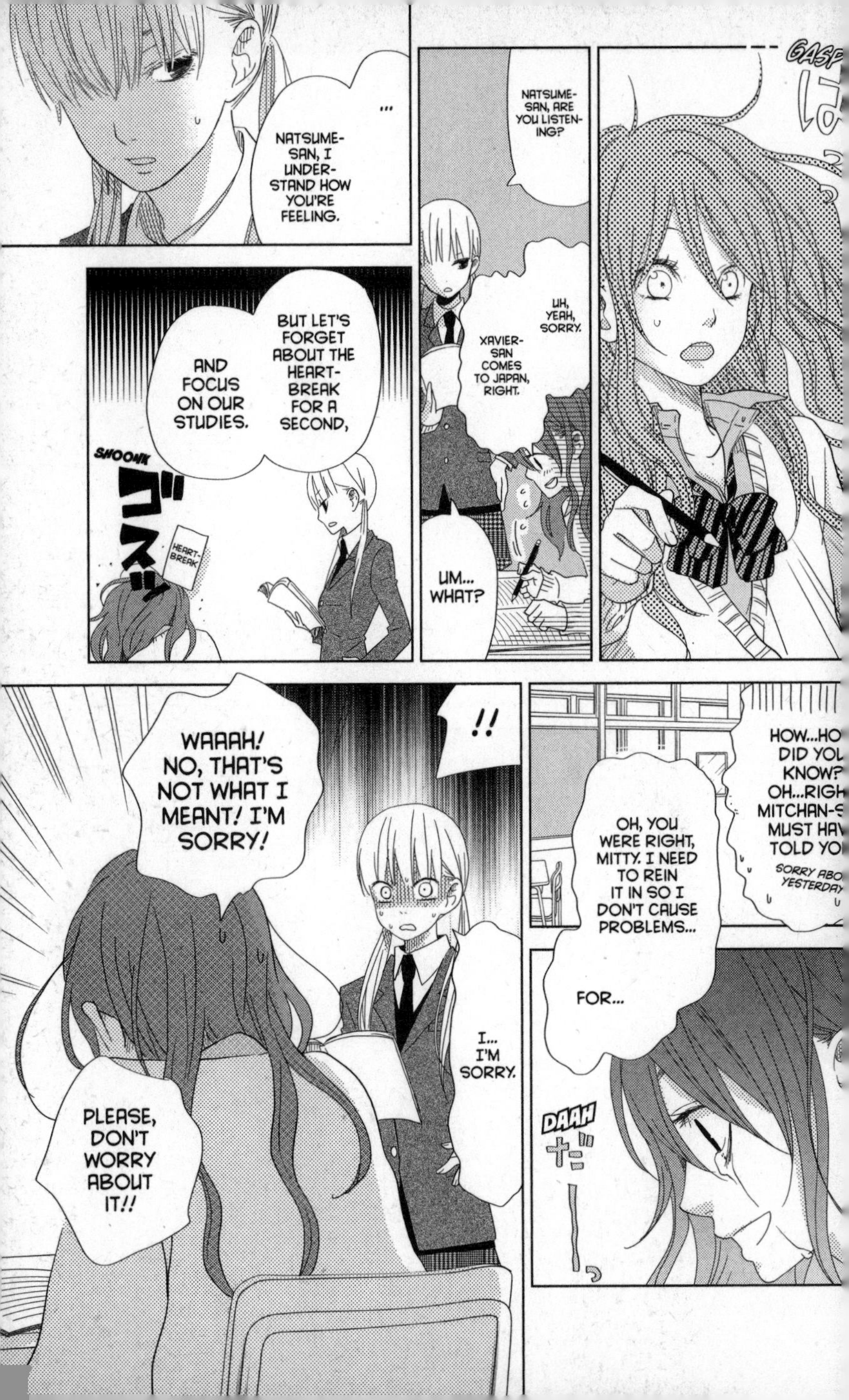
GASP
...
NATSUME-SAN, ARE YOU LISTENING?
UH, YEAH, SORRY.
XAVIER-SAN COMES TO JAPAN, RIGHT.
UM... WHAT?
...
NATSUME-SAN, I UNDERSTAND HOW YOU'RE FEELING.
BUT LET'S FORGET ABOUT THE HEARTBREAK FOR A SECOND,
AND FOCUS ON OUR STUDIES.
SHOONK
HEART-BREAK
HOW...HO DID YOU KNOW? OH...RIGH MITCHAN-S MUST HAV TOLD YO
SORRY ABO YESTERDAY
OH, YOU WERE RIGHT, MITTY. I NEED TO REIN IT IN SO I DON'T CAUSE PROBLEMS...
FOR...
DAAH
!!
WAAAH! NO, THAT'S NOT WHAT I MEANT! I'M SORRY!
I... I'M SORRY.
PLEASE, DON'T WORRY ABOUT IT!!

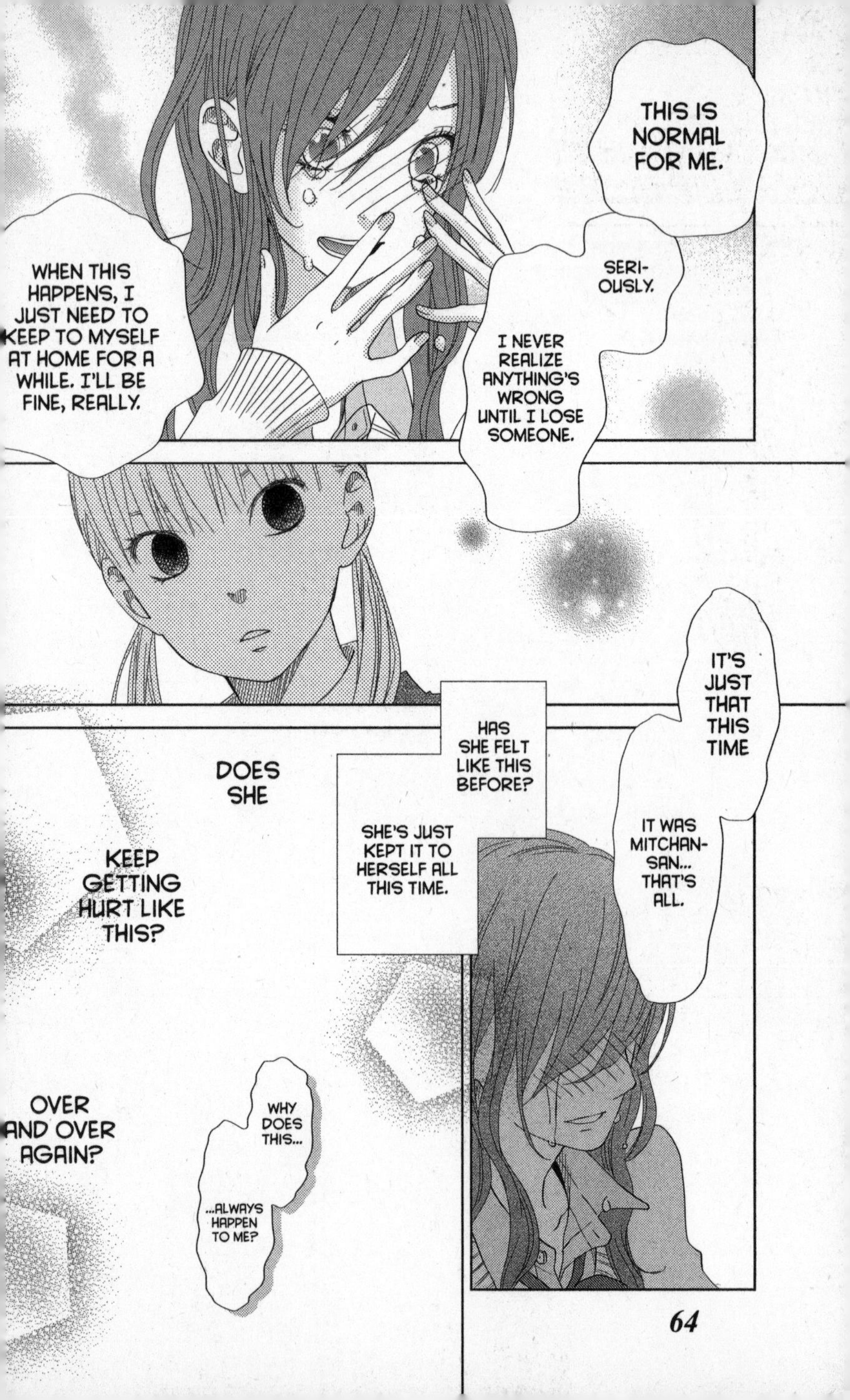
THIS IS NORMAL FOR ME.
SERI-OUSLY.
I NEVER REALIZE ANYTHING'S WRONG UNTIL I LOSE SOMEONE.
WHEN THIS HAPPENS, I JUST NEED TO KEEP TO MYSELF AT HOME FOR A WHILE. I'LL BE FINE, REALLY.
IT'S JUST THAT THIS TIME
IT WAS MITCHAN-SAN... THAT'S ALL.
HAS SHE FELT LIKE THIS BEFORE?
SHE'S JUST KEPT IT TO HERSELF ALL THIS TIME.
DOES SHE
KEEP GETTING HURT LIKE THIS?
WHY DOES THIS...
...ALWAYS HAPPEN TO ME?
OVER AND OVER AGAIN?

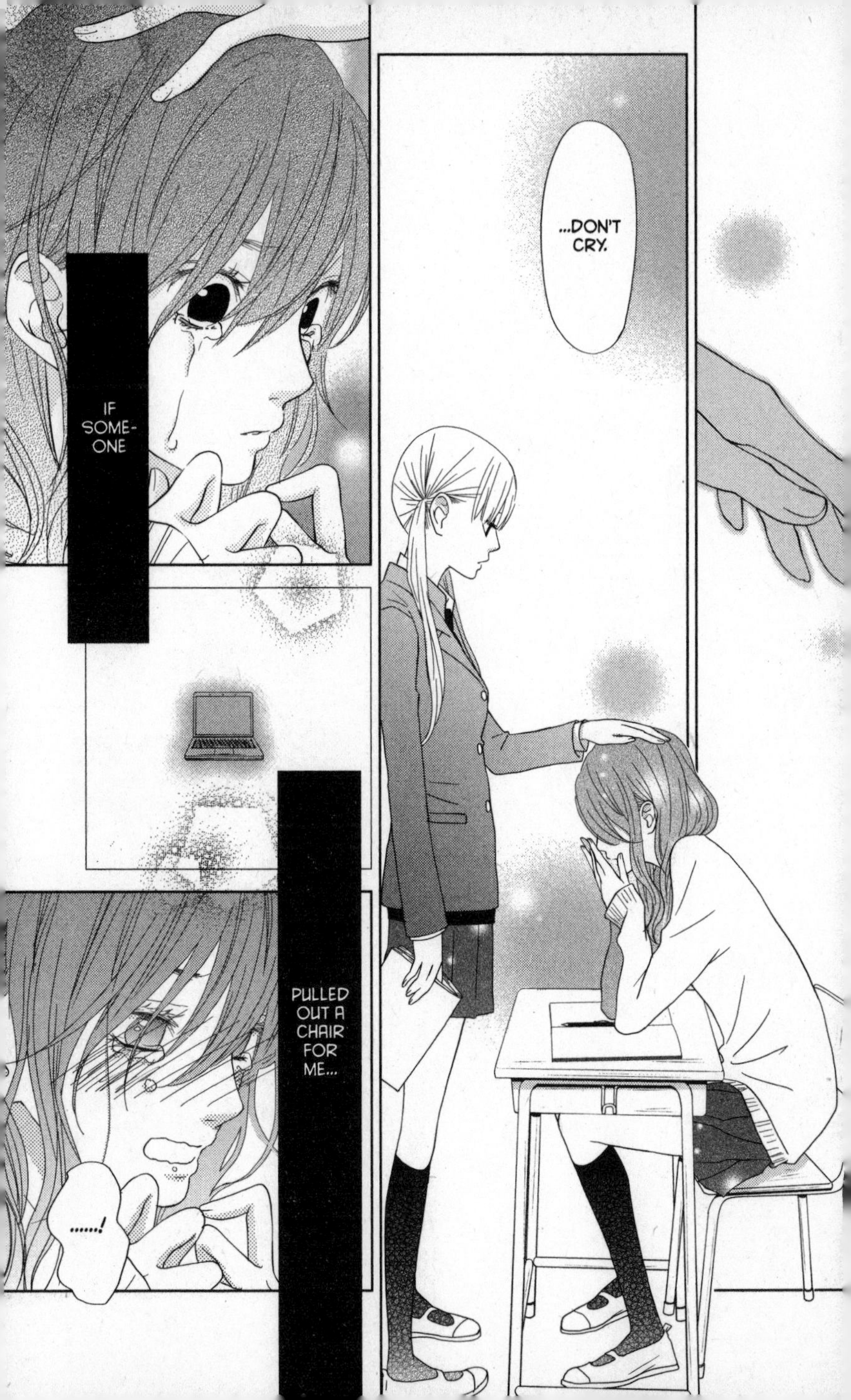
...DON'T CRY.
IF SOME-ONE
PULLED OUT A CHAIR FOR ME...
......!

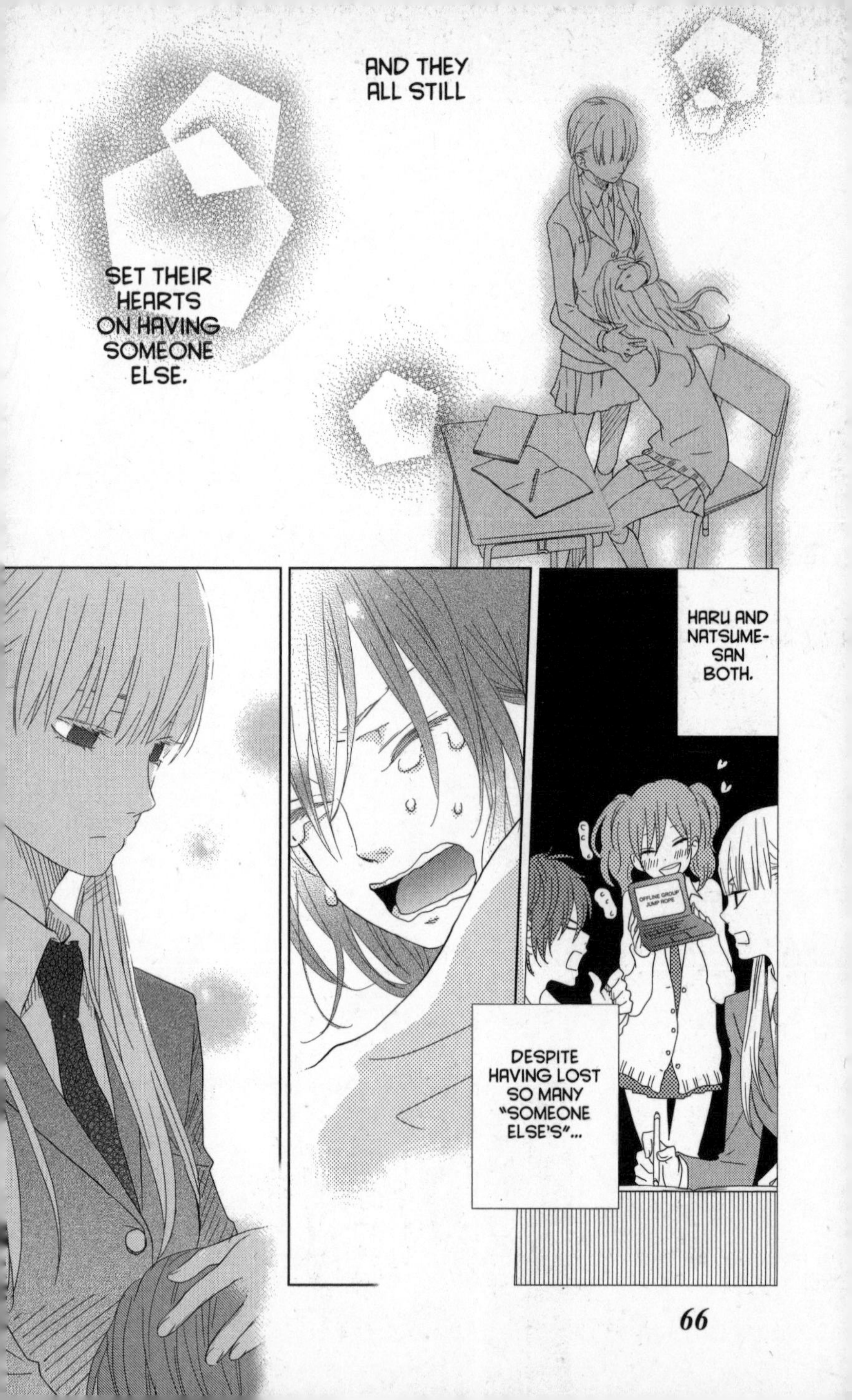
AND THEY ALL STILL
SET THEIR HEARTS ON HAVING SOMEONE ELSE.
HARU AND NATSUME-SAN BOTH.
OFFLINE GROUP JUMP ROPE
DESPITE HAVING LOST SO MANY "SOMEONE ELSE'S"...

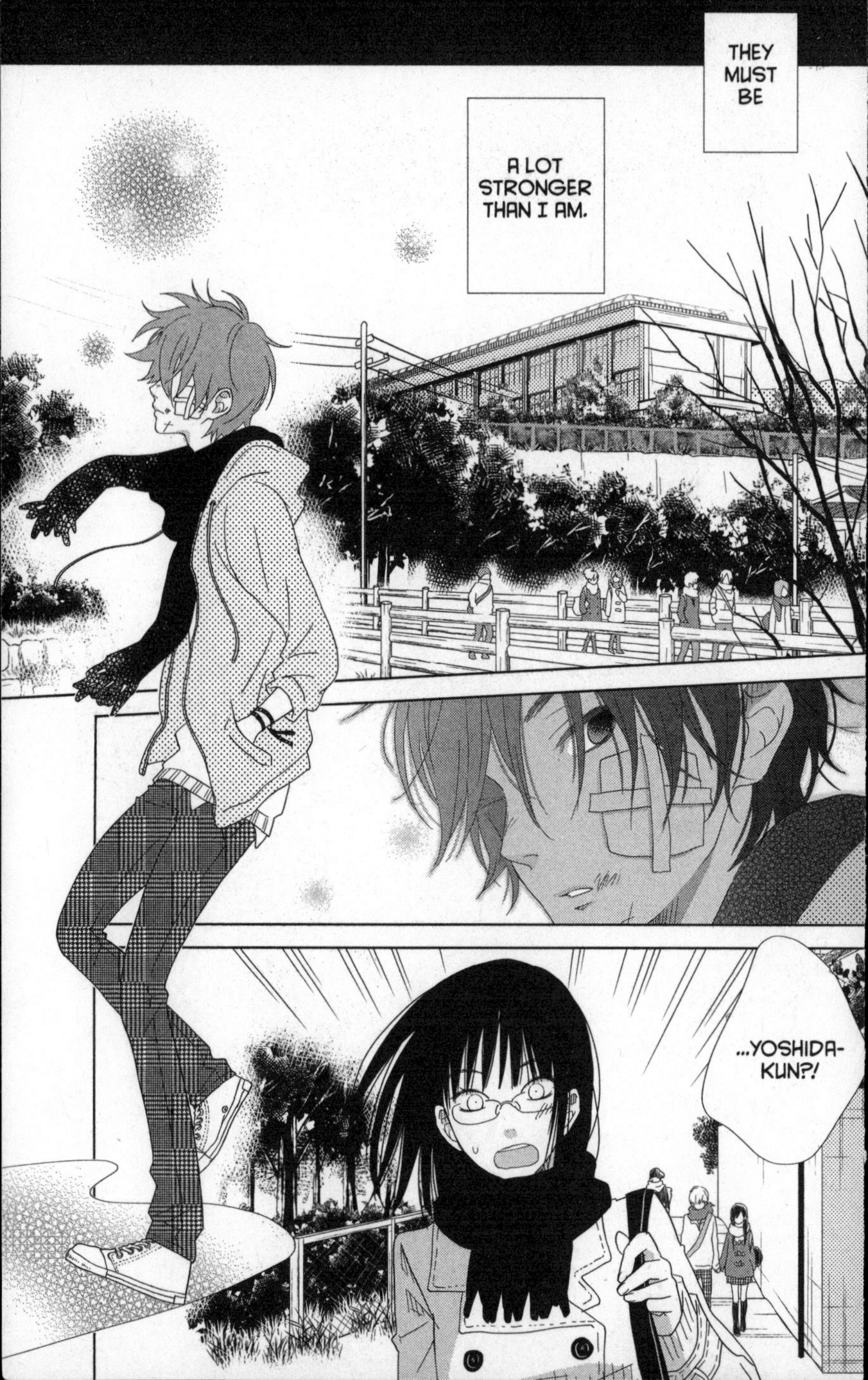
THEY MUST BE
A LOT STRONGER THAN I AM.
...YOSHIDA-KUN?!

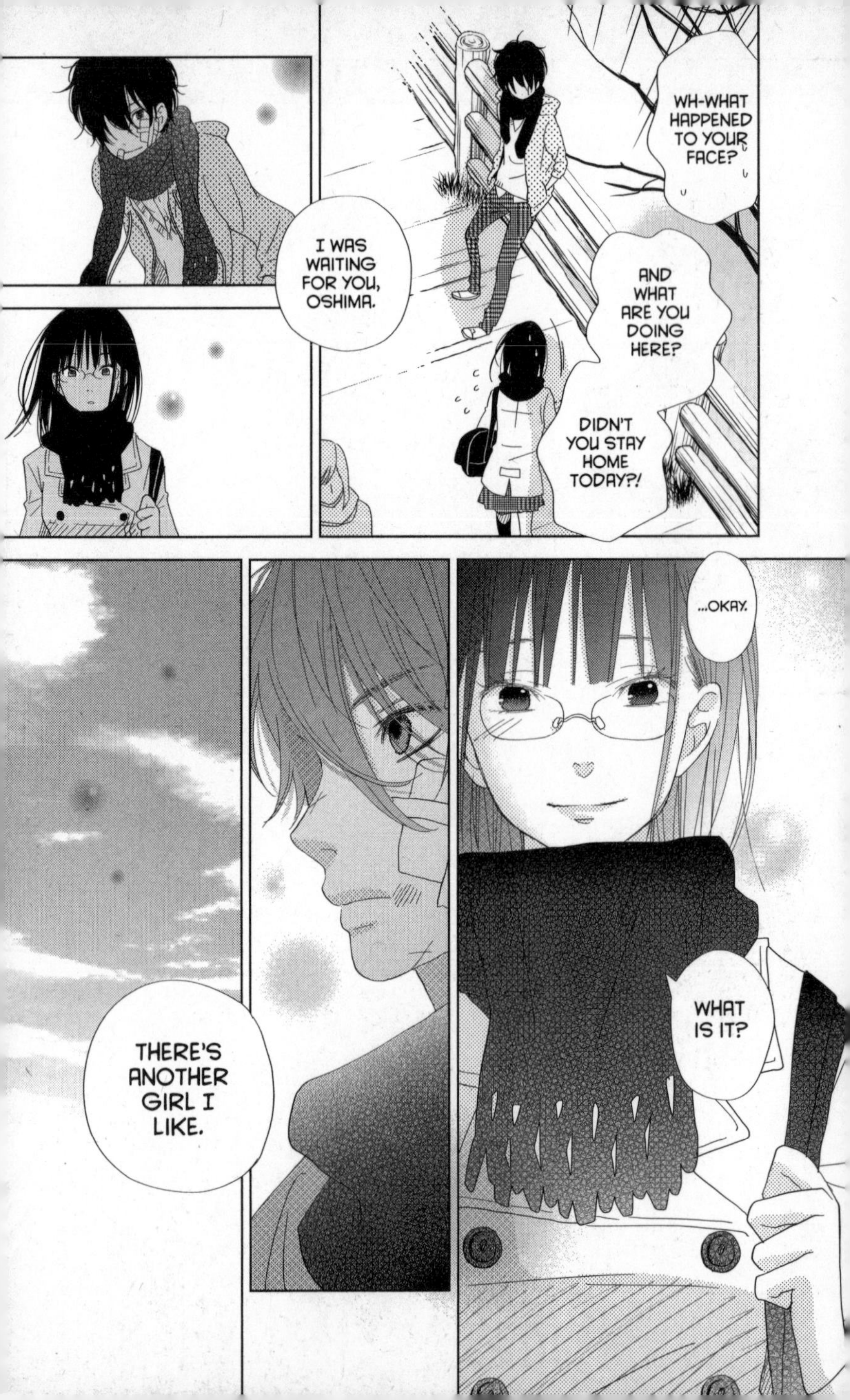
WH-WHAT HAPPENED TO YOUR FACE?
AND WHAT ARE YOU DOING HERE?
DIDN'T YOU STAY HOME TODAY?!
I WAS WAITING FOR YOU, OSHIMA.
...OKAY.
WHAT IS IT?
THERE'S ANOTHER GIRL I LIKE.

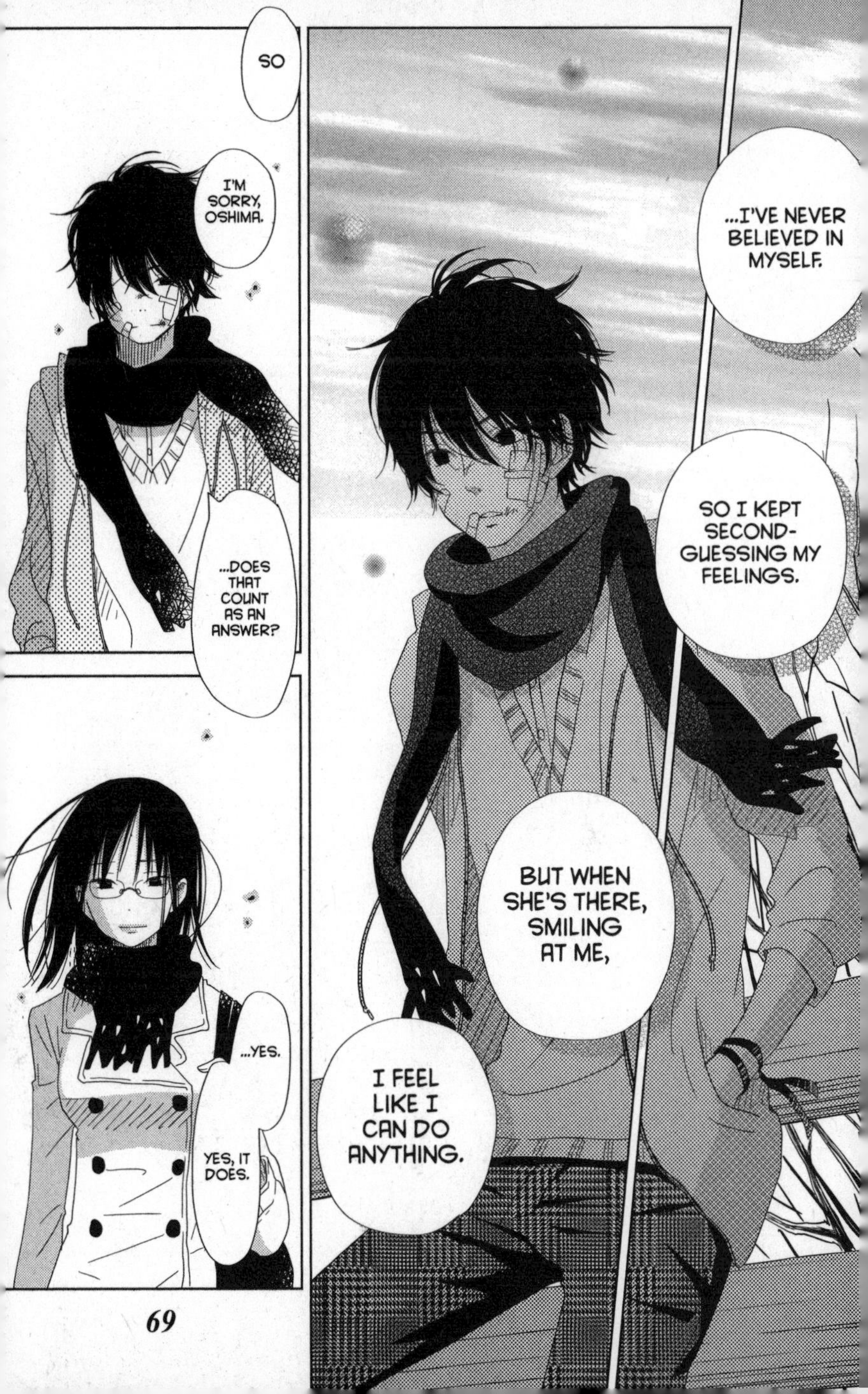
...I'VE NEVER BELIEVED IN MYSELF.
SO I KEPT SECOND-GUESSING MY FEELINGS.
BUT WHEN SHE'S THERE, SMILING AT ME,
I FEEL LIKE I CAN DO ANYTHING.
SO
I'M SORRY, OSHIMA.
...DOES THAT COUNT AS AN ANSWER?
...YES.
YES, IT DOES.

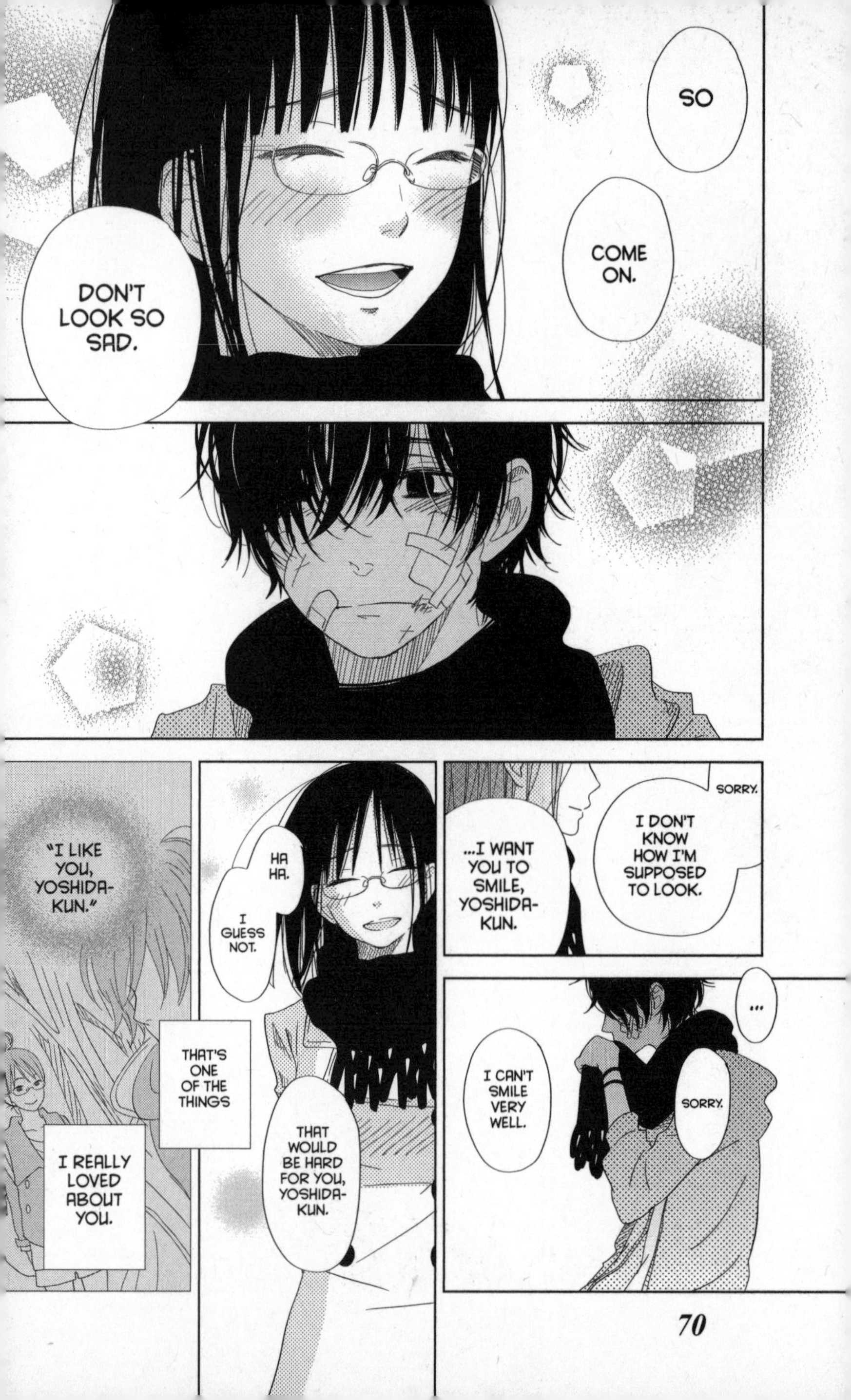
SO
COME ON.
DON'T LOOK SO SAD.
SORRY.
I DON'T KNOW HOW I'M SUPPOSED TO LOOK.
...I WANT YOU TO SMILE, YOSHIDA-KUN.
...
SORRY.
I CAN'T SMILE VERY WELL.
HA HA.
I GUESS NOT.
THAT WOULD BE HARD FOR YOU, YOSHIDA-KUN.
"I LIKE YOU, YOSHIDA-KUN."
THAT'S ONE OF THE THINGS
I REALLY LOVED ABOUT YOU.

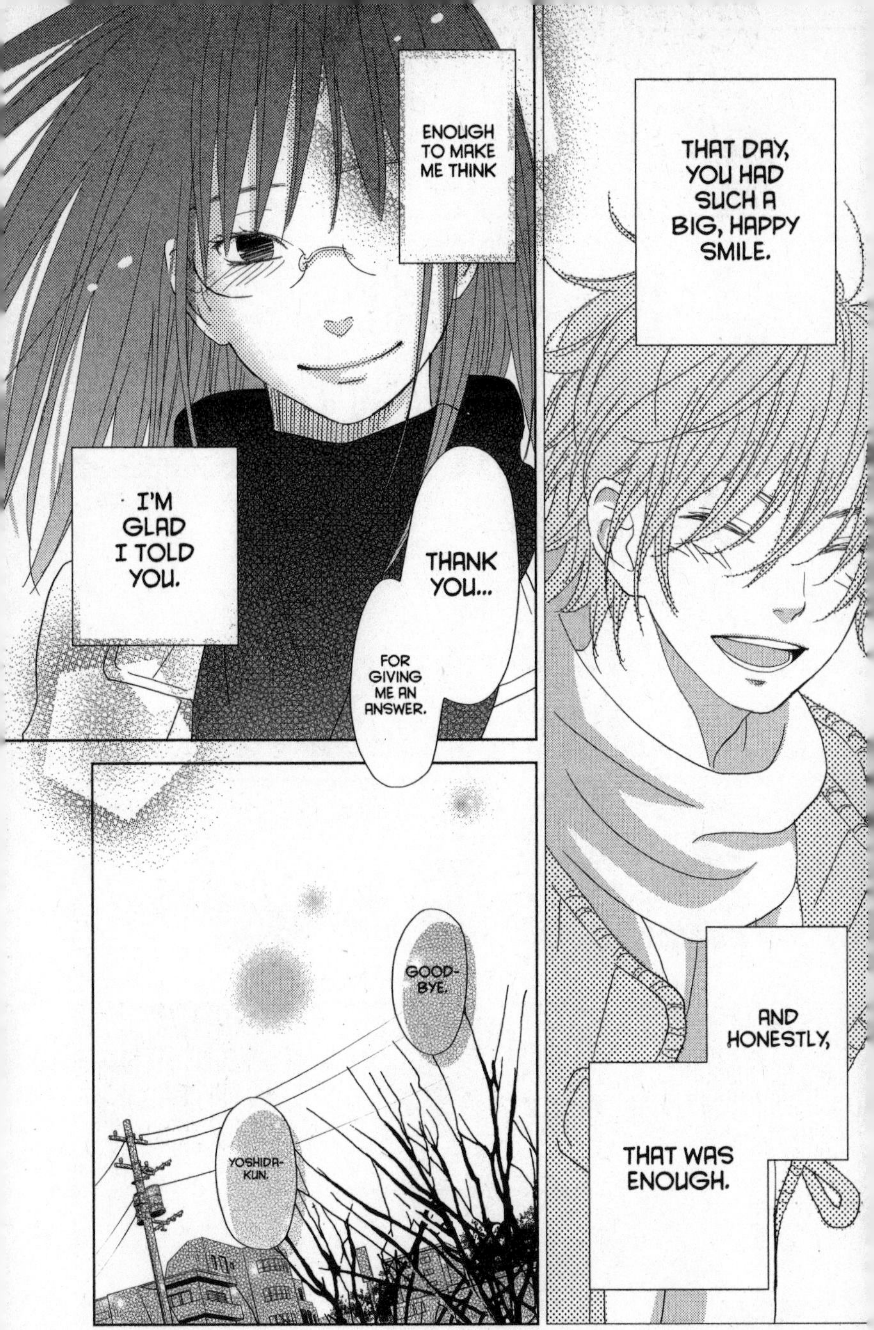
THAT DAY, YOU HAD SUCH A BIG, HAPPY SMILE.
AND HONESTLY,
THAT WAS ENOUGH.
ENOUGH TO MAKE ME THINK
I'M GLAD I TOLD YOU.
THANK YOU...
FOR GIVING ME AN ANSWER.
GOOD-BYE.
YOSHIDA-KUN.

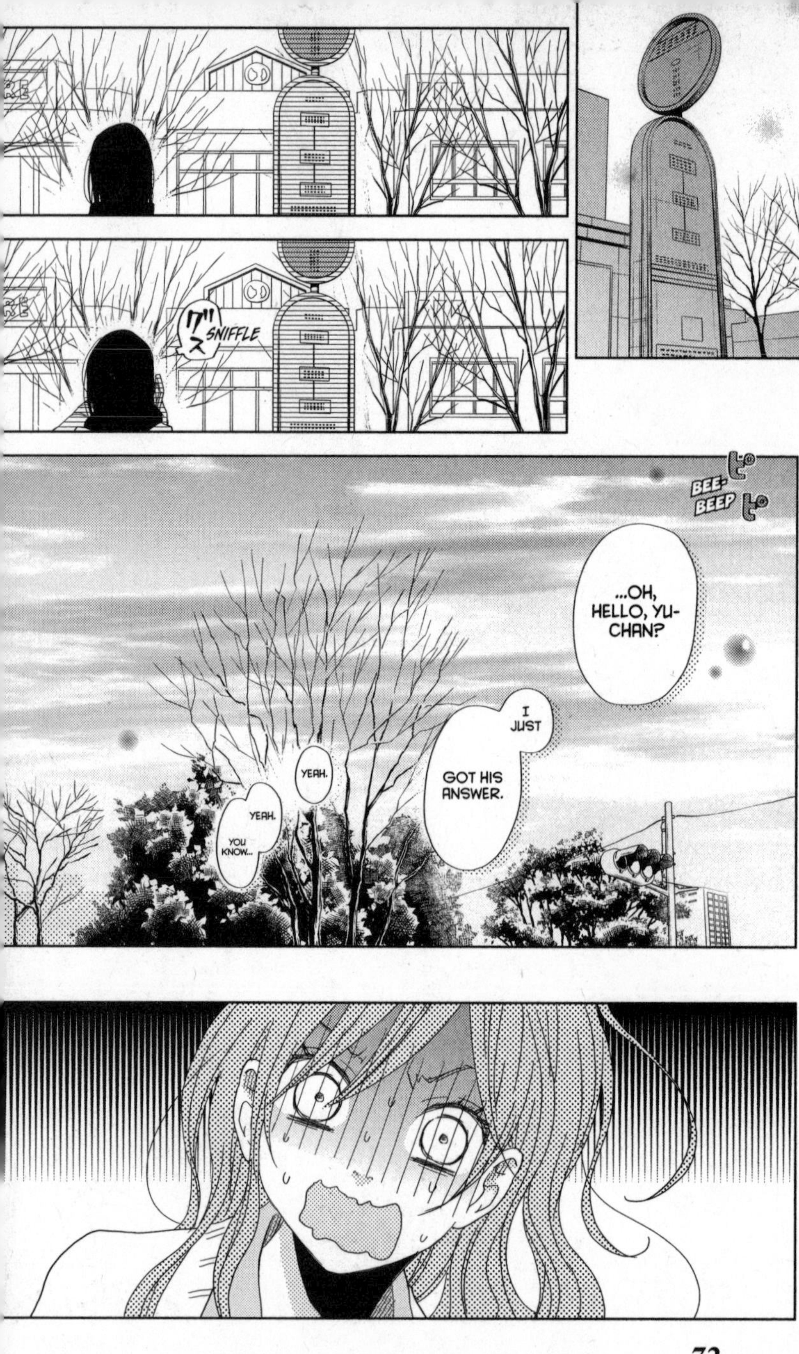
グス
SNIFFLE
ピ BEE-
ピ BEEP
...OH, HELLO, YU-CHAN?
I JUST
GOT HIS ANSWER.
YEAH.
YEAH.
YOU KNOW...

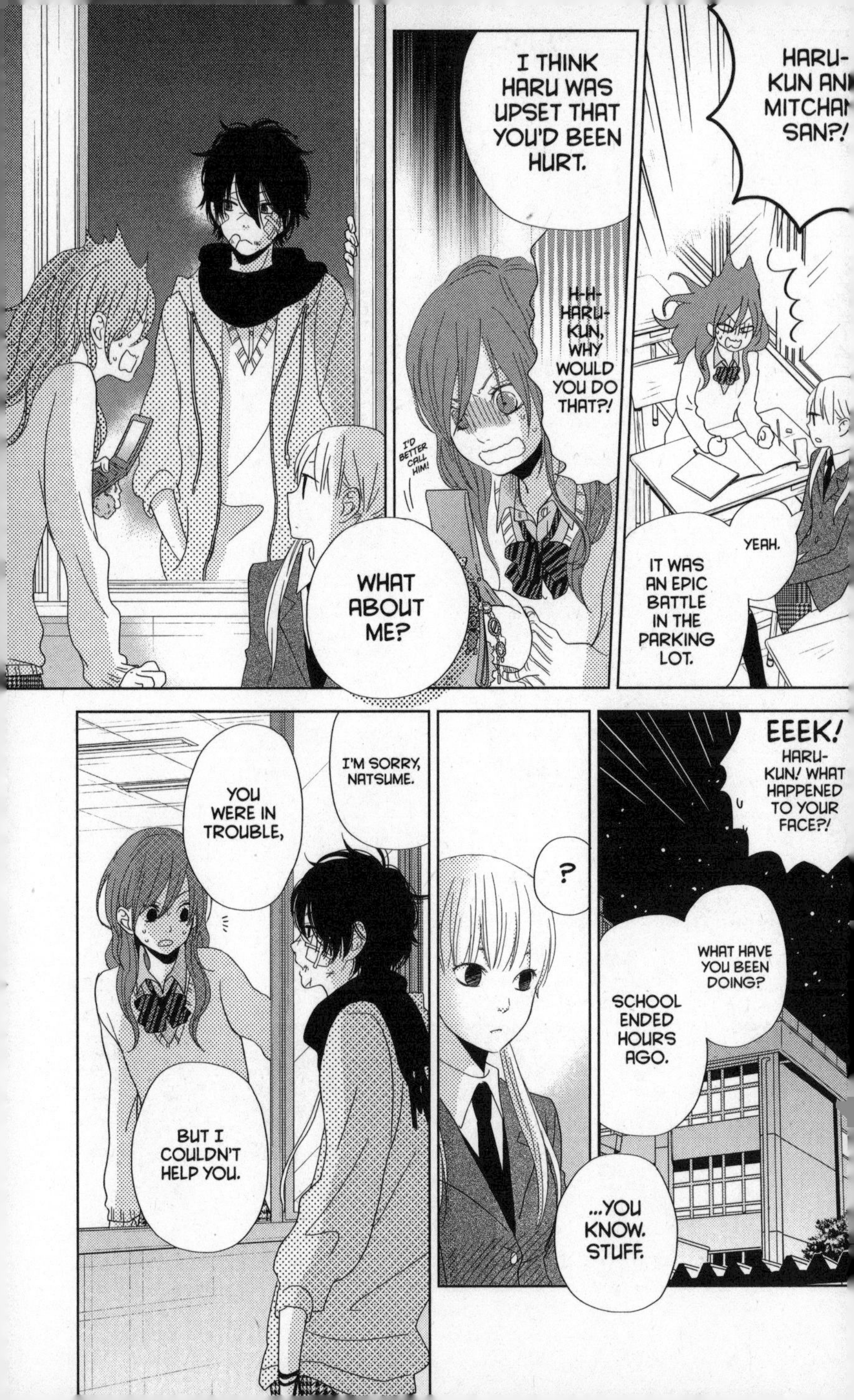
HARU-KUN AN MITCHAN SAN?!
YEAH.
IT WAS AN EPIC BATTLE IN THE PARKING LOT.
I THINK HARU WAS UPSET THAT YOU'D BEEN HURT.
H-H-HARU-KUN, WHY WOULD YOU DO THAT?!
I'D BETTER CALL HIM!
WHAT ABOUT ME?
EEEK! HARU-KUN! WHAT HAPPENED TO YOUR FACE?!
WHAT HAVE YOU BEEN DOING?
SCHOOL ENDED HOURS AGO.
?
...YOU KNOW. STUFF.
I'M SORRY, NATSUME.
YOU WERE IN TROUBLE,
BUT I COULDN'T HELP YOU.

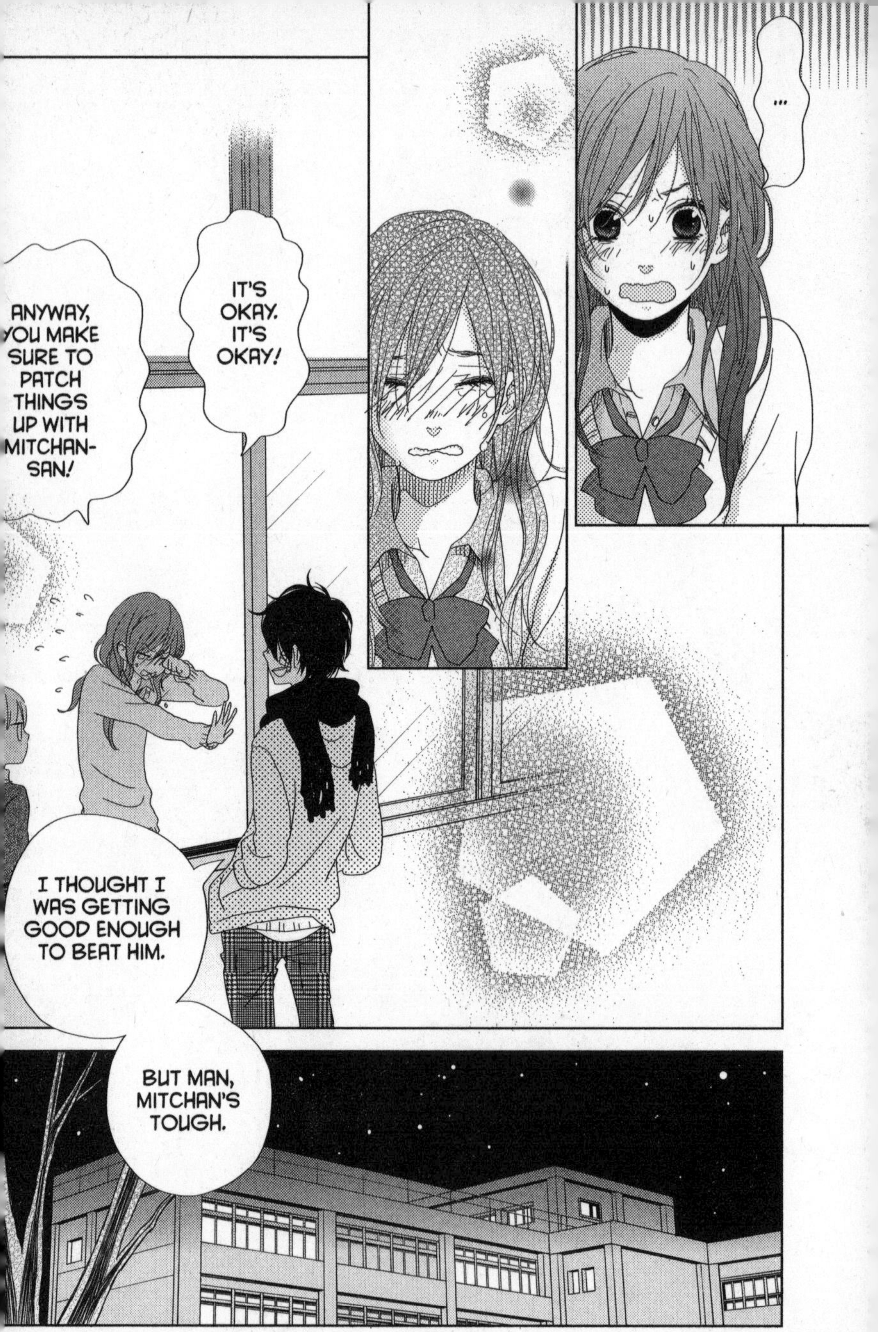
...
IT'S OKAY. IT'S OKAY!
ANYWAY, YOU MAKE SURE TO PATCH THINGS UP WITH MITCHAN-SAN!
I THOUGHT I WAS GETTING GOOD ENOUGH TO BEAT HIM.
BUT MAN, MITCHAN'S TOUGH.

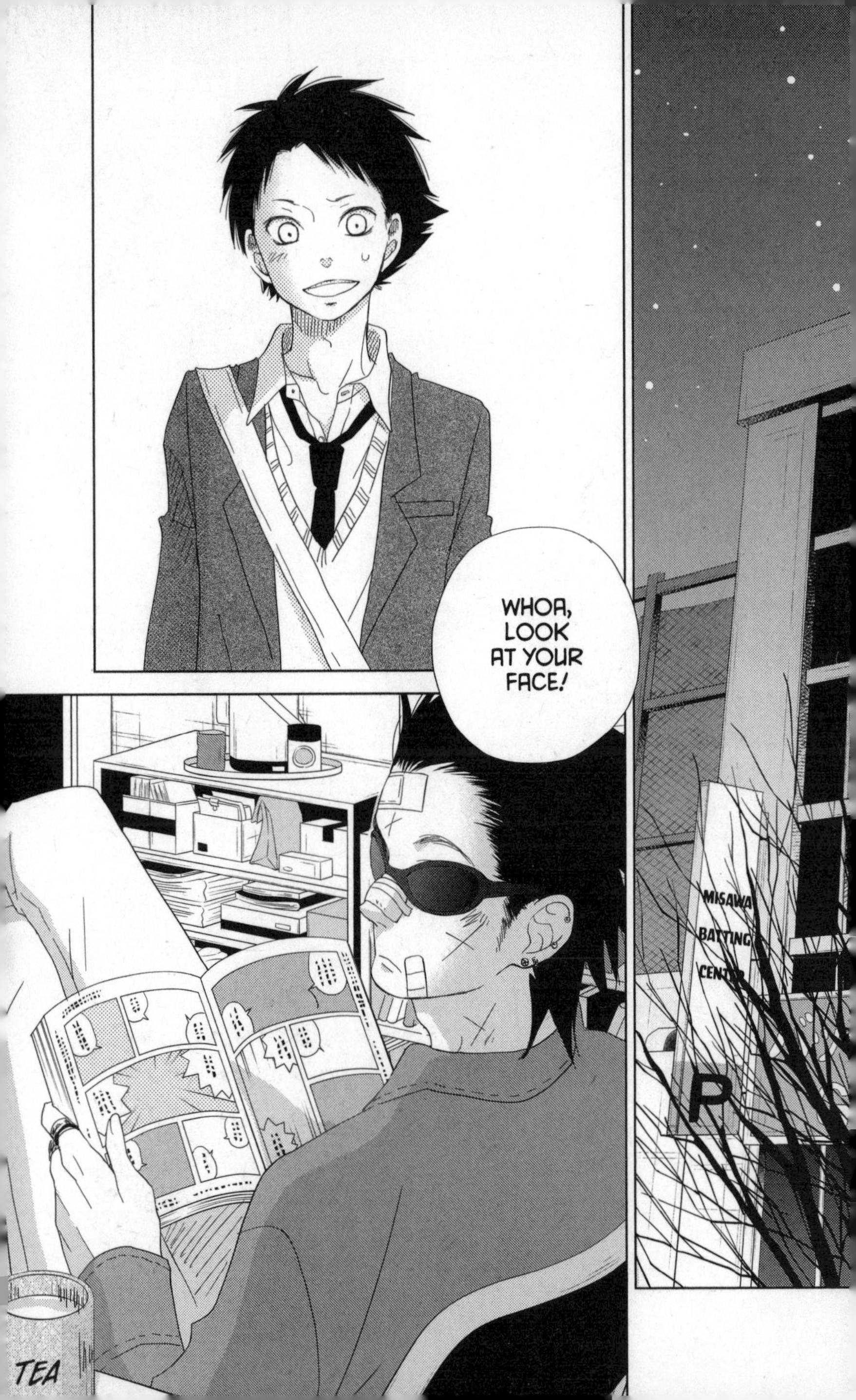
MISAWA BATTING CENTER
P
WHOA, LOOK AT YOUR FACE!
TEA

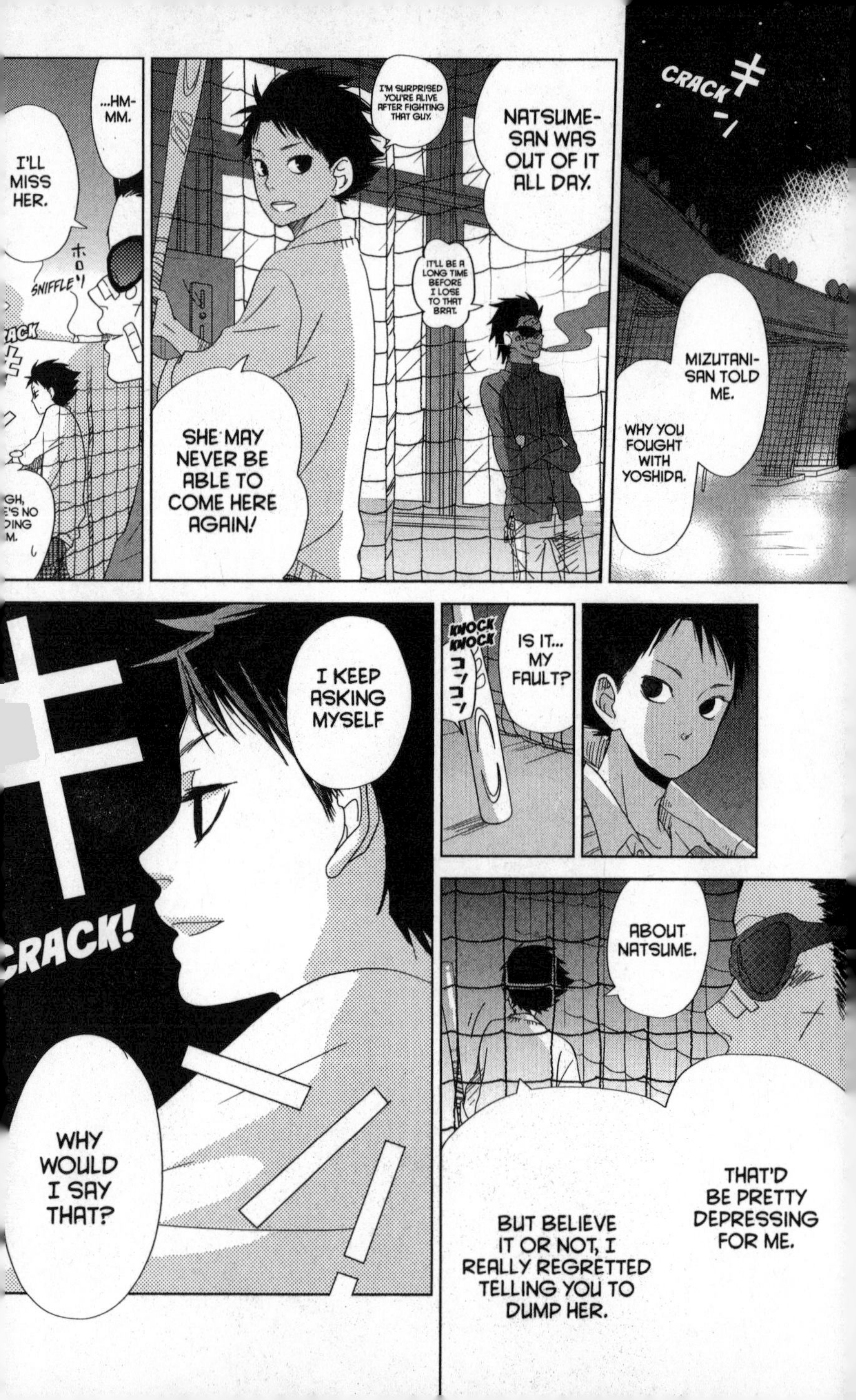
CRACK
MIZUTANI-SAN TOLD ME.
WHY YOU FOUGHT WITH YOSHIDA.
NATSUME-SAN WAS OUT OF IT ALL DAY.
I'M SURPRISED YOU'RE ALIVE AFTER FIGHTING THAT GUY.
IT'LL BE A LONG TIME BEFORE I LOSE TO THAT BRAT.
SHE MAY NEVER BE ABLE TO COME HERE AGAIN!
...HM-MM.
I'LL MISS HER.
SNIFFLE
KNOCK KNOCK
IS IT... MY FAULT?
ABOUT NATSUME.
THAT'D BE PRETTY DEPRESSING FOR ME.
BUT BELIEVE IT OR NOT, I REALLY REGRETTED TELLING YOU TO DUMP HER.
I KEEP ASKING MYSELF
CRACK!
WHY WOULD I SAY THAT?

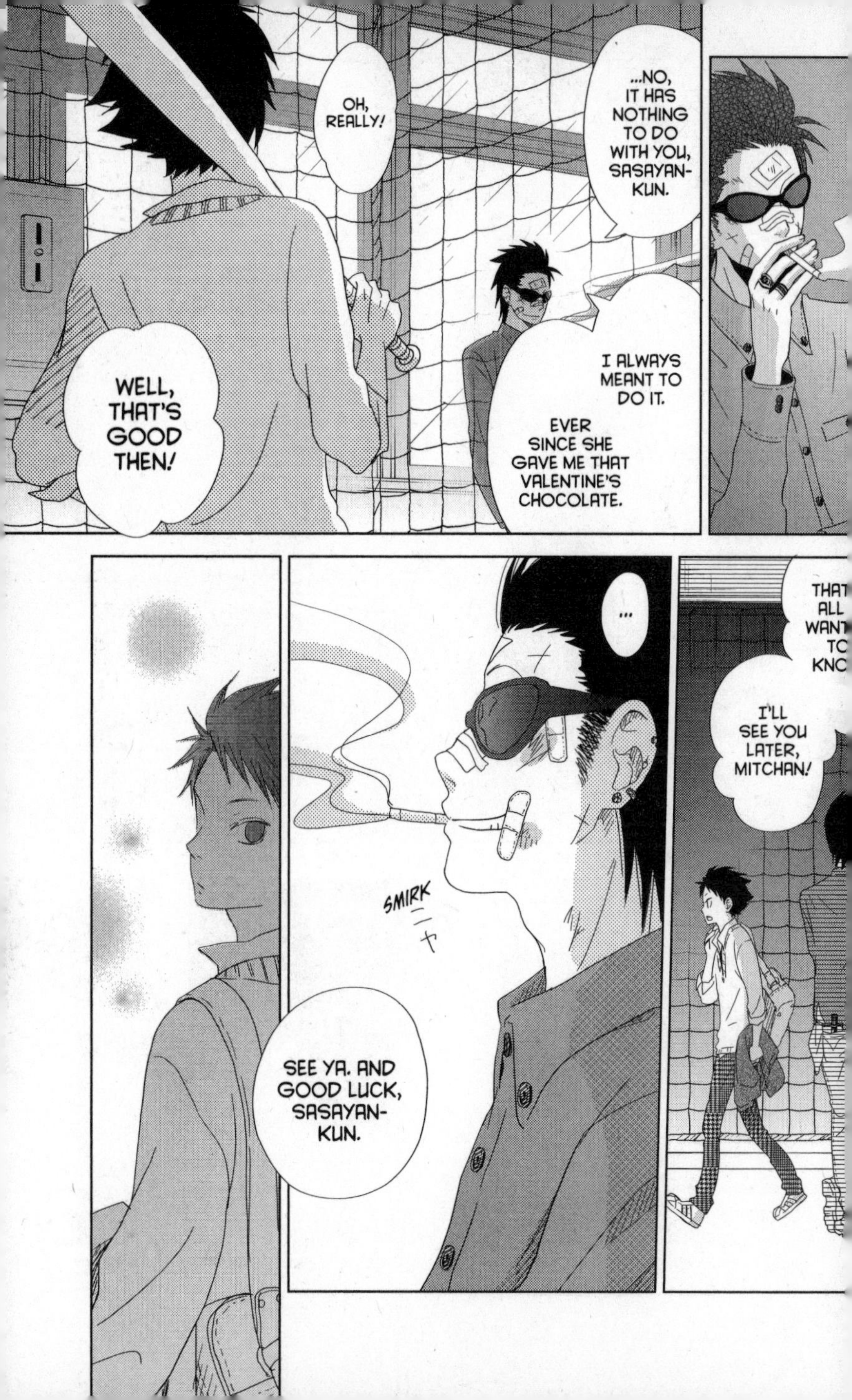
...NO, IT HAS NOTHING TO DO WITH YOU, SASAYAN-KUN.
OH, REALLY!
I ALWAYS MEANT TO DO IT.
EVER SINCE SHE GAVE ME THAT VALENTINE'S CHOCOLATE.
WELL, THAT'S GOOD THEN!
THAT ALL WANT TO KNO
I'LL SEE YOU LATER, MITCHAN!
...
SMIRK
ニヤ
SEE YA. AND GOOD LUCK, SASAYAN-KUN.

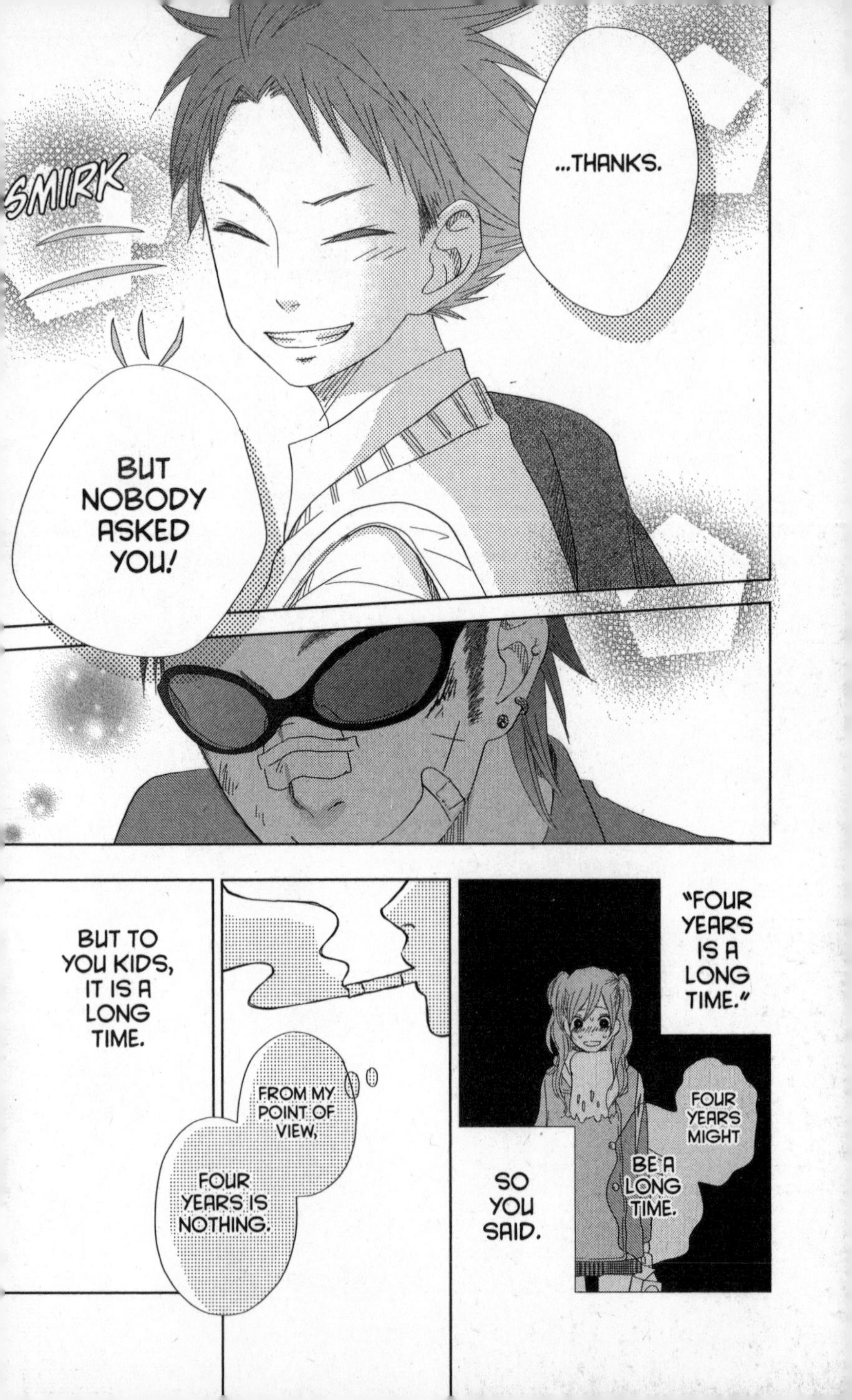
...THANKS.
SMIRK
BUT NOBODY ASKED YOU!
"FOUR YEARS IS A LONG TIME."
FOUR YEARS MIGHT BE A LONG TIME.
SO YOU SAID.
FROM MY POINT OF VIEW,
FOUR YEARS IS NOTHING.
BUT TO YOU KIDS, IT IS A LONG TIME.

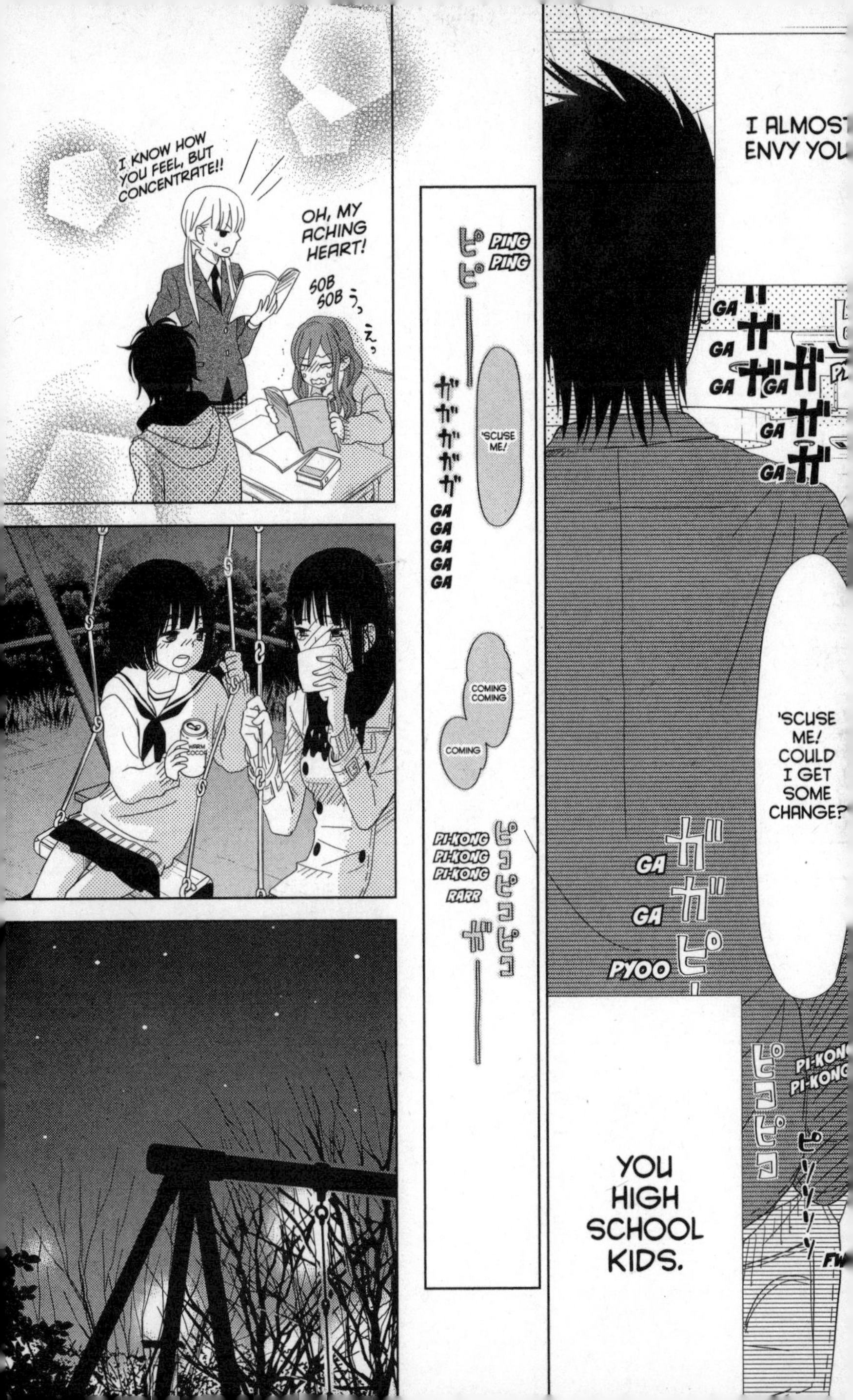
I ALMOS
ENVY YOU
GA GA GA GA GA
ガガガガガ
'SCUSE ME! COULD I GET SOME CHANGE?
GA GA
ガガピー
PYOO
PI-KON PI-KON
ピコピコピーン
YOU HIGH SCHOOL KIDS.
ピピー
PING PING
'SCUSE ME!
ガガガガガ
GA GA GA GA GA
COMING COMING
COMING
ピコピコピコガー
PI-KONG PI-KONG PI-KONG RARR
OH, MY ACHING HEART!
I KNOW HOW YOU FEEL, BUT CONCENTRATE!!
SOB SOB
WARM COCOA

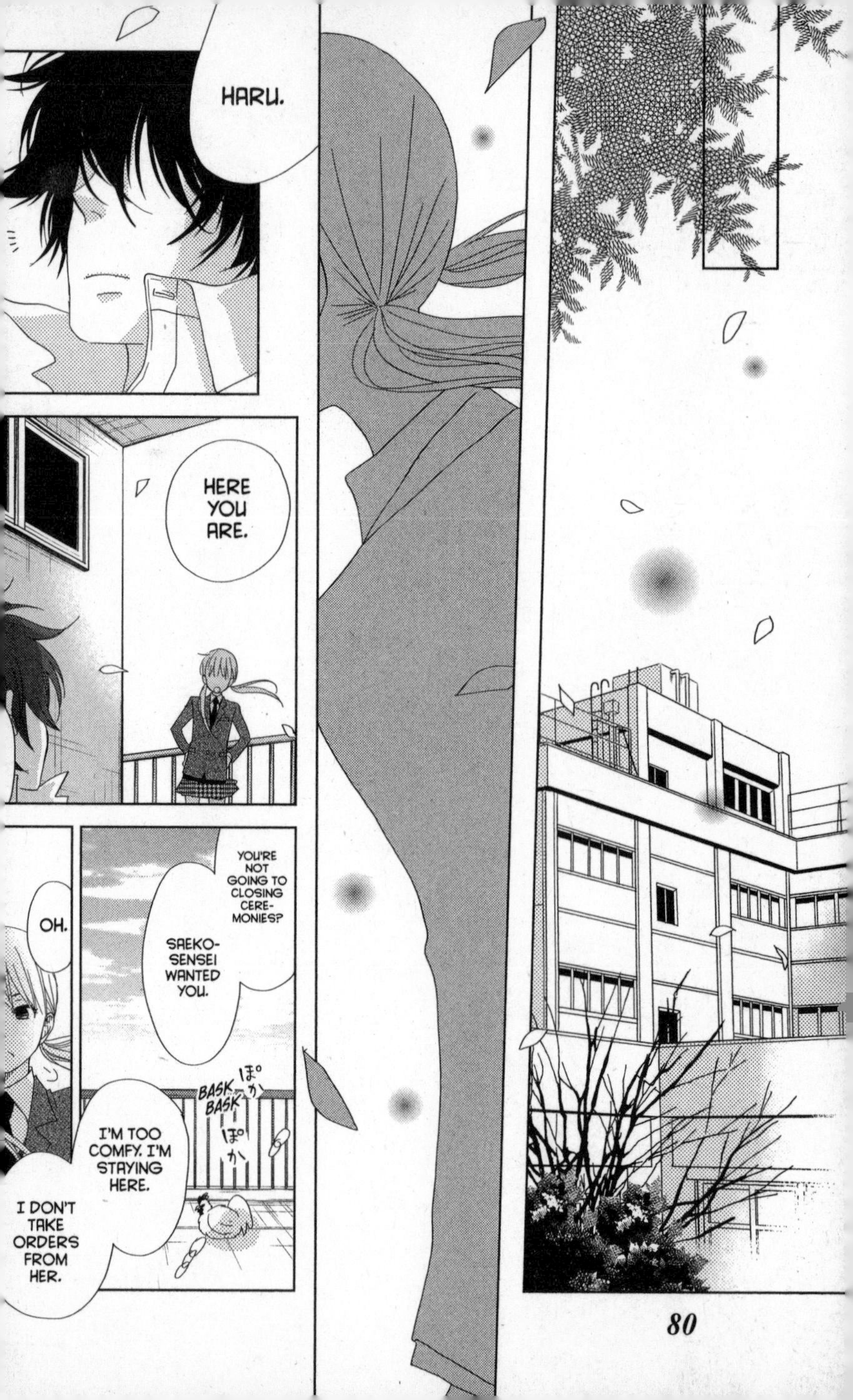
HARU.
HERE YOU ARE.
YOU'RE NOT GOING TO CLOSING CERE-MONIES?
SAEKO-SENSEI WANTED YOU.
BASK BASK
ぽかぽか
I'M TOO COMFY. I'M STAYING HERE.
OH.
I DON'T TAKE ORDERS FROM HER.

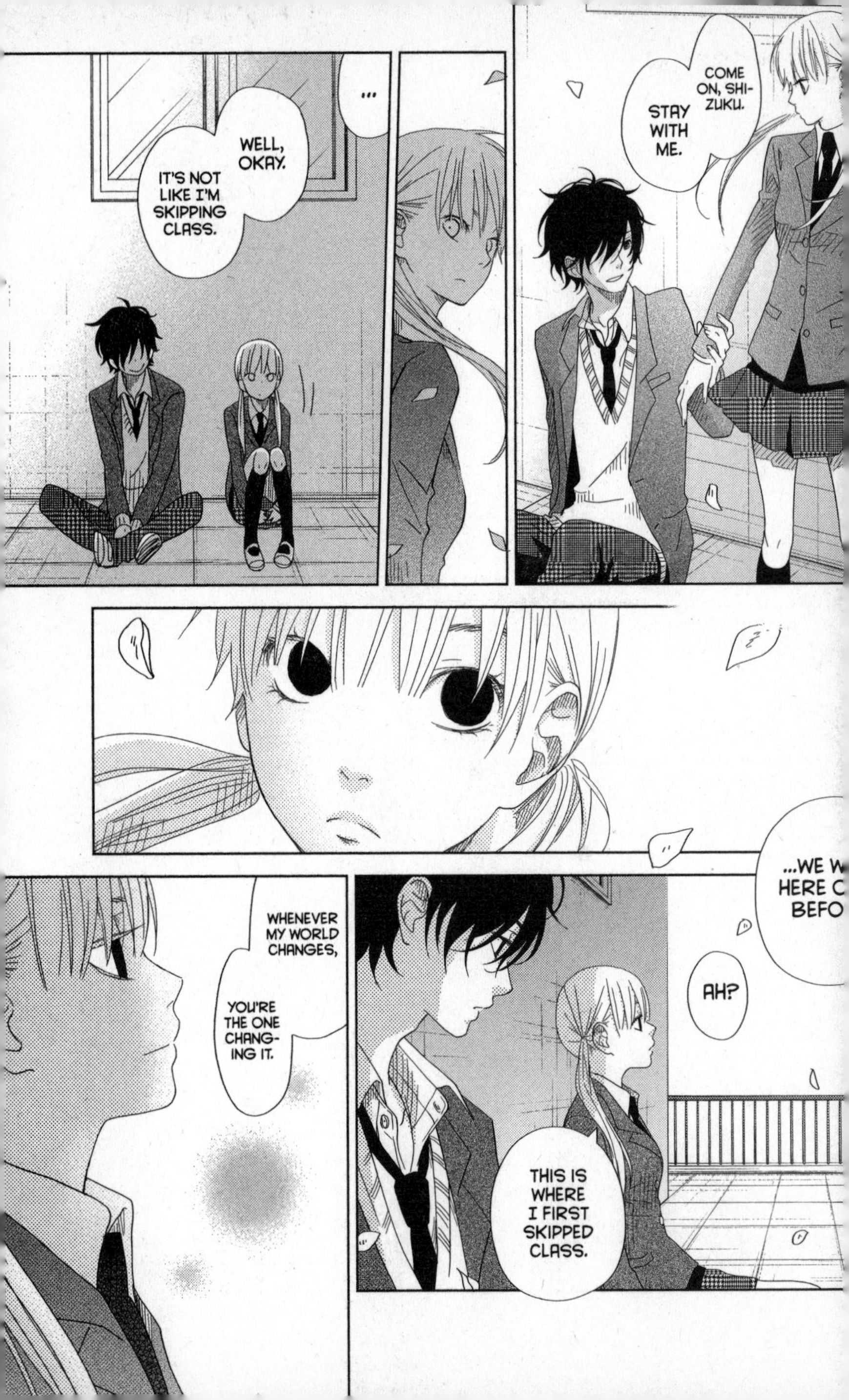

COME ON, SHIZUKU. STAY WITH ME.
...
WELL, OKAY.
IT'S NOT LIKE I'M SKIPPING CLASS.
...WE W HERE C BEFO
AH?
THIS IS WHERE I FIRST SKIPPED CLASS.
WHENEVER MY WORLD CHANGES,
YOU'RE THE ONE CHANGING IT.

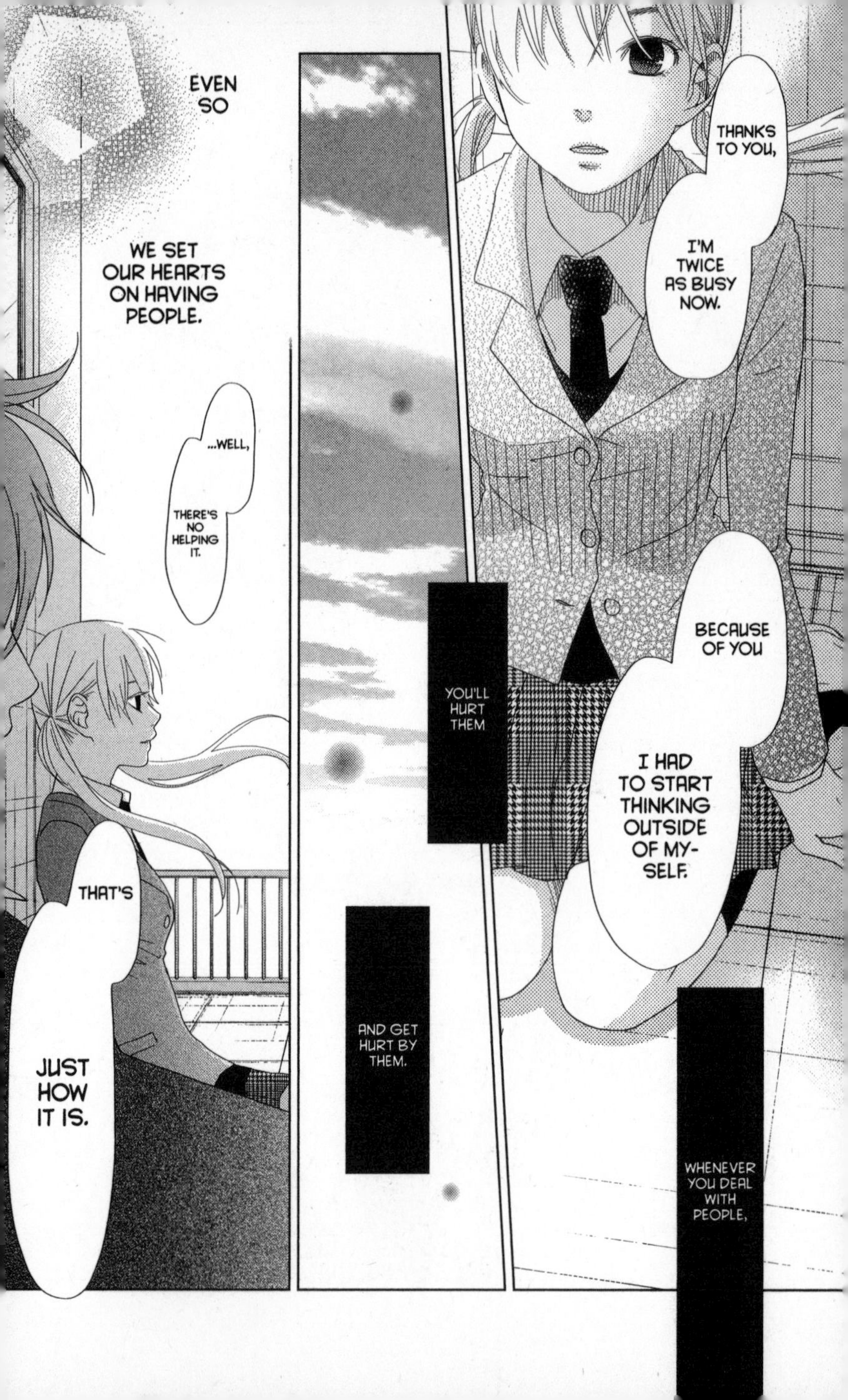
THANKS TO YOU,
I'M TWICE AS BUSY NOW.
BECAUSE OF YOU
I HAD TO START THINKING OUTSIDE OF MY-SELF.
WHENEVER YOU DEAL WITH PEOPLE,
YOU'LL HURT THEM
AND GET HURT BY THEM.
EVEN SO
WE SET OUR HEARTS ON HAVING PEOPLE.
...WELL,
THERE'S NO HELPING IT.
THAT'S
JUST HOW IT IS.

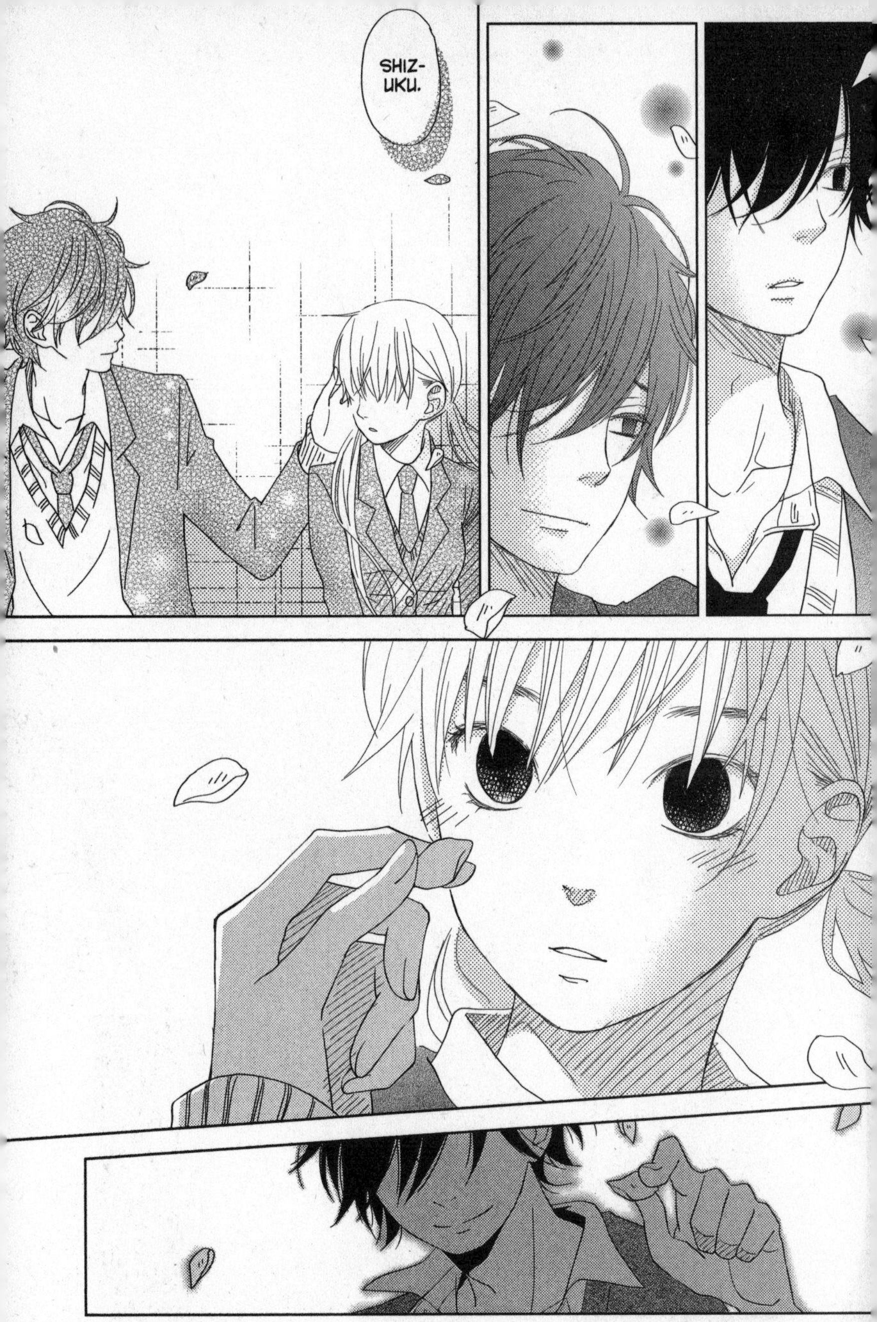
SHIZ-
UKU.

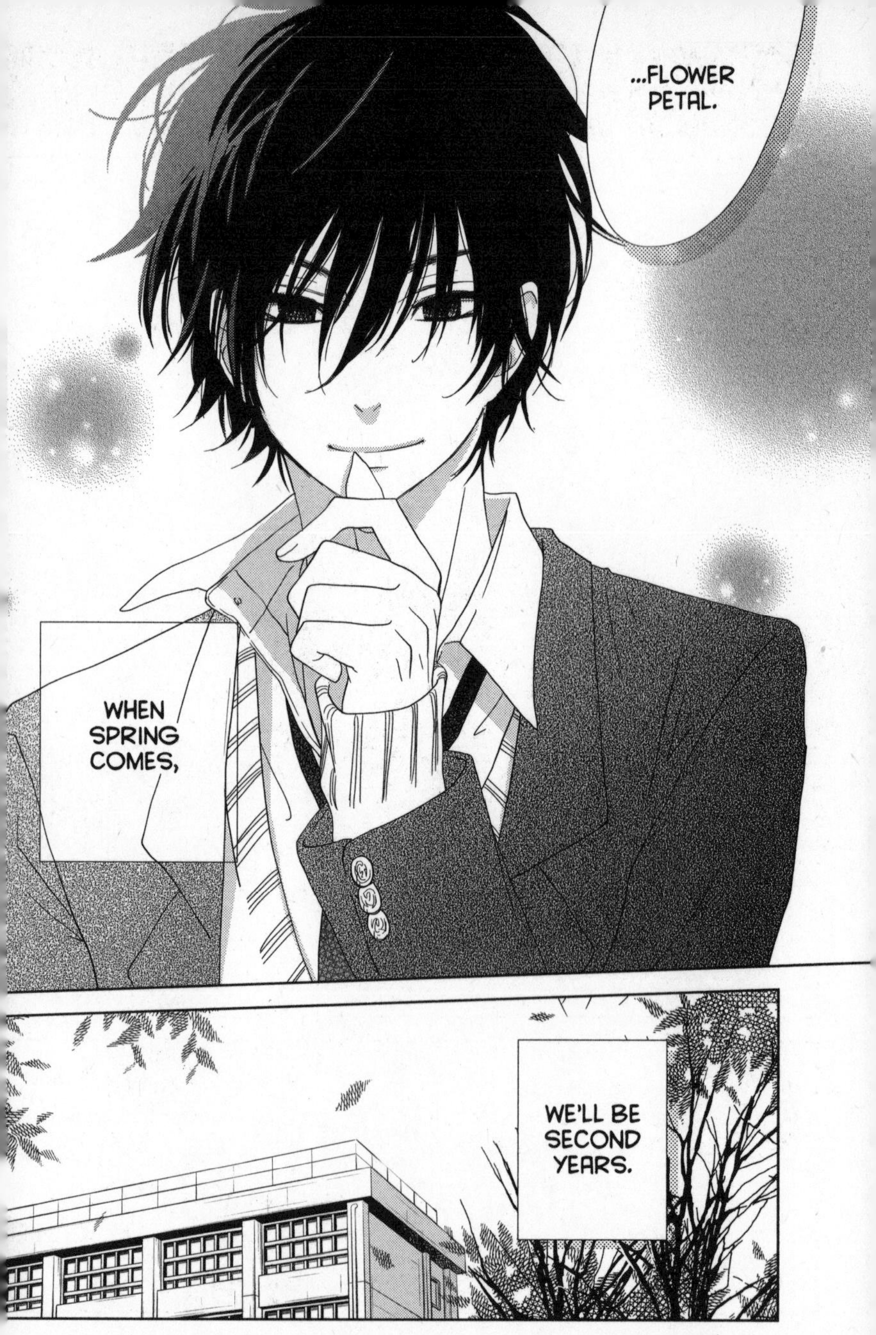
...FLOWER PETAL.
WHEN SPRING COMES,
WE'LL BE SECOND YEARS.

WRAP PARTY

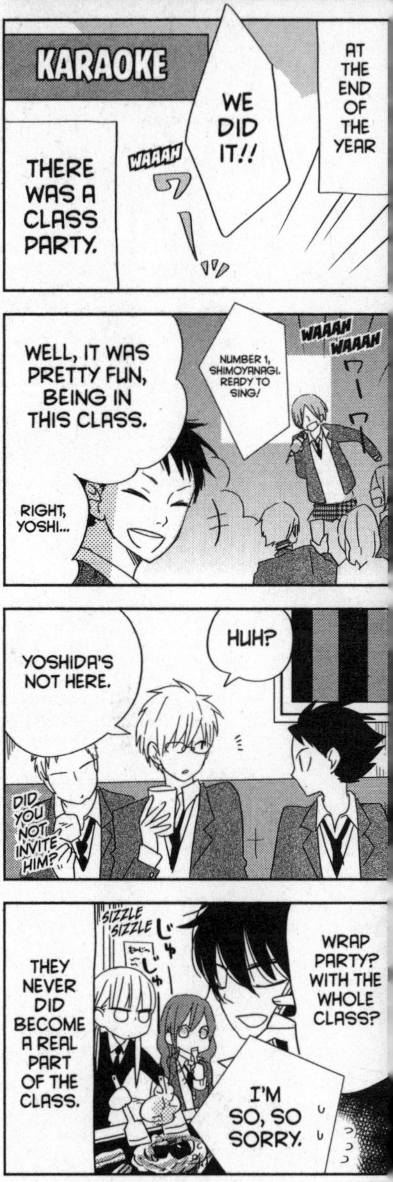

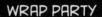

AT THE END OF THE YEAR
WE DID IT!!
WAAAH
KARAOKE
THERE WAS A CLASS PARTY.
WAAAH WAAAH
NUMBER 1, SHIMOYANAGI. READY TO SING!
WELL, IT WAS PRETTY FUN, BEING IN THIS CLASS.
RIGHT, YOSHI...
HUH?
YOSHIDA'S NOT HERE.
DID YOU NOT INVITE HIM?
WRAP PARTY? WITH THE WHOLE CLASS?
I'M SO, SO SORRY.
SIZZLE SIZZLE
THEY NEVER DID BECOME A REAL PART OF THE CLASS.

AT THE END OF FIRST YEAR

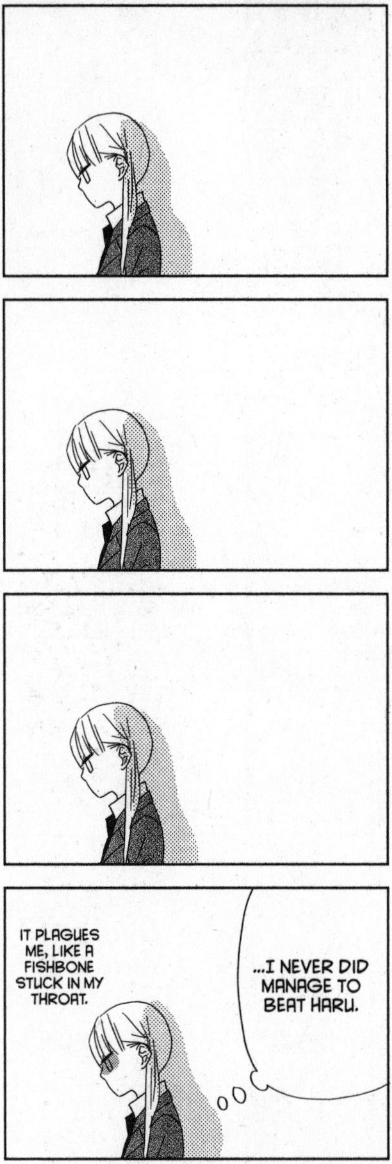

...I NEVER DID MANAGE TO BEAT HARU.
IT PLAGUES ME, LIKE A FISHBONE STUCK IN MY THROAT.

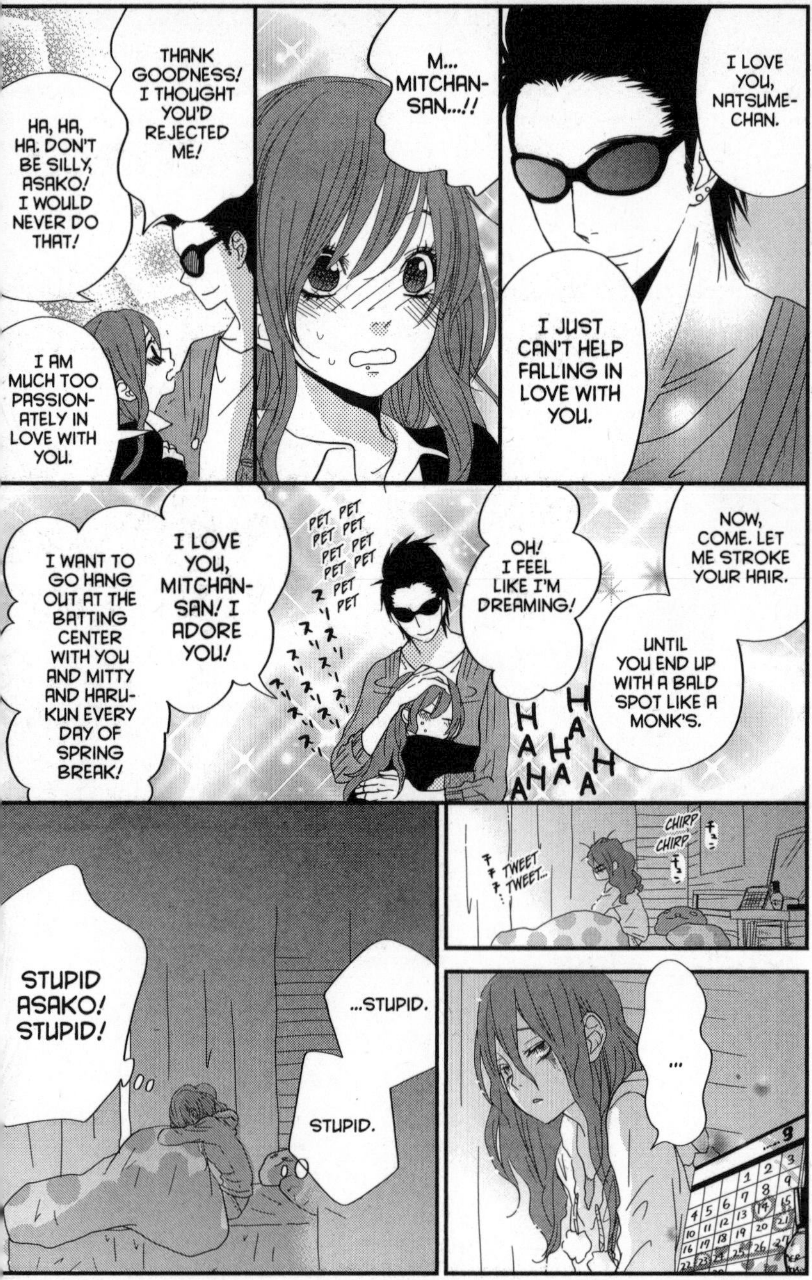
I LOVE YOU, NATSUME-CHAN.
I JUST CAN'T HELP FALLING IN LOVE WITH YOU.
M... MITCHAN-SAN...!!
THANK GOODNESS! I THOUGHT YOU'D REJECTED ME!
HA, HA, HA. DON'T BE SILLY, ASAKO! I WOULD NEVER DO THAT!
I AM MUCH TOO PASSIONATELY IN LOVE WITH YOU.
NOW, COME. LET ME STROKE YOUR HAIR.
OH! I FEEL LIKE I'M DREAMING!
UNTIL YOU END UP WITH A BALD SPOT LIKE A MONK'S.
HA HA HA HA HA
PET PET PET PET PET PET PET PET PET PET
I LOVE YOU, MITCHAN-SAN! I ADORE YOU!
I WANT TO GO HANG OUT AT THE BATTING CENTER WITH YOU AND MITTY AND HARU-KUN EVERY DAY OF SPRING BREAK!
CHIRP CHIRP
TWEET TWEET...
...
...STUPID.
STUPID ASAKO! STUPID!
STUPID.

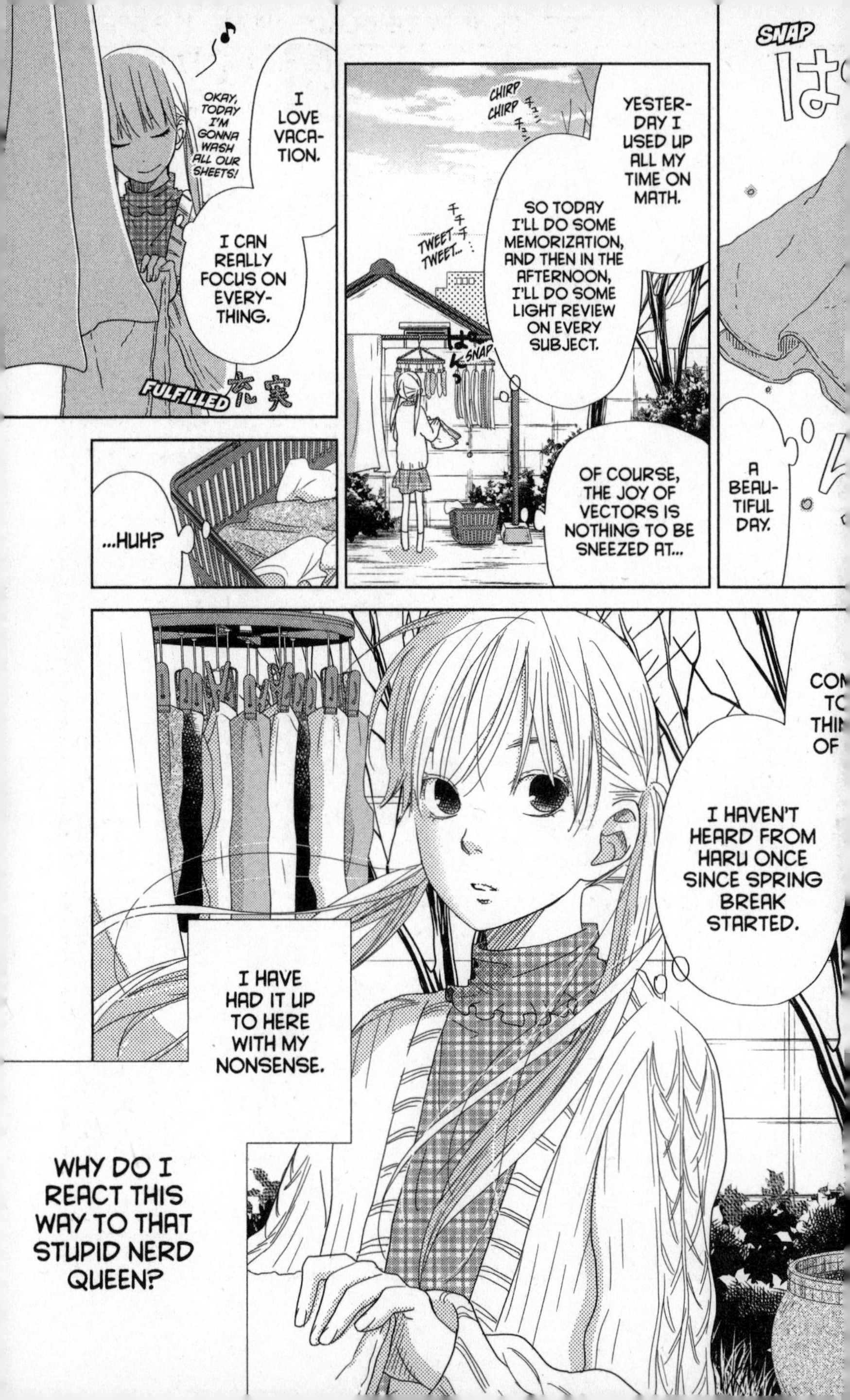
SNAP
A BEAUTIFUL DAY.
CHIRP CHIRP
YESTERDAY I USED UP ALL MY TIME ON MATH.
SO TODAY I'LL DO SOME MEMORIZATION, AND THEN IN THE AFTERNOON, I'LL DO SOME LIGHT REVIEW ON EVERY SUBJECT.
TWEET TWEET...
SNAP
OF COURSE, THE JOY OF VECTORS IS NOTHING TO BE SNEEZED AT...
I LOVE VACATION.
OKAY, TODAY I'M GONNA WASH ALL OUR SHEETS!
I CAN REALLY FOCUS ON EVERYTHING.
FULFILLED
...HUH?
I HAVEN'T HEARD FROM HARU ONCE SINCE SPRING BREAK STARTED.
I HAVE HAD IT UP TO HERE WITH MY NONSENSE.
WHY DO I REACT THIS WAY TO THAT STUPID NERD QUEEN?

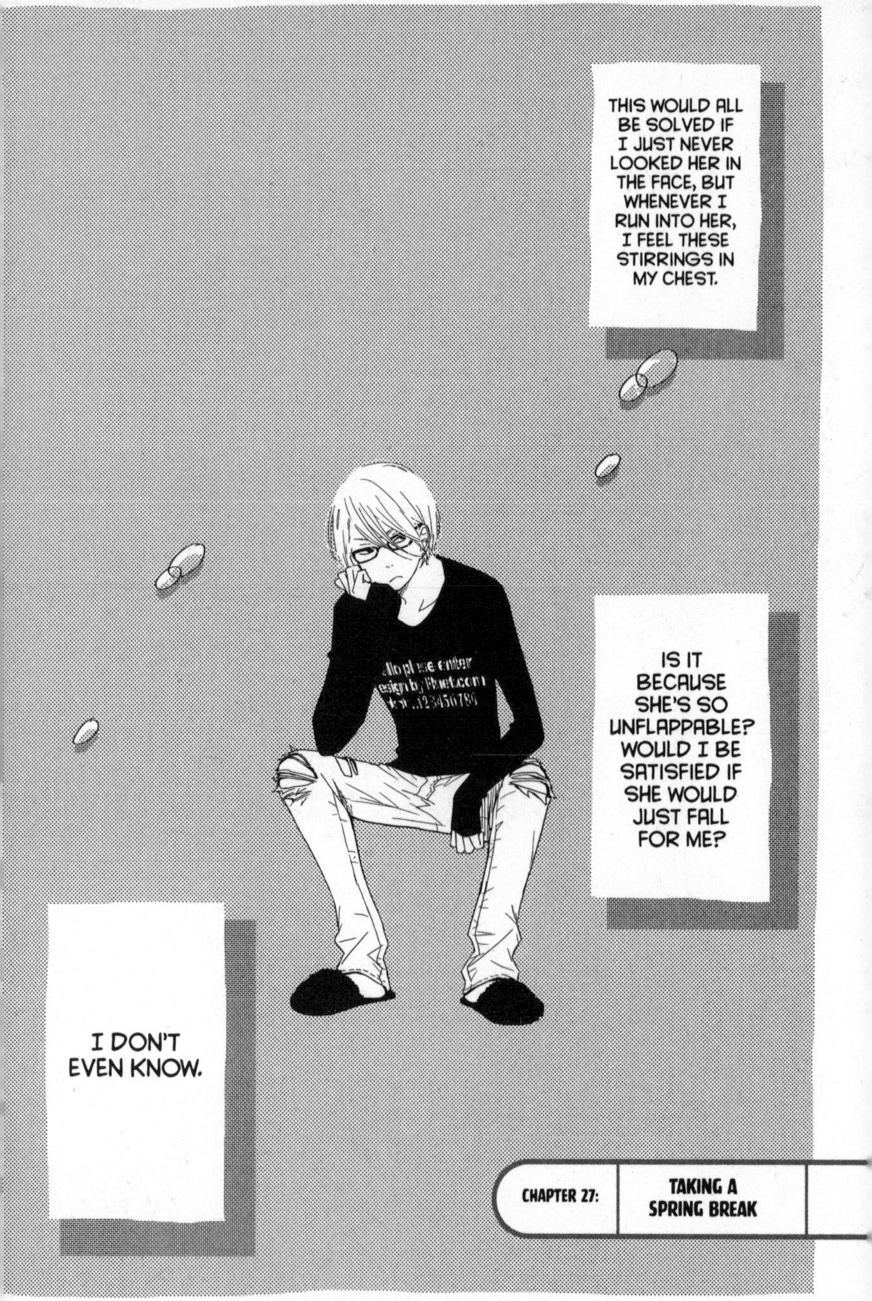
THIS WOULD ALL BE SOLVED IF I JUST NEVER LOOKED HER IN THE FACE, BUT WHENEVER I RUN INTO HER, I FEEL THESE STIRRINGS IN MY CHEST.
IS IT BECAUSE SHE'S SO UNFLAPPABLE? WOULD I BE SATISFIED IF SHE WOULD JUST FALL FOR ME?
I DON'T EVEN KNOW.
CHAPTER 27: TAKING A SPRING BREAK

OH, HELLO. MY NAME IS YAMAGUCHI. IS SHIZUKU-SAN AT HOME?

BUT DAWDLING AROUND HERE ISN'T GOING TO GET ME ANYWHERE!

...MAY I ASK WHO'S SPEAKING?

IF I *CAN* MAKE HER MINE, THEN I WILL!!!

THIS IS YAMA-GUCHI.

TURURU... TURURU...

LITTLE BROTHER?

WHEW...

FATHER?!

I'M SORRY, BUT I'M ONLY A LITTLE KID. I DON'T REALLY GET IT, SO I'M GOING TO LET YOU TALK TO MY FATHER.

...

WHAT.

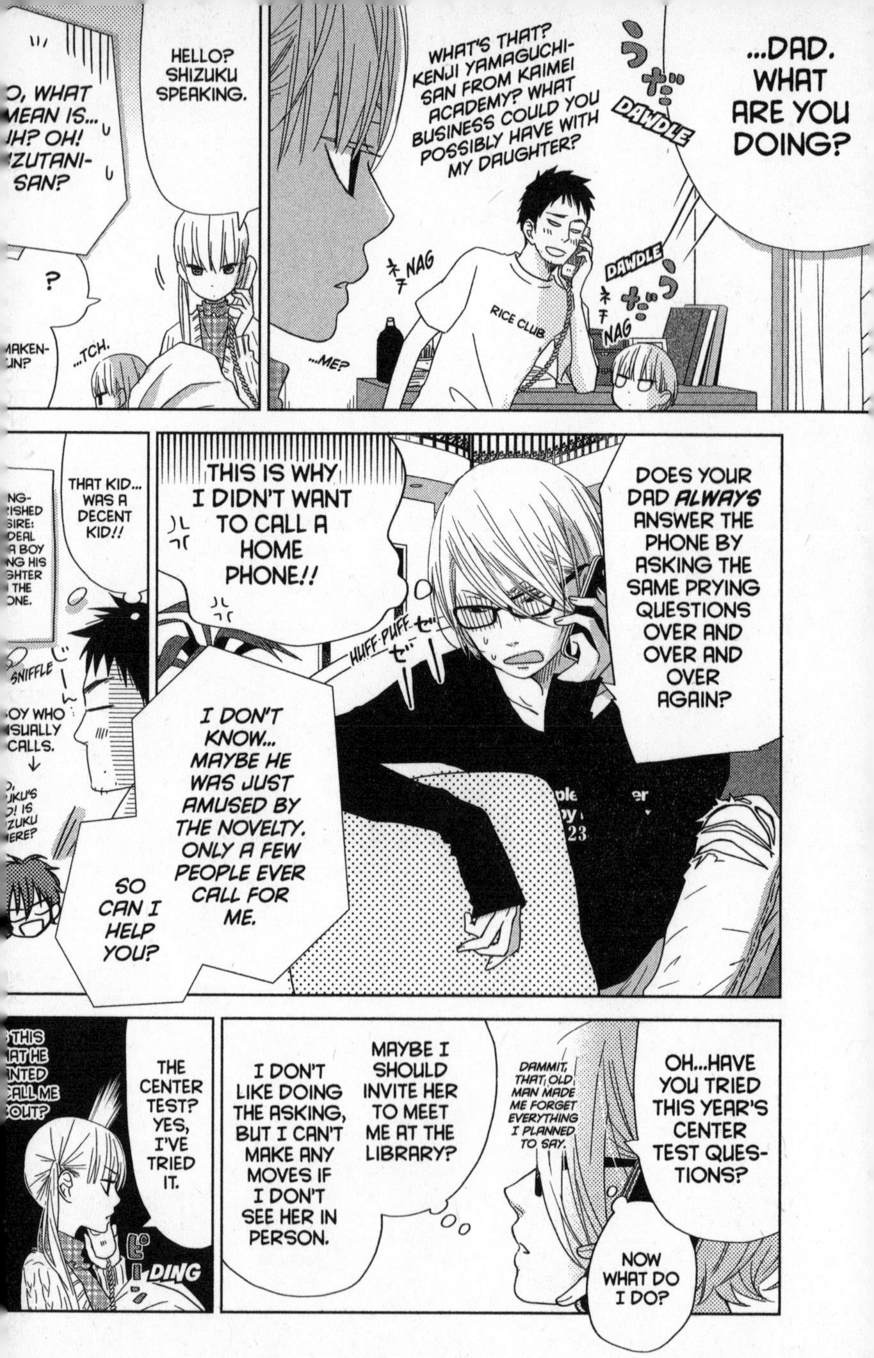
...DAD. WHAT ARE YOU DOING?
DAWDLE
DAWDLE
WHAT'S THAT? KENJI YAMAGUCHI-SAN FROM KAIMEI ACADEMY? WHAT BUSINESS COULD YOU POSSIBLY HAVE WITH MY DAUGHTER?
NAG
NAG
...ME?
HELLO? SHIZUKU SPEAKING.
?
...TCH.
O, WHAT MEAN IS... H? OH! ZUTANI-SAN?
MAKEN-UN?
DOES YOUR DAD *ALWAYS* ANSWER THE PHONE BY ASKING THE SAME PRYING QUESTIONS OVER AND OVER AND OVER AGAIN?
THIS IS WHY I DIDN'T WANT TO CALL A HOME PHONE!!
HUFF PUFF
I DON'T KNOW... MAYBE HE WAS JUST AMUSED BY THE NOVELTY. ONLY A FEW PEOPLE EVER CALL FOR ME.
SO CAN I HELP YOU?
THAT KID... WAS A DECENT KID!!
SNIFFLE
OH...HAVE YOU TRIED THIS YEAR'S CENTER TEST QUESTIONS?
DAMMIT, THAT OLD MAN MADE ME FORGET EVERYTHING I PLANNED TO SAY.
NOW WHAT DO I DO?
MAYBE I SHOULD INVITE HER TO MEET ME AT THE LIBRARY?
I DON'T LIKE DOING THE ASKING, BUT I CAN'T MAKE ANY MOVES IF I DON'T SEE HER IN PERSON.
THE CENTER TEST? YES, I'VE TRIED IT.
DING

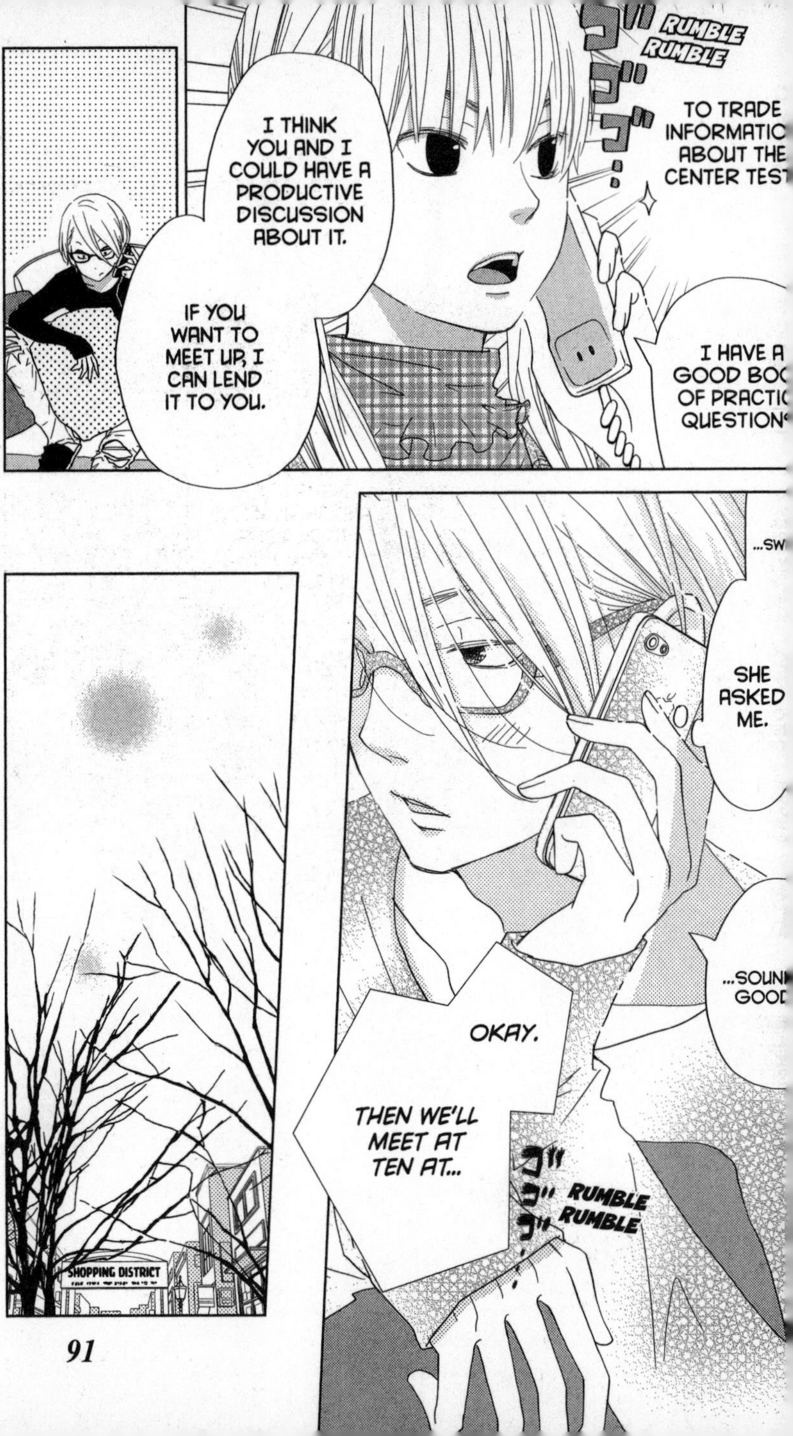

RUMBLE RUMBLE
TO TRADE INFORMATIC ABOUT THE CENTER TEST
I THINK YOU AND I COULD HAVE A PRODUCTIVE DISCUSSION ABOUT IT.
I HAVE A GOOD BOO OF PRACTIC QUESTION
IF YOU WANT TO MEET UP, I CAN LEND IT TO YOU.
...SW
SHE ASKED ME.
...SOUN GOOD
OKAY.
THEN WE'LL MEET AT TEN AT...
RUMBLE RUMBLE
SHOPPING DISTRICT

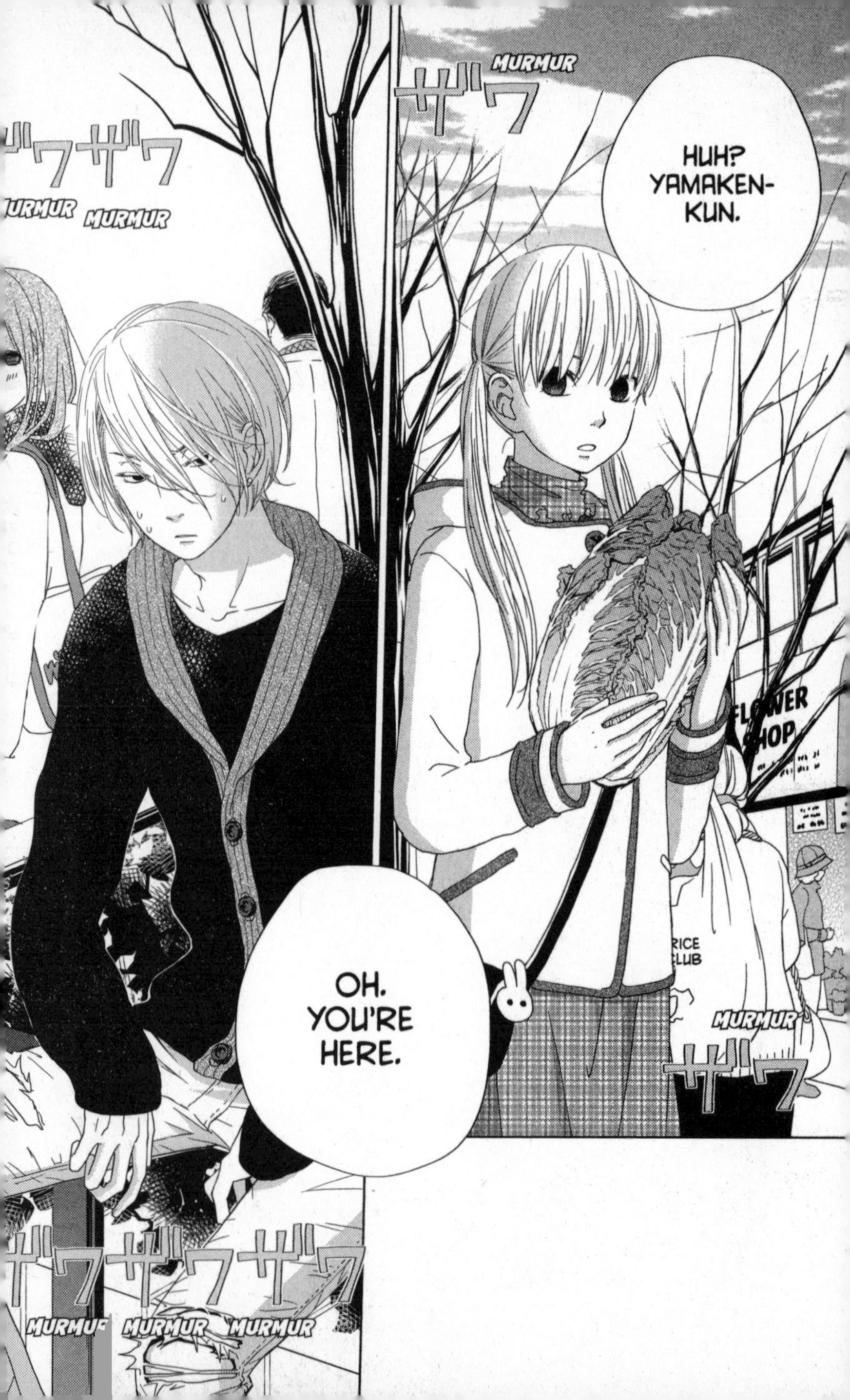
ザワ
MURMUR
HUH? YAMAKEN-KUN.
FLOWER SHOP
RICE CLUB
ザワ
MURMUR
ザワザワ
MURMUR MURMUR
OH. YOU'RE HERE.
ザワザワザワ
MURMUR MURMUR MURMUR

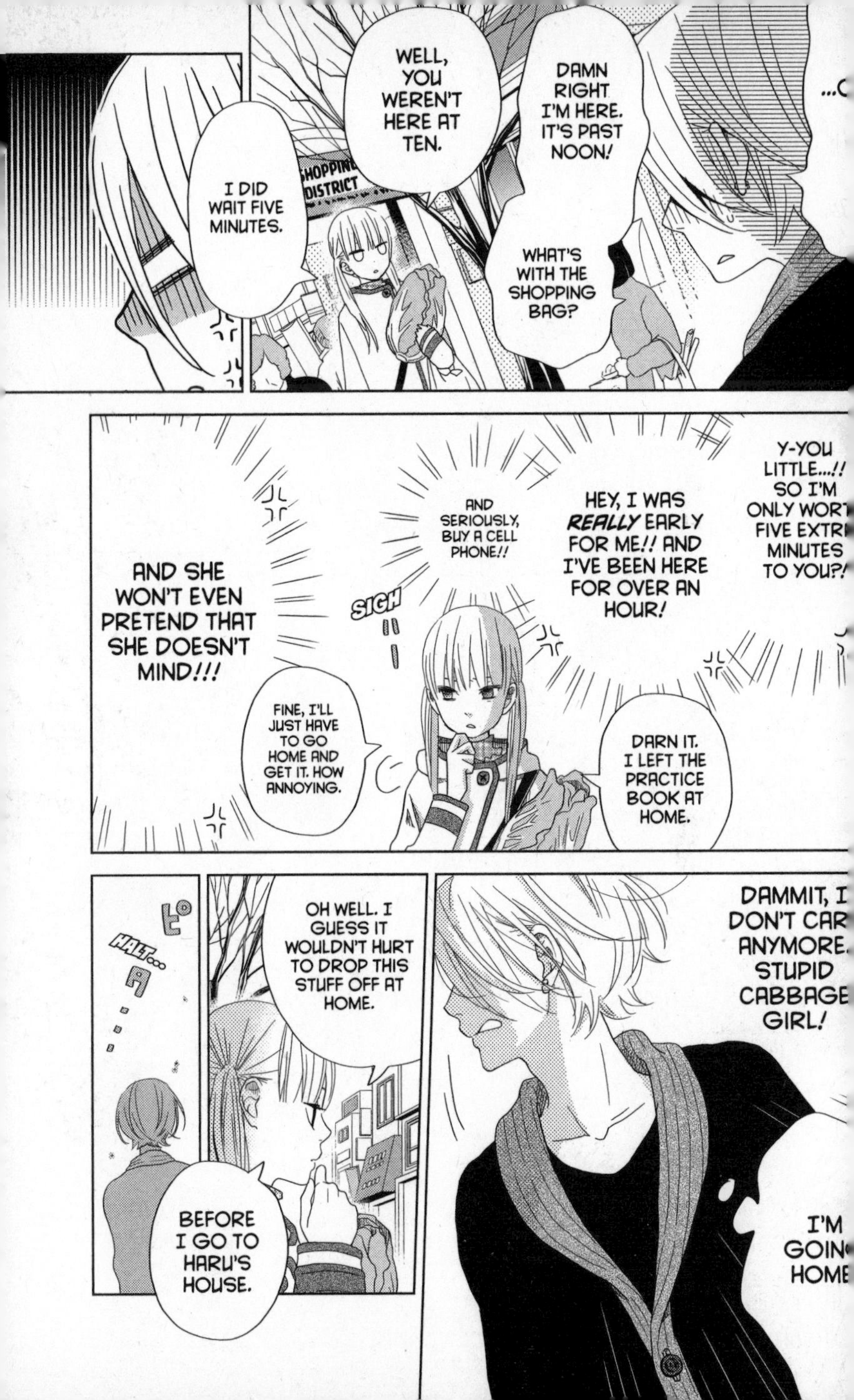
...C
DAMN RIGHT I'M HERE. IT'S PAST NOON!
WHAT'S WITH THE SHOPPING BAG?
WELL, YOU WEREN'T HERE AT TEN.
SHOPPIN DISTRICT
I DID WAIT FIVE MINUTES.
Y-YOU LITTLE...!! SO I'M ONLY WORT FIVE EXTR MINUTES TO YOU?!
HEY, I WAS REALLY EARLY FOR ME!! AND I'VE BEEN HERE FOR OVER AN HOUR!
AND SERIOUSLY, BUY A CELL PHONE!!
SIGH
DARN IT. I LEFT THE PRACTICE BOOK AT HOME.
FINE, I'LL JUST HAVE TO GO HOME AND GET IT. HOW ANNOYING.
AND SHE WON'T EVEN PRETEND THAT SHE DOESN'T MIND!!!
DAMMIT, I DON'T CAR ANYMORE. STUPID CABBAGE GIRL!
I'M GOIN HOME
OH WELL. I GUESS IT WOULDN'T HURT TO DROP THIS STUFF OFF AT HOME.
BEFORE I GO TO HARU'S HOUSE.
HALT...

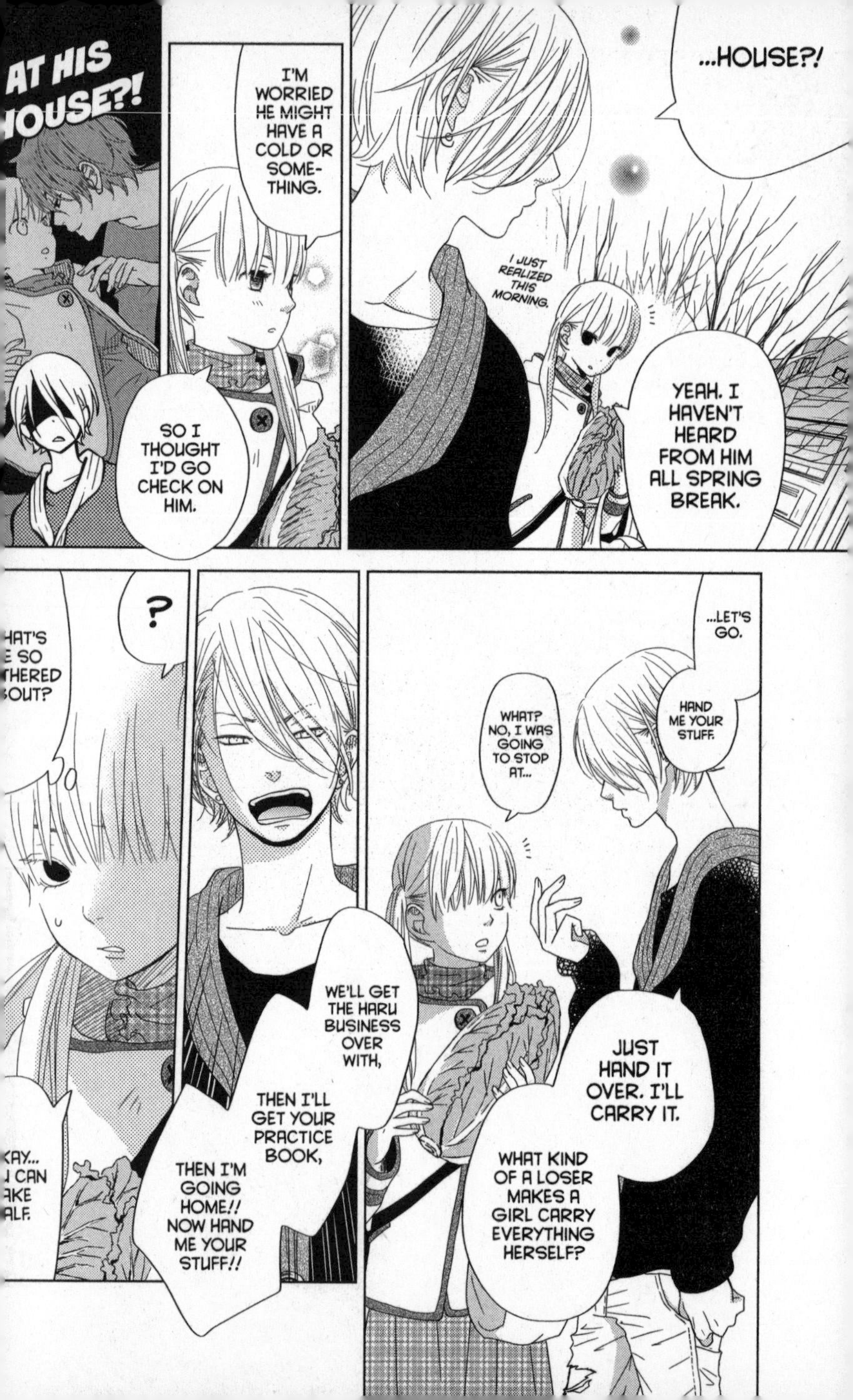
...HOUSE?!
YEAH. I HAVEN'T HEARD FROM HIM ALL SPRING BREAK.
I JUST REALIZED THIS MORNING.
I'M WORRIED HE MIGHT HAVE A COLD OR SOME-THING.
SO I THOUGHT I'D GO CHECK ON HIM.
AT HIS HOUSE?!
...LET'S GO.
HAND ME YOUR STUFF.
WHAT? NO, I WAS GOING TO STOP AT...
JUST HAND IT OVER. I'LL CARRY IT.
WHAT KIND OF A LOSER MAKES A GIRL CARRY EVERYTHING HERSELF?
WE'LL GET THE HARU BUSINESS OVER WITH,
THEN I'LL GET YOUR PRACTICE BOOK,
THEN I'M GOING HOME!! NOW HAND ME YOUR STUFF!!
?
HAT'S E SO THERED OUT?
KAY... U CAN AKE ALF.

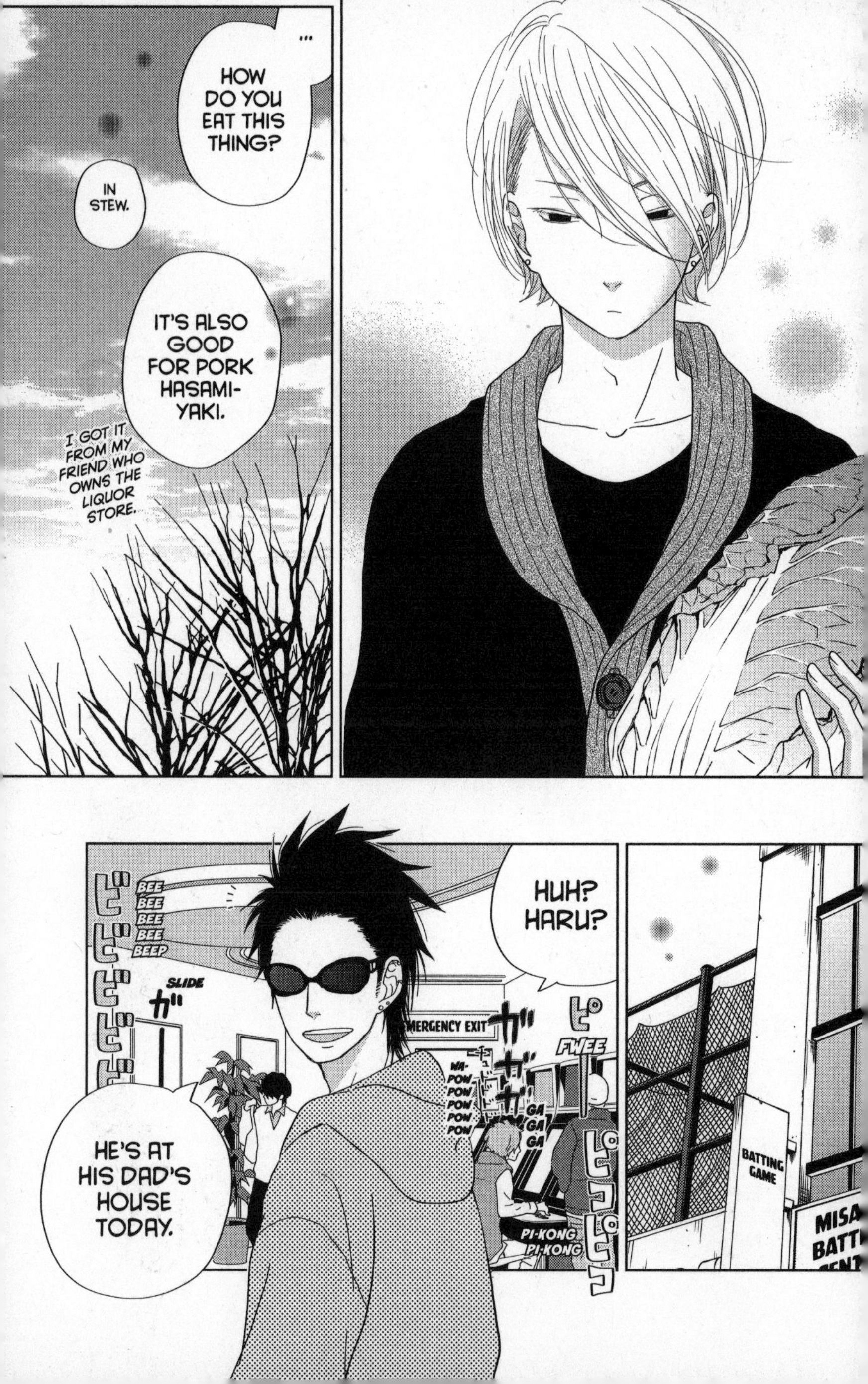

...
HOW DO YOU EAT THIS THING?
IN STEW.
IT'S ALSO GOOD FOR PORK HASAMI-YAKI.
I GOT IT FROM MY FRIEND WHO OWNS THE LIQUOR STORE.
BATTING GAME
HUH? HARU?
ピ FWEE
ガガガ
EMERGENCY EXIT
WA-POW POW POW POW POW
GA GA GA
ピコピコ
PI-KONG PI-KONG
ビビビビビ
BEE BEE BEE BEE BEEP
ガ SLIDE
HE'S AT HIS DAD'S HOUSE TODAY.

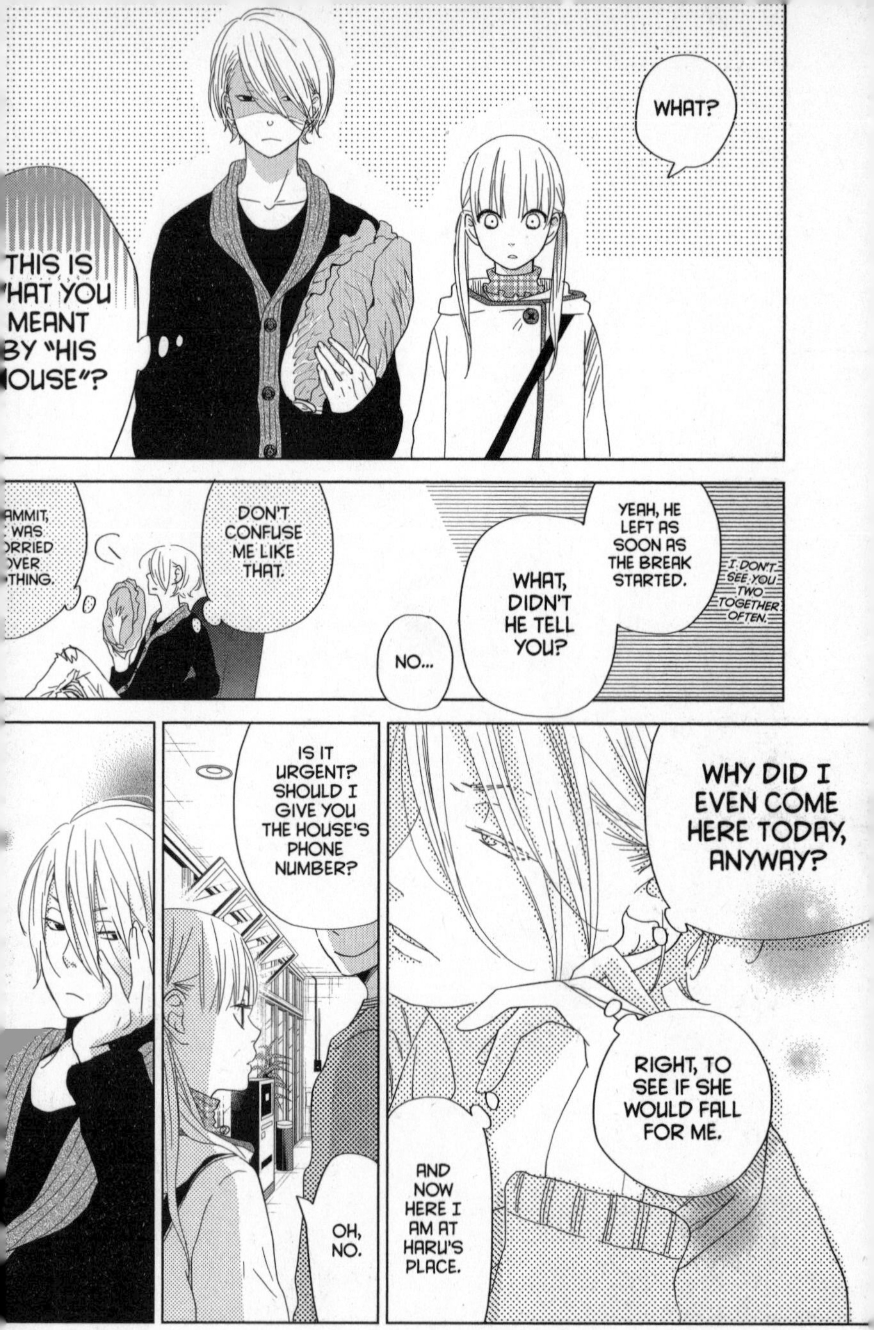
WHAT?
THIS IS HAT YOU MEANT BY "HIS OUSE"?
I DON'T SEE YOU TWO TOGETHER OFTEN.
YEAH, HE LEFT AS SOON AS THE BREAK STARTED.
WHAT, DIDN'T HE TELL YOU?
NO...
DON'T CONFUSE ME LIKE THAT.
AMMIT, WAS ORRIED OVER THING.
WHY DID I EVEN COME HERE TODAY, ANYWAY?
RIGHT, TO SEE IF SHE WOULD FALL FOR ME.
AND NOW HERE I AM AT HARU'S PLACE.
IS IT URGENT? SHOULD I GIVE YOU THE HOUSE'S PHONE NUMBER?
OH, NO.

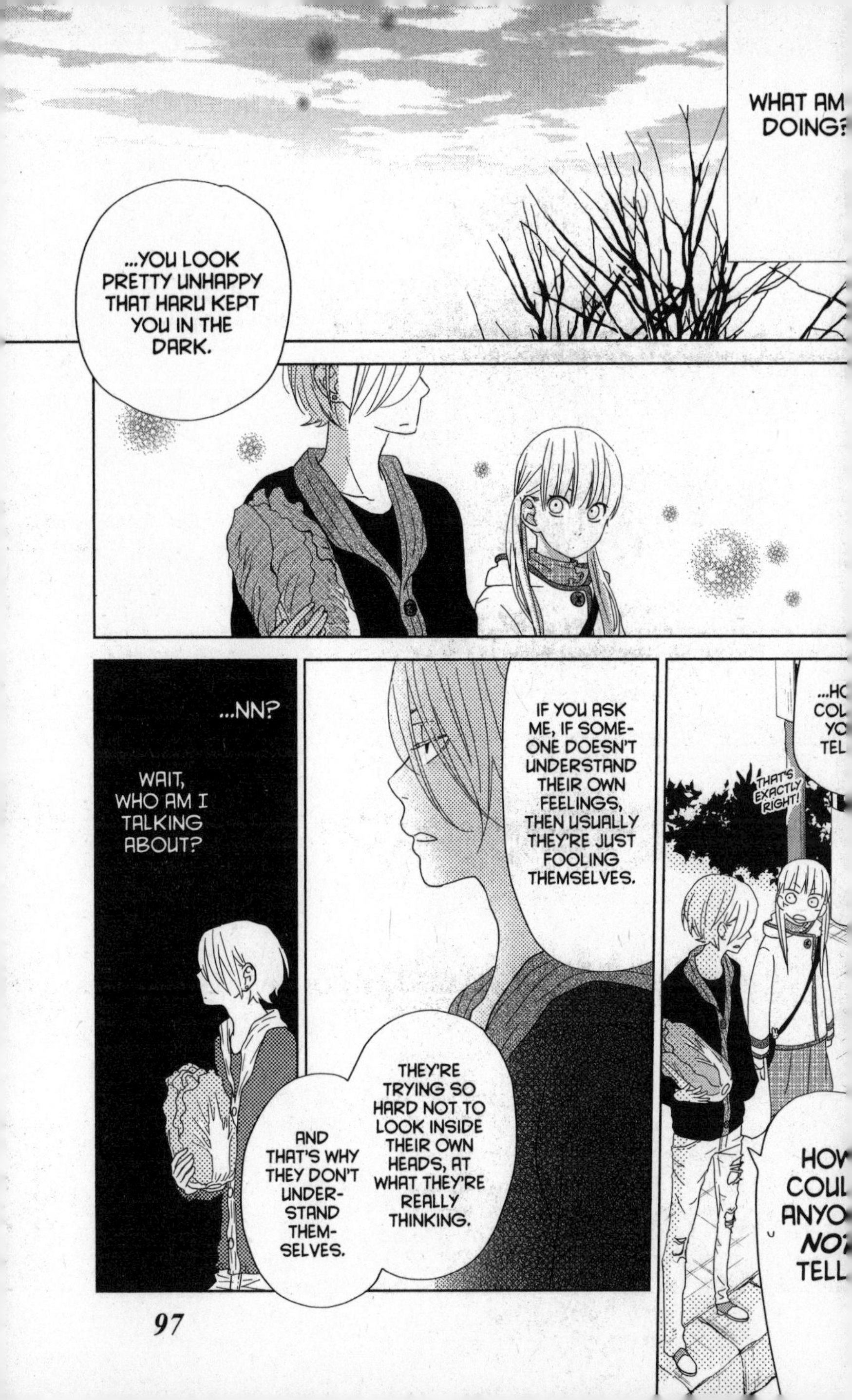

WHAT AM DOING?
...YOU LOOK PRETTY UNHAPPY THAT HARU KEPT YOU IN THE DARK.
...HO COUL YO TEL
THAT'S EXACTLY RIGHT!
HOW COUL ANYO NOT TELL
IF YOU ASK ME, IF SOME-ONE DOESN'T UNDERSTAND THEIR OWN FEELINGS, THEN USUALLY THEY'RE JUST FOOLING THEMSELVES.
THEY'RE TRYING SO HARD NOT TO LOOK INSIDE THEIR OWN HEADS, AT WHAT THEY'RE REALLY THINKING.
AND THAT'S WHY THEY DON'T UNDER-STAND THEM-SELVES.
...NN?
WAIT, WHO AM I TALKING ABOUT?

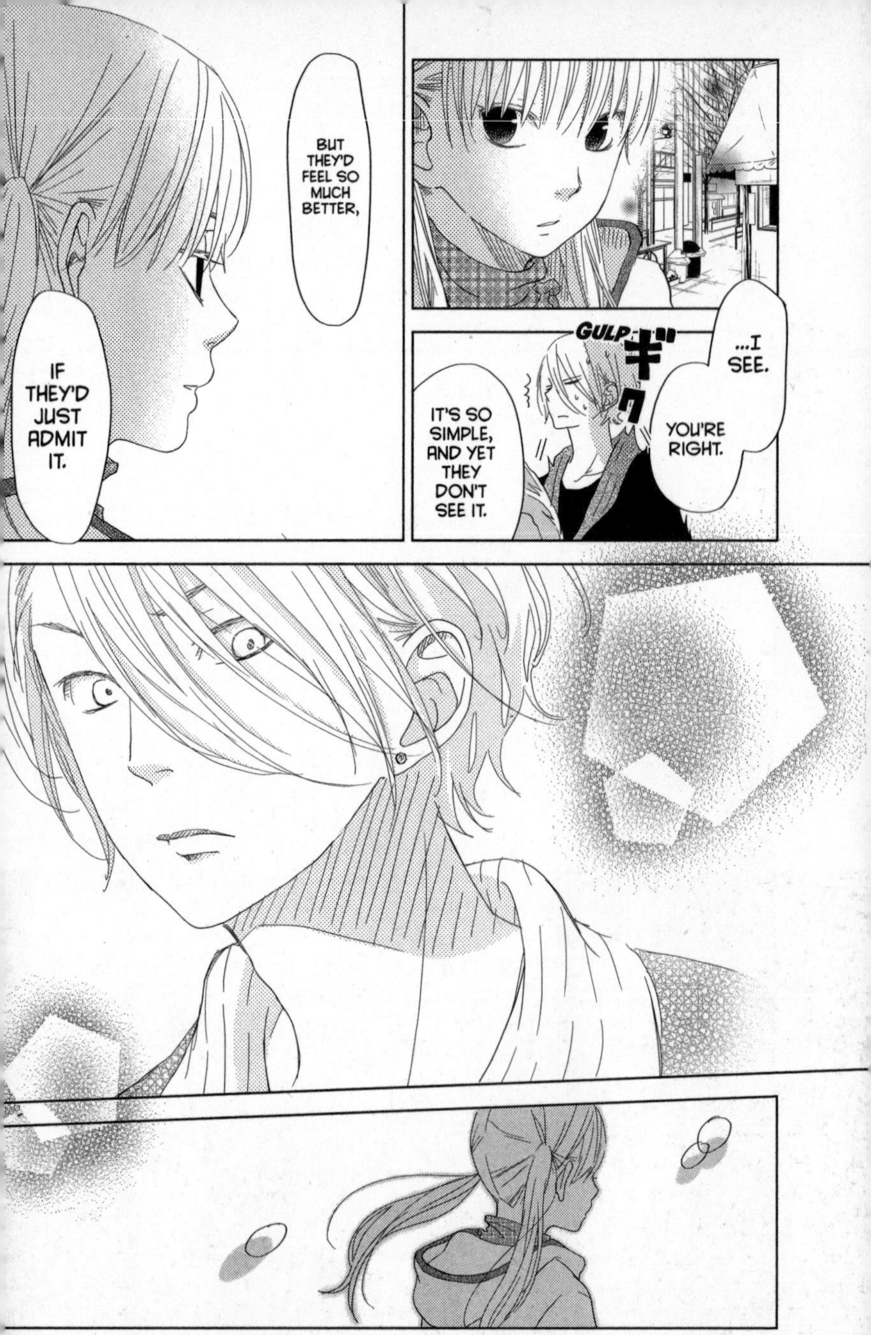
...I SEE.
YOU'RE RIGHT.
GULP
ギク
IT'S SO SIMPLE, AND YET THEY DON'T SEE IT.
BUT THEY'D FEEL SO MUCH BETTER,
IF THEY'D JUST ADMIT IT.

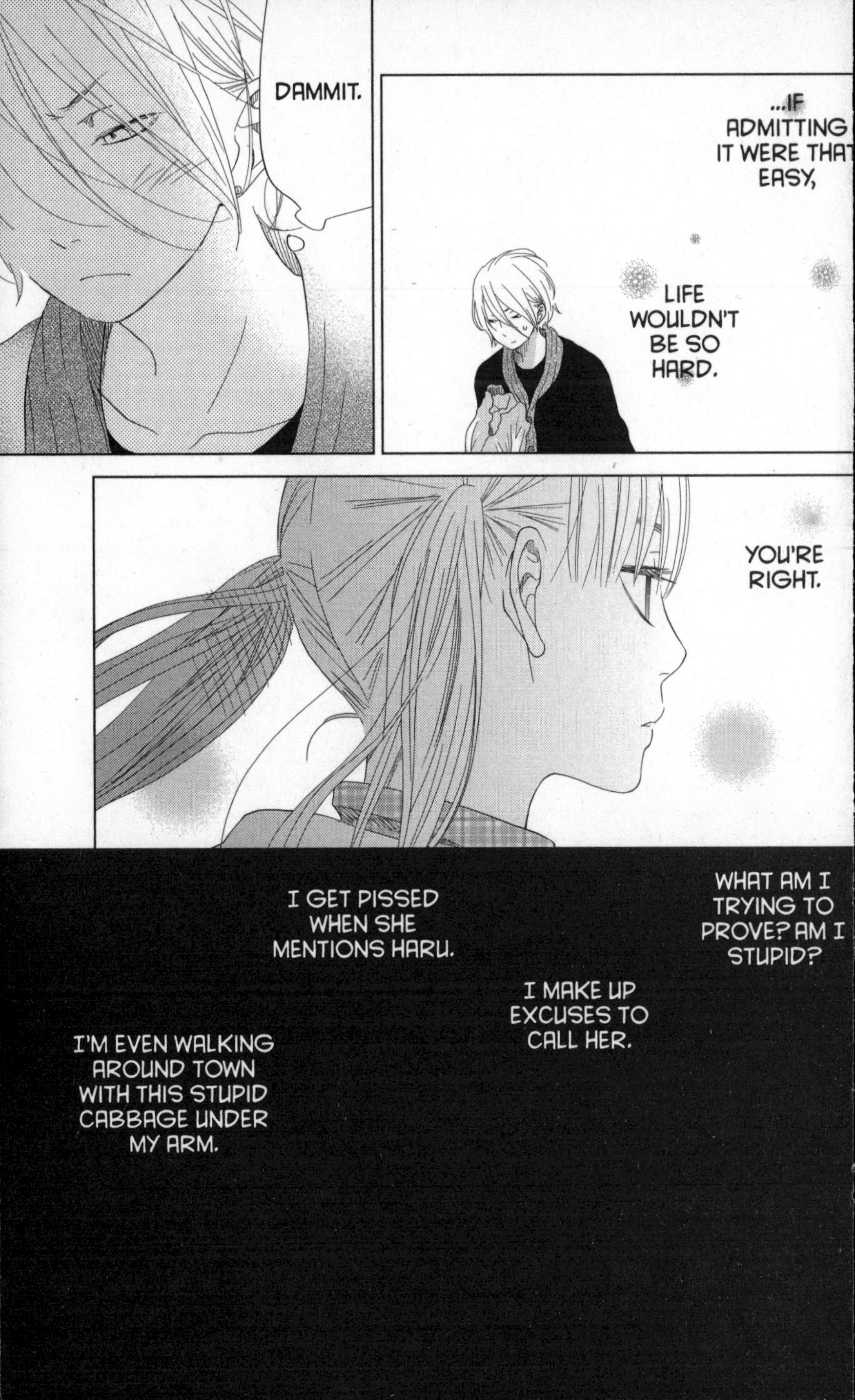
...IF ADMITTING IT WERE THAT EASY,
LIFE WOULDN'T BE SO HARD.
DAMMIT.
YOU'RE RIGHT.
WHAT AM I TRYING TO PROVE? AM I STUPID?
I MAKE UP EXCUSES TO CALL HER.
I GET PISSED WHEN SHE MENTIONS HARU.
I'M EVEN WALKING AROUND TOWN WITH THIS STUPID CABBAGE UNDER MY ARM.

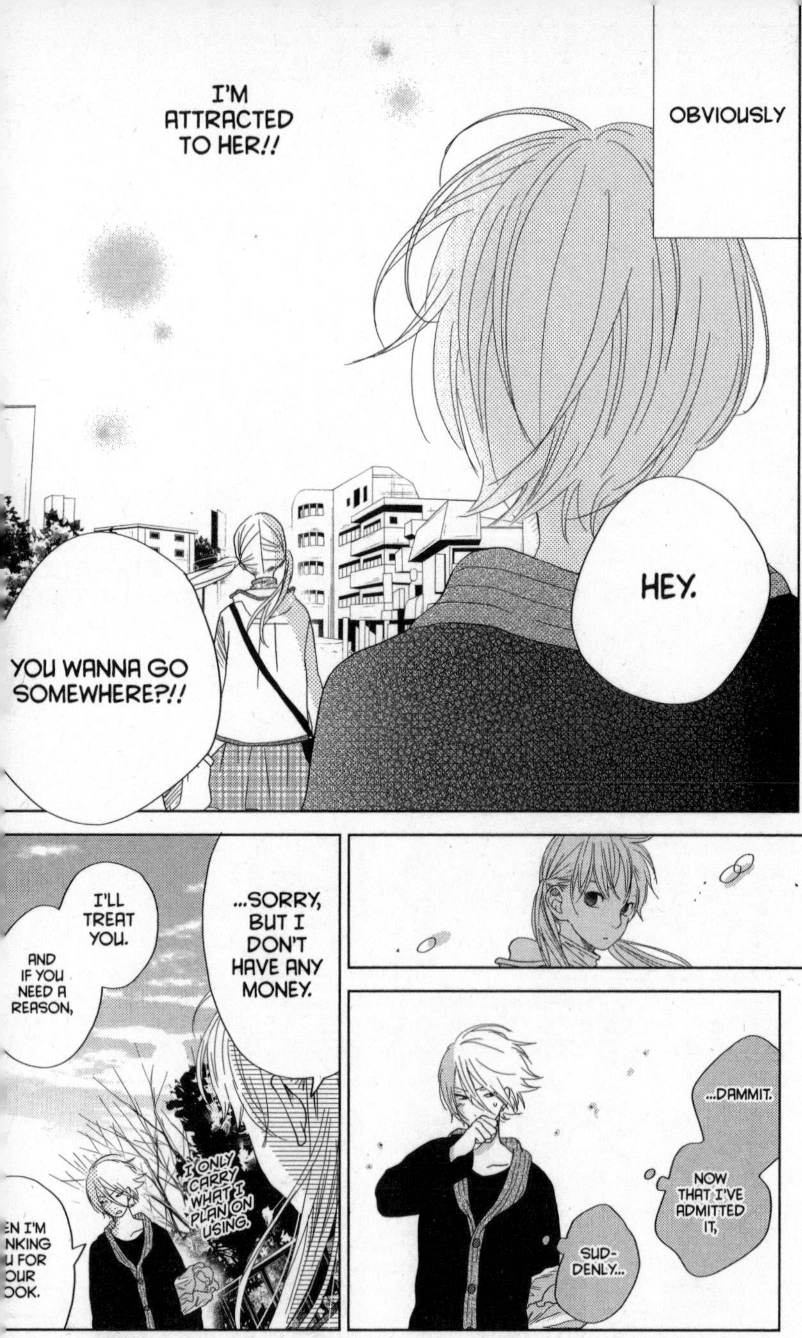
OBVIOUSLY
I'M ATTRACTED TO HER!!
HEY.
YOU WANNA GO SOMEWHERE?!!
...DAMMIT.
NOW THAT I'VE ADMITTED IT,
SUD-DENLY...
...SORRY, BUT I DON'T HAVE ANY MONEY.
I'LL TREAT YOU.
AND IF YOU NEED A REASON,
I ONLY CARRY WHAT I PLAN ON USING.
EN I'M NKING U FOR OUR OOK.

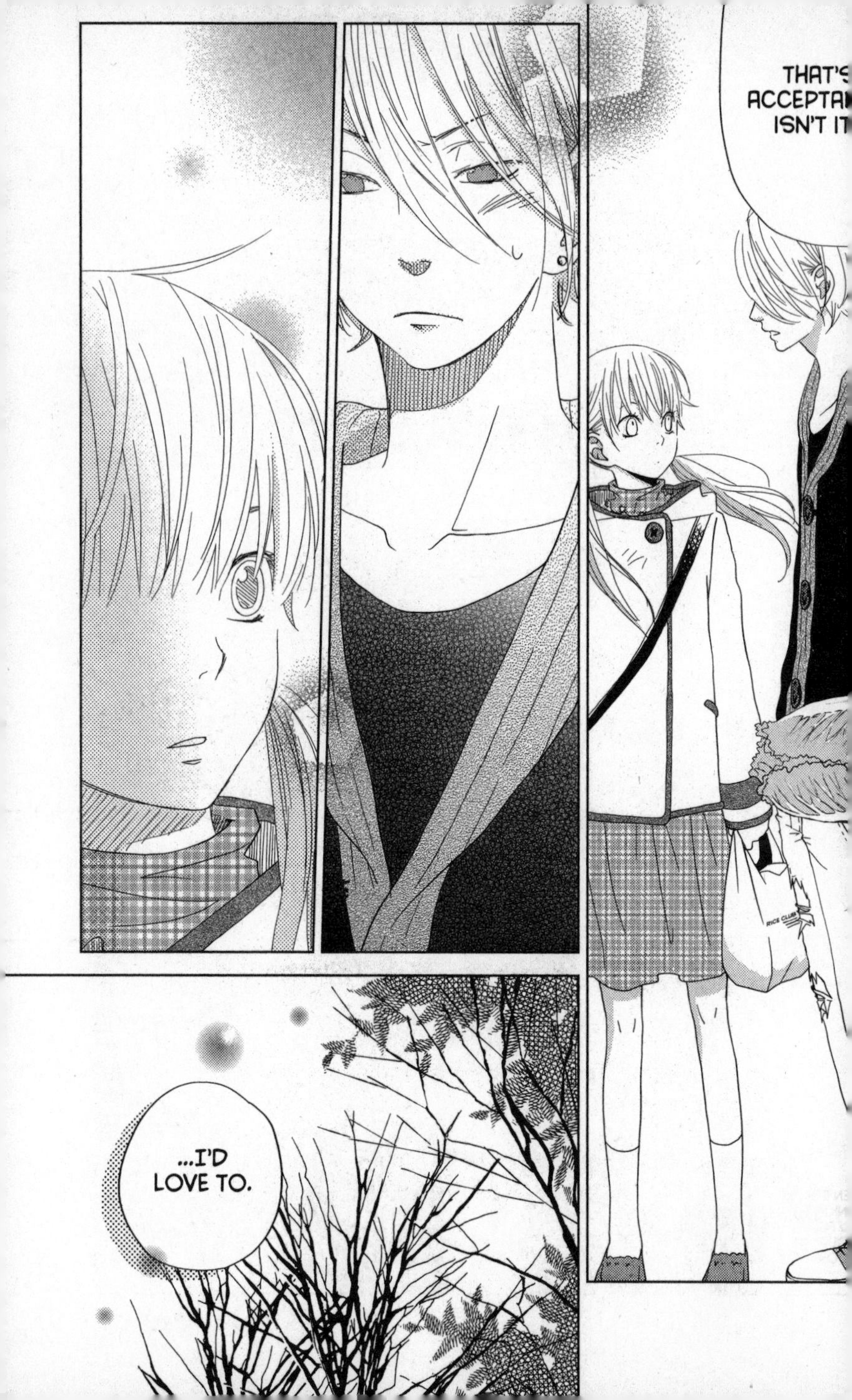
THAT'S ACCEPTA ISN'T IT
...I'D LOVE TO.

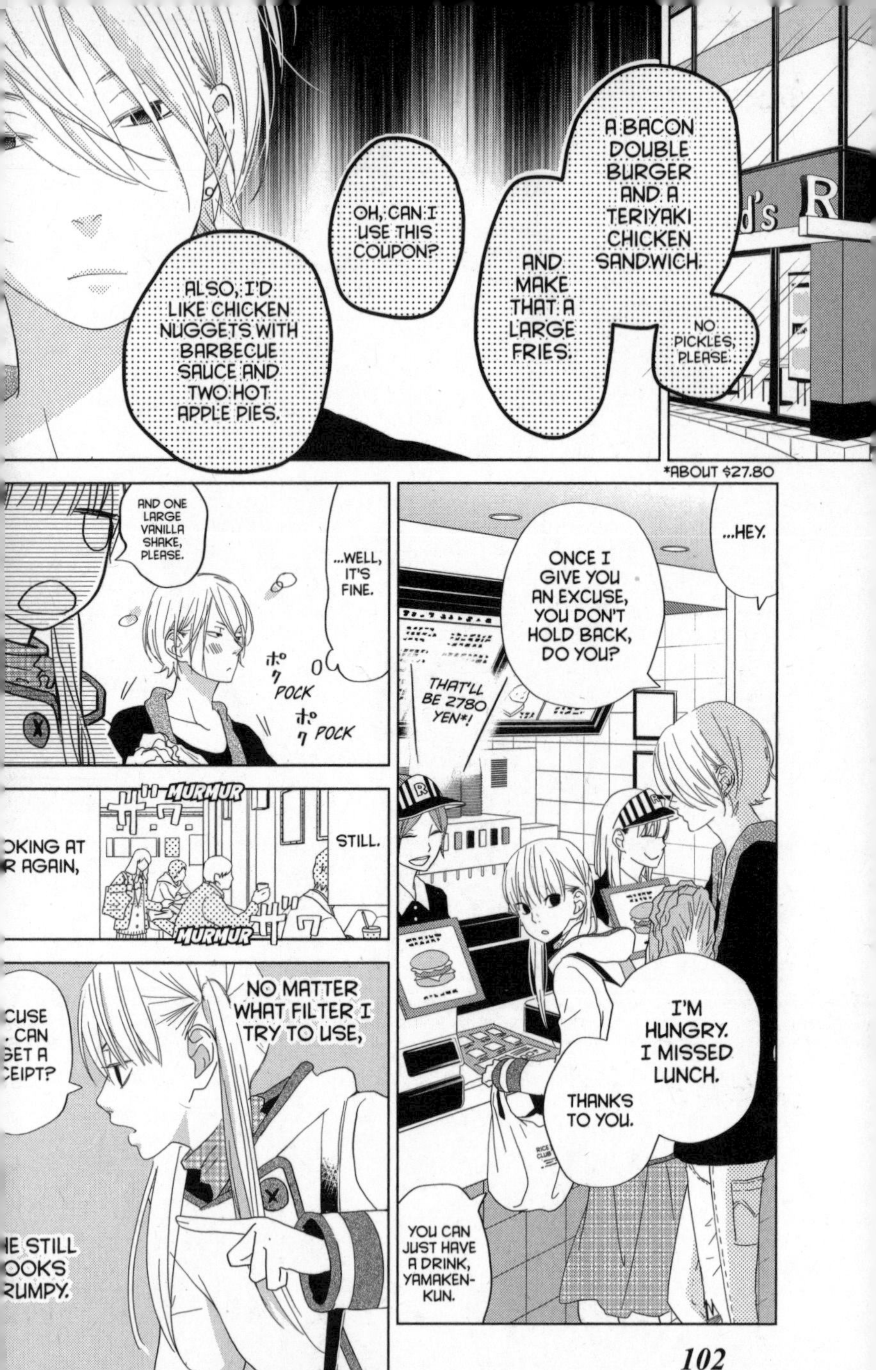
A BACON DOUBLE BURGER AND A TERIYAKI CHICKEN SANDWICH.
NO PICKLES, PLEASE.
AND MAKE THAT A LARGE FRIES.
OH, CAN I USE THIS COUPON?
ALSO, I'D LIKE CHICKEN NUGGETS WITH BARBECUE SAUCE AND TWO HOT APPLE PIES.
...HEY.
ONCE I GIVE YOU AN EXCUSE, YOU DON'T HOLD BACK, DO YOU?
THAT'LL BE 2780 YEN*!
I'M HUNGRY. I MISSED LUNCH.
THANKS TO YOU.
YOU CAN JUST HAVE A DRINK, YAMAKEN-KUN.
...WELL, IT'S FINE.
AND ONE LARGE VANILLA SHAKE, PLEASE.
POCK
POCK
MURMUR
STILL.
OKING AT R AGAIN,
MURMUR
NO MATTER WHAT FILTER I TRY TO USE,
CUSE . CAN GET A CEIPT?
HE STILL OOKS RUMPY.

*ABOUT $27.80

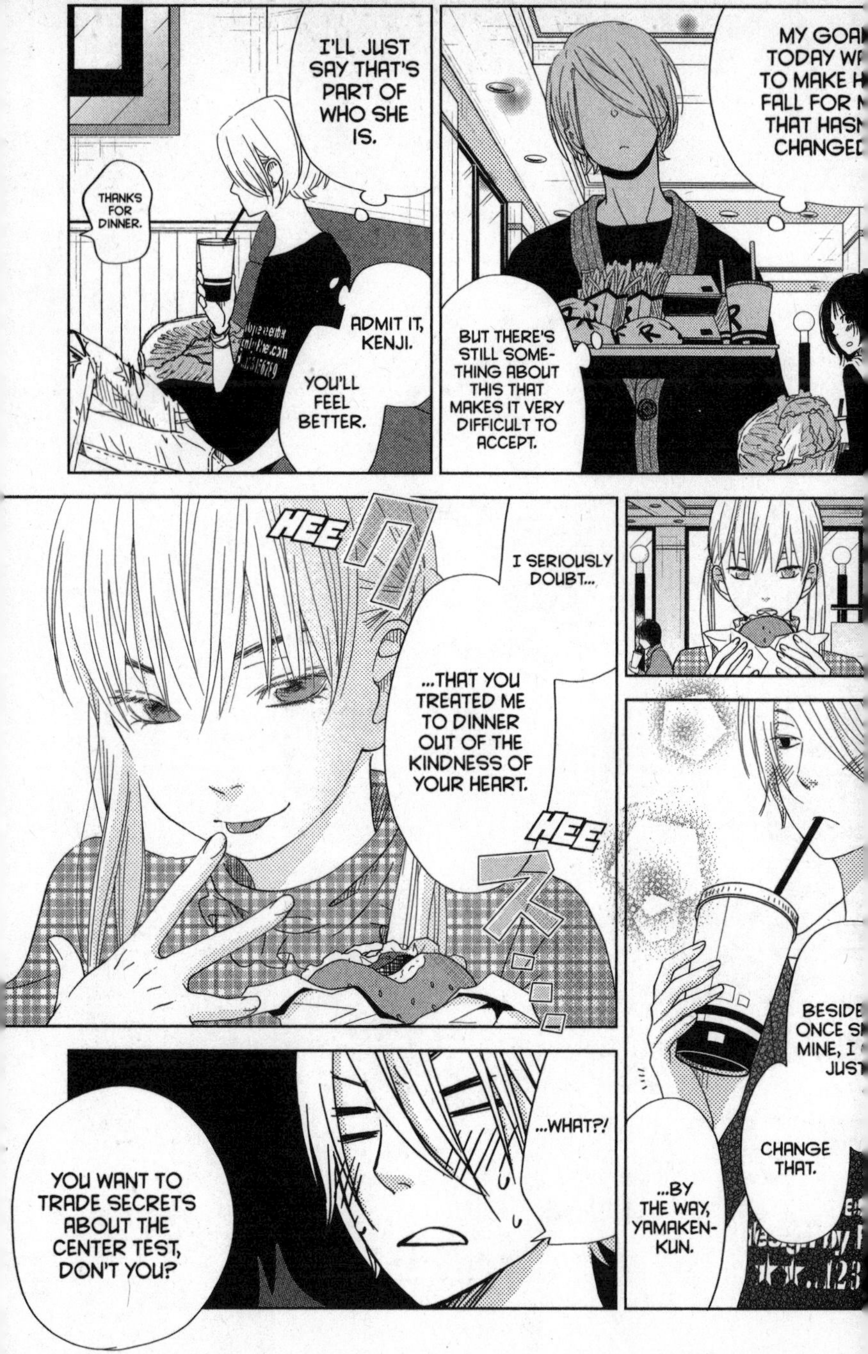
MY GOA TODAY WA TO MAKE H FALL FOR M THAT HASN CHANGED
BUT THERE'S STILL SOME-THING ABOUT THIS THAT MAKES IT VERY DIFFICULT TO ACCEPT.
I'LL JUST SAY THAT'S PART OF WHO SHE IS.
ADMIT IT, KENJI.
YOU'LL FEEL BETTER.
THANKS FOR DINNER.
BESIDE ONCE S MINE, I JUST
CHANGE THAT.
...BY THE WAY, YAMAKEN-KUN.
I SERIOUSLY DOUBT...
HEE
...THAT YOU TREATED ME TO DINNER OUT OF THE KINDNESS OF YOUR HEART.
HEE
...WHAT?!
YOU WANT TO TRADE SECRETS ABOUT THE CENTER TEST, DON'T YOU?

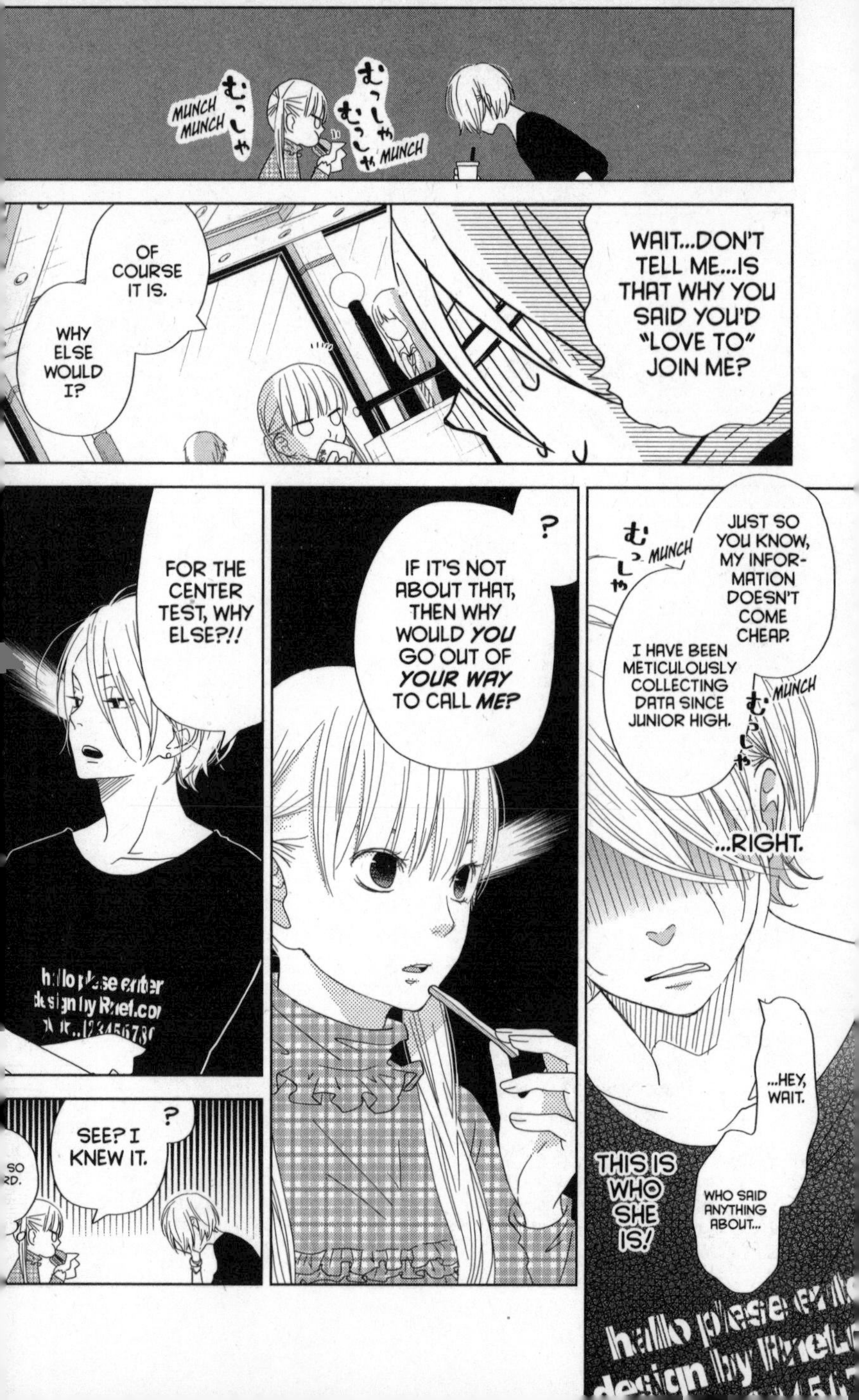

むっしゃむっしゃ
MUNCH
むっしゃ
MUNCH MUNCH
WAIT...DON'T TELL ME...IS THAT WHY YOU SAID YOU'D "LOVE TO" JOIN ME?
OF COURSE IT IS.
WHY ELSE WOULD I?
JUST SO YOU KNOW, MY INFORMATION DOESN'T COME CHEAP.
むっしゃ
MUNCH
I HAVE BEEN METICULOUSLY COLLECTING DATA SINCE JUNIOR HIGH.
むっしゃ
MUNCH
...RIGHT.
...HEY, WAIT.
WHO SAID ANYTHING ABOUT...
THIS IS WHO SHE IS!
?
IF IT'S NOT ABOUT THAT, THEN WHY WOULD *YOU* GO OUT OF ***YOUR WAY*** TO CALL ***ME?***
FOR THE CENTER TEST, WHY ELSE?!!
?
SEE? I KNEW IT.

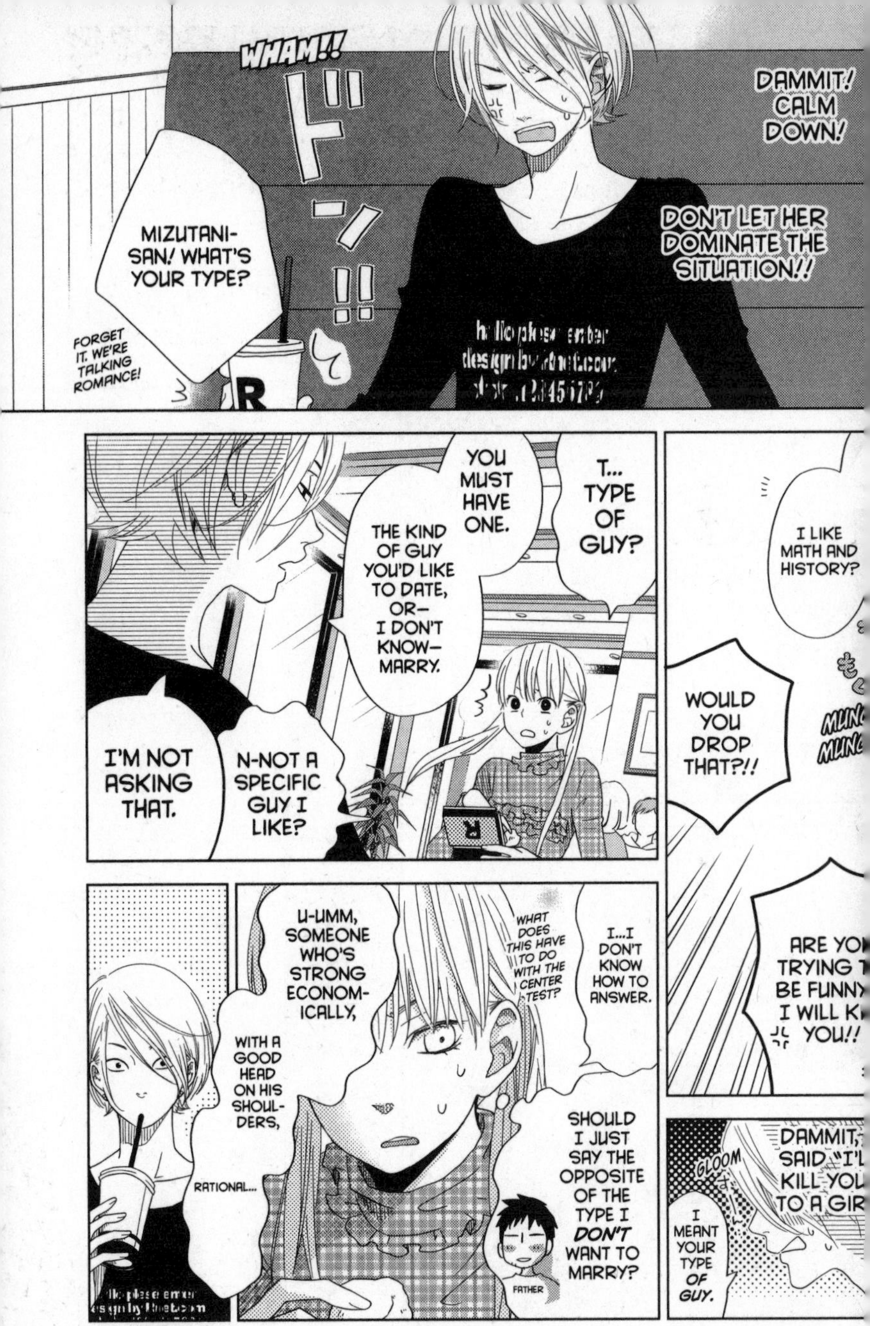
WHAM!!
ドーン!!
DAMMIT! CALM DOWN!
DON'T LET HER DOMINATE THE SITUATION!!
MIZUTANI-SAN! WHAT'S YOUR TYPE?
FORGET IT. WE'RE TALKING ROMANCE!
T... TYPE OF GUY?
YOU MUST HAVE ONE.
THE KIND OF GUY YOU'D LIKE TO DATE, OR— I DON'T KNOW— MARRY.
N-NOT A SPECIFIC GUY I LIKE?
I'M NOT ASKING THAT.
I LIKE MATH AND HISTORY?
WOULD YOU DROP THAT?!!
ARE YO TRYING T BE FUNNY I WILL K YOU!!
DAMMIT, SAID "I'L KILL YOU TO A GIR
GLOOM
I MEANT YOUR TYPE OF GUY.
I...I DON'T KNOW HOW TO ANSWER.
WHAT DOES THIS HAVE TO DO WITH THE CENTER TEST?
U-UMM, SOMEONE WHO'S STRONG ECONOMICALLY,
SHOULD I JUST SAY THE OPPOSITE OF THE TYPE I DON'T WANT TO MARRY?
WITH A GOOD HEAD ON HIS SHOULDERS,
RATIONAL...
FATHER

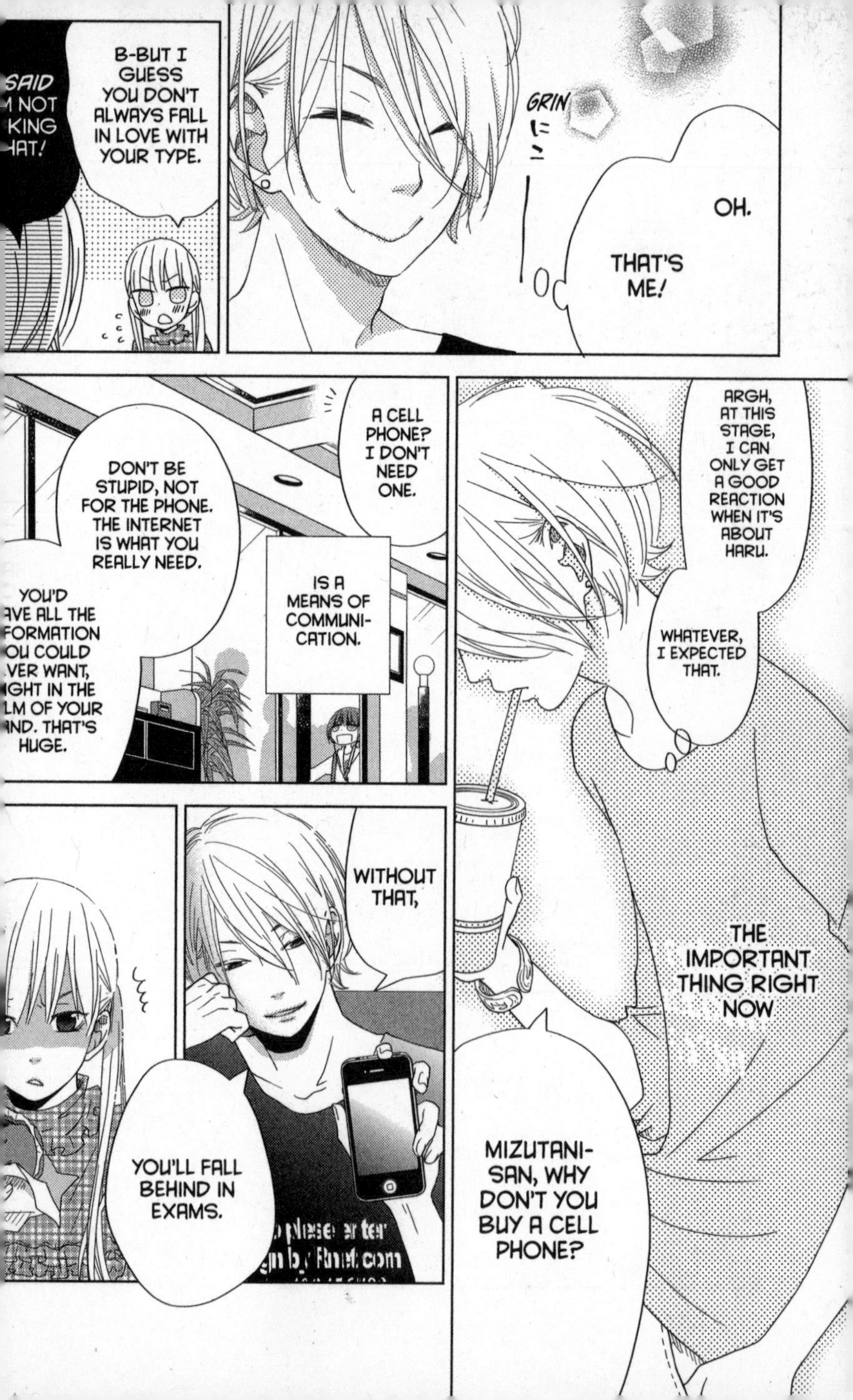
GRIN にこ
OH.
THAT'S ME!
B-BUT I GUESS YOU DON'T ALWAYS FALL IN LOVE WITH YOUR TYPE.
SAID
M NOT
KING
HAT!
ARGH, AT THIS STAGE, I CAN ONLY GET A GOOD REACTION WHEN IT'S ABOUT HARU.
WHATEVER, I EXPECTED THAT.
THE IMPORTANT THING RIGHT NOW
MIZUTANI-SAN, WHY DON'T YOU BUY A CELL PHONE?
A CELL PHONE? I DON'T NEED ONE.
DON'T BE STUPID, NOT FOR THE PHONE. THE INTERNET IS WHAT YOU REALLY NEED.
IS A MEANS OF COMMUNICATION.
YOU'D
AVE ALL THE
FORMATION
OU COULD
VER WANT,
GHT IN THE
LM OF YOUR
ND. THAT'S
HUGE.
WITHOUT THAT,
YOU'LL FALL BEHIND IN EXAMS.

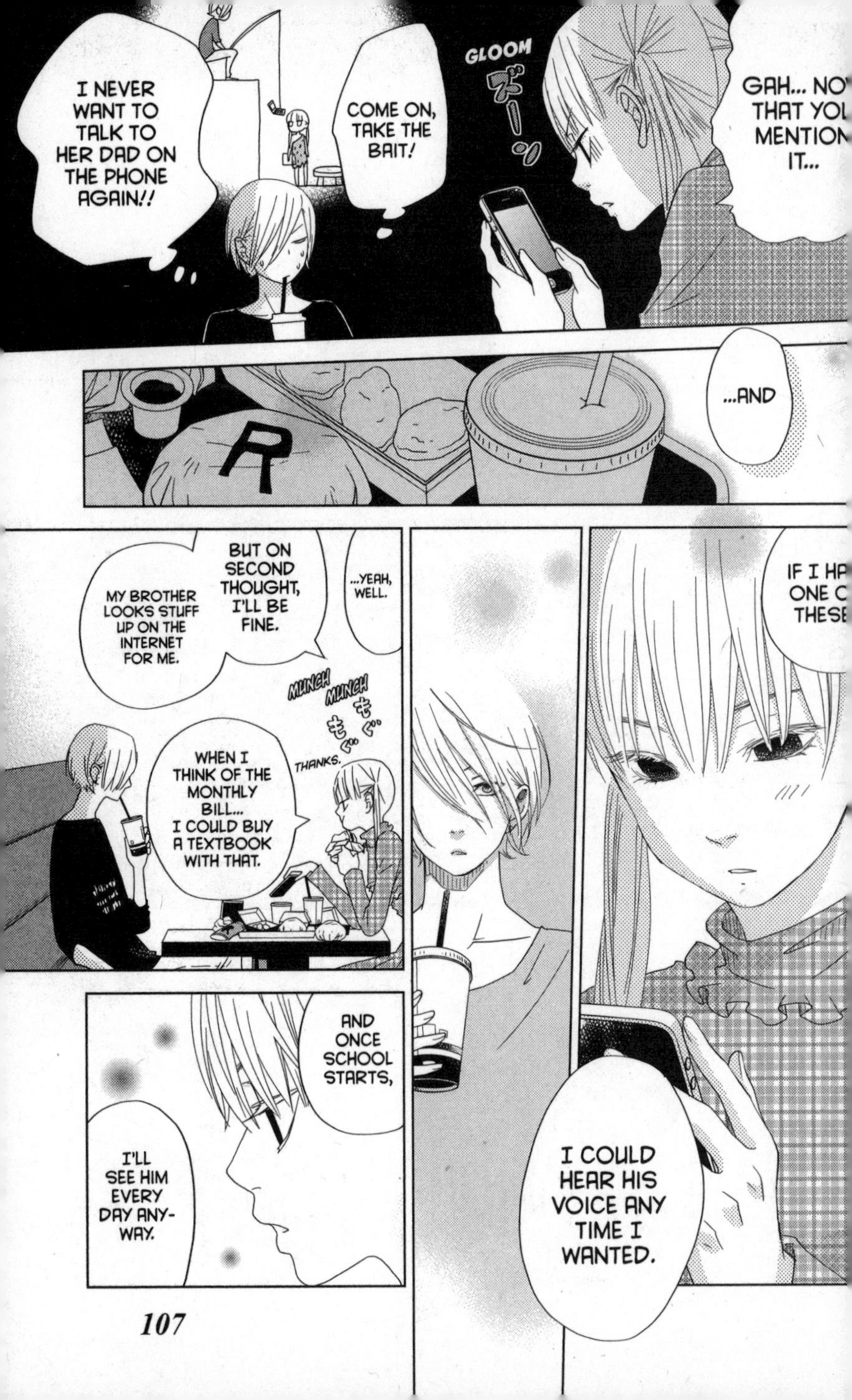
GLOOM
GAH... NO THAT YO MENTIO IT...
COME ON, TAKE THE BAIT!
I NEVER WANT TO TALK TO HER DAD ON THE PHONE AGAIN!!
...AND
IF I HA ONE O THESE
I COULD HEAR HIS VOICE ANY TIME I WANTED.
...YEAH, WELL.
BUT ON SECOND THOUGHT, I'LL BE FINE.
MY BROTHER LOOKS STUFF UP ON THE INTERNET FOR ME.
MUNCH MUNCH
THANKS.
WHEN I THINK OF THE MONTHLY BILL... I COULD BUY A TEXTBOOK WITH THAT.
AND ONCE SCHOOL STARTS,
I'LL SEE HIM EVERY DAY ANY-WAY.

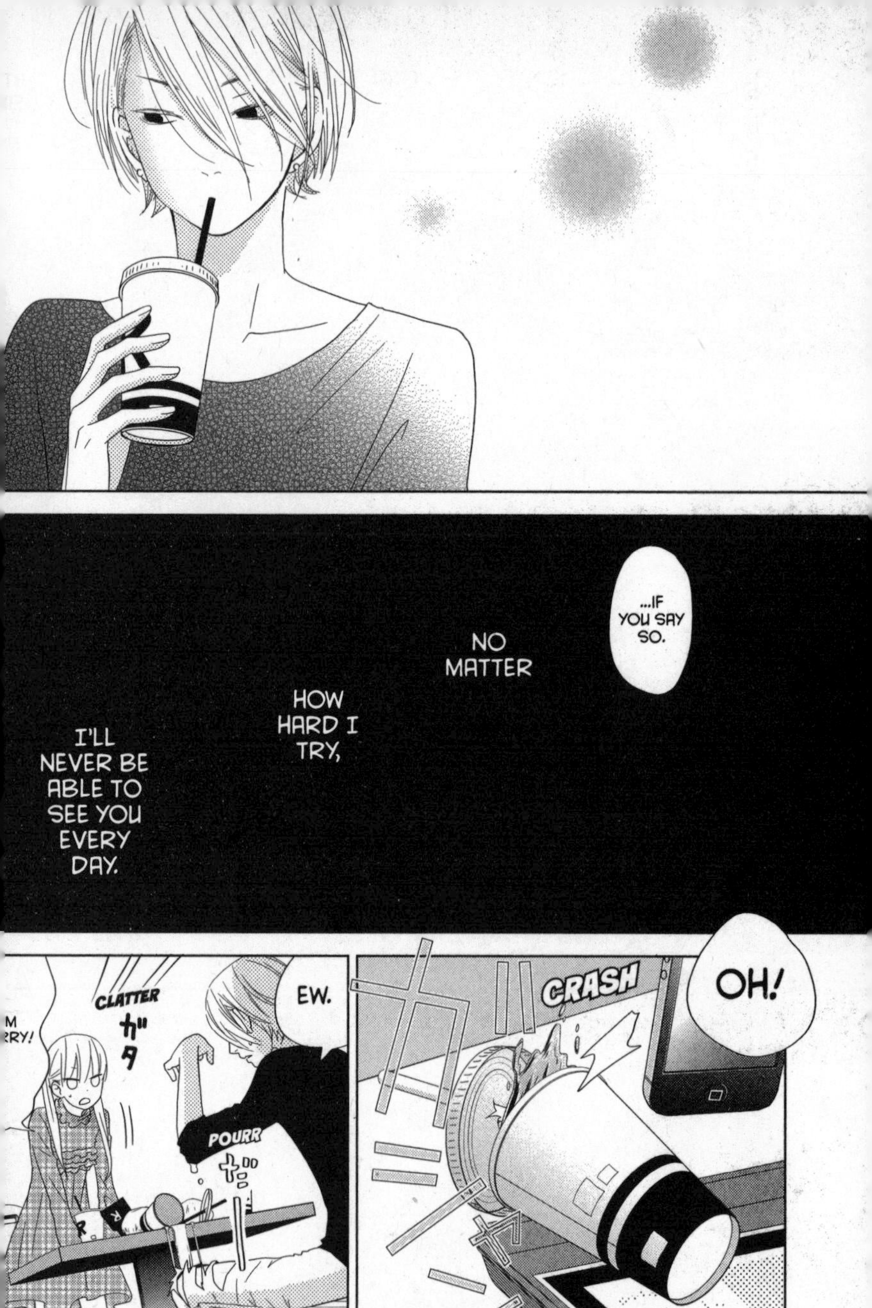
...IF YOU SAY SO.
NO MATTER
HOW HARD I TRY,
I'LL NEVER BE ABLE TO SEE YOU EVERY DAY.
OH!
CRASH
EW.
CLATTER
POURR

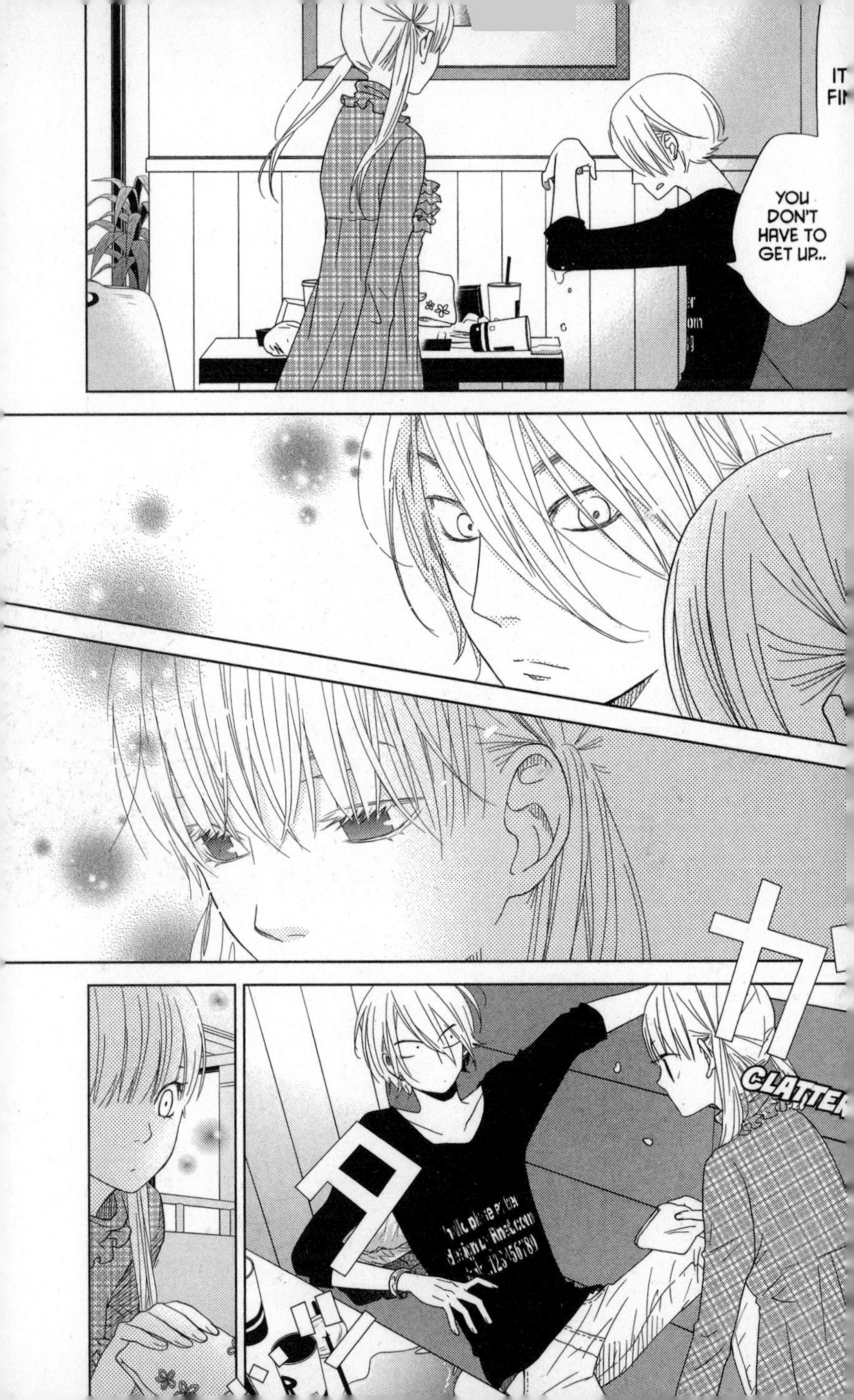
IT
FI
YOU DON'T HAVE TO GET UP...
CLATTER

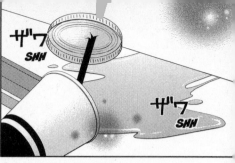

ザッ SHH

ザッ SHH

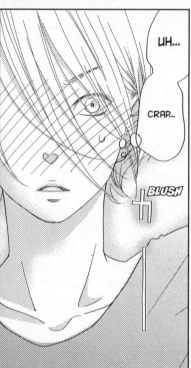

UH...

CRAP...

ヽ BLUSH

...

THAT REACTION BEFORE.

I'VE SEEN...

ザッ MURMUR

TELL ME...

...YAMA-KEN-KUN.

KYA HA HA HA...

MURMUR ザッ

DON'T

GULP ギ

o please enter
n by Raetcan
456780

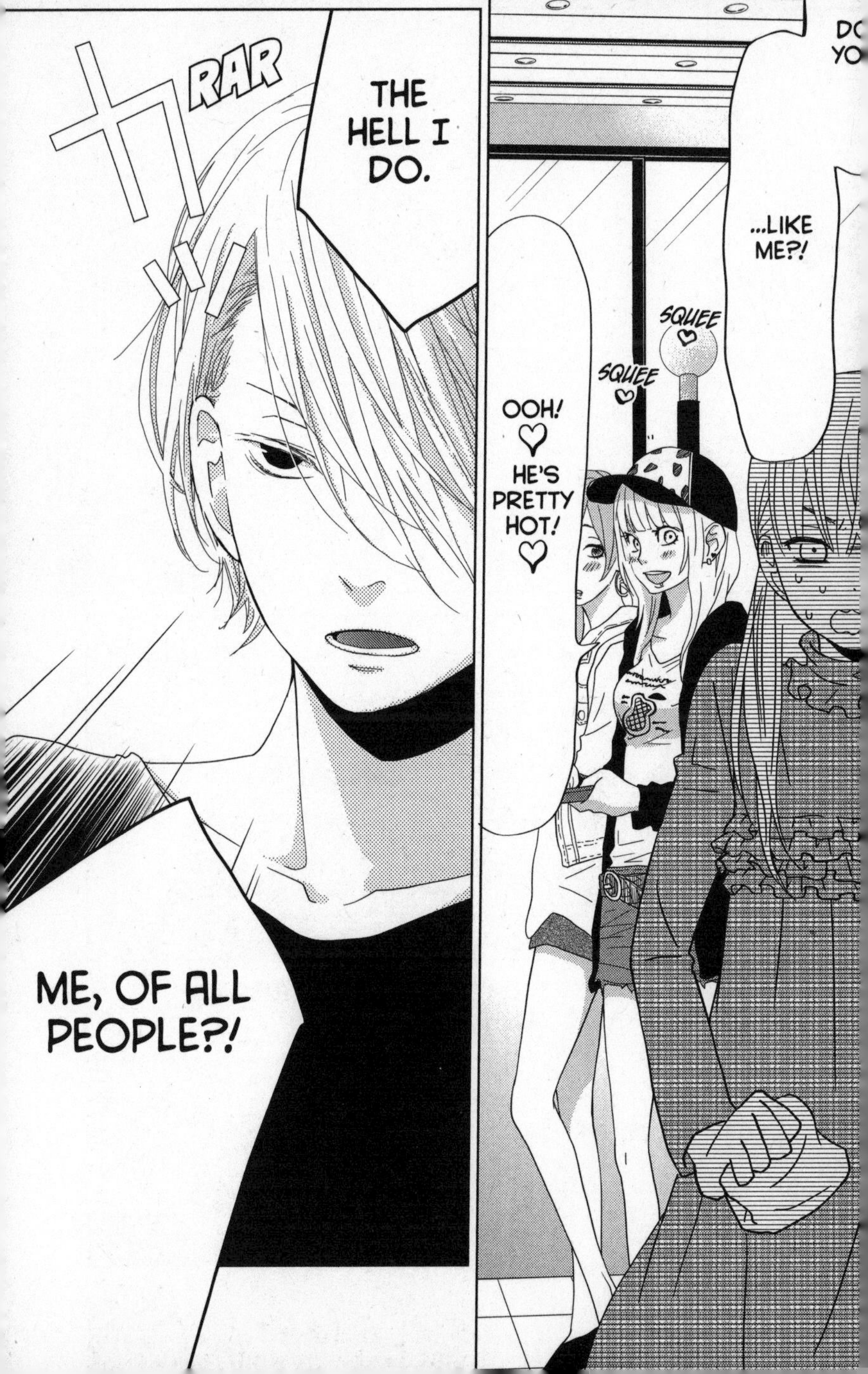
...LIKE ME?!
SQUEE
SQUEE
OOH! HE'S PRETTY HOT!
THE HELL I DO.
RAR
ME, OF ALL PEOPLE?!

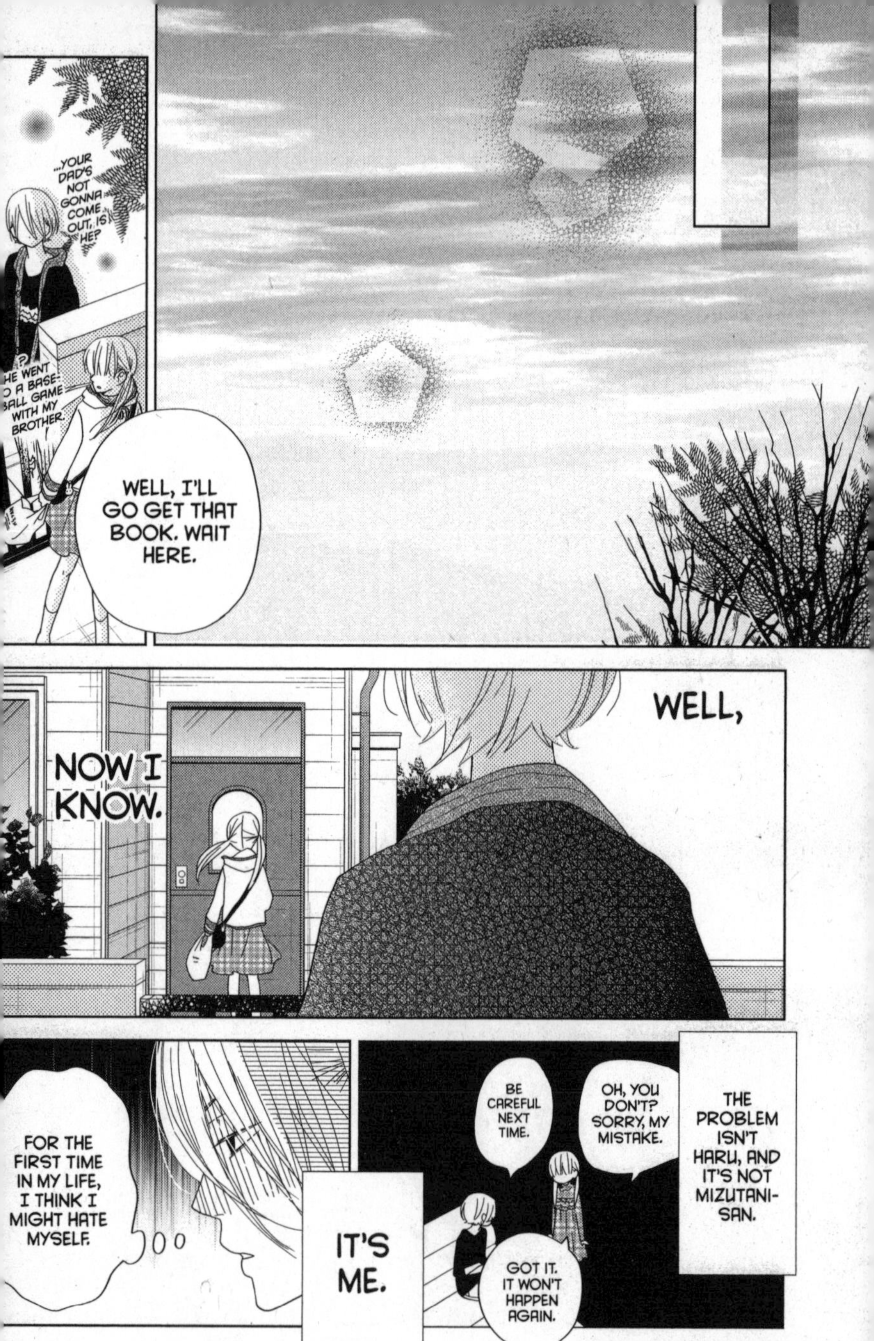
...YOUR DAD'S NOT GONNA COME OUT, IS HE?
? HE WENT TO A BASEBALL GAME WITH MY BROTHER.
WELL, I'LL GO GET THAT BOOK. WAIT HERE.
WELL,
NOW I KNOW.
THE PROBLEM ISN'T HARU, AND IT'S NOT MIZUTANI-SAN.
OH, YOU DON'T? SORRY, MY MISTAKE.
BE CAREFUL NEXT TIME.
GOT IT. IT WON'T HAPPEN AGAIN.
IT'S ME.
FOR THE FIRST TIME IN MY LIFE, I THINK I MIGHT HATE MYSELF.

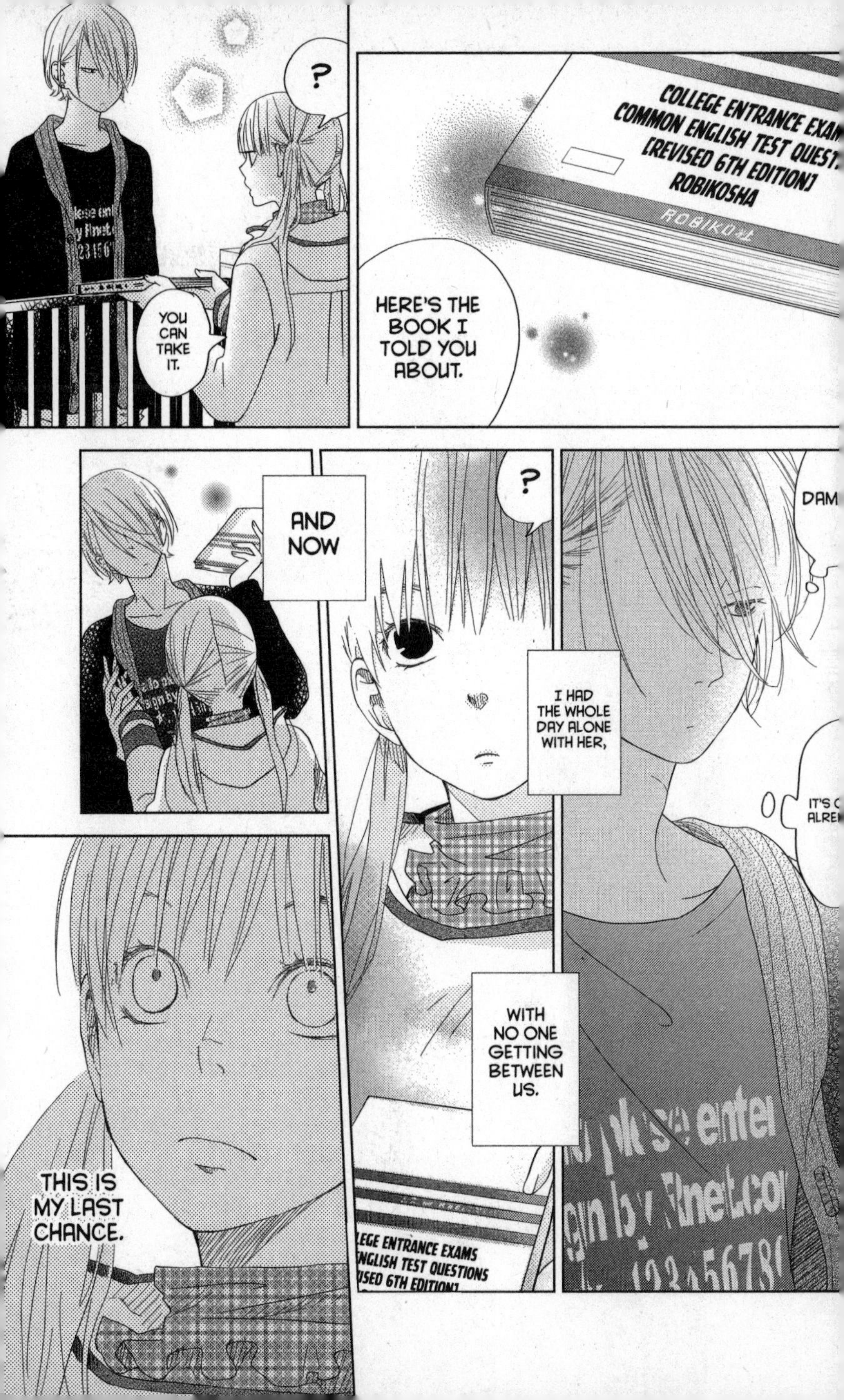

COLLEGE ENTRANCE EXAM
COMMON ENGLISH TEST QUEST
[REVISED 6TH EDITION]
ROBIKOSHA
HERE'S THE BOOK I TOLD YOU ABOUT.
?
YOU CAN TAKE IT.
DAM
IT'S
ALRE
?
I HAD THE WHOLE DAY ALONE WITH HER,
WITH NO ONE GETTING BETWEEN US.
LLEGE ENTRANCE EXAMS
ENGLISH TEST QUESTIONS
ISED 6TH EDITION]
AND NOW
THIS IS MY LAST CHANCE.

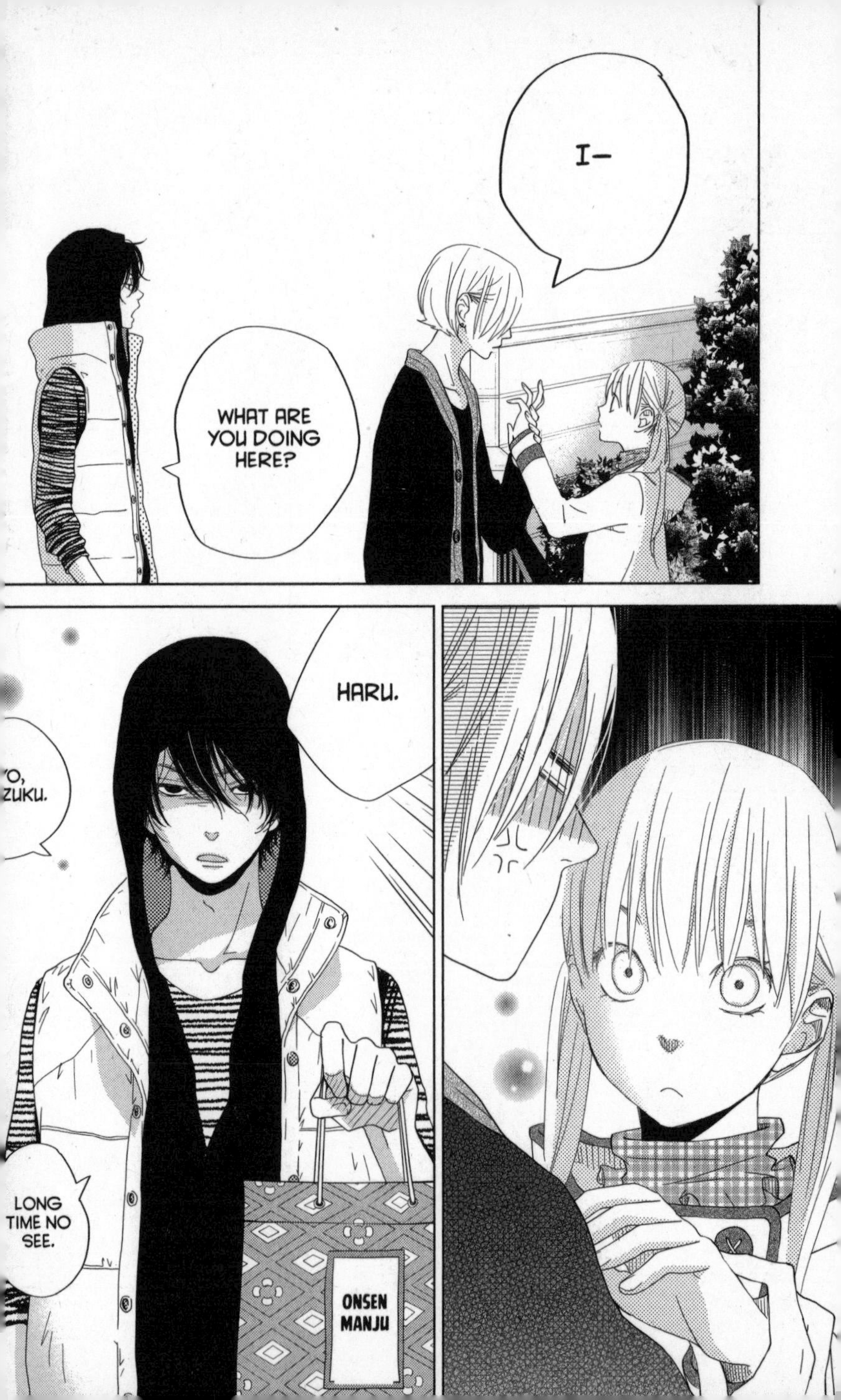
I—
WHAT ARE YOU DOING HERE?
HARU.
O, ZUKU.
LONG TIME NO SEE.
ONSEN MANJU

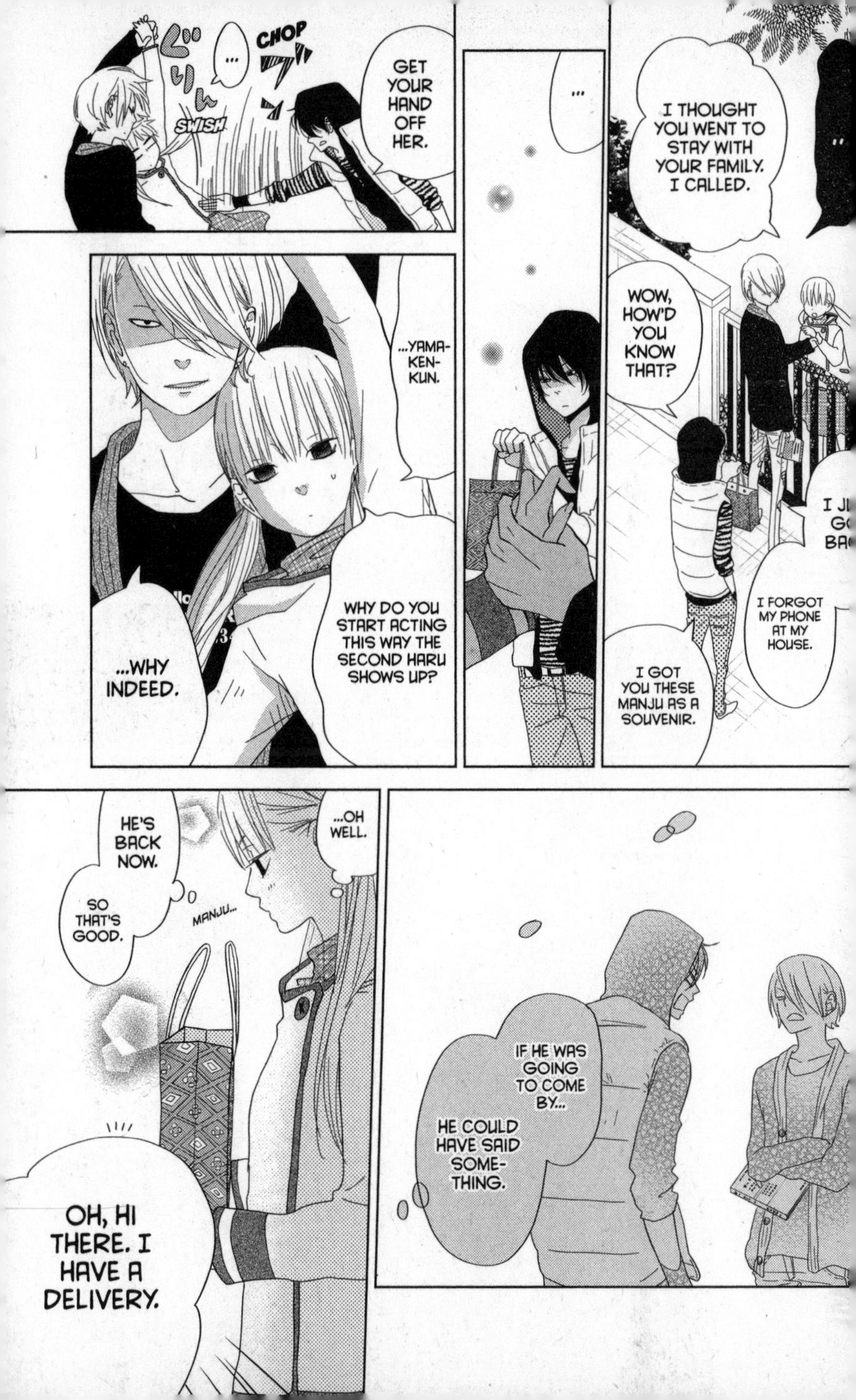
...
I THOUGHT YOU WENT TO STAY WITH YOUR FAMILY. I CALLED.
WOW, HOW'D YOU KNOW THAT?
I FORGOT MY PHONE AT MY HOUSE.
I GOT YOU THESE MANJU AS A SOUVENIR.
...
GET YOUR HAND OFF HER.
CHOP
...
ぐりん
SWISH
...YAMA-KEN-KUN.
WHY DO YOU START ACTING THIS WAY THE SECOND HARU SHOWS UP?
...WHY INDEED.
IF HE WAS GOING TO COME BY...
HE COULD HAVE SAID SOME-THING.
...OH WELL.
HE'S BACK NOW.
SO THAT'S GOOD.
MANJU...
OH, HI THERE. I HAVE A DELIVERY.

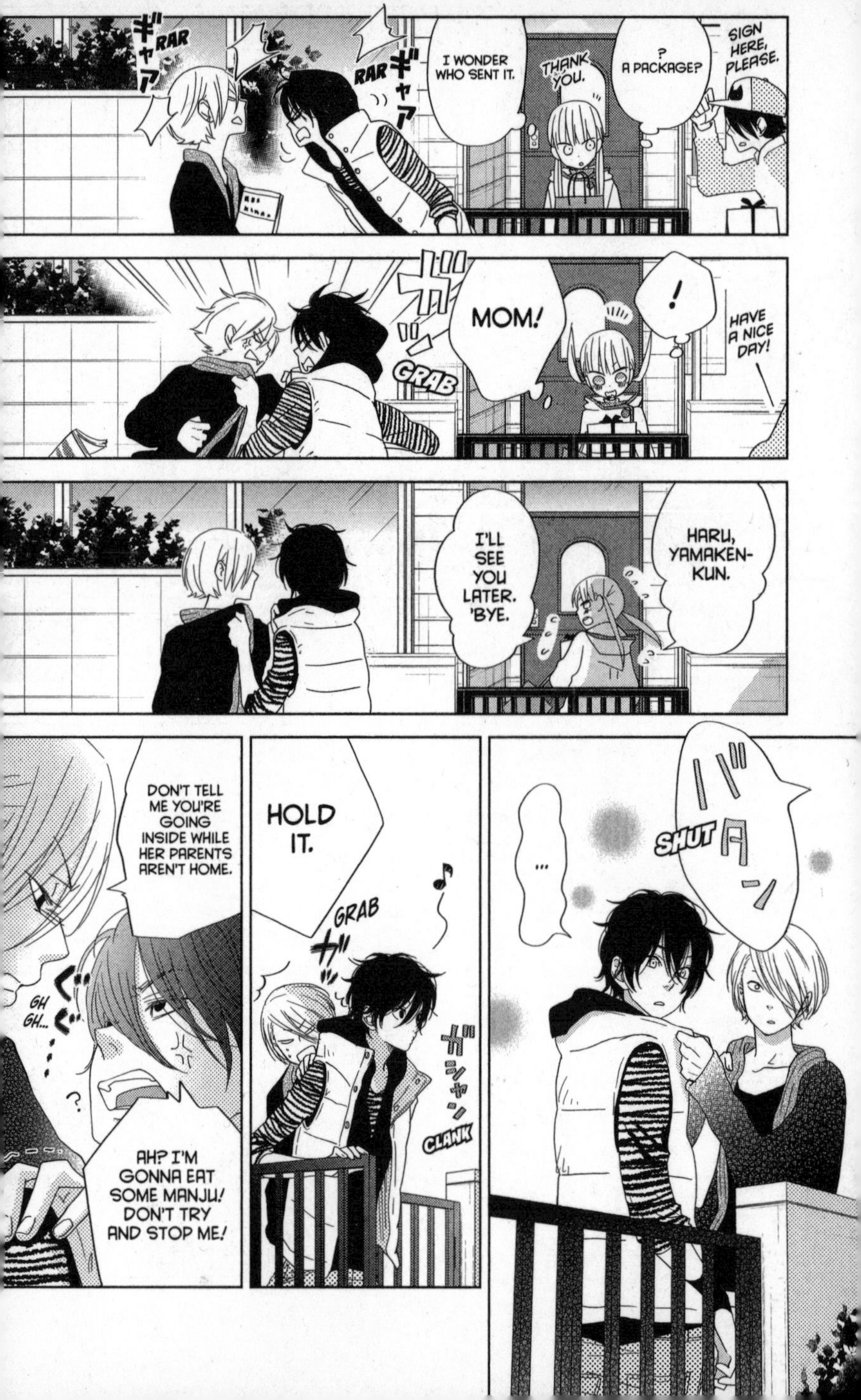
SIGN HERE, PLEASE.
? A PACKAGE?
THANK YOU.
I WONDER WHO SENT IT.
RAR
RAR
HAVE A NICE DAY!
!
MOM!
GRAB
HARU, YAMAKEN-KUN.
I'LL SEE YOU LATER. 'BYE.
SHUT
...
HOLD IT.
GRAB
CLANK
DON'T TELL ME YOU'RE GOING INSIDE WHILE HER PARENTS AREN'T HOME.
GH GH...
?
AH? I'M GONNA EAT SOME MANJU! DON'T TRY AND STOP ME!

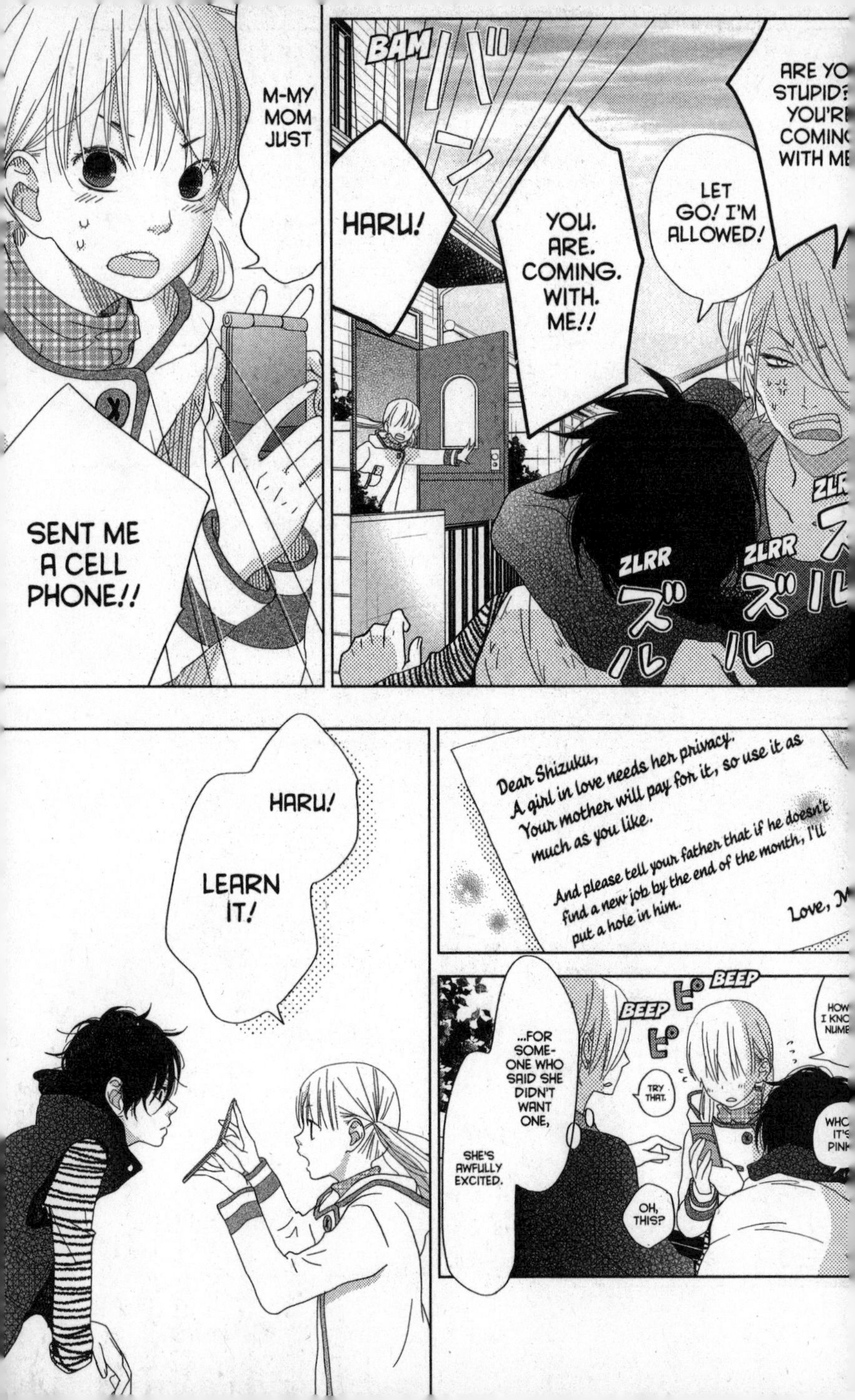
ARE YO STUPID? YOU'R COMIN WITH ME
BAM
LET GO! I'M ALLOWED!
YOU. ARE. COMING. WITH. ME!!
HARU!
ZLRR
ZLRR
ZLRR
M-MY MOM JUST
SENT ME A CELL PHONE!!
Dear Shizuku,
A girl in love needs her privacy.
Your mother will pay for it, so use it as much as you like.
And please tell your father that if he doesn't find a new job by the end of the month, I'll put a hole in him.
Love, M
HOW I KNO NUMB
BEEP
BEEP
TRY THAT.
WHO IT'S PINK
...FOR SOME-ONE WHO SAID SHE DIDN'T WANT ONE,
SHE'S AWFULLY EXCITED.
OH, THIS?
HARU!
LEARN IT!

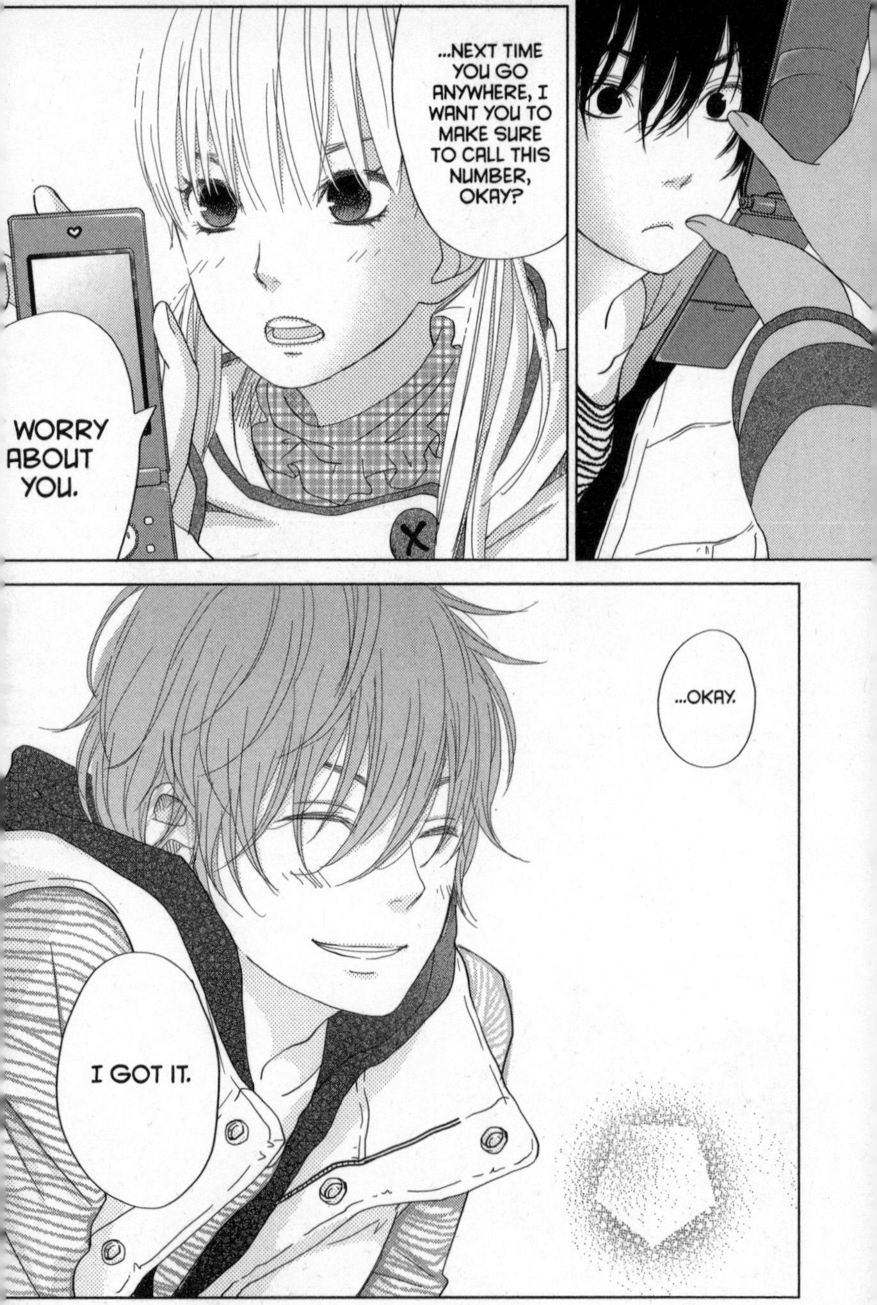
...NEXT TIME YOU GO ANYWHERE, I WANT YOU TO MAKE SURE TO CALL THIS NUMBER, OKAY?
WORRY ABOUT YOU.
...OKAY.
I GOT IT.

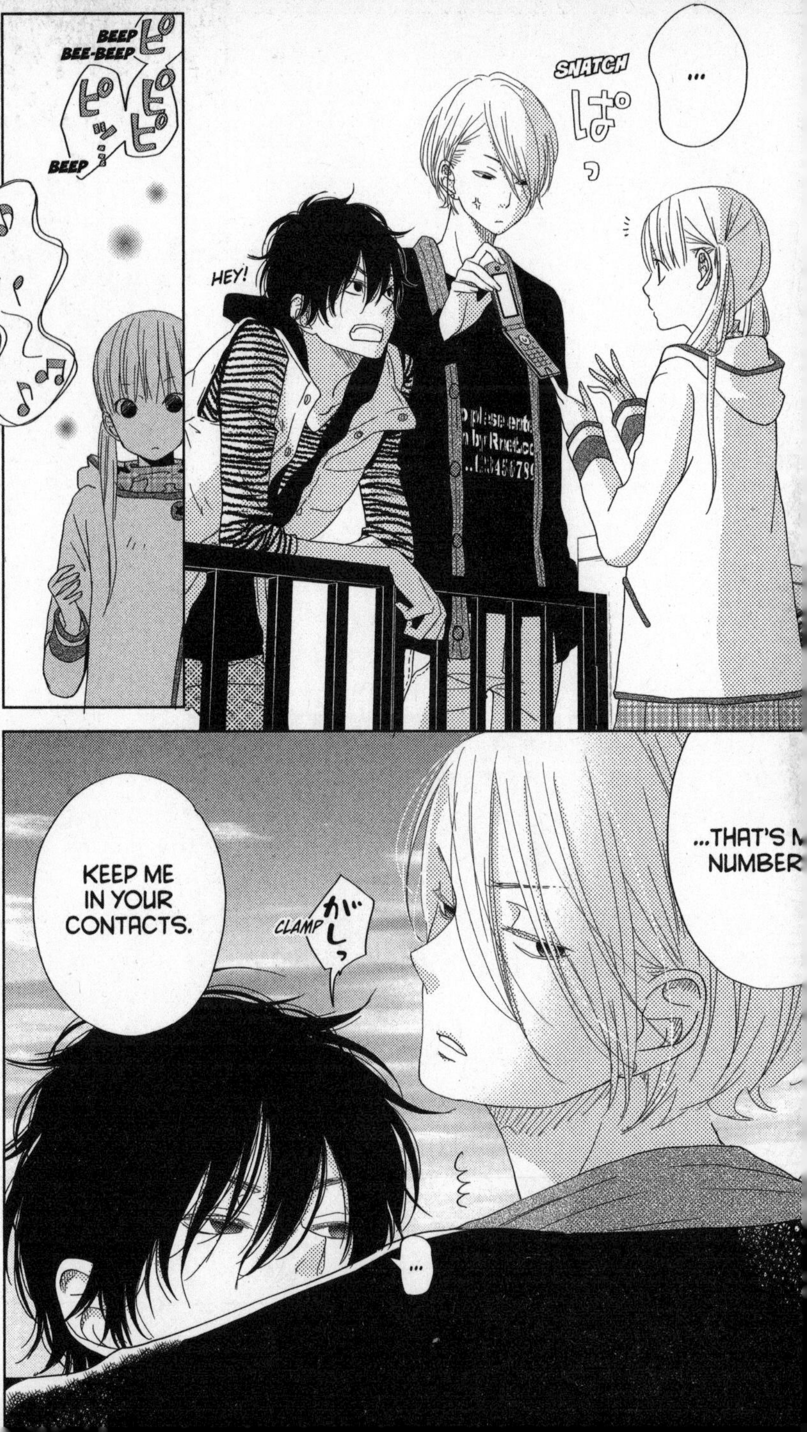
...
SNATCH ぱっ
HEY!
BEEP ピ
BEE-BEEP ピピ
BEEP ピッ
...THAT'S M
NUMBER
KEEP ME IN YOUR CONTACTS.
CLAMP がしっ
...

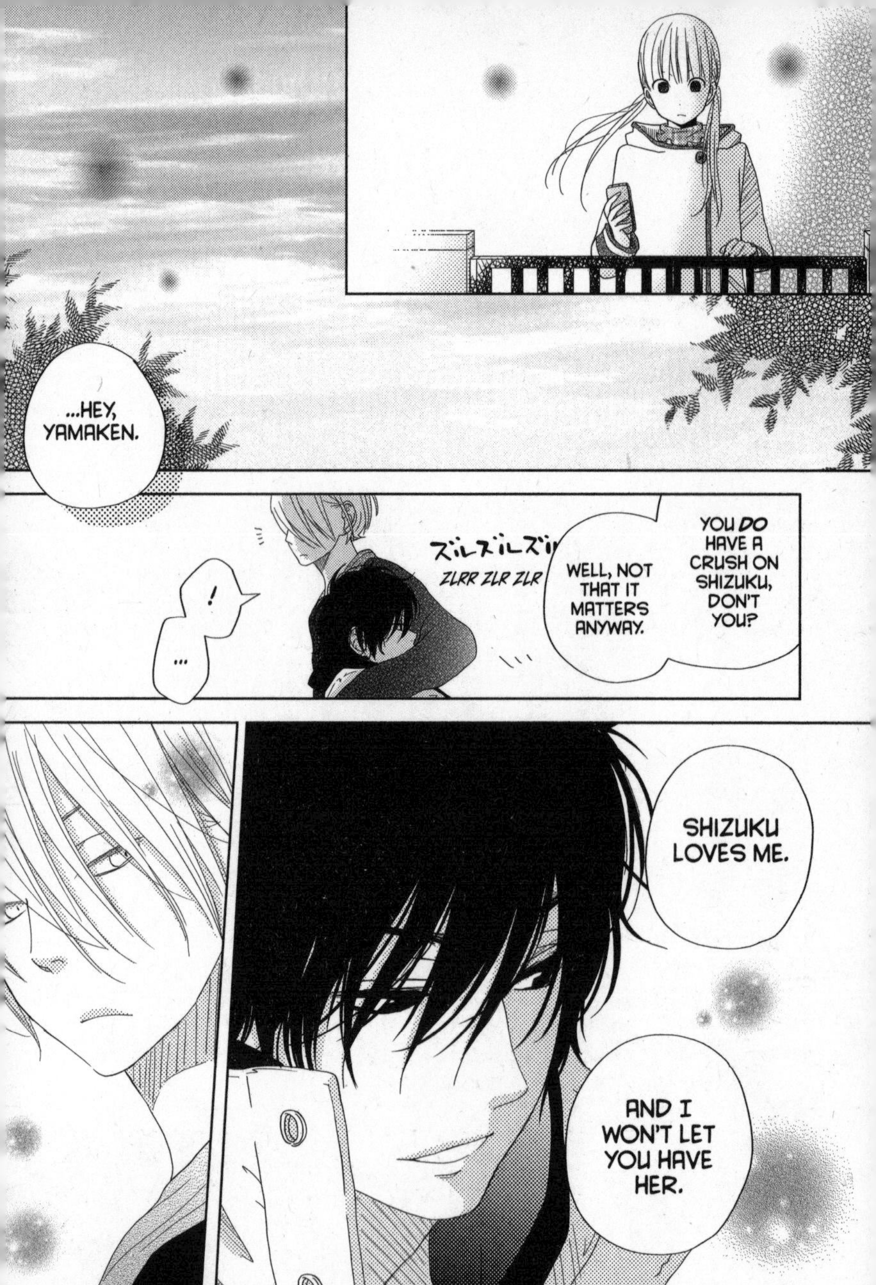
...HEY, YAMAKEN.
YOU *DO* HAVE A CRUSH ON SHIZUKU, DON'T YOU?
WELL, NOT THAT IT MATTERS ANYWAY.
ズルズルズ
ZLRR ZLR ZLR
!
...
SHIZUKU LOVES ME.
AND I WON'T LET YOU HAVE HER.

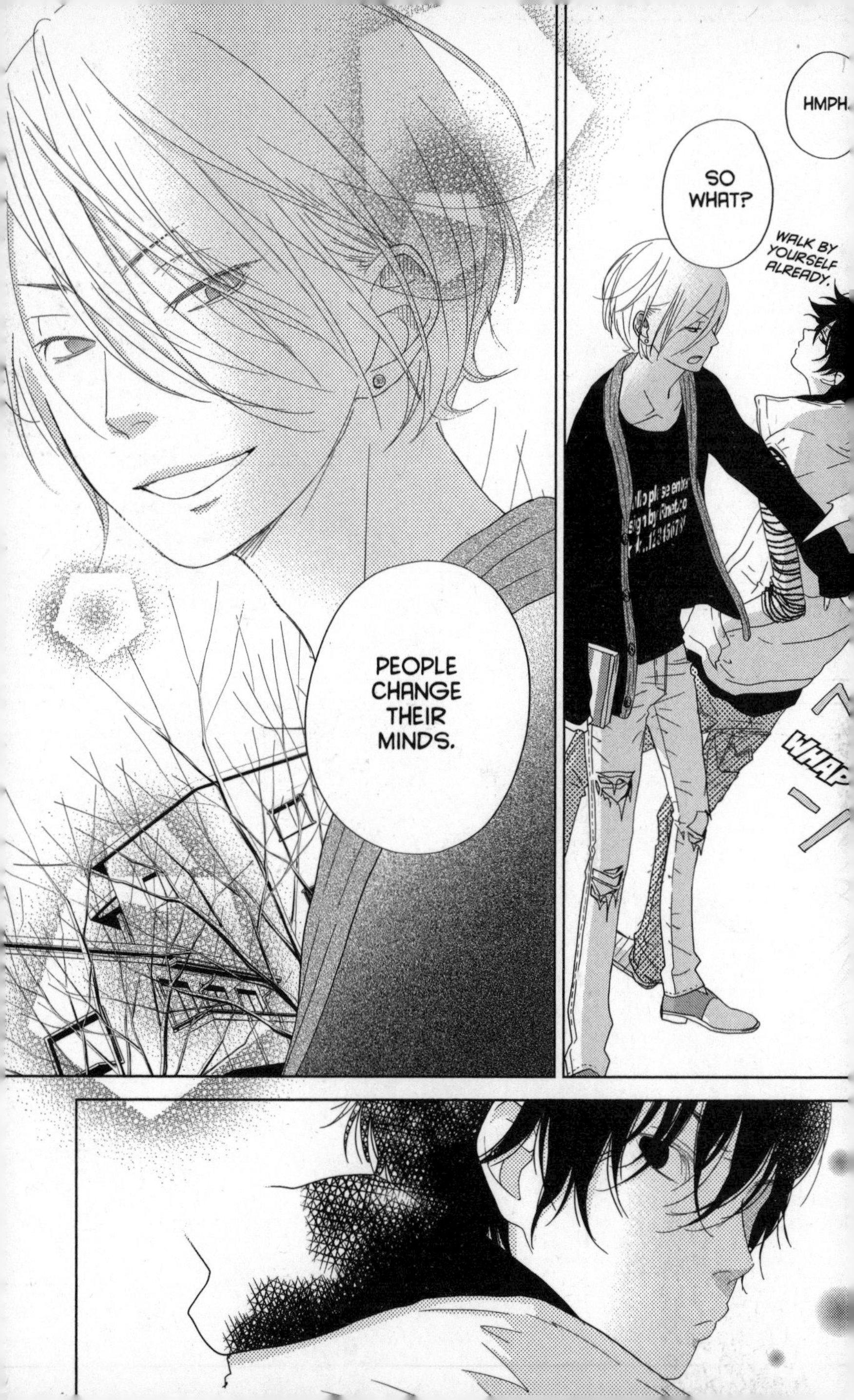
HMPH.
SO WHAT?
WALK BY YOURSELF ALREADY.
WHAP
PEOPLE CHANGE THEIR MINDS.

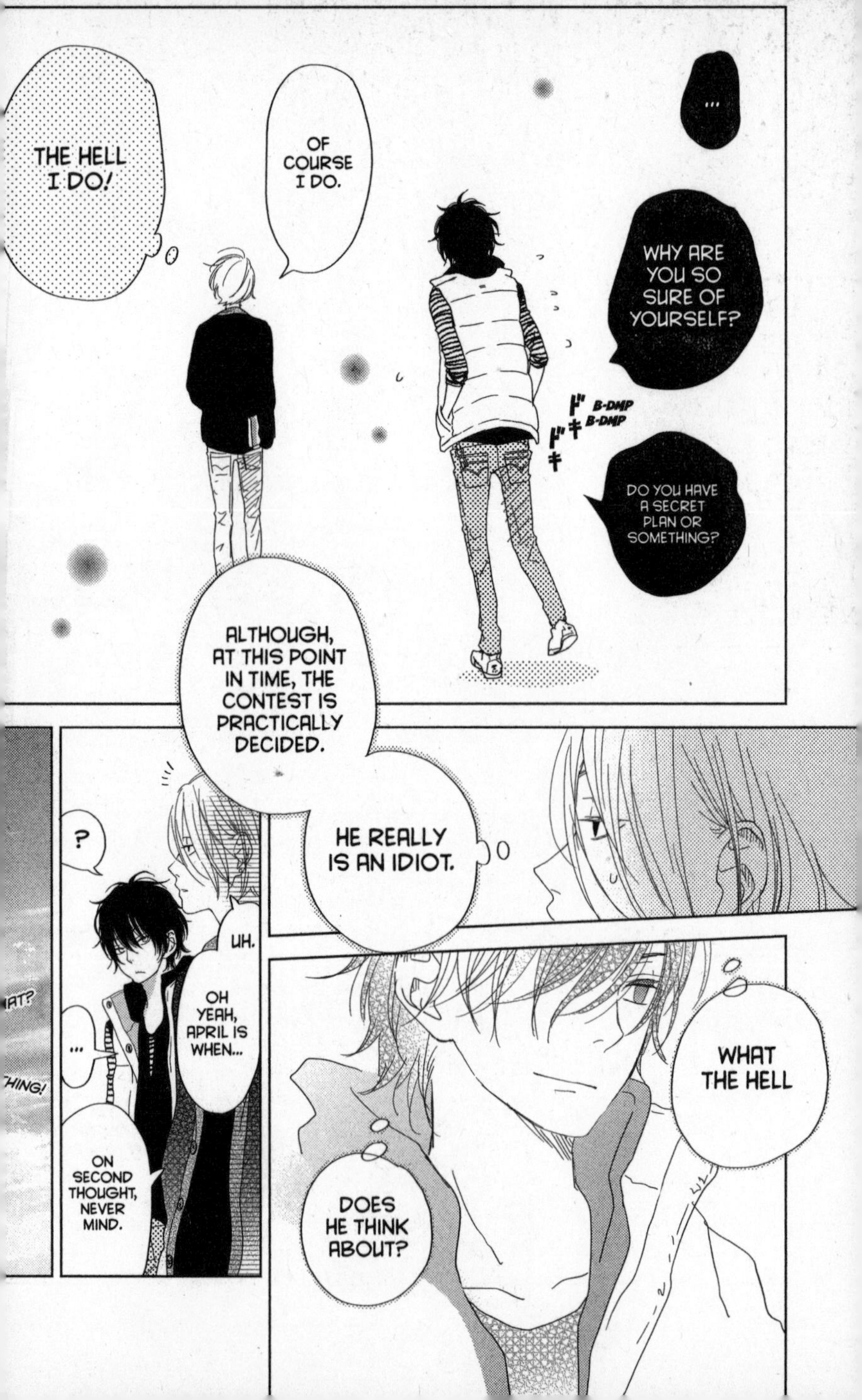
...
WHY ARE YOU SO SURE OF YOURSELF?
ドキ ドキ
B-DMP B-DMP
DO YOU HAVE A SECRET PLAN OR SOMETHING?
OF COURSE I DO.
THE HELL I DO!
ALTHOUGH, AT THIS POINT IN TIME, THE CONTEST IS PRACTICALLY DECIDED.
HE REALLY IS AN IDIOT.
WHAT THE HELL
DOES HE THINK ABOUT?
?
UH.
OH YEAH, APRIL IS WHEN...
...
ON SECOND THOUGHT, NEVER MIND.

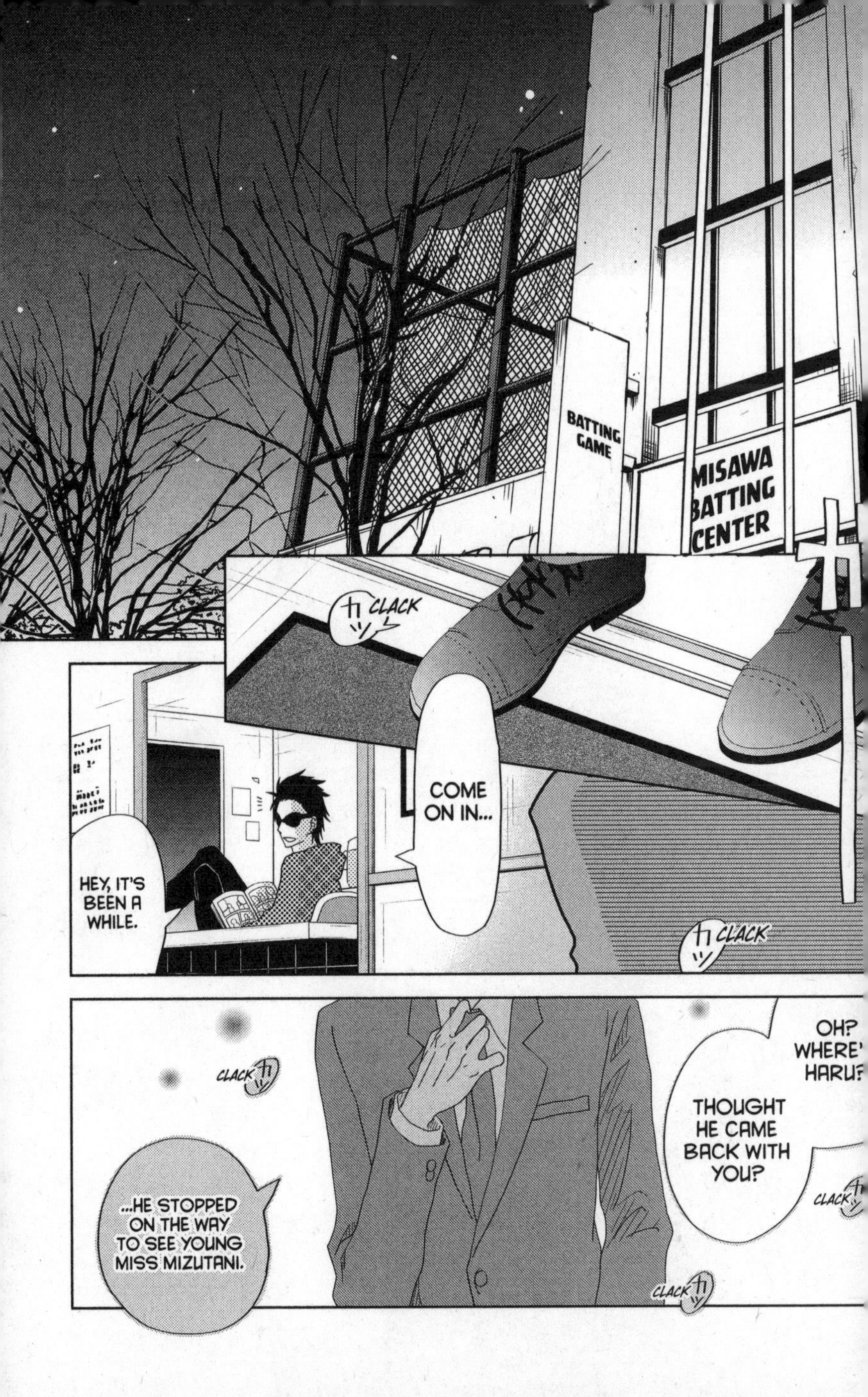
BATTING GAME
MISAWA BATTING CENTER
CLACK
COME ON IN...
CLACK
HEY, IT'S BEEN A WHILE.
OH? WHERE' HARU?
THOUGHT HE CAME BACK WITH YOU?
CLACK
CLACK
CLACK
...HE STOPPED ON THE WAY TO SEE YOUNG MISS MIZUTANI.

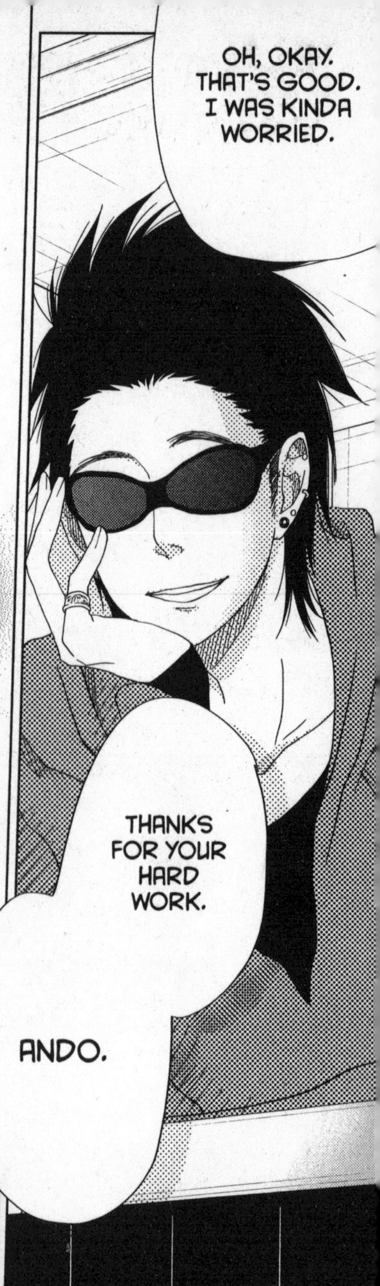
OH, OKAY. THAT'S GOOD. I WAS KINDA WORRIED.
THANKS FOR YOUR HARD WORK.
ANDO.
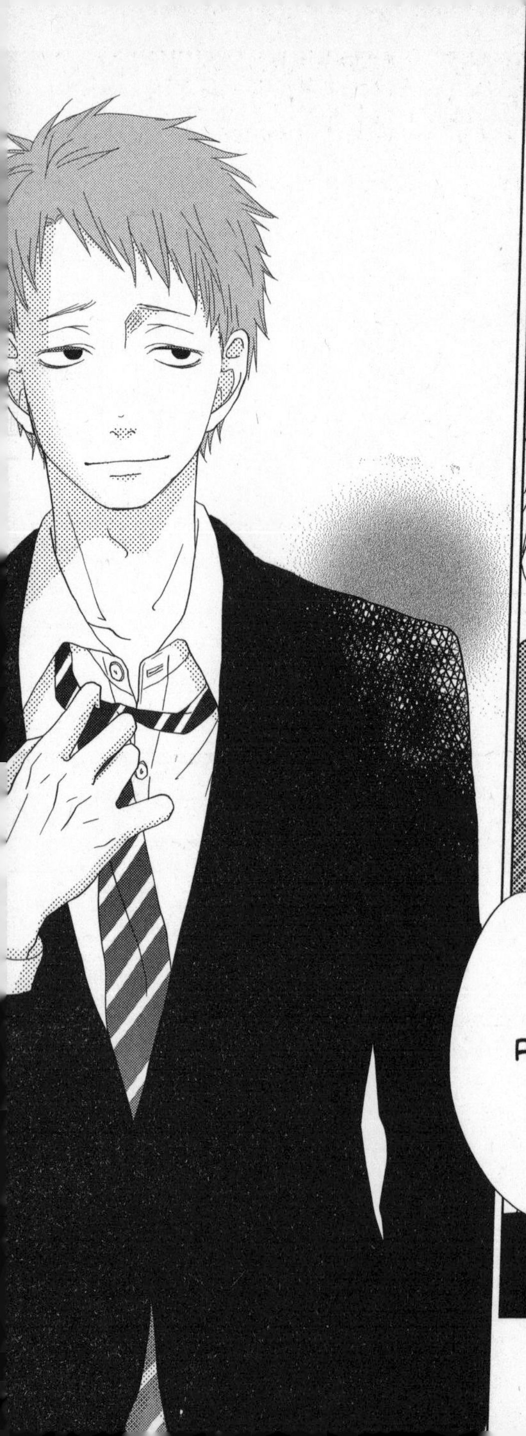

TEXTING

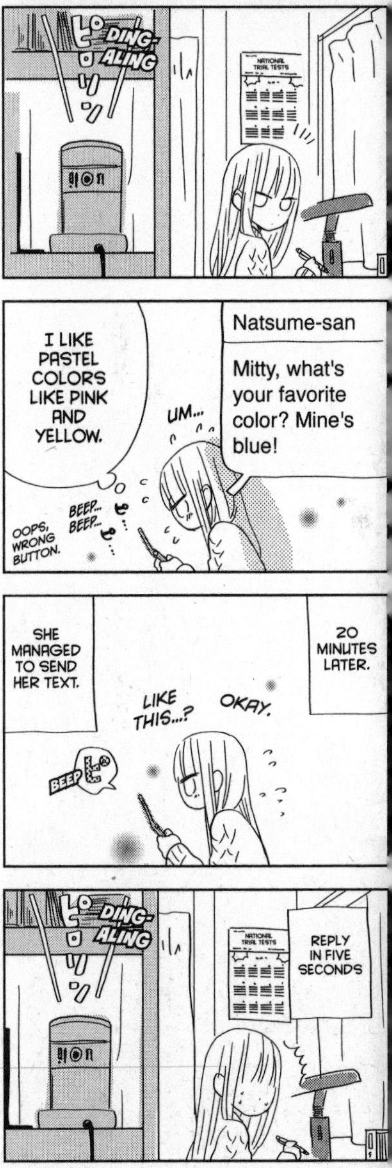
DING-ALING
NATIONAL TRIAL TESTS
Natsume-san
Mitty, what's your favorite color? Mine's blue!
UM...
I LIKE PASTEL COLORS LIKE PINK AND YELLOW.
BEEP... BEEP...
OOPS, WRONG BUTTON.
20 MINUTES LATER.
SHE MANAGED TO SEND HER TEXT.
OKAY.
LIKE THIS...?
BEEP
DING-ALING
REPLY IN FIVE SECONDS
NATIONAL TRIAL TESTS

HINDRANCE

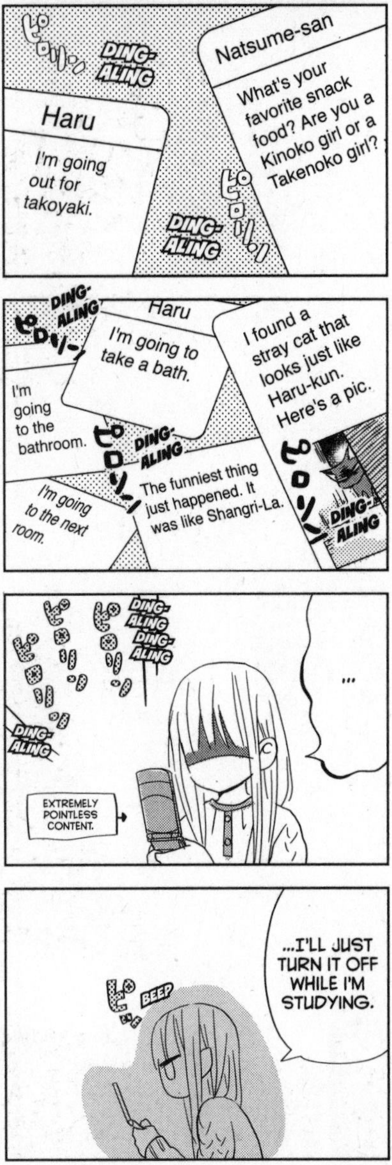
Natsume-san
What's your favorite snack food? Are you a Kinoko girl or a Takenoko girl?
DING-ALING
Haru
I'm going out for takoyaki.
DING-ALING
I found a stray cat that looks just like Haru-kun. Here's a pic.
Haru
I'm going to take a bath.
DING-ALING
I'm going to the bathroom.
DING-ALING
The funniest thing just happened. It was like Shangri-La.
DING-ALING
I'm going to the next room.
...
DING-ALING
DING-ALING
DING-ALING
EXTREMELY POINTLESS CONTENT.
...I'LL JUST TURN IT OFF WHILE I'M STUDYING.
BEEP

VOICE

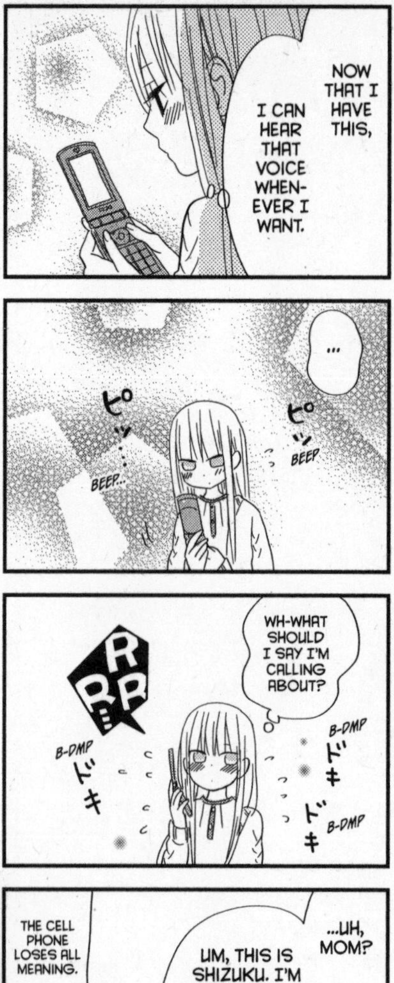
NOW THAT I HAVE THIS,
I CAN HEAR THAT VOICE WHENEVER I WANT.
...
ピッ
BEEP
ピッ
BEEP...
WH-WHAT SHOULD I SAY I'M CALLING ABOUT?
RRR
ドキ
B-DMP
ドキ
B-DMP
ドキ
B-DMP
...UH, MOM?
UM, THIS IS SHIZUKU. I'M GOING TO TURN MY PHONE OFF WHEN I'M AT HOME OR SCHOOL, SO IF YOU NEED ME, CALL THE HOUSE.
THE CELL PHONE LOSES ALL MEANING.

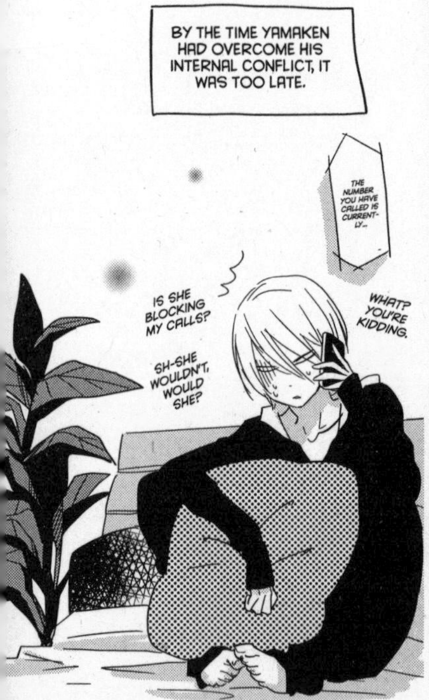
BY THE TIME YAMAKEN HAD OVERCOME HIS INTERNAL CONFLICT, IT WAS TOO LATE.
THE NUMBER YOU HAVE CALLED IS CURRENTLY...
WHAT? YOU'RE KIDDING.
IS SHE BLOCKING MY CALLS?
SH-SHE WOULDN'T, WOULD SHE?

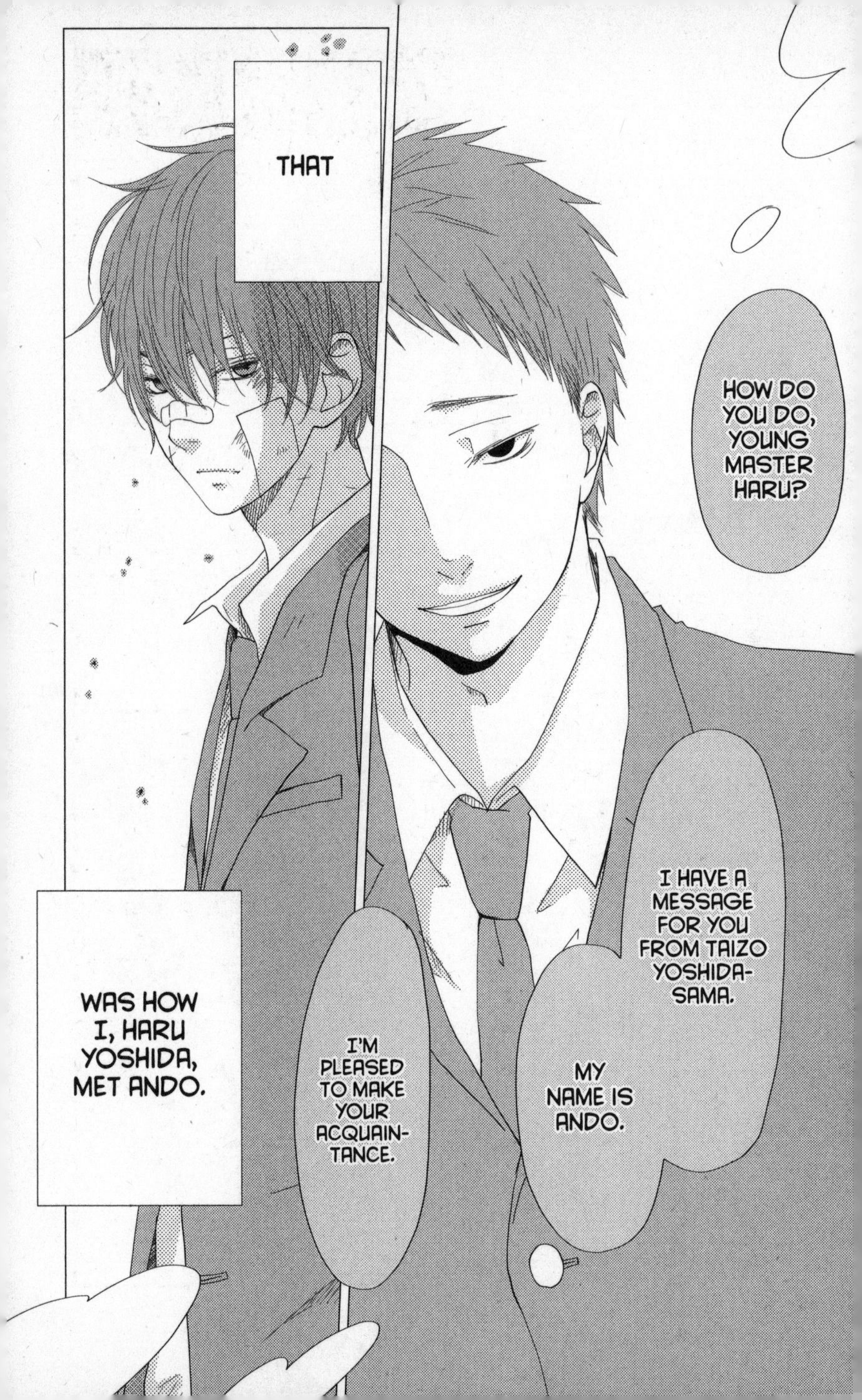
HOW DO YOU DO, YOUNG MASTER HARU?
I HAVE A MESSAGE FOR YOU FROM TAIZO YOSHIDA-SAMA.
MY NAME IS ANDO.
I'M PLEASED TO MAKE YOUR ACQUAIN-TANCE.
THAT
WAS HOW I, HARU YOSHIDA, MET ANDO.

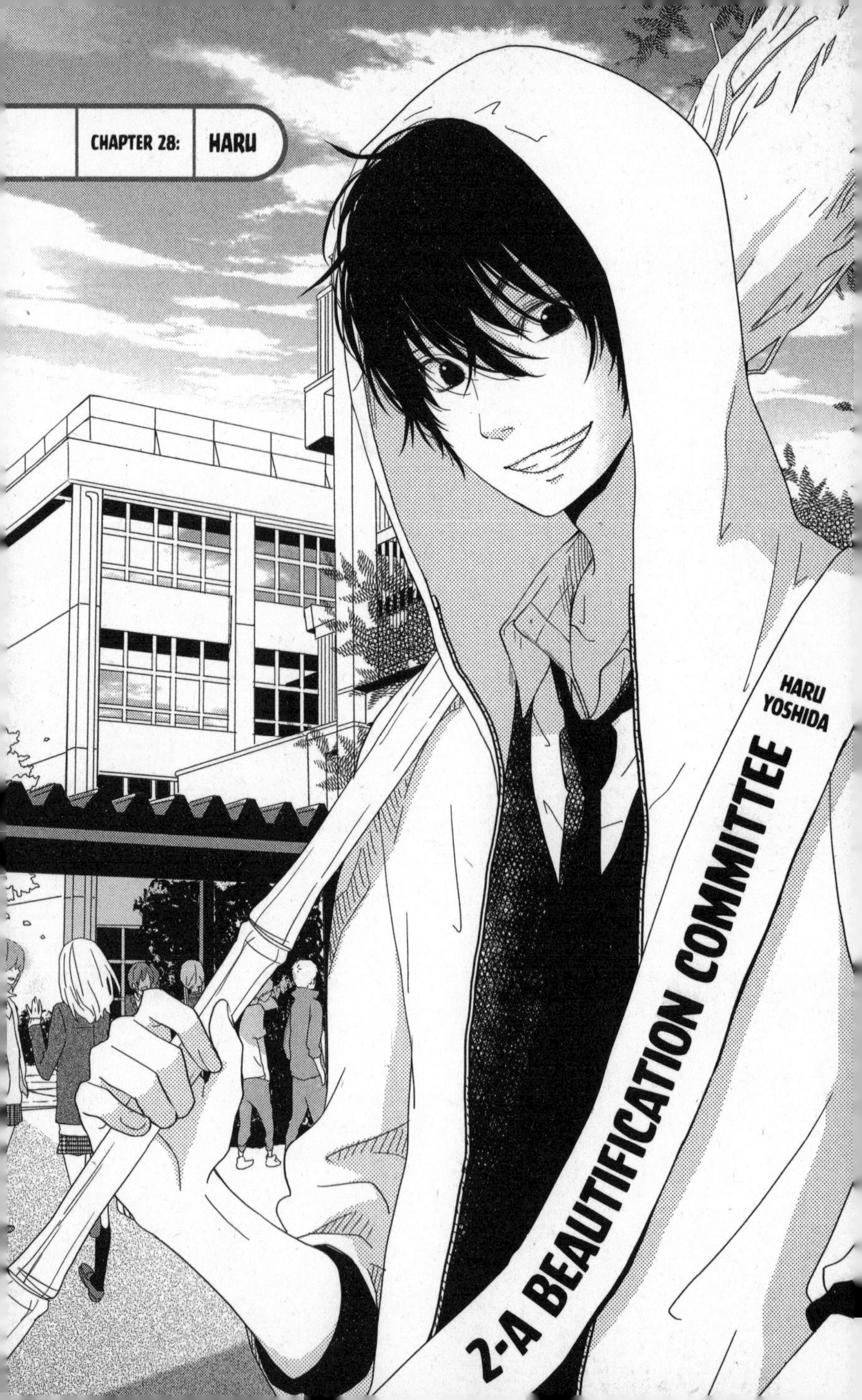
CHAPTER 28: HARU
HARU YOSHIDA
2-A BEAUTIFICATION COMMITTEE

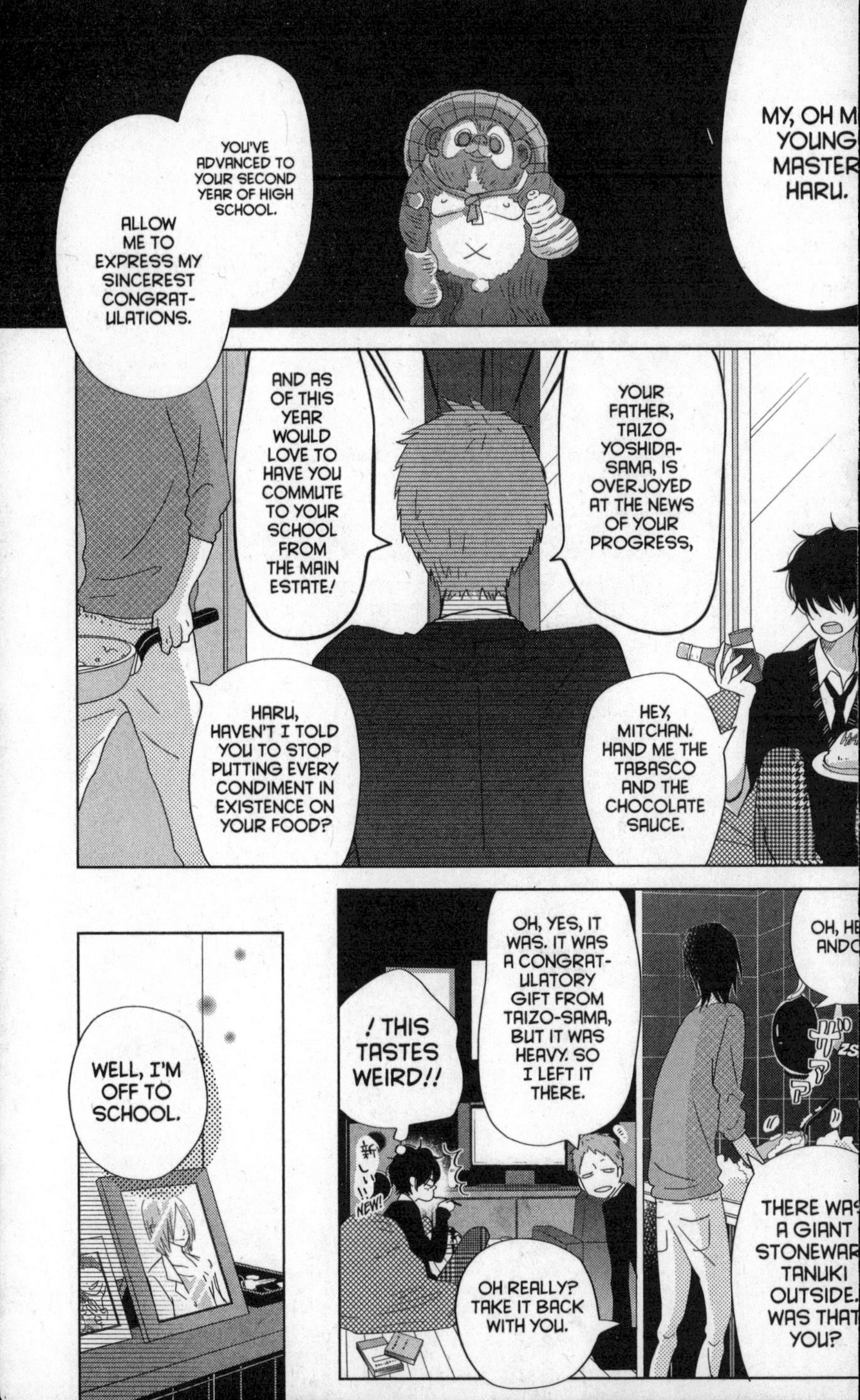
MY, OH M YOUNG MASTER HARU.
YOU'VE ADVANCED TO YOUR SECOND YEAR OF HIGH SCHOOL.
ALLOW ME TO EXPRESS MY SINCEREST CONGRAT-ULATIONS.
YOUR FATHER, TAIZO YOSHIDA-SAMA, IS OVERJOYED AT THE NEWS OF YOUR PROGRESS,
AND AS OF THIS YEAR WOULD LOVE TO HAVE YOU COMMUTE TO YOUR SCHOOL FROM THE MAIN ESTATE!
HEY, MITCHAN. HAND ME THE TABASCO AND THE CHOCOLATE SAUCE.
HARU, HAVEN'T I TOLD YOU TO STOP PUTTING EVERY CONDIMENT IN EXISTENCE ON YOUR FOOD?
OH, HE ANDO
ザァァ ZS
THERE WAS A GIANT STONEWAR TANUKI OUTSIDE. WAS THAT YOU?
OH, YES, IT WAS. IT WAS A CONGRAT-ULATORY GIFT FROM TAIZO-SAMA, BUT IT WAS HEAVY. SO I LEFT IT THERE.
! THIS TASTES WEIRD!!
新しい!! NEW!
OH REALLY? TAKE IT BACK WITH YOU.
WELL, I'M OFF TO SCHOOL.

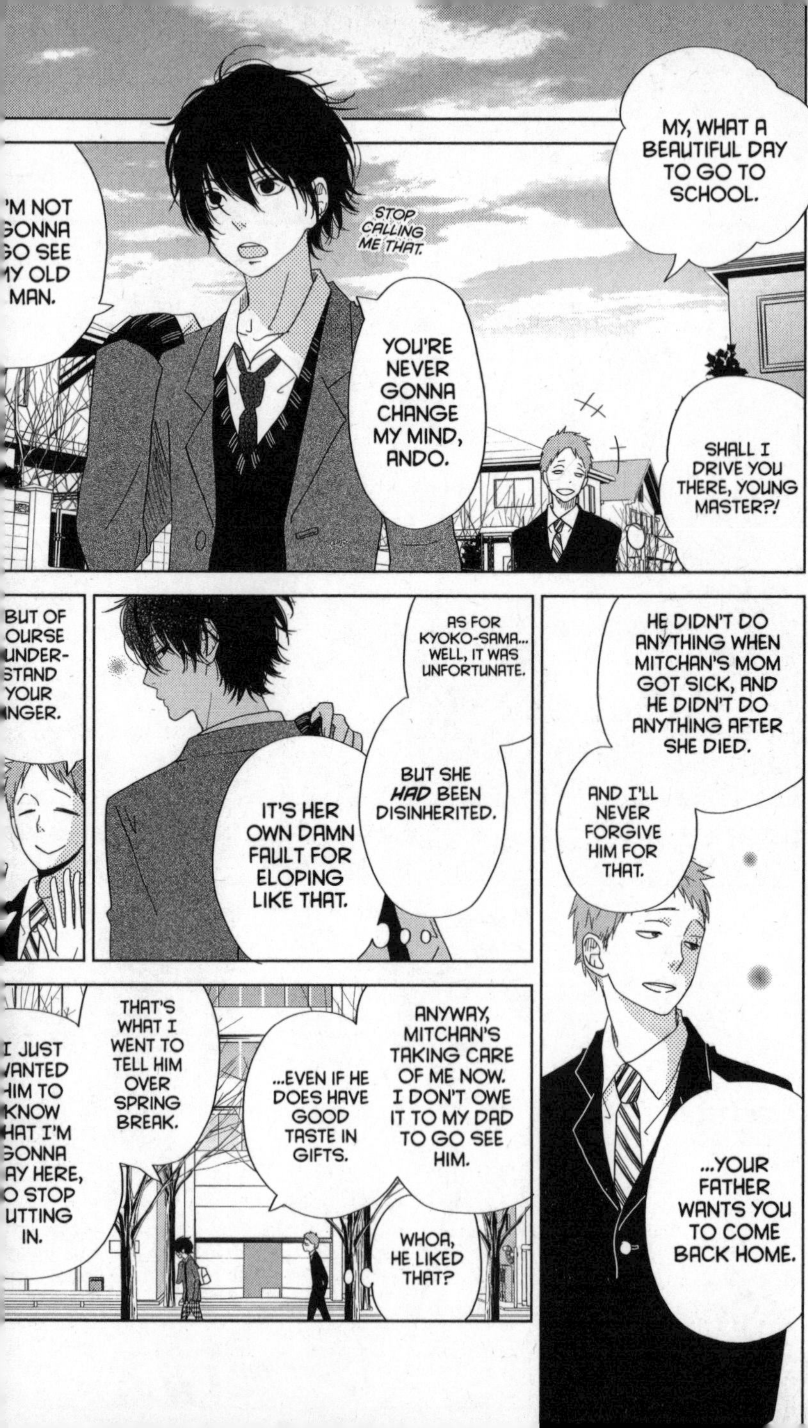
MY, WHAT A BEAUTIFUL DAY TO GO TO SCHOOL.
SHALL I DRIVE YOU THERE, YOUNG MASTER?!
STOP CALLING ME THAT.
YOU'RE NEVER GONNA CHANGE MY MIND, ANDO.
'M NOT GONNA GO SEE MY OLD MAN.
HE DIDN'T DO ANYTHING WHEN MITCHAN'S MOM GOT SICK, AND HE DIDN'T DO ANYTHING AFTER SHE DIED.
AND I'LL NEVER FORGIVE HIM FOR THAT.
...YOUR FATHER WANTS YOU TO COME BACK HOME.
AS FOR KYOKO-SAMA... WELL, IT WAS UNFORTUNATE.
BUT SHE *HAD* BEEN DISINHERITED.
IT'S HER OWN DAMN FAULT FOR ELOPING LIKE THAT.
BUT OF OURSE UNDER-STAND YOUR NGER.
ANYWAY, MITCHAN'S TAKING CARE OF ME NOW. I DON'T OWE IT TO MY DAD TO GO SEE HIM.
WHOA, HE LIKED THAT?
...EVEN IF HE DOES HAVE GOOD TASTE IN GIFTS.
THAT'S WHAT I WENT TO TELL HIM OVER SPRING BREAK.
I JUST ANTED IM TO NOW HAT I'M ONNA AY HERE, O STOP UTTING IN.

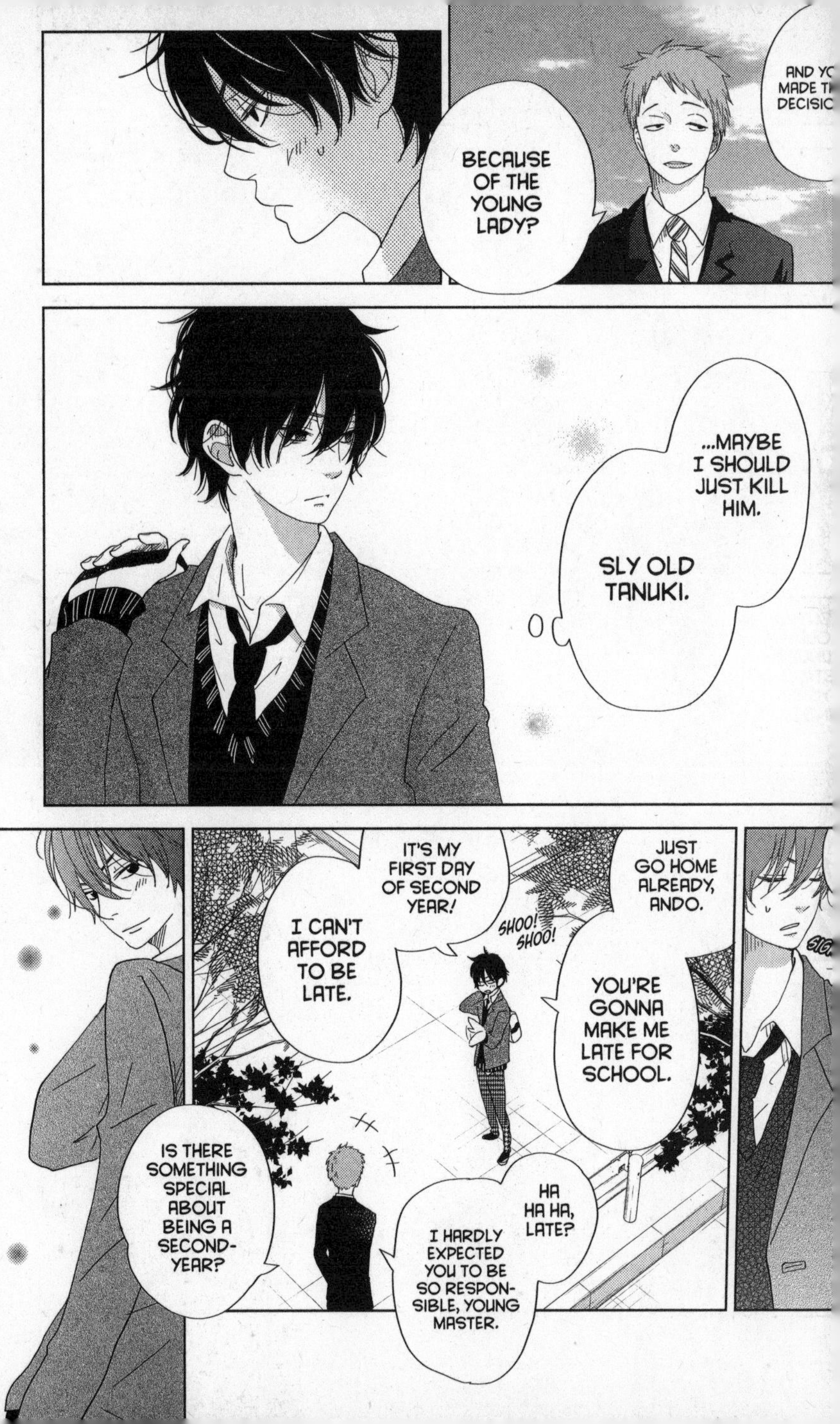
AND YO MADE T DECISIO
BECAUSE OF THE YOUNG LADY?
...MAYBE I SHOULD JUST KILL HIM.
SLY OLD TANUKI.
JUST GO HOME ALREADY, ANDO.
YOU'RE GONNA MAKE ME LATE FOR SCHOOL.
SHOO! SHOO!
IT'S MY FIRST DAY OF SECOND YEAR!
I CAN'T AFFORD TO BE LATE.
HA HA HA, LATE?
I HARDLY EXPECTED YOU TO BE SO RESPONSIBLE, YOUNG MASTER.
IS THERE SOMETHING SPECIAL ABOUT BEING A SECOND-YEAR?

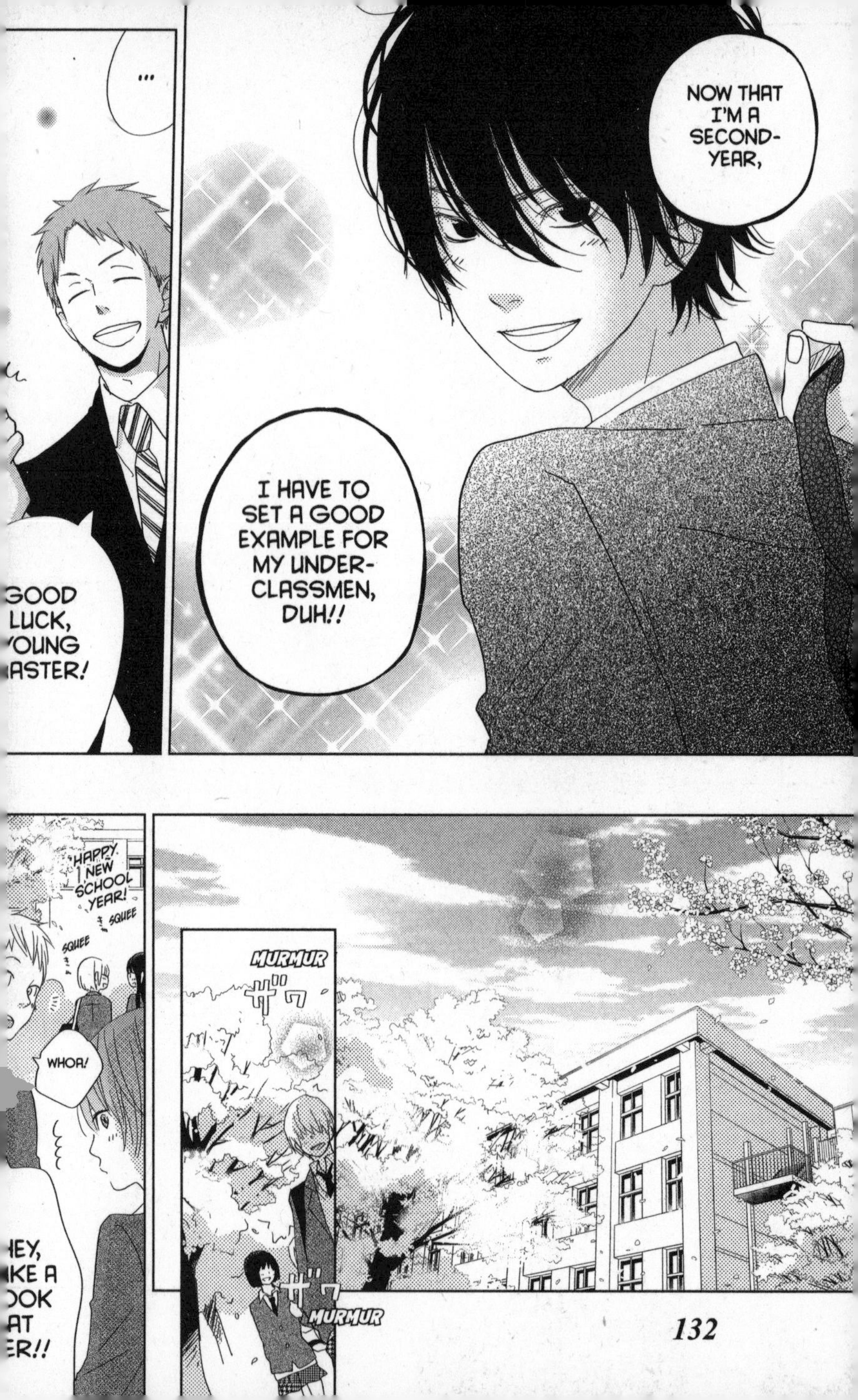
NOW THAT I'M A SECOND-YEAR,
I HAVE TO SET A GOOD EXAMPLE FOR MY UNDER-CLASSMEN, DUH!!
...
GOOD LUCK, YOUNG ASTER!
MURMUR
ザワ
ザワ
MURMUR
HAPPY NEW SCHOOL YEAR!
SQUEE
SQUEE
WHOA!
HEY, AKE A OOK AT ER!!

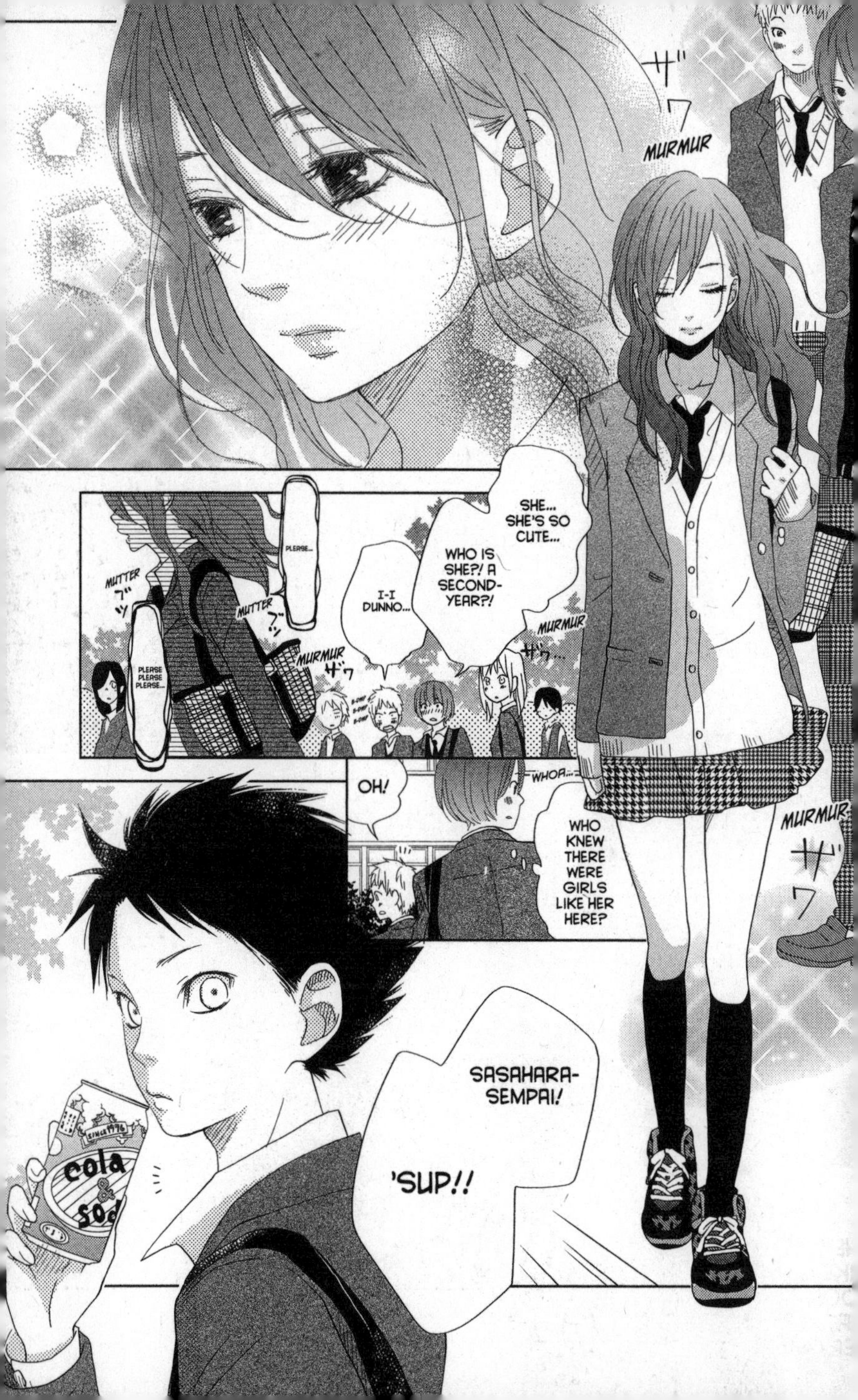

ザワ
MURMUR
SHE... SHE'S SO CUTE...
WHO IS SHE?! A SECOND-YEAR?!
MURMUR
ザワ...
I-I DUNNO...
MURMUR
ザワ
PLEASE...
MUTTER
ブツ
MUTTER
ブツ
PLEASE PLEASE PLEASE...
WHOA...
WHO KNEW THERE WERE GIRLS LIKE HER HERE?
OH!
MURMUR
ザワ
SASAHARA-SEMPAI!
'SUP!!

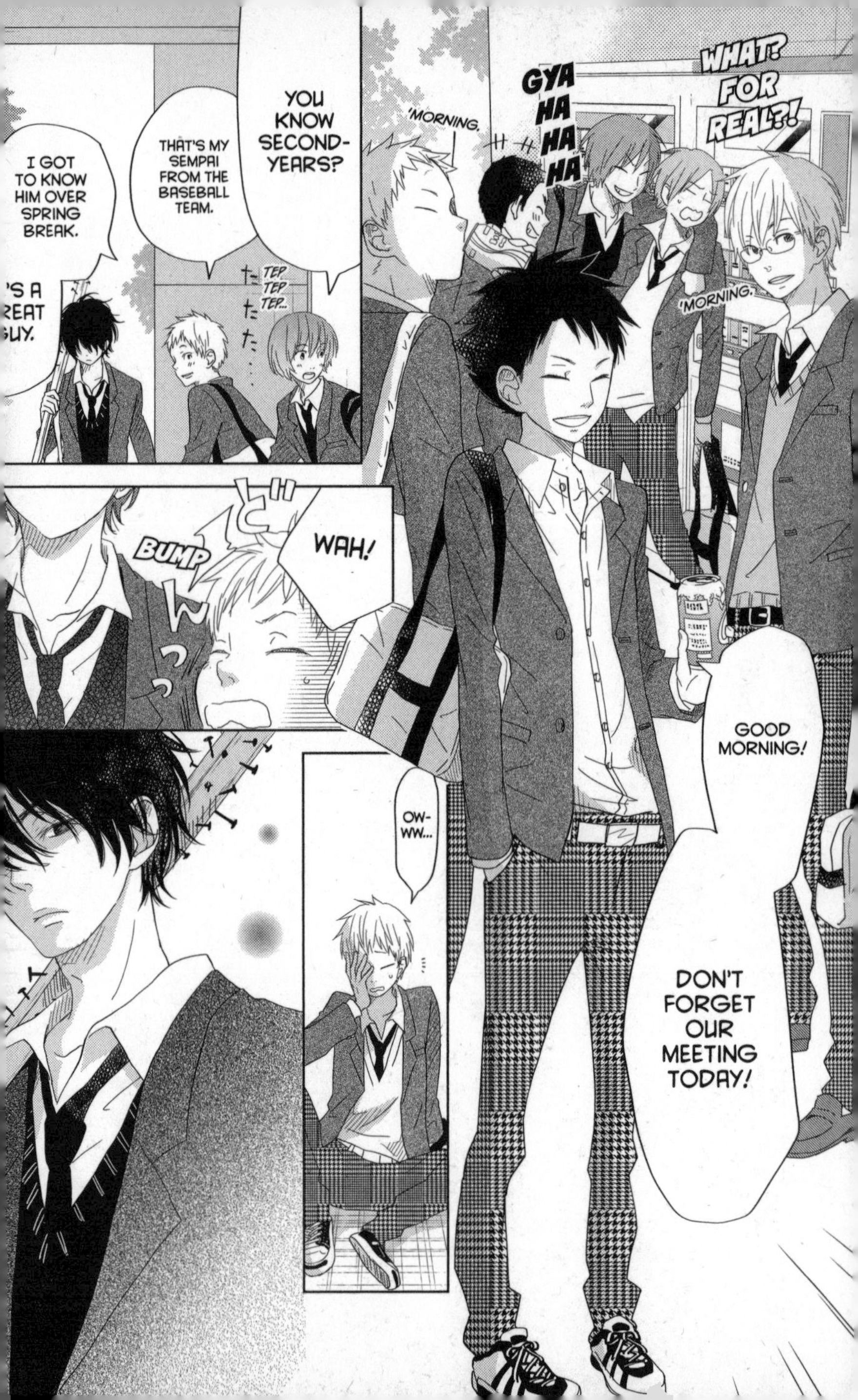
WHAT? FOR REAL?!
GYA HA HA HA
'MORNING.
'MORNING.
GOOD MORNING!
DON'T FORGET OUR MEETING TODAY!
YOU KNOW SECOND-YEARS?
TEP TEP TEP...
THAT'S MY SEMPAI FROM THE BASEBALL TEAM.
I GOT TO KNOW HIM OVER SPRING BREAK.
'S A REAT GUY.
WAH!
BUMP
OW-WW...

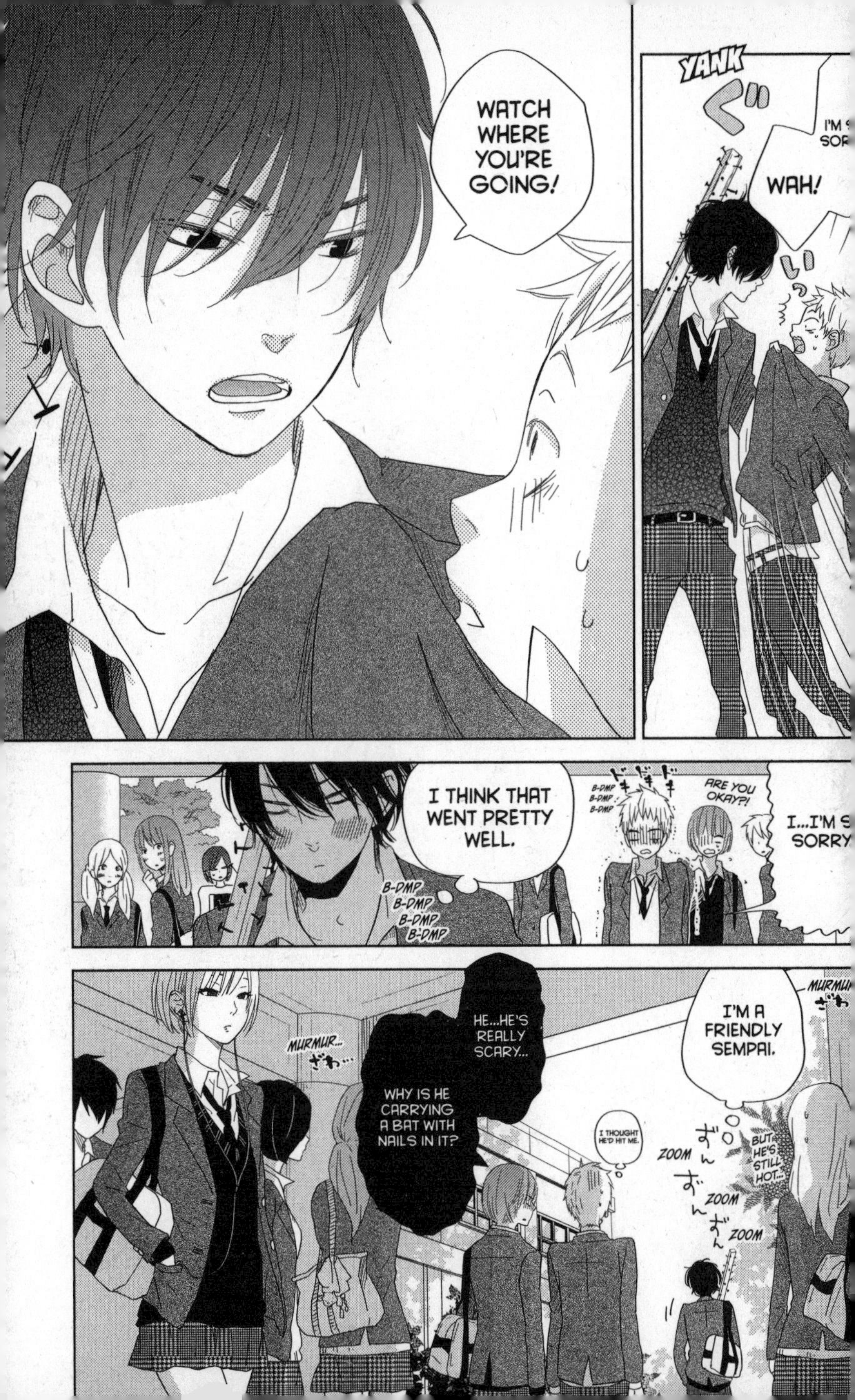
YANK
ぐい
I'M S
SOR
WAH!
WATCH WHERE YOU'RE GOING!
I...I'M S
SORRY
ARE YOU OKAY?!
B-DMP
B-DMP
B-DMP
ドキ ドキ ドキ
I THINK THAT WENT PRETTY WELL.
B-DMP
B-DMP
B-DMP
B-DMP
MURMUR
ざわ
I'M A FRIENDLY SEMPAI.
BUT HE'S STILL HOT...
I THOUGHT HE'D HIT ME.
ZOOM
ずん
ZOOM
ずん
ZOOM
HE...HE'S REALLY SCARY...
WHY IS HE CARRYING A BAT WITH NAILS IN IT?
MURMUR...
ざわ...

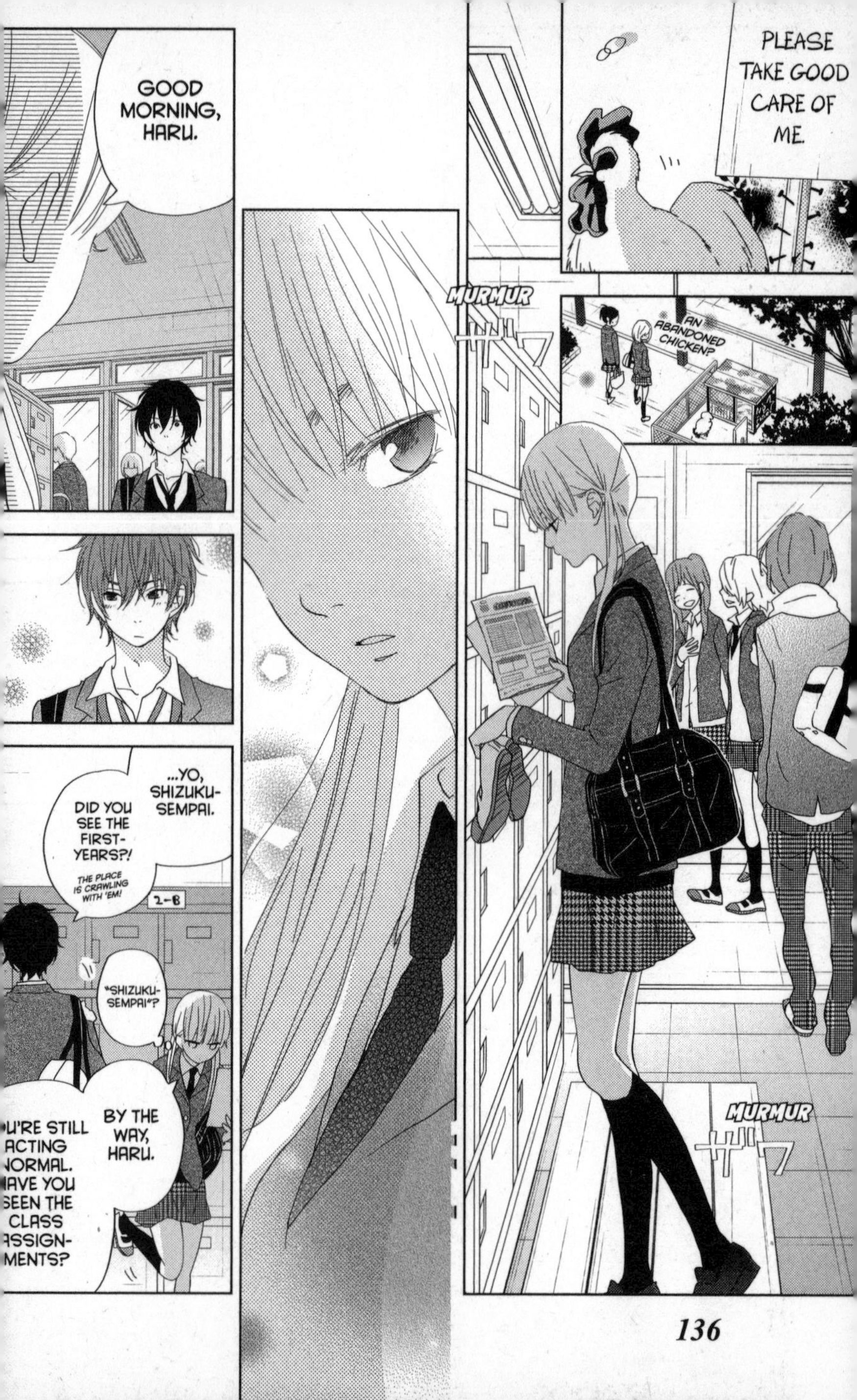
PLEASE TAKE GOOD CARE OF ME.
AN ABANDONED CHICKEN?
MURMUR
MURMUR
GOOD MORNING, HARU.
...YO, SHIZUKU-SEMPAI.
DID YOU SEE THE FIRST-YEARS?!
THE PLACE IS CRAWLING WITH 'EM!
2-B
"SHIZUKU-SEMPAI"?
BY THE WAY, HARU.
U'RE STILL ACTING NORMAL. AVE YOU SEEN THE CLASS SSIGN-MENTS?

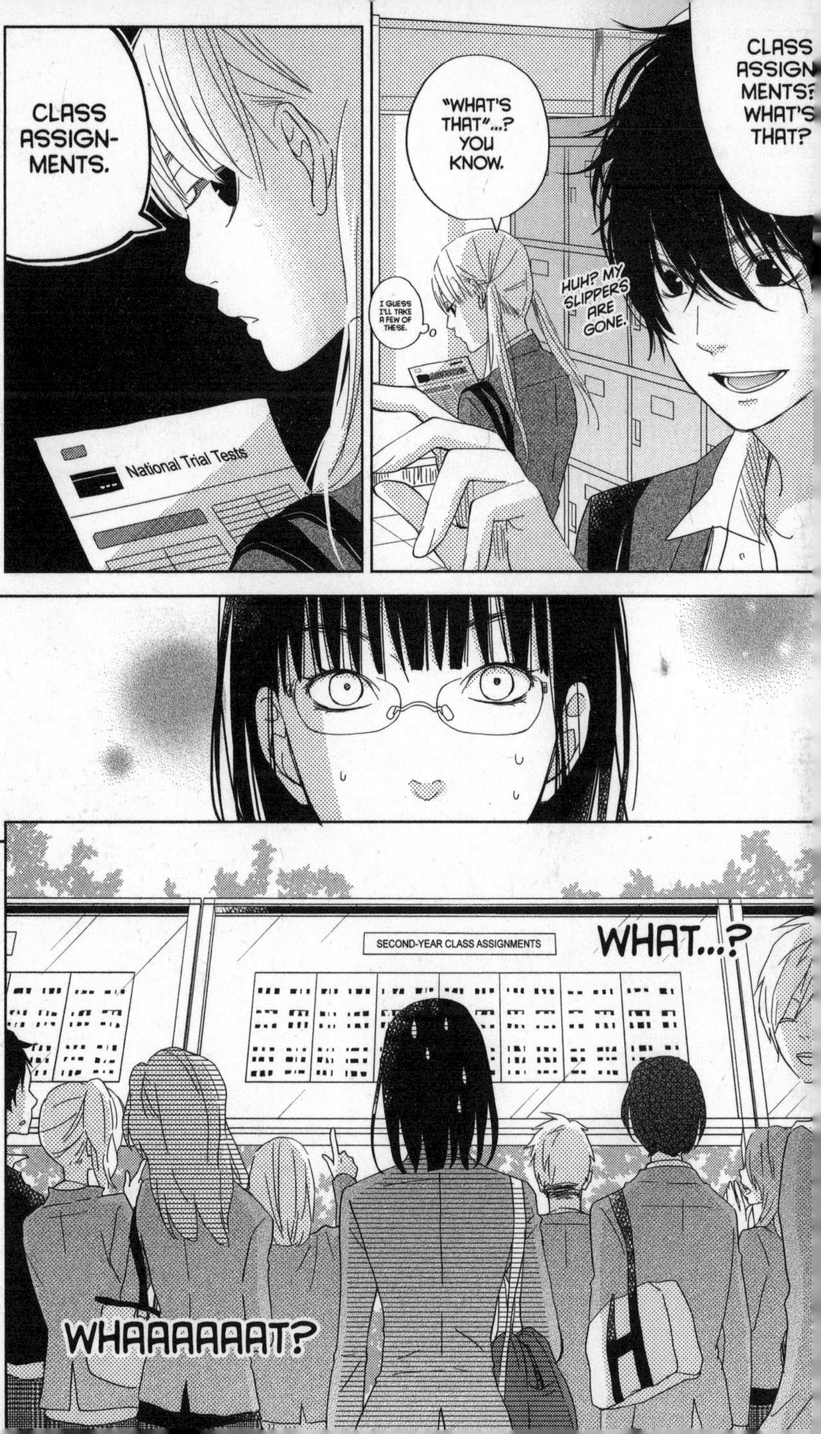
CLASS ASSIGNMENTS? WHAT'S THAT?
HUH? MY SLIPPERS ARE GONE.
"WHAT'S THAT"...? YOU KNOW.
I GUESS I'LL TAKE A FEW OF THESE.
CLASS ASSIGNMENTS.
National Trial Tests
SECOND-YEAR CLASS ASSIGNMENTS
WHAT...?
WHAAAAAAAT?

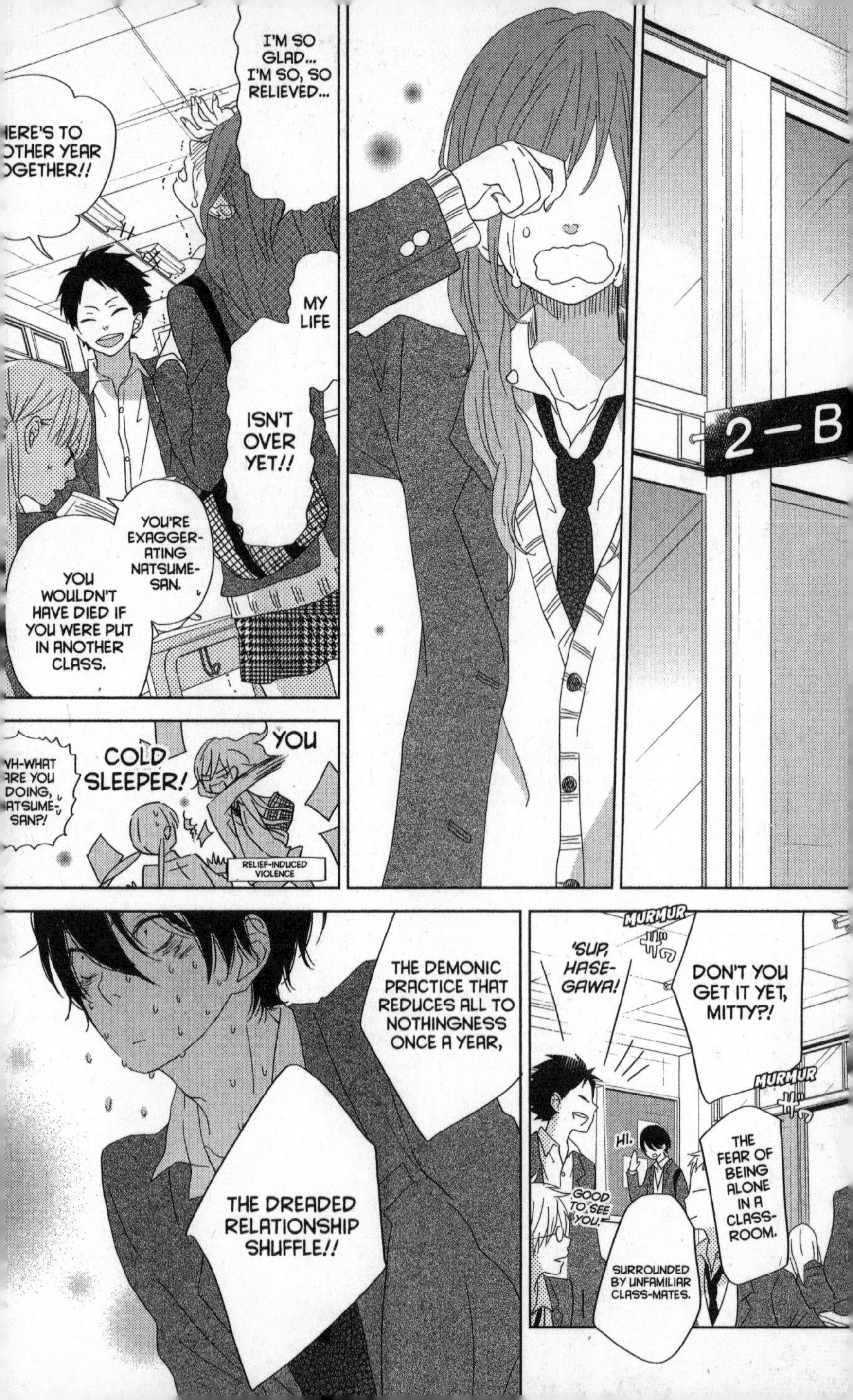
2-B
I'M SO GLAD... I'M SO, SO RELIEVED...
MY LIFE ISN'T OVER YET!!
HERE'S TO OTHER YEAR OGETHER!!
YOU'RE EXAGGER-ATING NATSUME-SAN.
YOU WOULDN'T HAVE DIED IF YOU WERE PUT IN ANOTHER CLASS.
YOU COLD SLEEPER!
WH-WHAT ARE YOU DOING, ATSUME-SAN?!
RELIEF-INDUCED VIOLENCE
MURMUR
DON'T YOU GET IT YET, MITTY?!
'SUP, HASE-GAWA!
MURMUR
HI.
GOOD TO SEE YOU.
THE FEAR OF BEING ALONE IN A CLASS-ROOM.
SURROUNDED BY UNFAMILIAR CLASS-MATES.
THE DEMONIC PRACTICE THAT REDUCES ALL TO NOTHINGNESS ONCE A YEAR,
THE DREADED RELATIONSHIP SHUFFLE!!

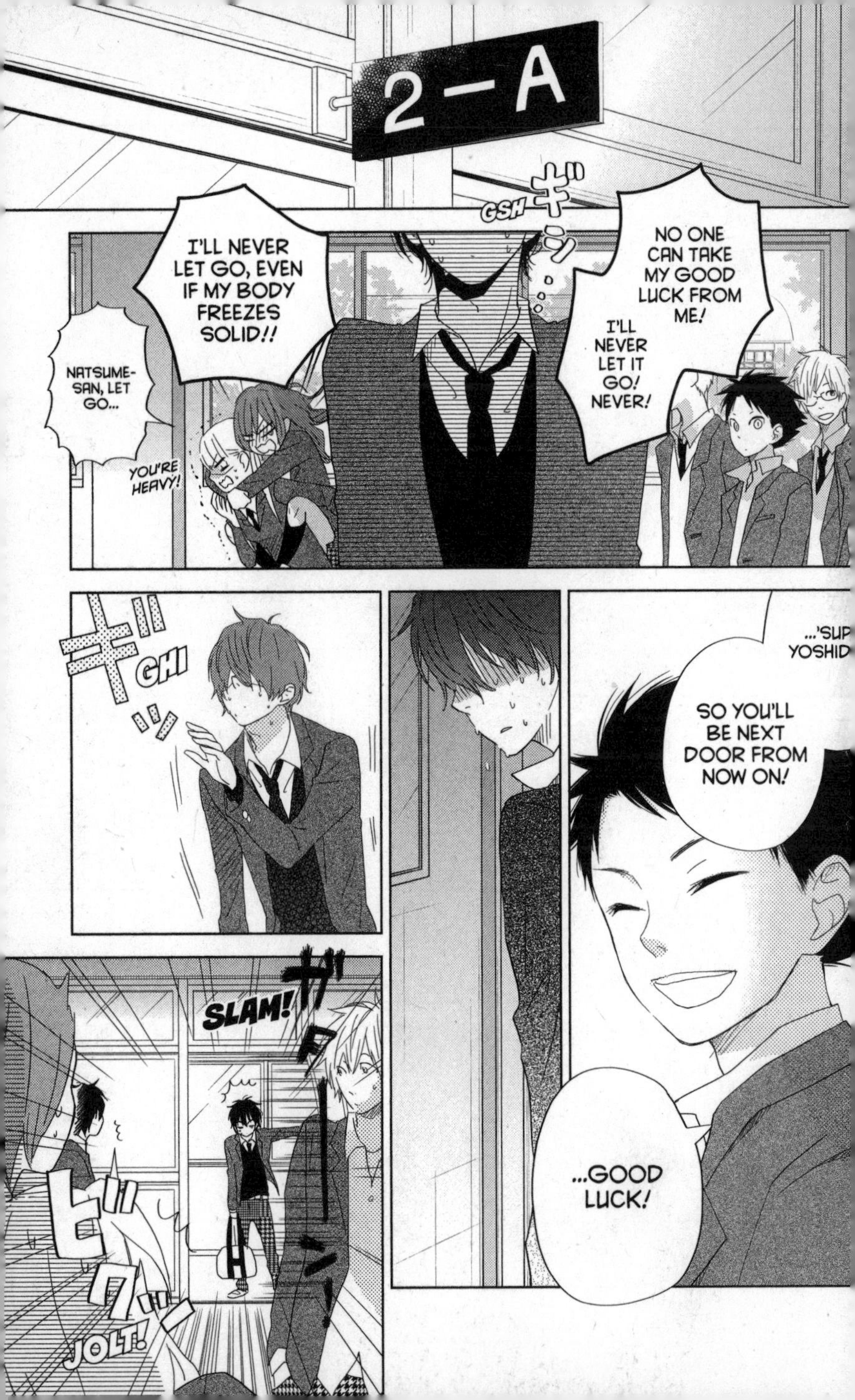
2-A
NO ONE CAN TAKE MY GOOD LUCK FROM ME!
I'LL NEVER LET IT GO! NEVER!
GSH
I'LL NEVER LET GO, EVEN IF MY BODY FREEZES SOLID!!
NATSUME-SAN, LET GO...
YOU'RE HEAVY!
...'SUP YOSHID
SO YOU'LL BE NEXT DOOR FROM NOW ON!
...GOOD LUCK!
GHI
SLAM!
JOLT!

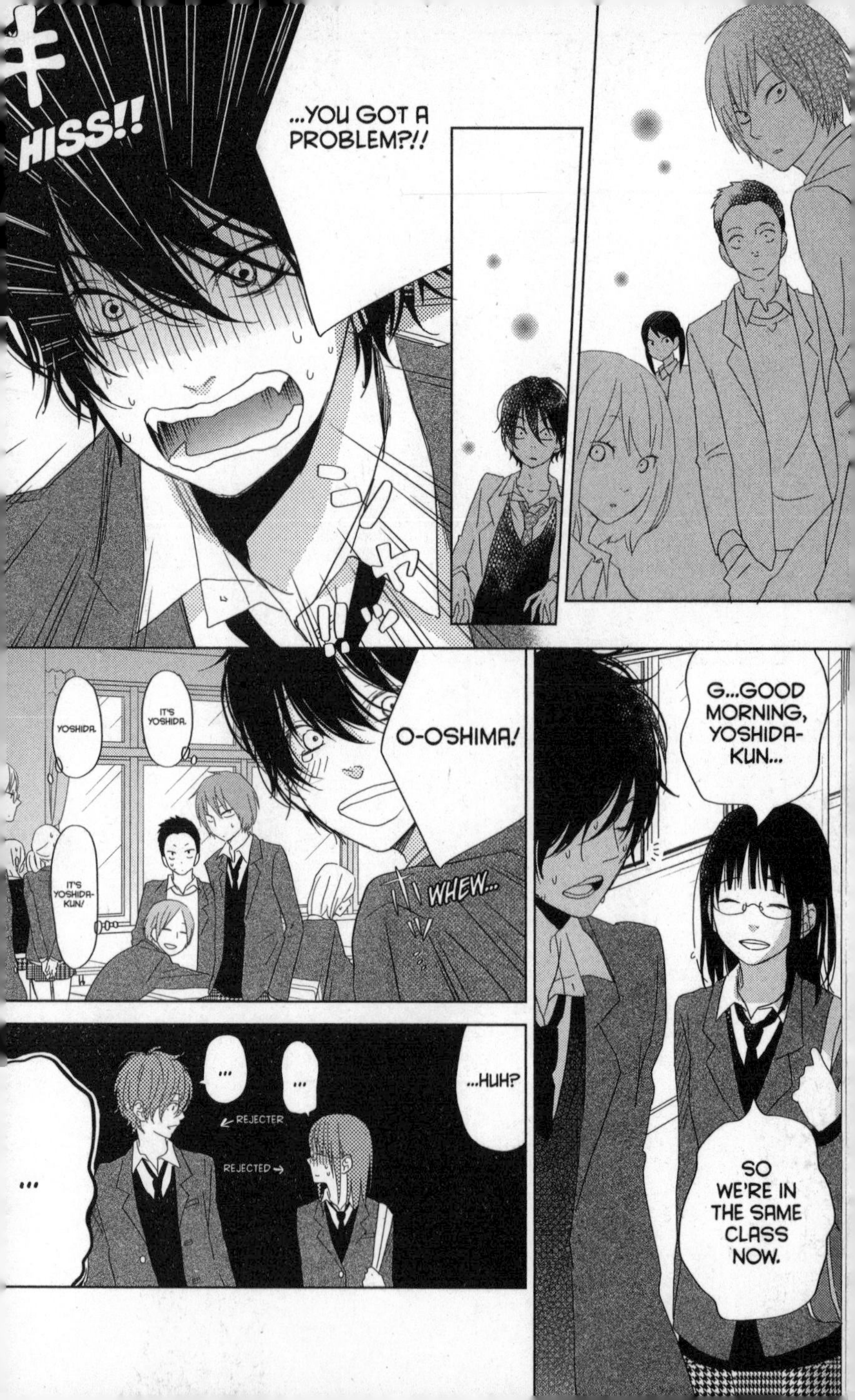
...YOU GOT A PROBLEM?!!
HISS!!
G...GOOD MORNING, YOSHIDA-KUN...
SO WE'RE IN THE SAME CLASS NOW.
O-OSHIMA!
IT'S YOSHIDA.
YOSHIDA.
IT'S YOSHIDA-KUN!
WHEW...
...HUH?
...
...
REJECTER
REJECTED
...

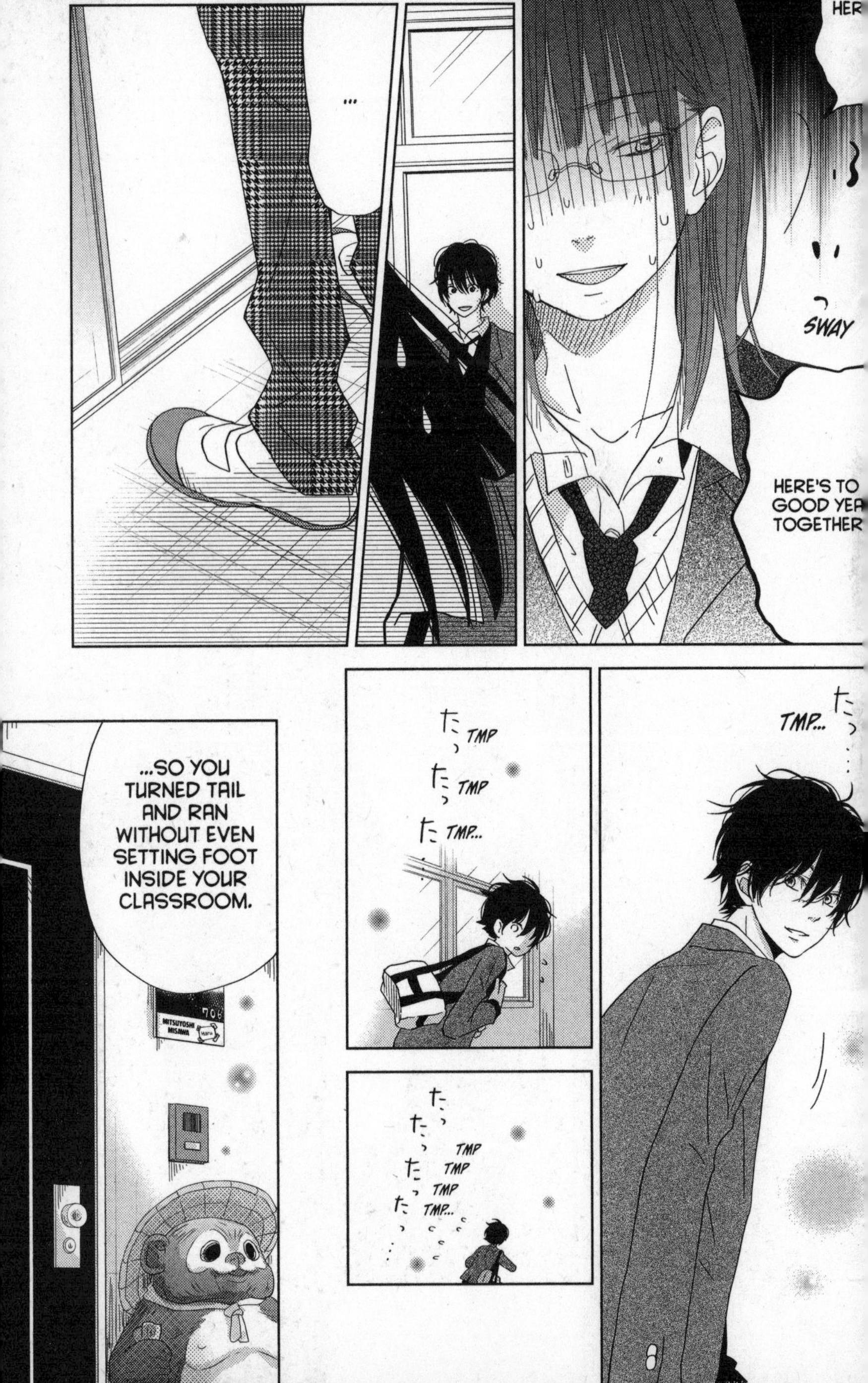
HER
SWAY
HERE'S TO
GOOD YEA
TOGETHER
...
TMP...
たっ TMP
たっ TMP
た TMP...
たっ TMP
たっ TMP
たっ TMP
たっ TMP...
...SO YOU TURNED TAIL AND RAN WITHOUT EVEN SETTING FOOT INSIDE YOUR CLASSROOM.
706
MITSUYOSHI MISAWA

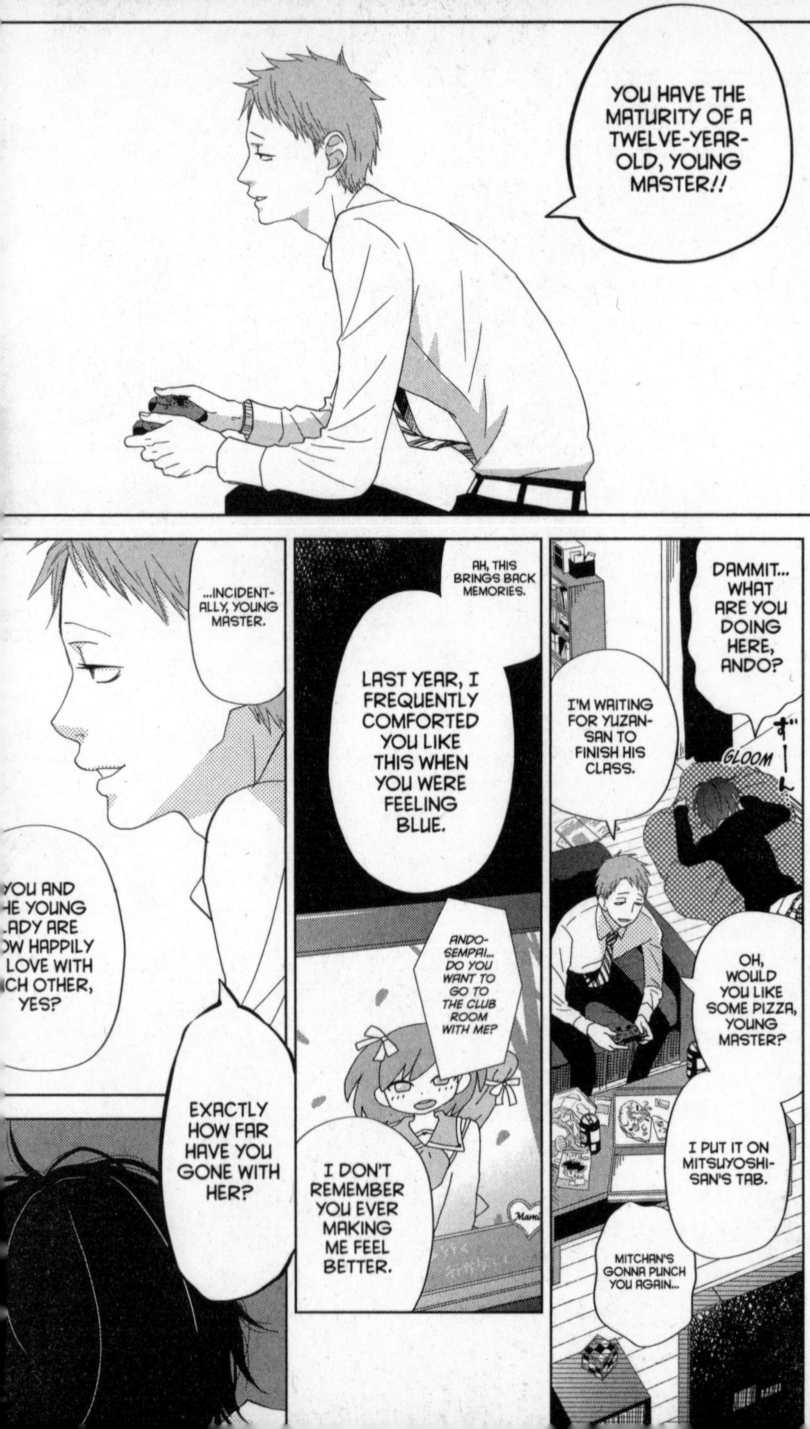

YOU HAVE THE MATURITY OF A TWELVE-YEAR-OLD, YOUNG MASTER!!
DAMMIT... WHAT ARE YOU DOING HERE, ANDO?
I'M WAITING FOR YUZAN-SAN TO FINISH HIS CLASS.
ずーん
GLOOM
OH, WOULD YOU LIKE SOME PIZZA, YOUNG MASTER?
I PUT IT ON MITSUYOSHI-SAN'S TAB.
MITCHAN'S GONNA PUNCH YOU AGAIN...
AH, THIS BRINGS BACK MEMORIES.
LAST YEAR, I FREQUENTLY COMFORTED YOU LIKE THIS WHEN YOU WERE FEELING BLUE.
ANDO-SEMPAI... DO YOU WANT TO GO TO THE CLUB ROOM WITH ME?
Mami
I DON'T REMEMBER YOU EVER MAKING ME FEEL BETTER.
...INCIDENT-ALLY, YOUNG MASTER.
YOU AND HE YOUNG ADY ARE OW HAPPILY LOVE WITH CH OTHER, YES?
EXACTLY HOW FAR HAVE YOU GONE WITH HER?

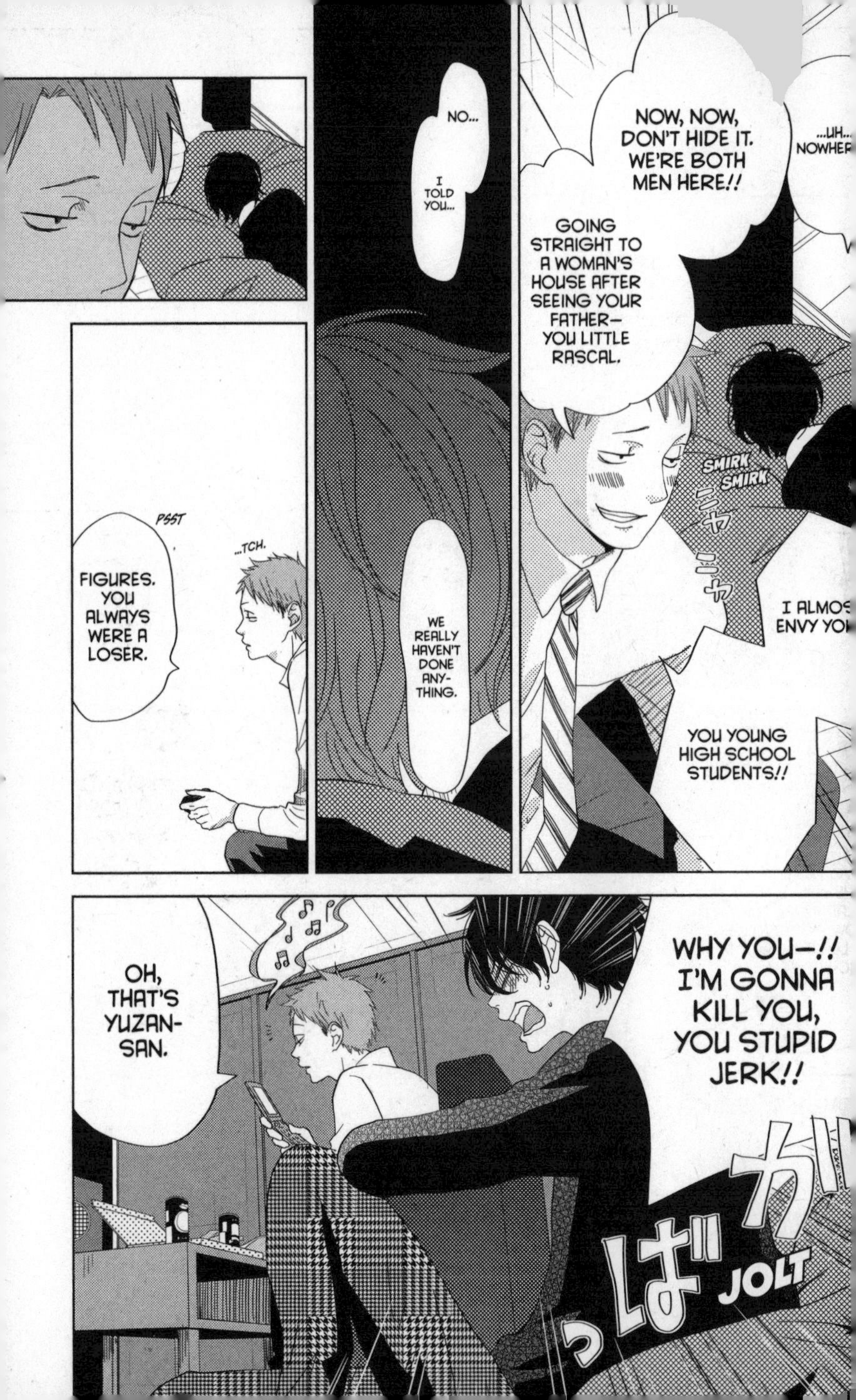
...UH... NOWHER
NOW, NOW, DON'T HIDE IT. WE'RE BOTH MEN HERE!!
GOING STRAIGHT TO A WOMAN'S HOUSE AFTER SEEING YOUR FATHER— YOU LITTLE RASCAL.
SMIRK SMIRK
I ALMOS ENVY YO
YOU YOUNG HIGH SCHOOL STUDENTS!!
NO...
I TOLD YOU...
WE REALLY HAVEN'T DONE ANYTHING.
PSST
...TCH.
FIGURES. YOU ALWAYS WERE A LOSER.
WHY YOU—!! I'M GONNA KILL YOU, YOU STUPID JERK!!
JOLT
OH, THAT'S YUZAN-SAN.

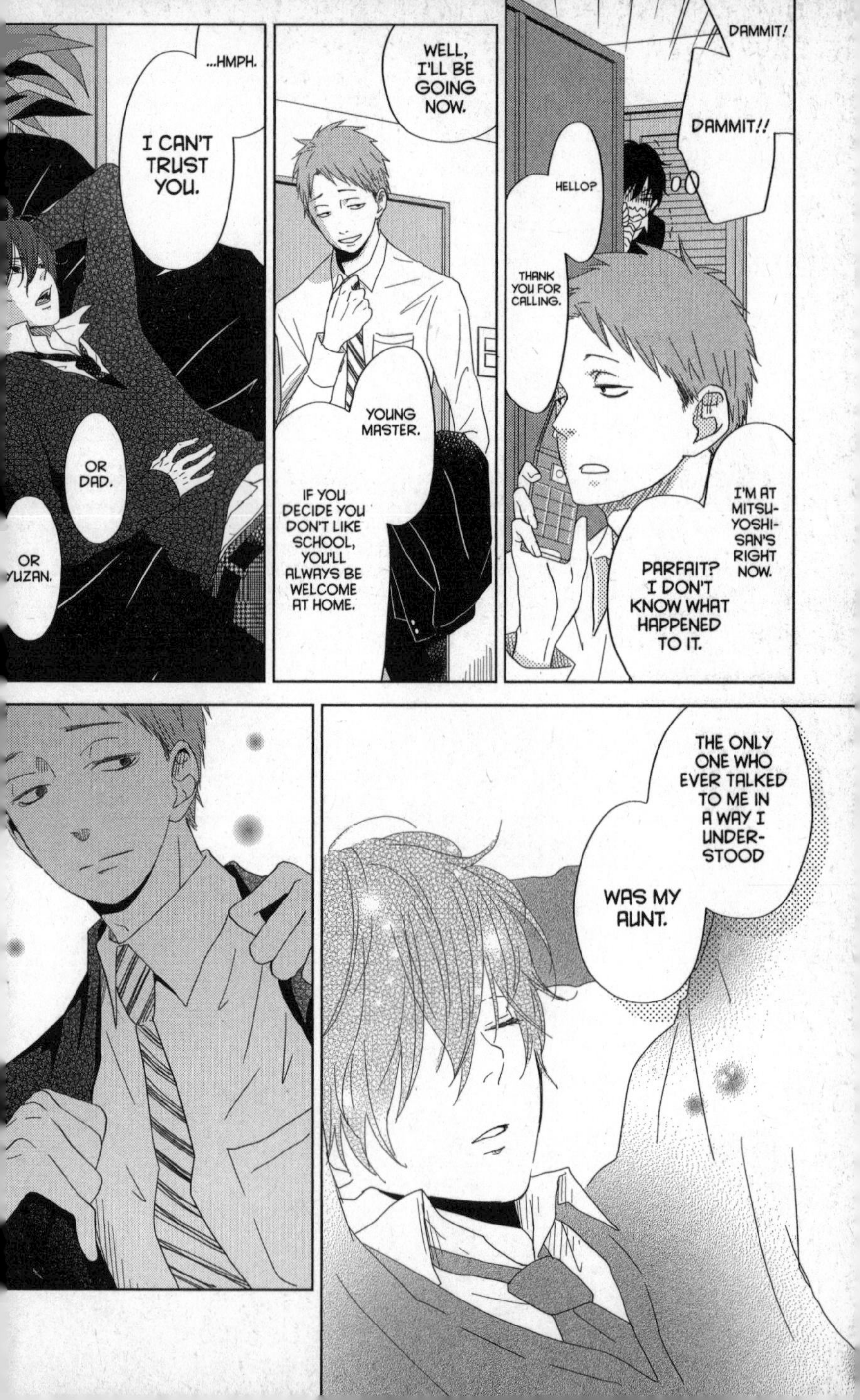
DAMMIT!
DAMMIT!!
HELLO?
THANK YOU FOR CALLING.
I'M AT MITSU-YOSHI-SAN'S RIGHT NOW.
PARFAIT? I DON'T KNOW WHAT HAPPENED TO IT.
WELL, I'LL BE GOING NOW.
YOUNG MASTER.
IF YOU DECIDE YOU DON'T LIKE SCHOOL, YOU'LL ALWAYS BE WELCOME AT HOME.
...HMPH.
I CAN'T TRUST YOU.
OR DAD.
OR YUZAN.
THE ONLY ONE WHO EVER TALKED TO ME IN A WAY I UNDER-STOOD
WAS MY AUNT.

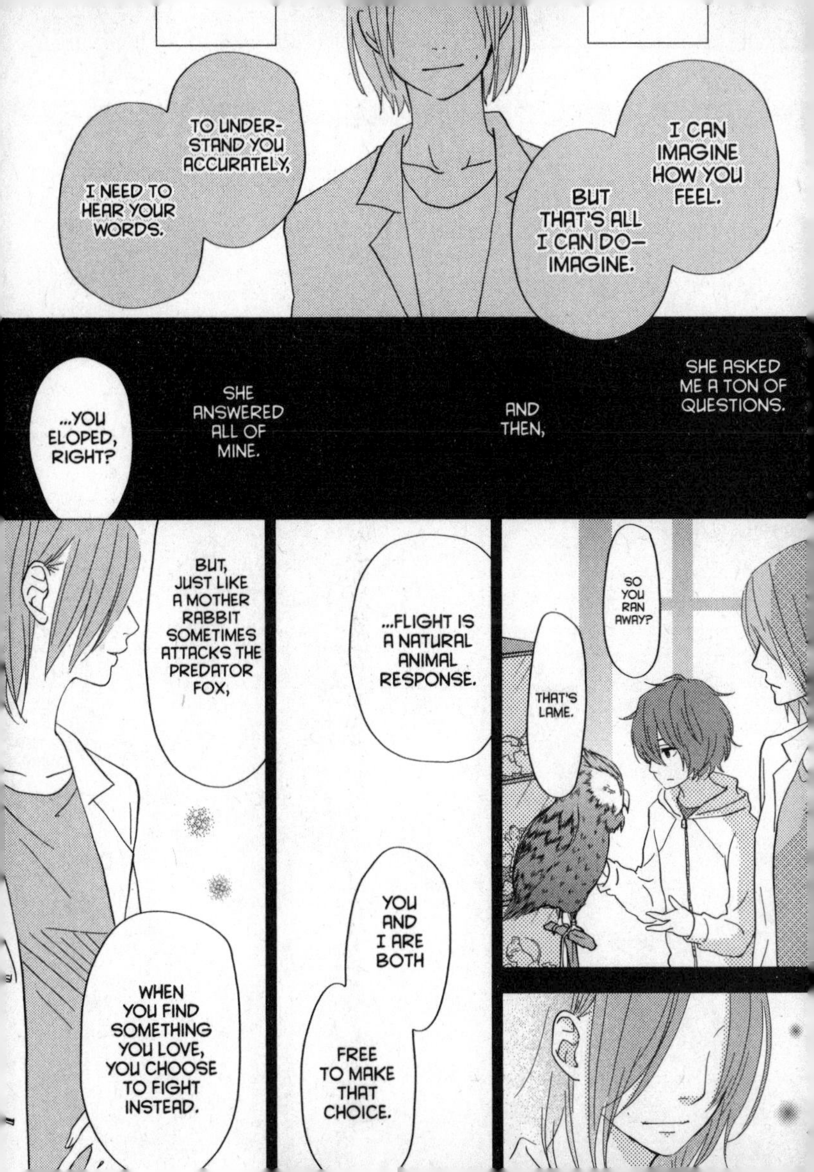
I CAN IMAGINE HOW YOU FEEL.
BUT THAT'S ALL I CAN DO— IMAGINE.
TO UNDER-STAND YOU ACCURATELY,
I NEED TO HEAR YOUR WORDS.
SHE ASKED ME A TON OF QUESTIONS.
AND THEN,
SHE ANSWERED ALL OF MINE.
...YOU ELOPED, RIGHT?
SO YOU RAN AWAY?
THAT'S LAME.
...FLIGHT IS A NATURAL ANIMAL RESPONSE.
YOU AND I ARE BOTH
FREE TO MAKE THAT CHOICE.
BUT, JUST LIKE A MOTHER RABBIT SOMETIMES ATTACKS THE PREDATOR FOX,
WHEN YOU FIND SOMETHING YOU LOVE, YOU CHOOSE TO FIGHT INSTEAD.

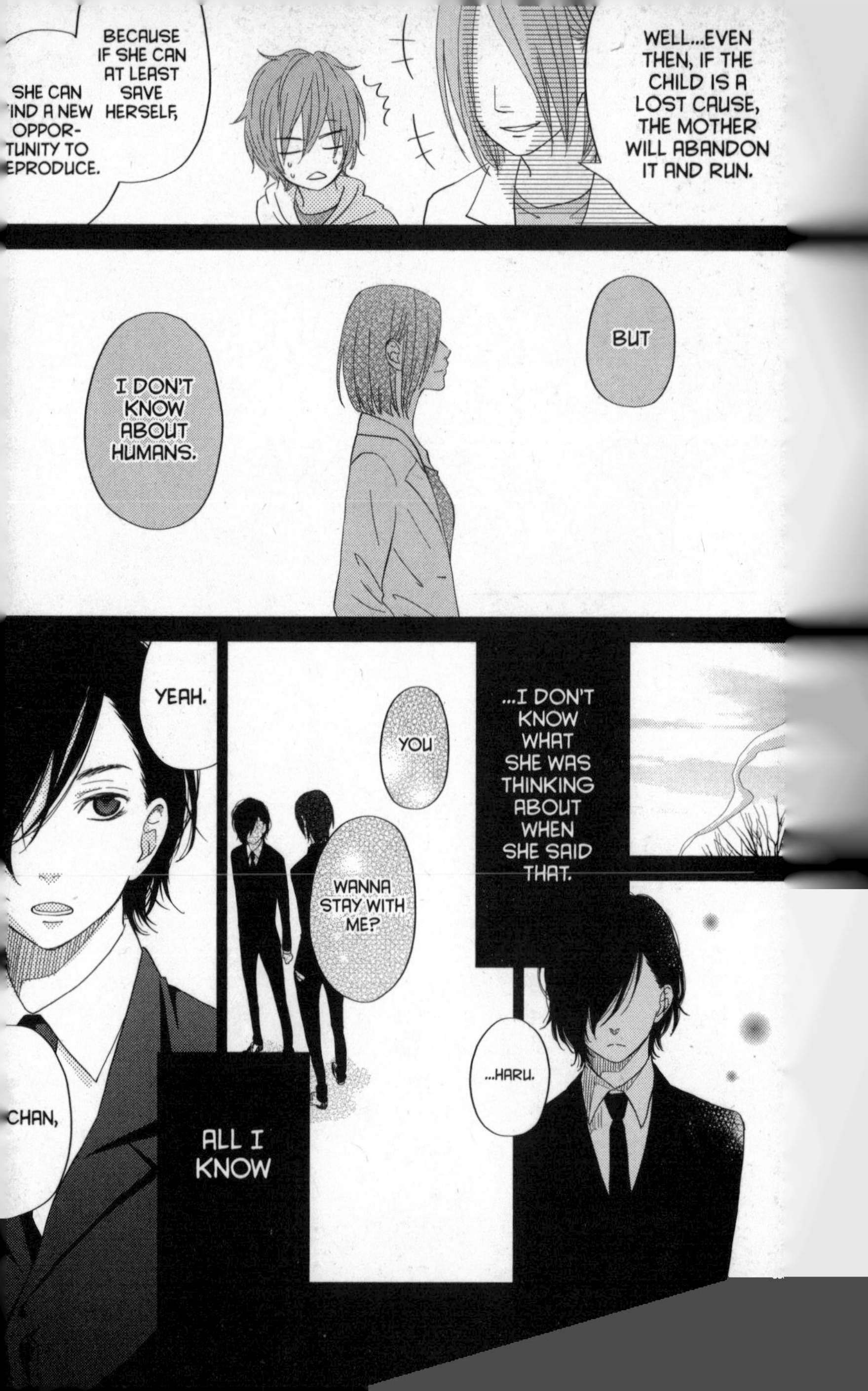
WELL...EVEN THEN, IF THE CHILD IS A LOST CAUSE, THE MOTHER WILL ABANDON IT AND RUN.
BECAUSE IF SHE CAN AT LEAST SAVE HERSELF,
SHE CAN IND A NEW OPPOR-TUNITY TO EPRODUCE.
BUT
I DON'T KNOW ABOUT HUMANS.
...I DON'T KNOW WHAT SHE WAS THINKING ABOUT WHEN SHE SAID THAT.
...HARU.
YOU
WANNA STAY WITH ME?
YEAH.
CHAN,
ALL I KNOW

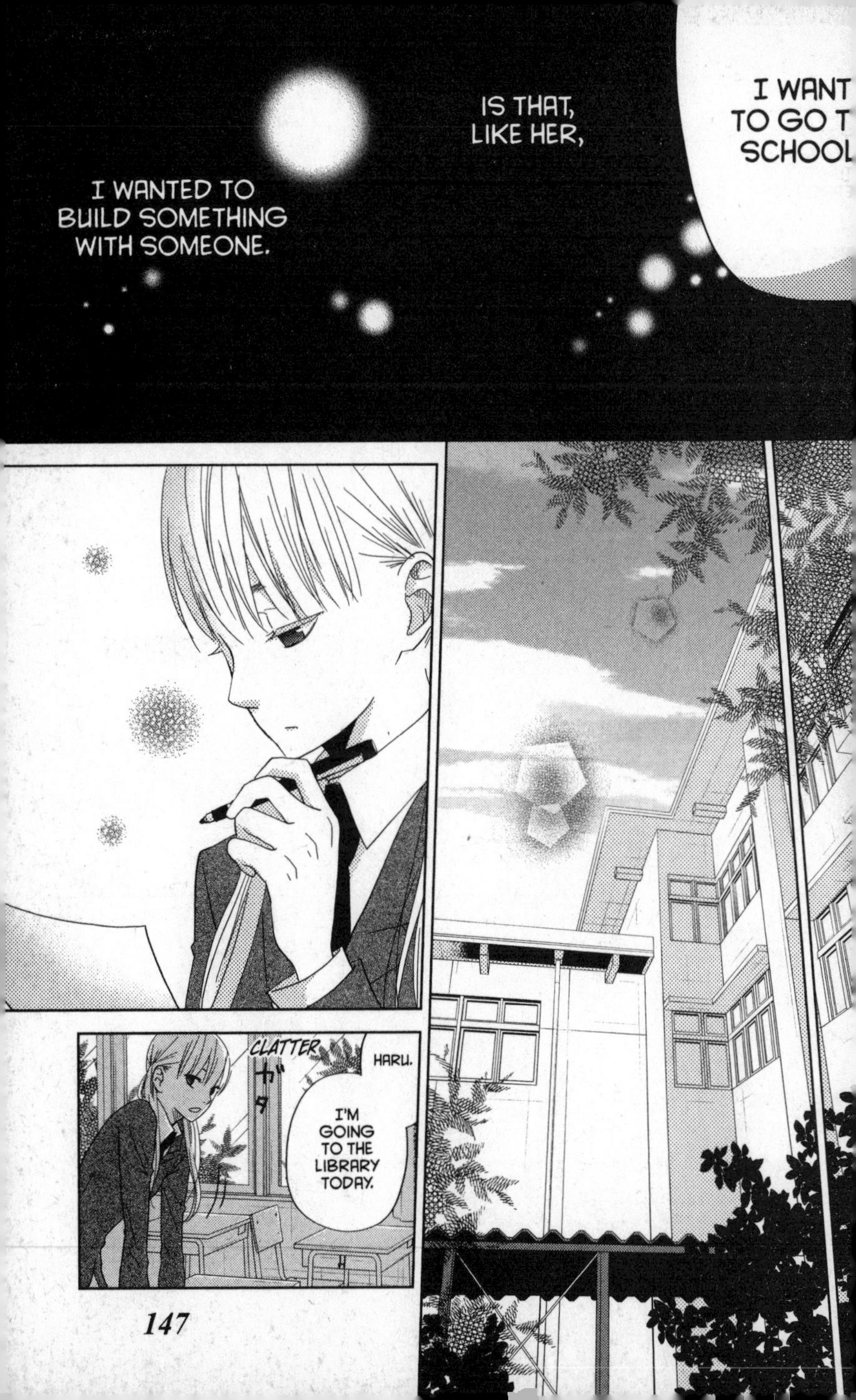
I WANT TO GO T SCHOOL
IS THAT, LIKE HER,
I WANTED TO BUILD SOMETHING WITH SOMEONE.
CLATTER
ガタ
HARU.
I'M GOING TO THE LIBRARY TODAY.

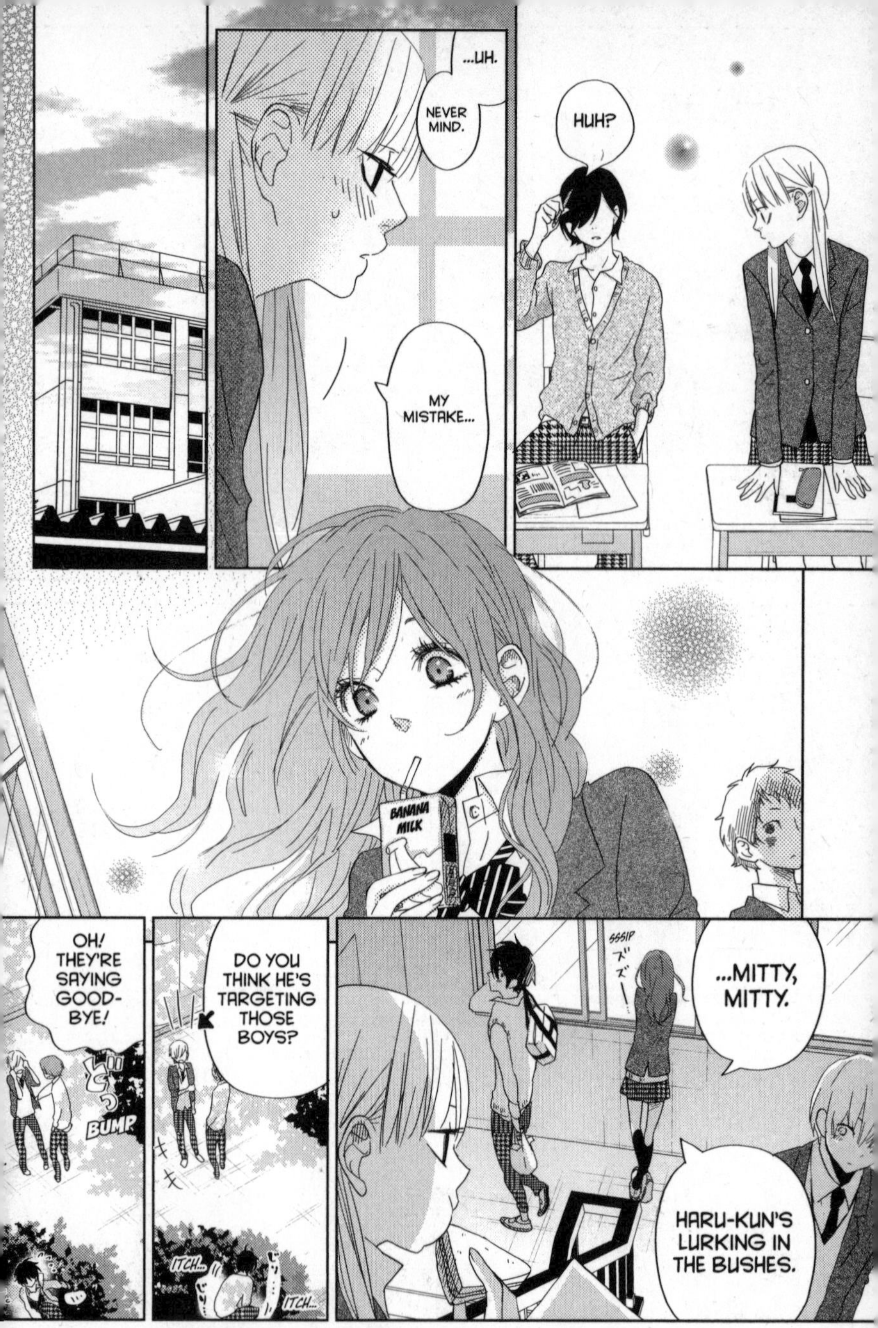
HUH?
...UH.
NEVER MIND.
MY MISTAKE...
...MITTY, MITTY.
SSSIP
HARU-KUN'S LURKING IN THE BUSHES.
DO YOU THINK HE'S TARGETING THOSE BOYS?
ITCH...
ITCH...
OH! THEY'RE SAYING GOOD-BYE!
BUMP

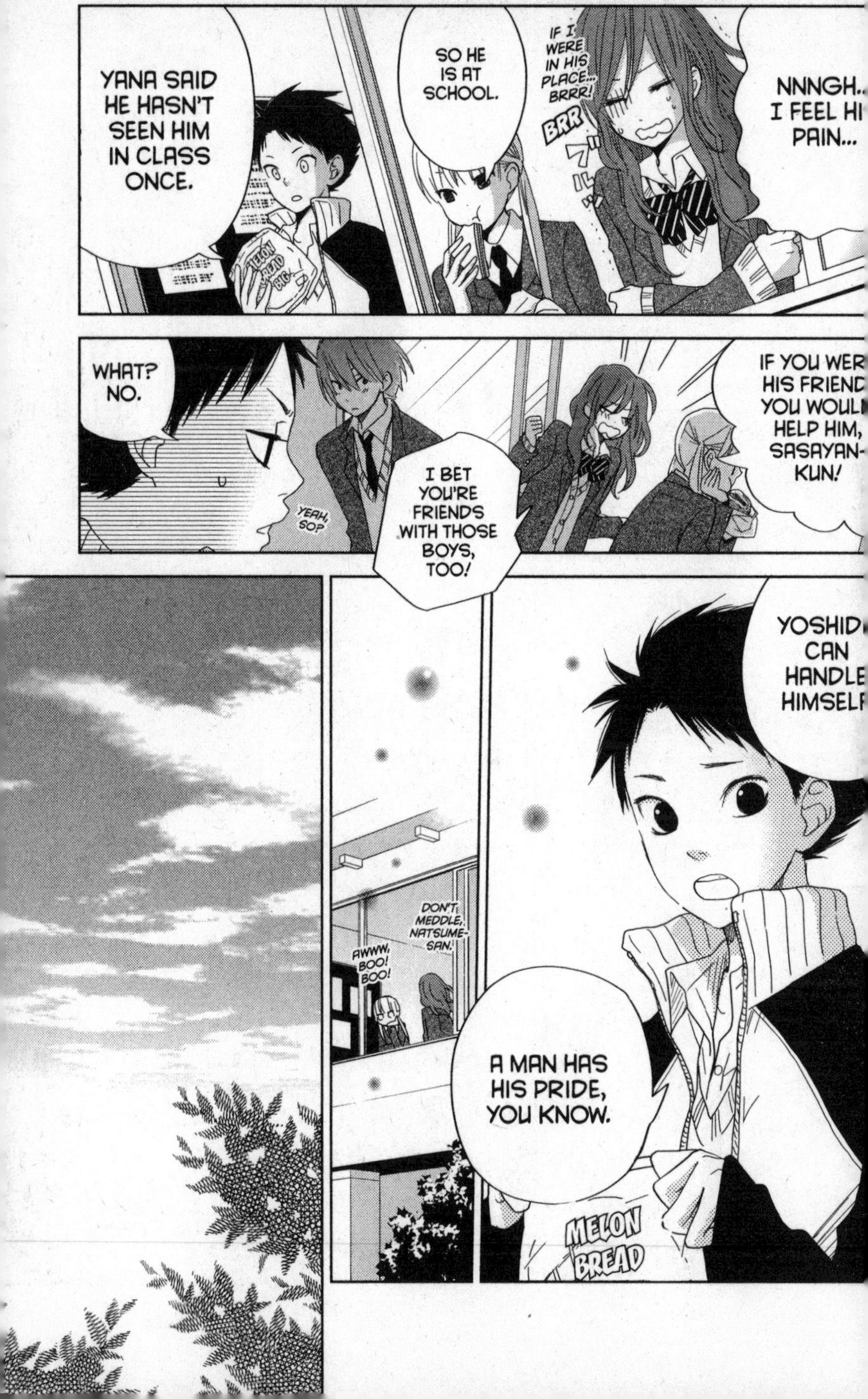
NNNGH.. I FEEL HI PAIN...
IF I WERE IN HIS PLACE... BRRR!
BRR
SO HE IS AT SCHOOL.
YANA SAID HE HASN'T SEEN HIM IN CLASS ONCE.
MELON BREAD BIG
IF YOU WER HIS FRIEND YOU WOUL HELP HIM, SASAYAN-KUN!
I BET YOU'RE FRIENDS WITH THOSE BOYS, TOO!
YEAH, SO?
WHAT? NO.
YOSHID CAN HANDLE HIMSELF
A MAN HAS HIS PRIDE, YOU KNOW.
MELON BREAD
DON'T MEDDLE, NATSUME-SAN.
AWWW, BOO! BOO!

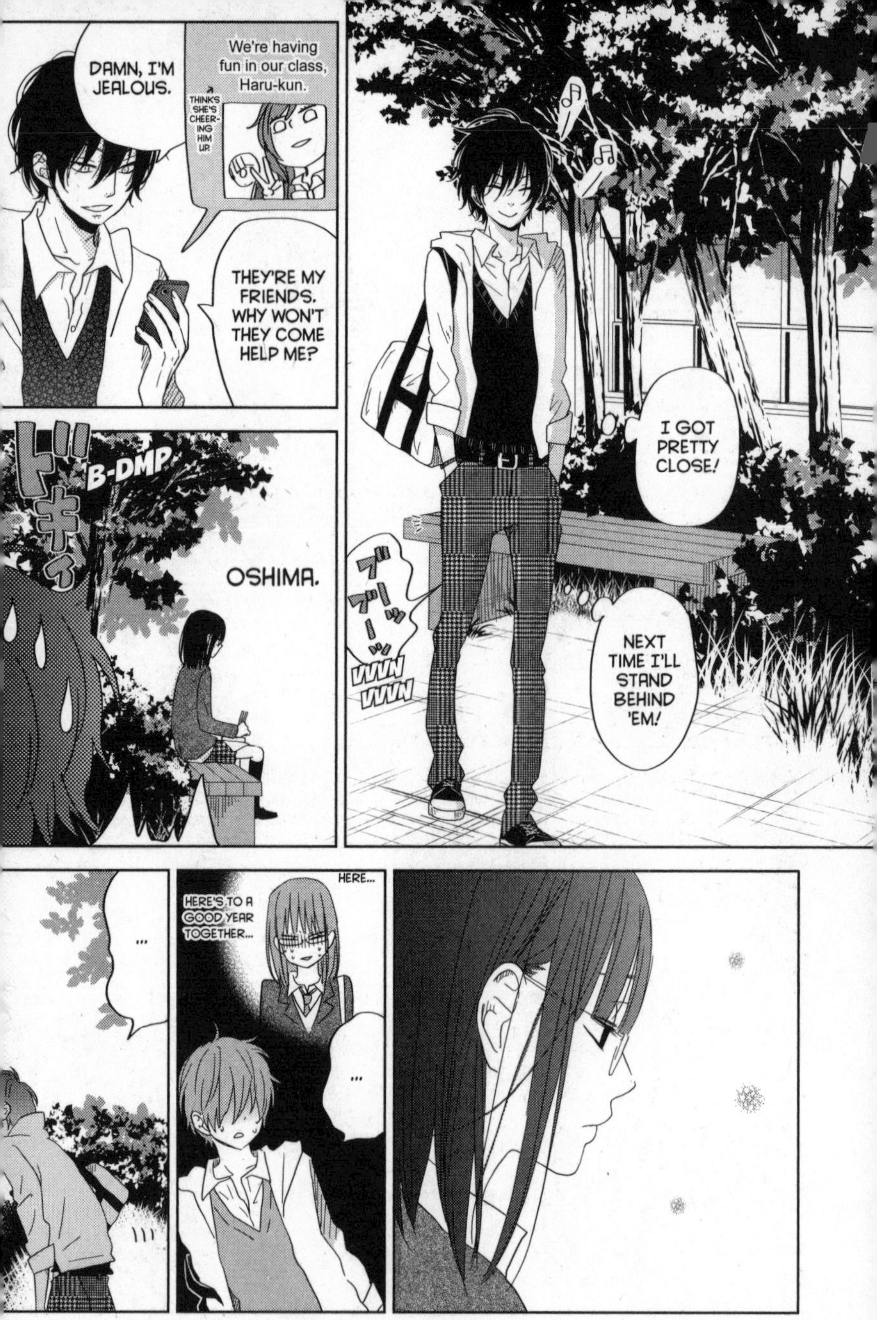
I GOT PRETTY CLOSE!
VVVN VVVN
NEXT TIME I'LL STAND BEHIND 'EM!
We're having fun in our class, Haru-kun.
THINKS SHE'S CHEERING HIM UP
DAMN, I'M JEALOUS.
THEY'RE MY FRIENDS. WHY WON'T THEY COME HELP ME?
B-DMP
OSHIMA.
HERE...
HERE'S TO A GOOD YEAR TOGETHER...
...
...

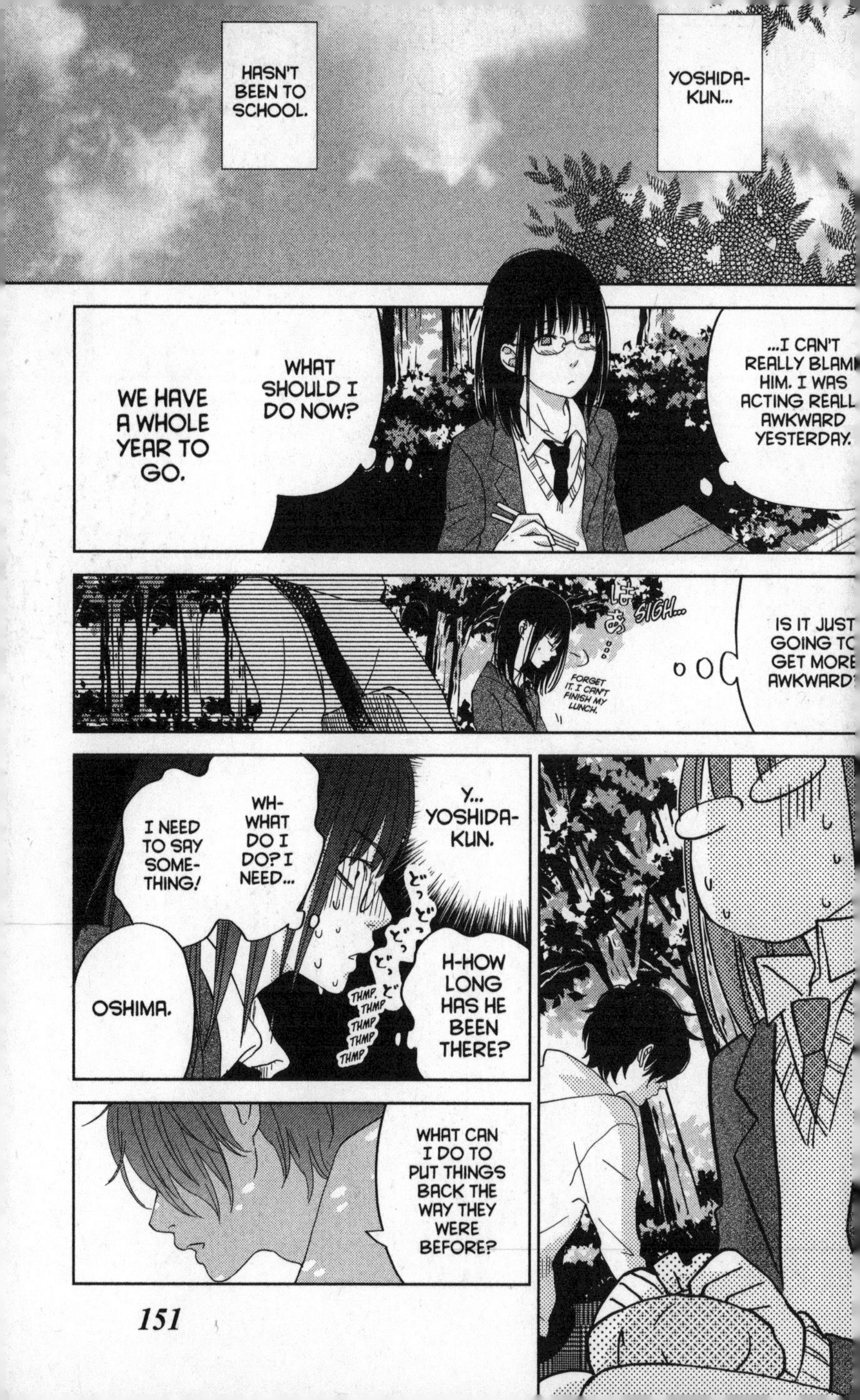
YOSHIDA-KUN...
HASN'T BEEN TO SCHOOL.
...I CAN'T REALLY BLAM HIM. I WAS ACTING REALL AWKWARD YESTERDAY.
WHAT SHOULD I DO NOW?
WE HAVE A WHOLE YEAR TO GO.
IS IT JUST GOING TO GET MORE AWKWARD
SIGH...
FORGET IT. I CAN'T FINISH MY LUNCH.
Y... YOSHIDA-KUN.
WH- WHAT DO I DO? I NEED...
I NEED TO SAY SOME-THING!
H-HOW LONG HAS HE BEEN THERE?
THMP THMP THMP THMP THMP
OSHIMA.
WHAT CAN I DO TO PUT THINGS BACK THE WAY THEY WERE BEFORE?

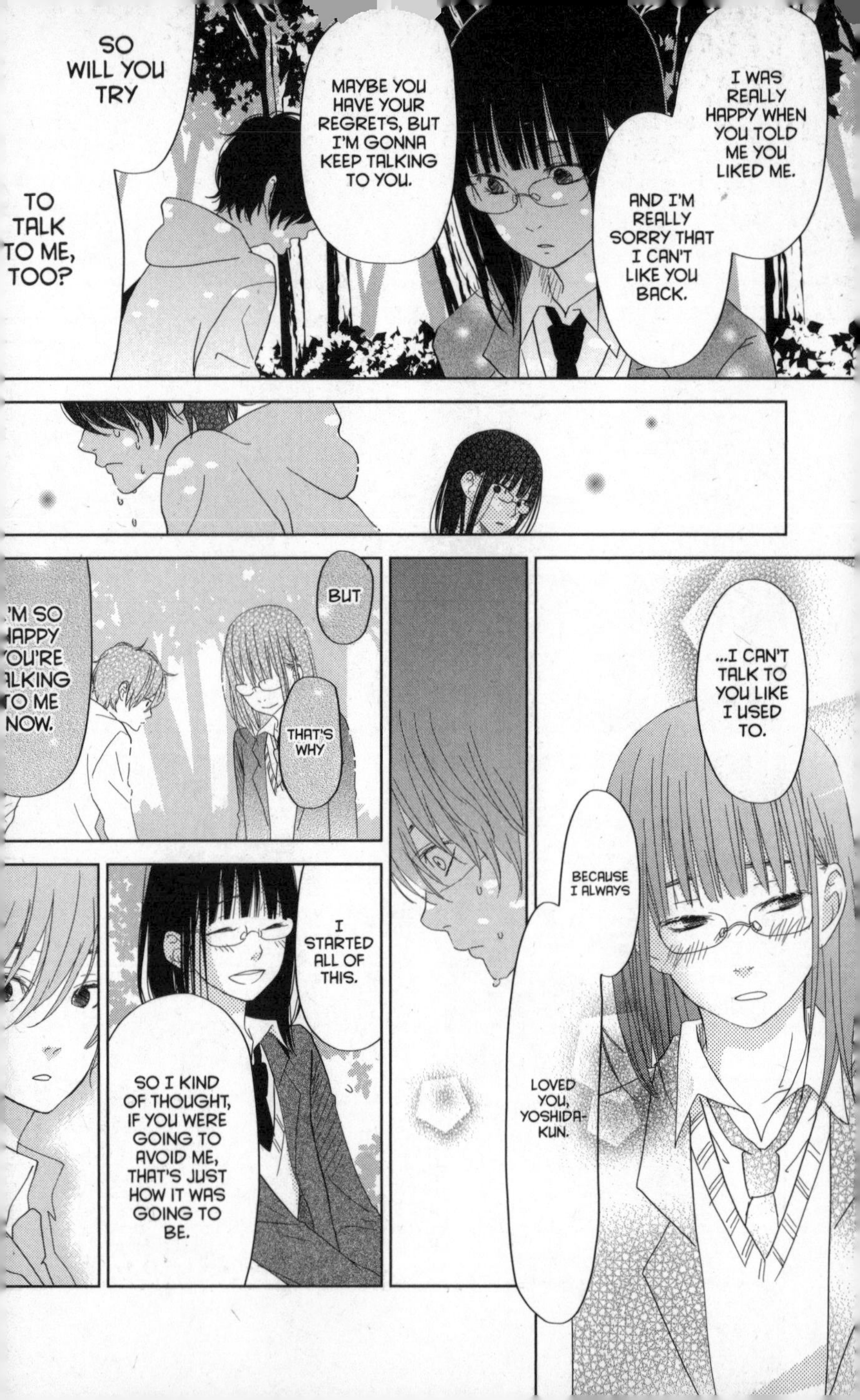
I WAS REALLY HAPPY WHEN YOU TOLD ME YOU LIKED ME.
AND I'M REALLY SORRY THAT I CAN'T LIKE YOU BACK.
MAYBE YOU HAVE YOUR REGRETS, BUT I'M GONNA KEEP TALKING TO YOU.
SO WILL YOU TRY
TO TALK TO ME, TOO?
...I CAN'T TALK TO YOU LIKE I USED TO.
BECAUSE I ALWAYS
LOVED YOU, YOSHIDA-KUN.
BUT
THAT'S WHY
'M SO HAPPY YOU'RE ALKING TO ME NOW.
I STARTED ALL OF THIS.
SO I KIND OF THOUGHT, IF YOU WERE GOING TO AVOID ME, THAT'S JUST HOW IT WAS GOING TO BE.

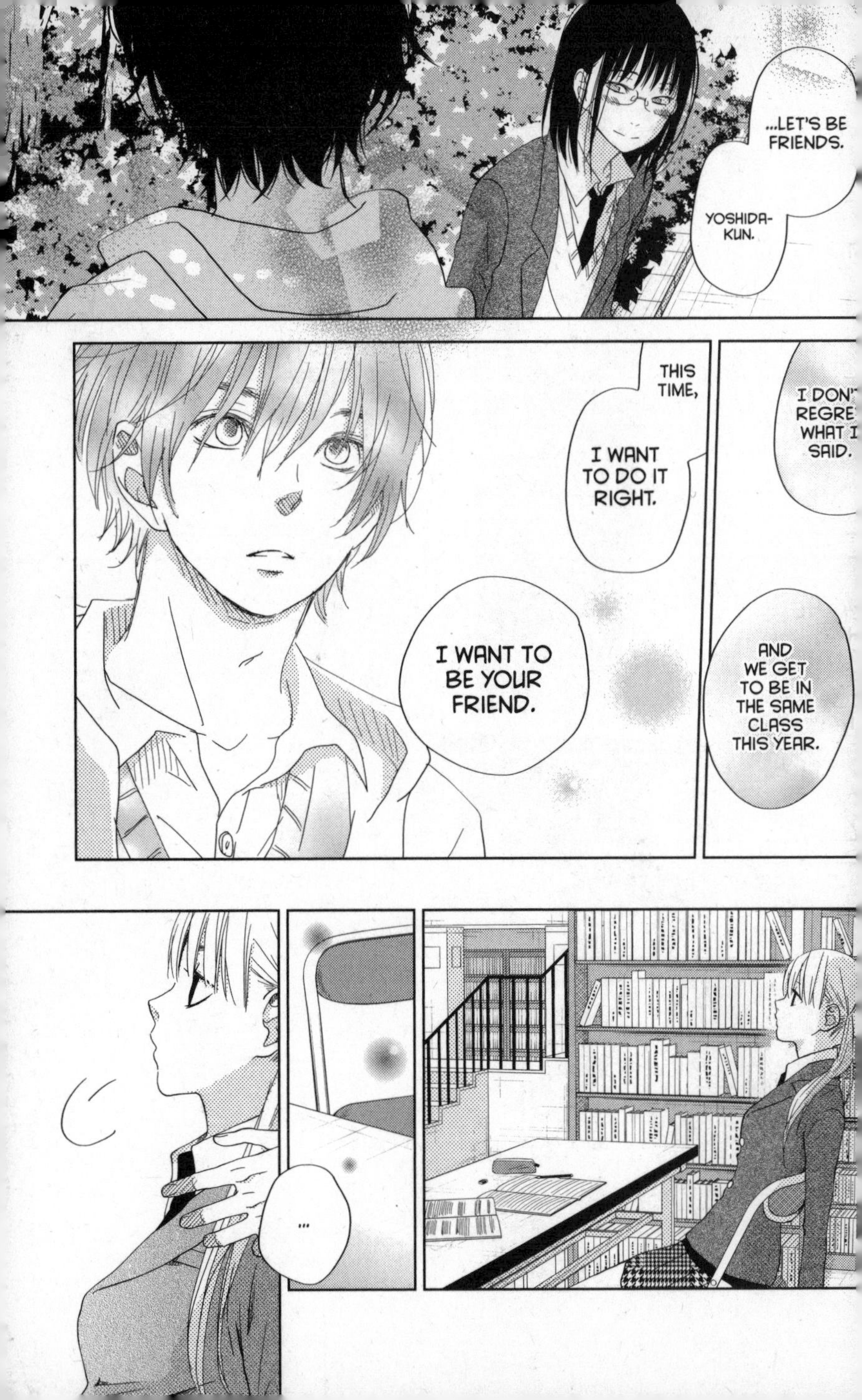
...LET'S BE FRIENDS.
YOSHIDA-KUN.
I DON' REGRE WHAT I SAID.
AND WE GET TO BE IN THE SAME CLASS THIS YEAR.
THIS TIME,
I WANT TO DO IT RIGHT.
I WANT TO BE YOUR FRIEND.
...

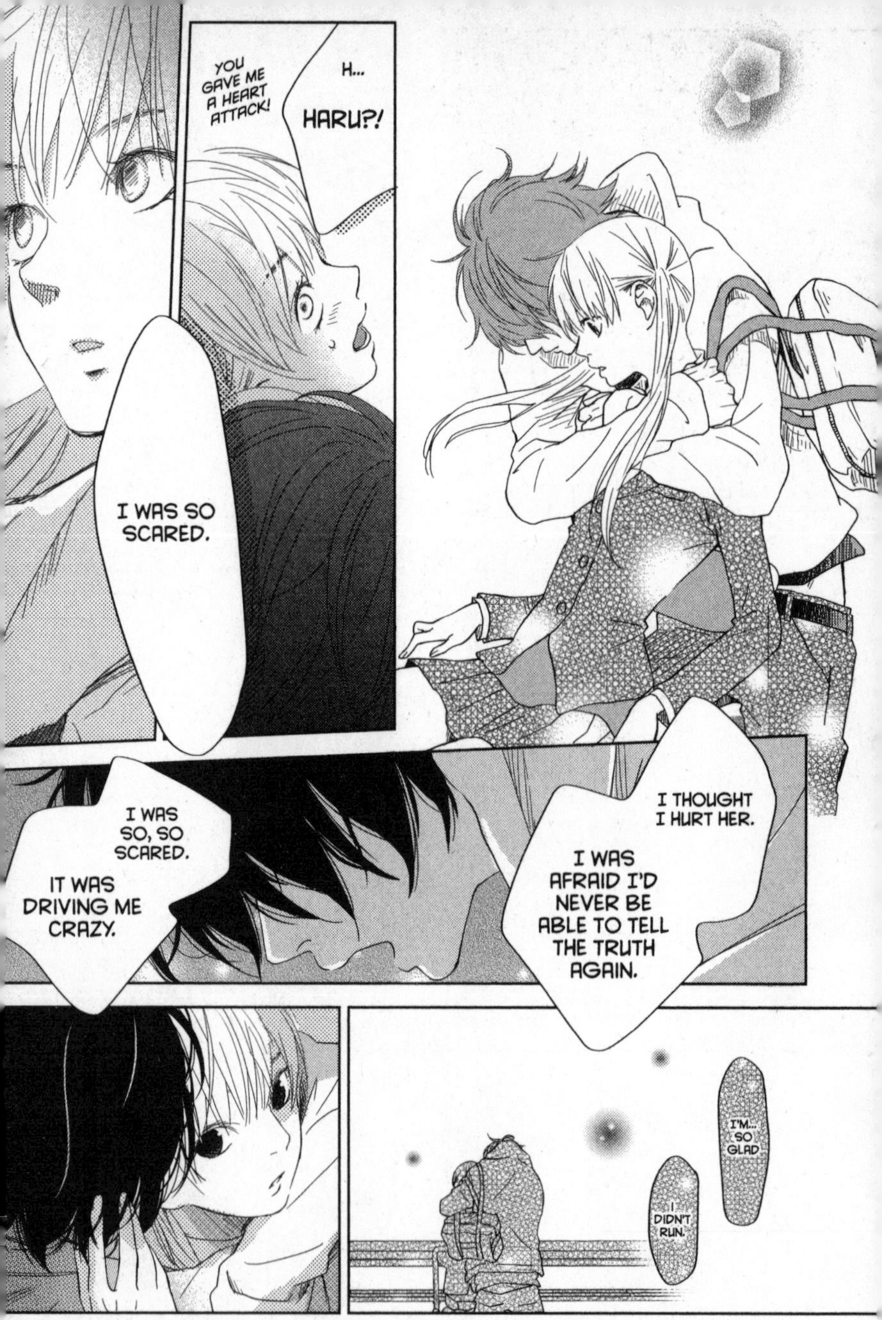
H...
HARU?!
YOU GAVE ME A HEART ATTACK!
I WAS SO SCARED.
I THOUGHT I HURT HER.
I WAS AFRAID I'D NEVER BE ABLE TO TELL THE TRUTH AGAIN.
I WAS SO, SO SCARED.
IT WAS DRIVING ME CRAZY.
I'M... SO GLAD.
I DIDN'T RUN.

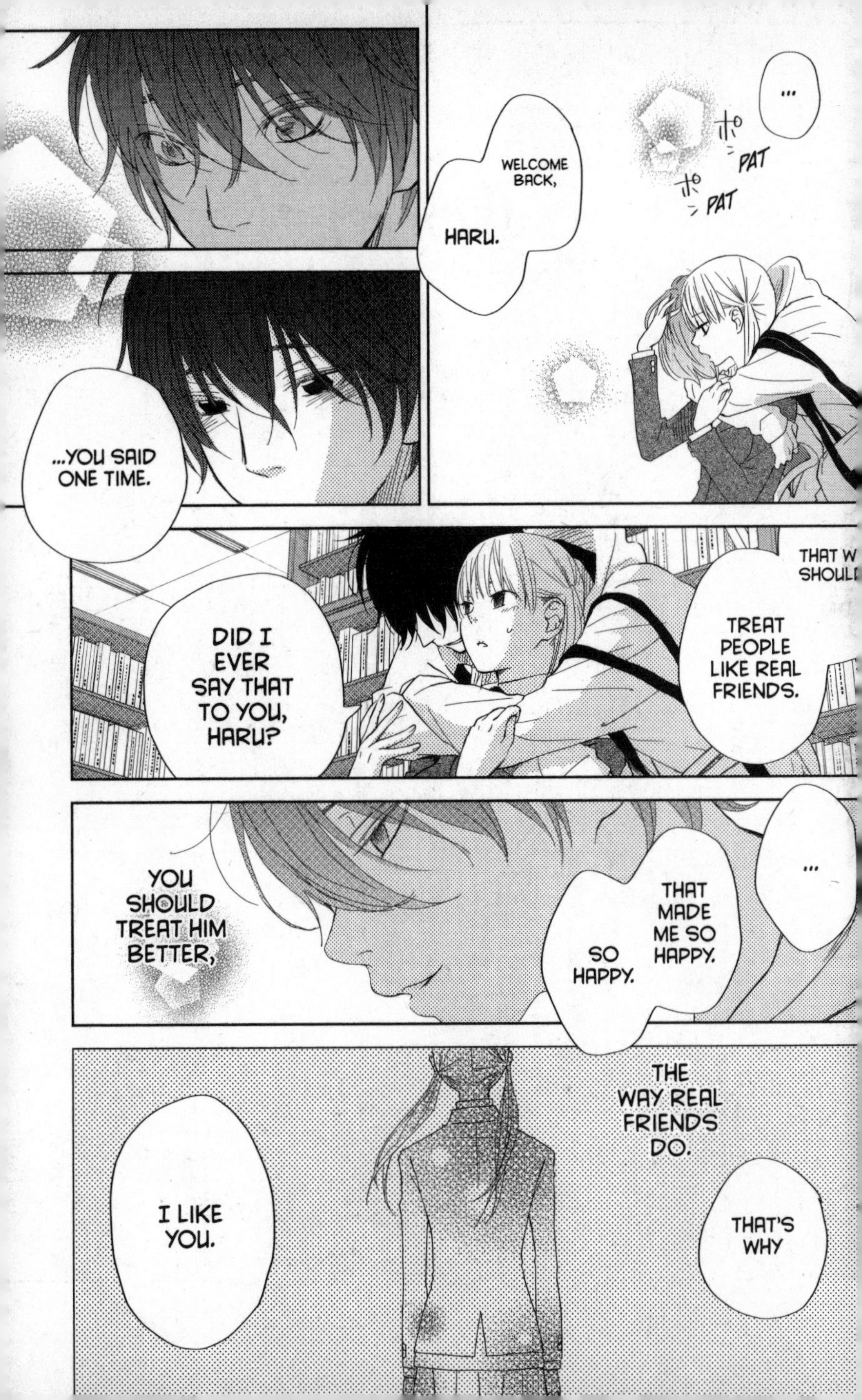
...
ポ PAT
ポ PAT
WELCOME BACK, HARU.
...YOU SAID ONE TIME.
THAT W SHOUL
TREAT PEOPLE LIKE REAL FRIENDS.
DID I EVER SAY THAT TO YOU, HARU?
...
THAT MADE ME SO HAPPY. SO HAPPY.
YOU SHOULD TREAT HIM BETTER,
THE WAY REAL FRIENDS DO.
THAT'S WHY
I LIKE YOU.

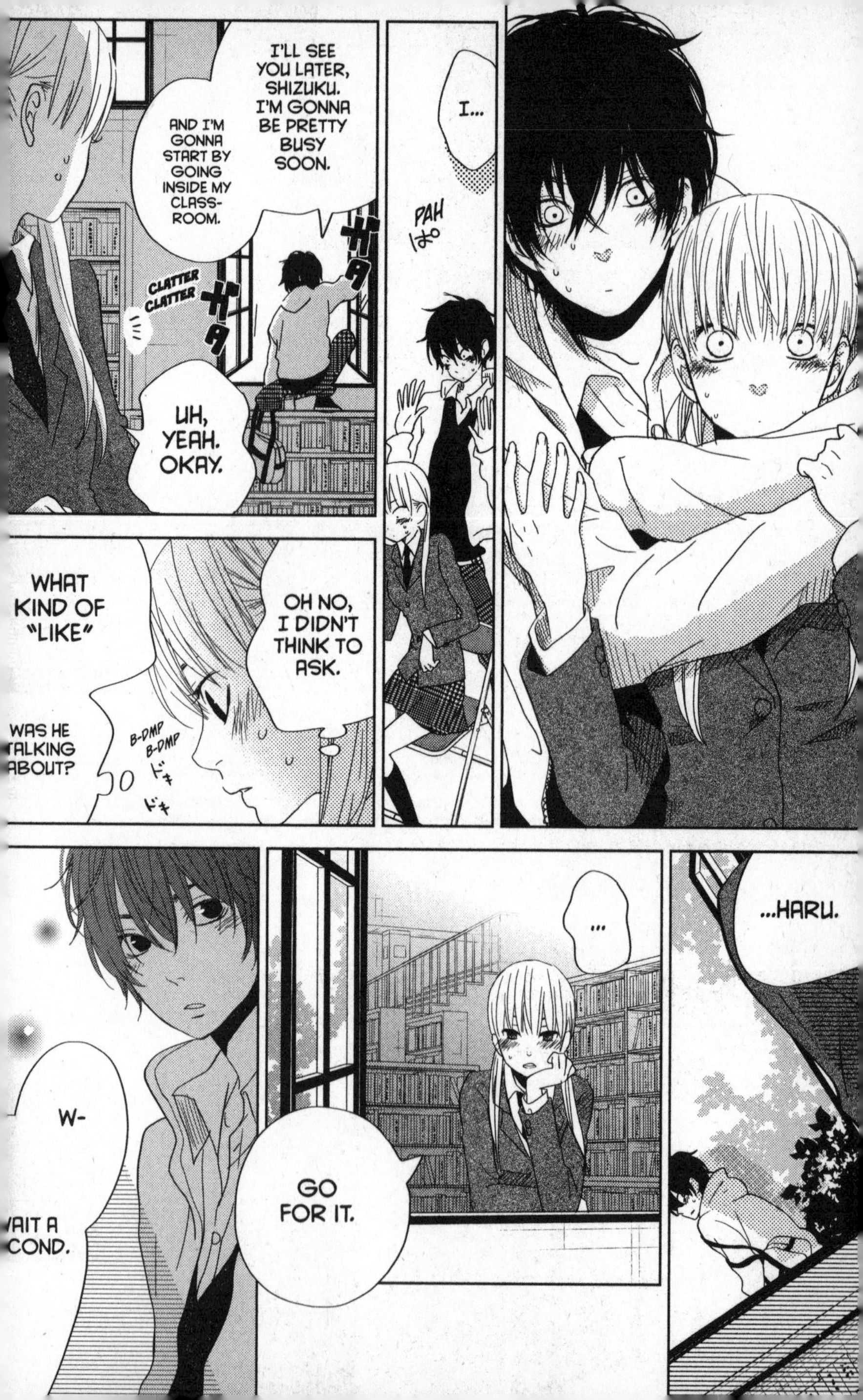
I...
PAH ぱっ
I'LL SEE YOU LATER, SHIZUKU. I'M GONNA BE PRETTY BUSY SOON.
AND I'M GONNA START BY GOING INSIDE MY CLASSROOM.
ガタ ガタ
CLATTER CLATTER
UH, YEAH. OKAY.
OH NO, I DIDN'T THINK TO ASK.
WHAT KIND OF "LIKE"
WAS HE TALKING ABOUT?
B-DMP B-DMP ドキ ドキ
...HARU.
...
GO FOR IT.
W-
VAIT A COND.

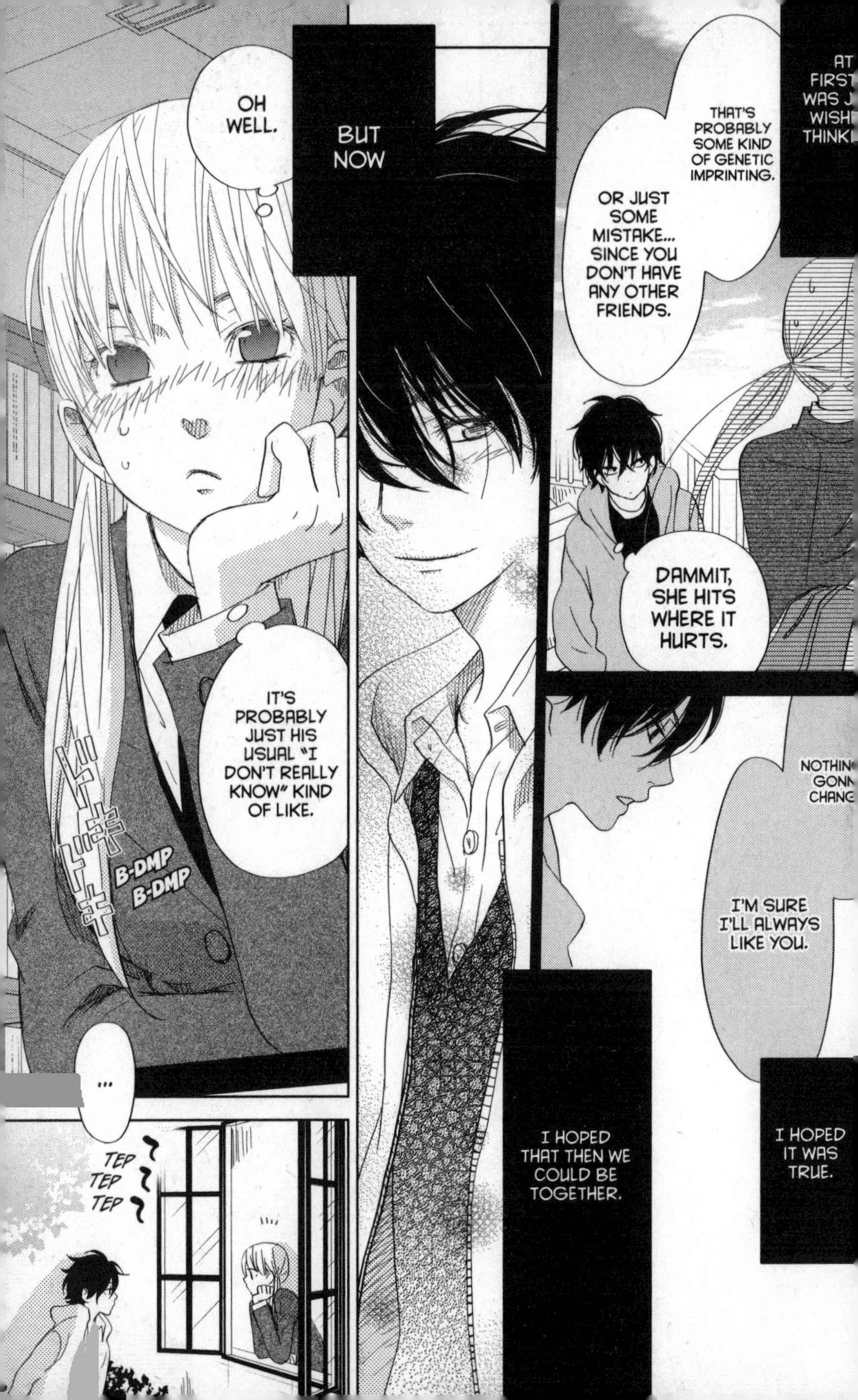
AT FIRST
THAT'S PROBABLY SOME KIND OF GENETIC IMPRINTING.
OR JUST SOME MISTAKE... SINCE YOU DON'T HAVE ANY OTHER FRIENDS.
DAMMIT, SHE HITS WHERE IT HURTS.
I'M SURE I'LL ALWAYS LIKE YOU.
I HOPED IT WAS TRUE.
I HOPED THAT THEN WE COULD BE TOGETHER.
BUT NOW
OH WELL.
IT'S PROBABLY JUST HIS USUAL "I DON'T REALLY KNOW" KIND OF LIKE.
B-DMP B-DMP
...
TEP TEP TEP

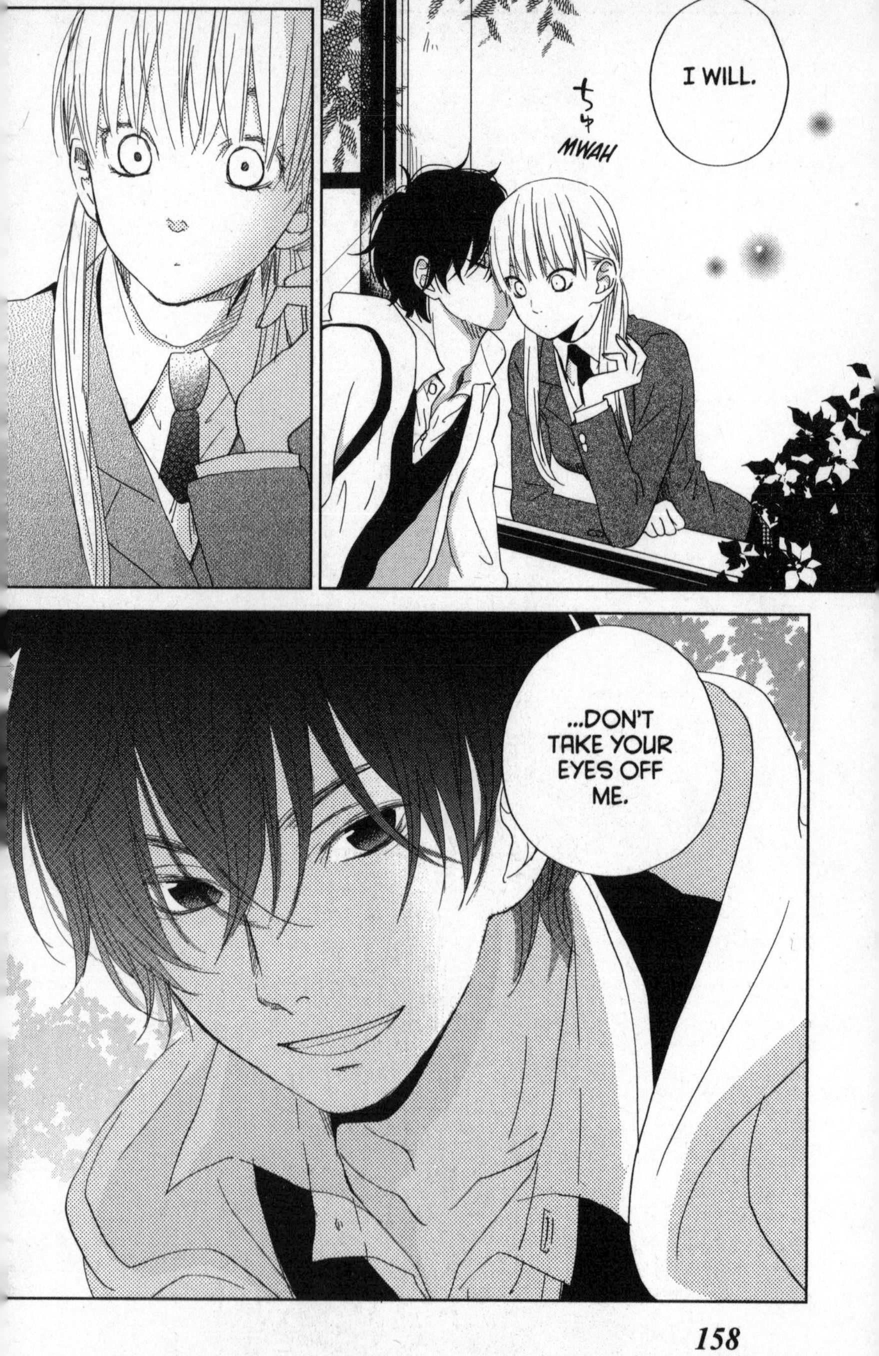
I WILL.
ちゅ
MWAH
...DON'T TAKE YOUR EYES OFF ME.

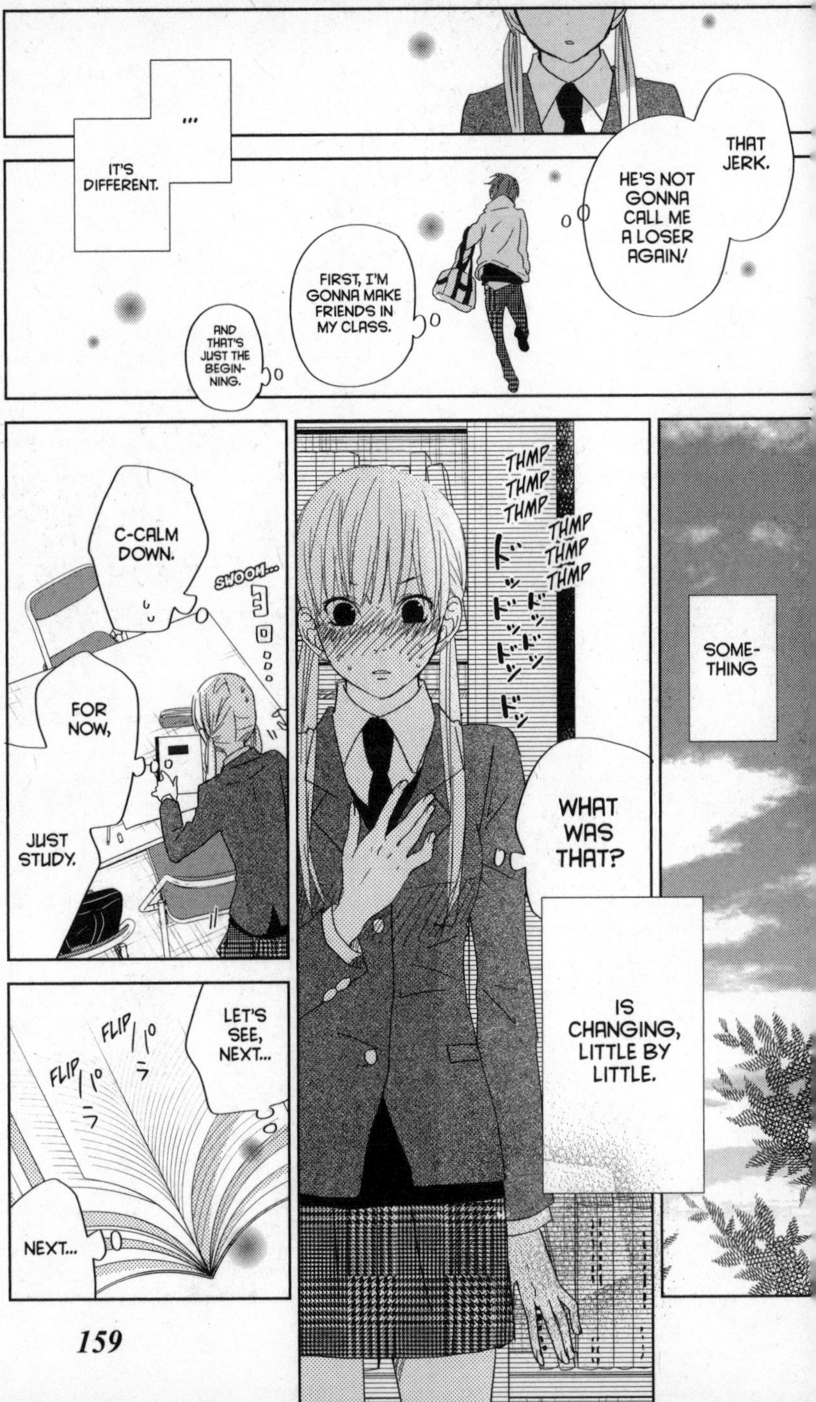
...
IT'S DIFFERENT.
THAT JERK.
HE'S NOT GONNA CALL ME A LOSER AGAIN!
FIRST, I'M GONNA MAKE FRIENDS IN MY CLASS.
AND THAT'S JUST THE BEGIN-NING.
SOME-THING
THMP THMP THMP
THMP THMP THMP
WHAT WAS THAT?
IS CHANGING, LITTLE BY LITTLE.
C-CALM DOWN.
SWOOM...
FOR NOW,
JUST STUDY.
LET'S SEE, NEXT...
FLIP
FLIP
NEXT...

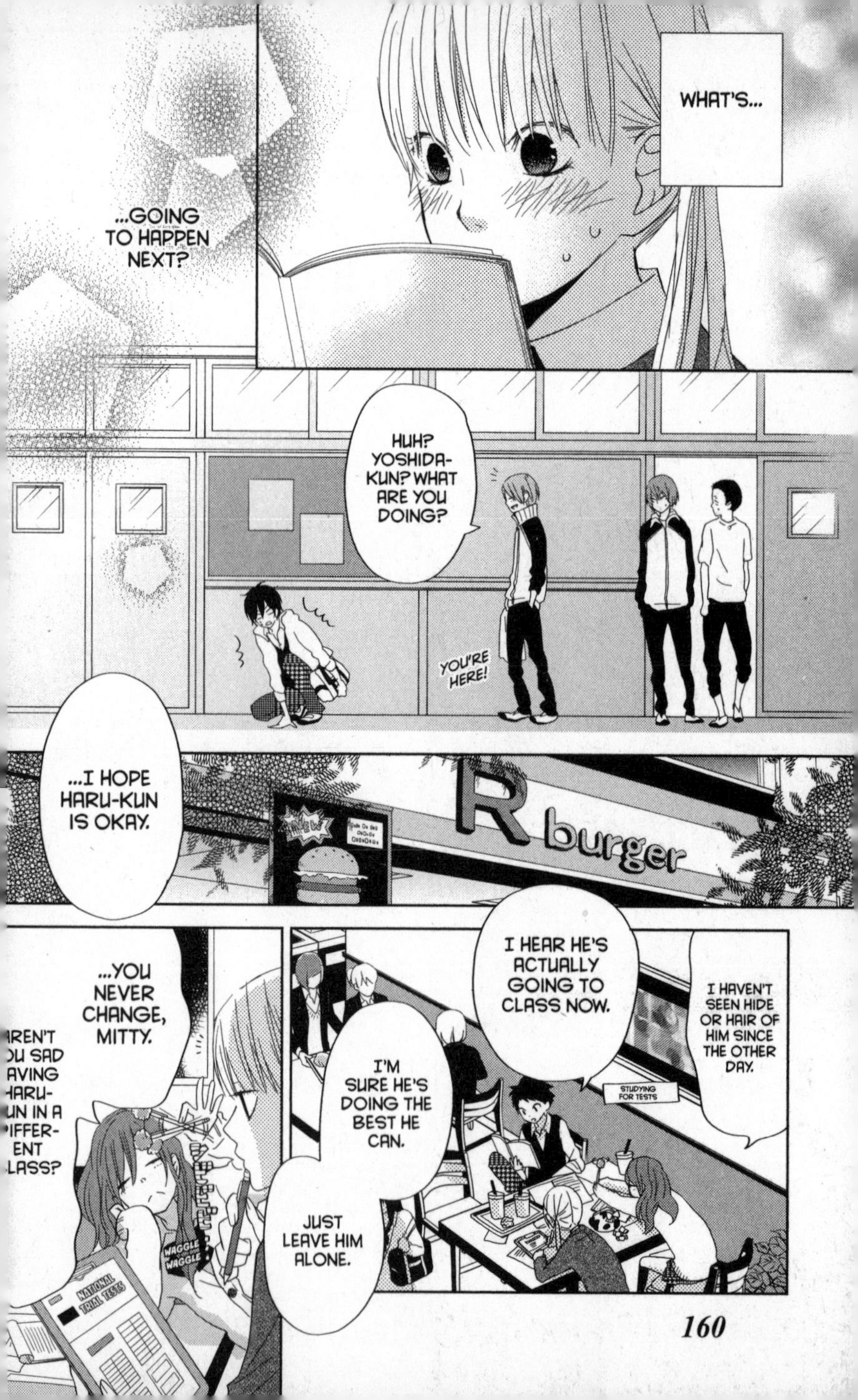
WHAT'S...
...GOING TO HAPPEN NEXT?
HUH? YOSHIDA-KUN? WHAT ARE YOU DOING?
YOU'RE HERE!
R burger
...I HOPE HARU-KUN IS OKAY.
I HAVEN'T SEEN HIDE OR HAIR OF HIM SINCE THE OTHER DAY.
I HEAR HE'S ACTUALLY GOING TO CLASS NOW.
STUDYING FOR TESTS
I'M SURE HE'S DOING THE BEST HE CAN.
JUST LEAVE HIM ALONE.
...YOU NEVER CHANGE, MITTY.
AREN'T OU SAD AVING HARU-UN IN A IFFER-ENT LASS?
WAGGLE WAGGLE
NATIONAL TRIAL TESTS

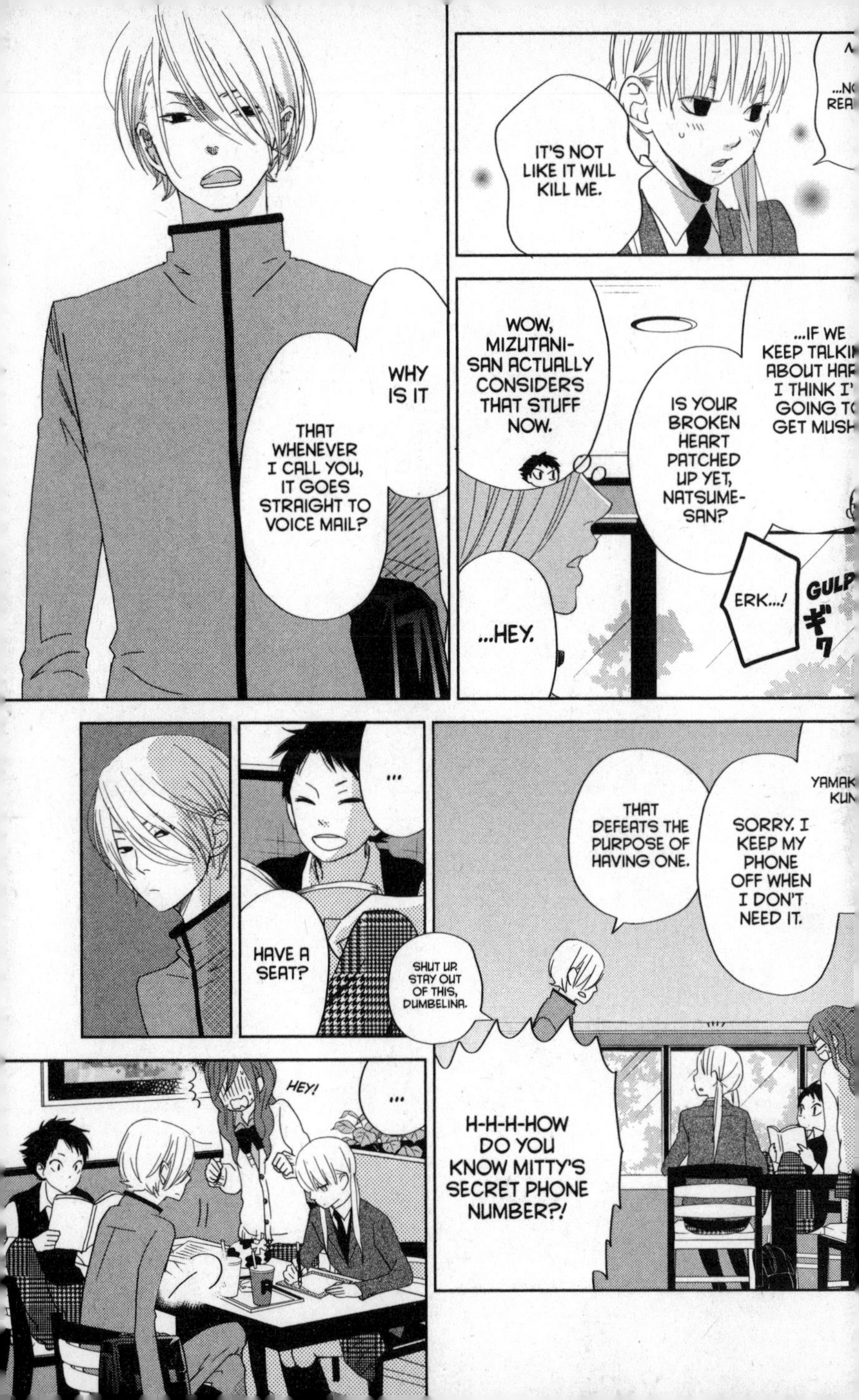

...N
REA
IT'S NOT LIKE IT WILL KILL ME.
...IF WE KEEP TALKI ABOUT HAR I THINK I' GOING T GET MUSH
IS YOUR BROKEN HEART PATCHED UP YET, NATSUME-SAN?
WOW, MIZUTANI-SAN ACTUALLY CONSIDERS THAT STUFF NOW.
ERK...!
GULP
ギク
...HEY.
WHY IS IT
THAT WHENEVER I CALL YOU, IT GOES STRAIGHT TO VOICE MAIL?
YAMAK KUN
SORRY. I KEEP MY PHONE OFF WHEN I DON'T NEED IT.
THAT DEFEATS THE PURPOSE OF HAVING ONE.
H-H-H-HOW DO YOU KNOW MITTY'S SECRET PHONE NUMBER?!
...
HAVE A SEAT?
SHUT UP. STAY OUT OF THIS, DUMBELINA.
...
HEY!

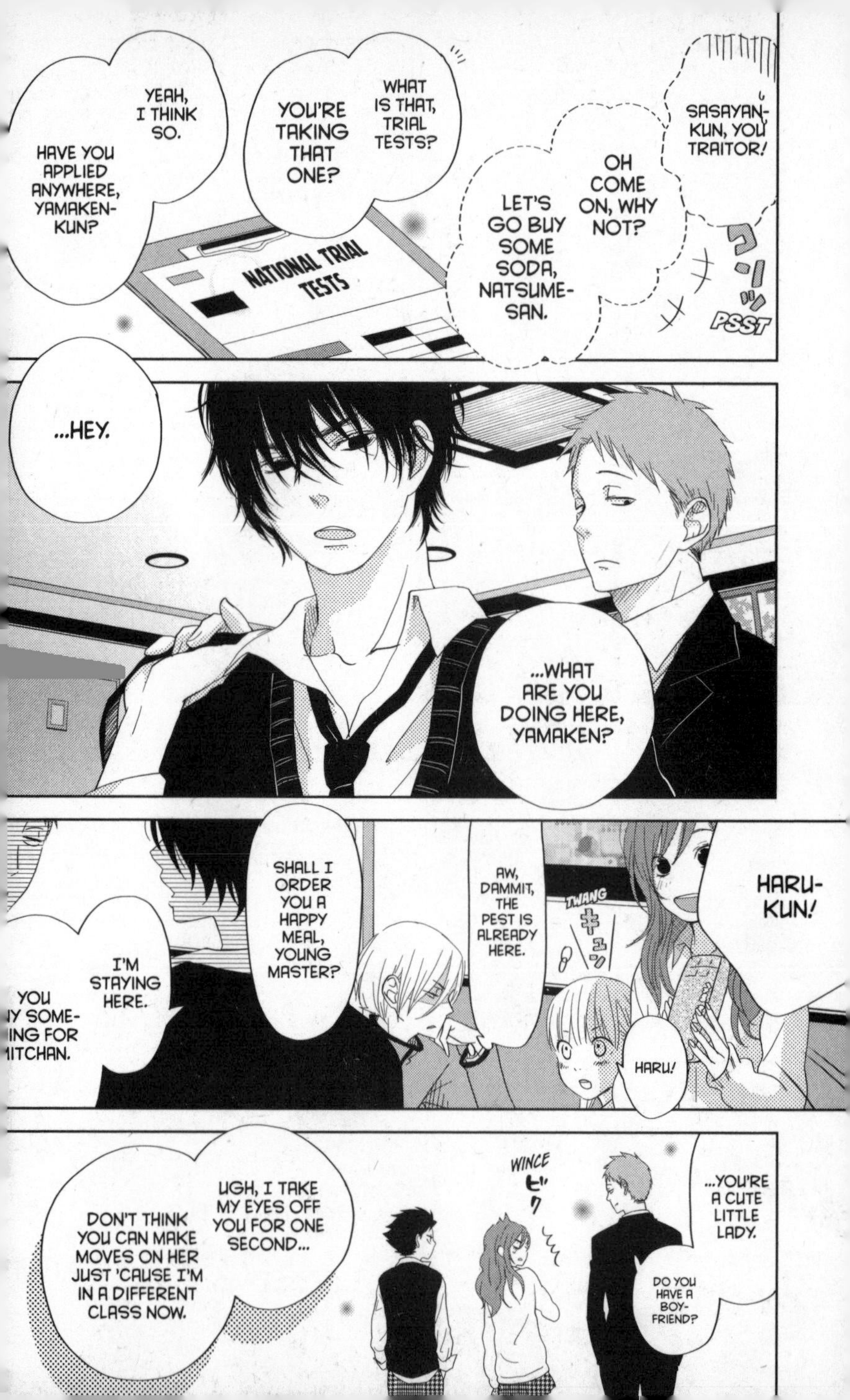
SASAYAN-KUN, YOU TRAITOR!
PSST
OH COME ON, WHY NOT?
LET'S GO BUY SOME SODA, NATSUME-SAN.
WHAT IS THAT, TRIAL TESTS?
YOU'RE TAKING THAT ONE?
NATIONAL TRIAL TESTS
YEAH, I THINK SO.
HAVE YOU APPLIED ANYWHERE, YAMAKEN-KUN?
...WHAT ARE YOU DOING HERE, YAMAKEN?
...HEY.
HARU-KUN!
TWANG
HARU!
AW, DAMMIT, THE PEST IS ALREADY HERE.
SHALL I ORDER YOU A HAPPY MEAL, YOUNG MASTER?
I'M STAYING HERE.
YOU
Y SOME-
ING FOR
MITCHAN.
...YOU'RE A CUTE LITTLE LADY.
DO YOU HAVE A BOY-FRIEND?
WINCE
UGH, I TAKE MY EYES OFF YOU FOR ONE SECOND...
DON'T THINK YOU CAN MAKE MOVES ON HER JUST 'CAUSE I'M IN A DIFFERENT CLASS NOW.

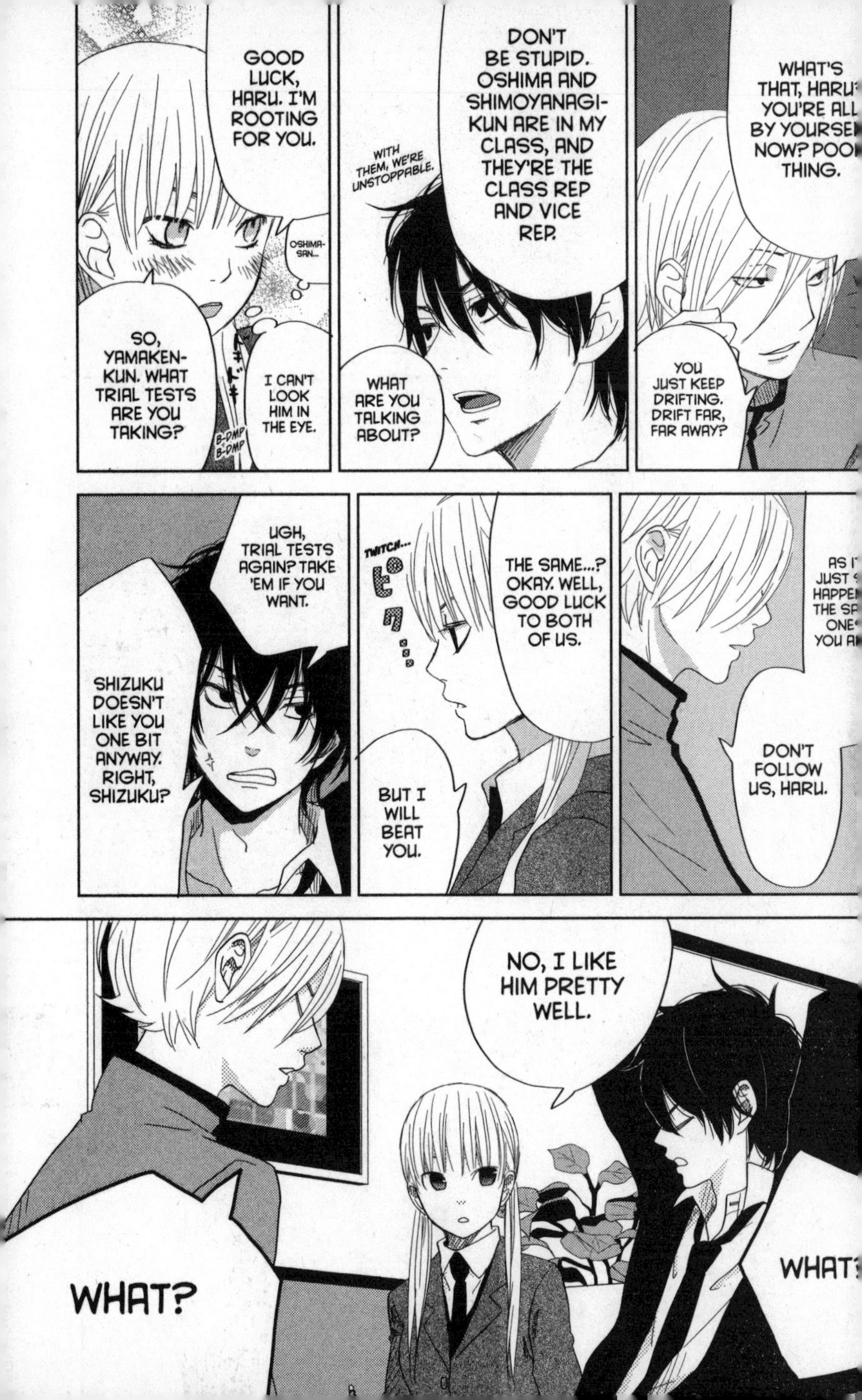
WHAT'S THAT, HARU YOU'RE ALL BY YOURSE NOW? POO THING.
YOU JUST KEEP DRIFTING. DRIFT FAR, FAR AWAY?
DON'T BE STUPID. OSHIMA AND SHIMOYANAGI-KUN ARE IN MY CLASS, AND THEY'RE THE CLASS REP AND VICE REP.
WITH THEM, WE'RE UNSTOPPABLE.
WHAT ARE YOU TALKING ABOUT?
GOOD LUCK, HARU. I'M ROOTING FOR YOU.
OSHIMA-SAN...
I CAN'T LOOK HIM IN THE EYE.
B-DMP B-DMP
SO, YAMAKEN-KUN. WHAT TRIAL TESTS ARE YOU TAKING?
DON'T FOLLOW US, HARU.
THE SAME...? OKAY. WELL, GOOD LUCK TO BOTH OF US.
TWITCH...
BUT I WILL BEAT YOU.
UGH, TRIAL TESTS AGAIN? TAKE 'EM IF YOU WANT.
SHIZUKU DOESN'T LIKE YOU ONE BIT ANYWAY. RIGHT, SHIZUKU?
WHAT
NO, I LIKE HIM PRETTY WELL.
WHAT?

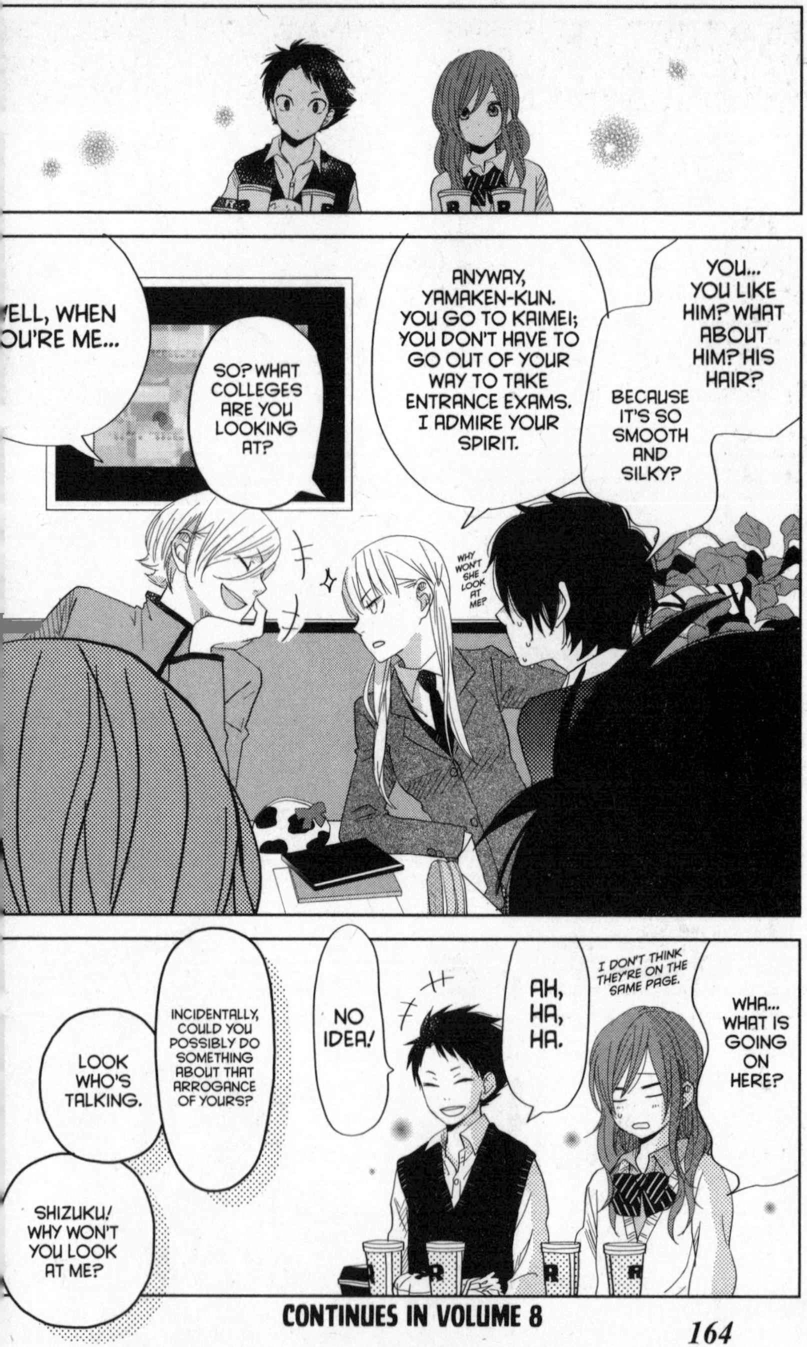
YOU... YOU LIKE HIM? WHAT ABOUT HIM? HIS HAIR?
BECAUSE IT'S SO SMOOTH AND SILKY?
WHY WON'T SHE LOOK AT ME?
ANYWAY, YAMAKEN-KUN. YOU GO TO KAIMEI; YOU DON'T HAVE TO GO OUT OF YOUR WAY TO TAKE ENTRANCE EXAMS. I ADMIRE YOUR SPIRIT.
SO? WHAT COLLEGES ARE YOU LOOKING AT?
ELL, WHEN OU'RE ME...
WHA... WHAT IS GOING ON HERE?
I DON'T THINK THEY'RE ON THE SAME PAGE.
AH, HA, HA.
NO IDEA!
INCIDENTALLY, COULD YOU POSSIBLY DO SOMETHING ABOUT THAT ARROGANCE OF YOURS?
LOOK WHO'S TALKING.
SHIZUKU! WHY WON'T YOU LOOK AT ME?

CONTINUES IN VOLUME 8

2-A

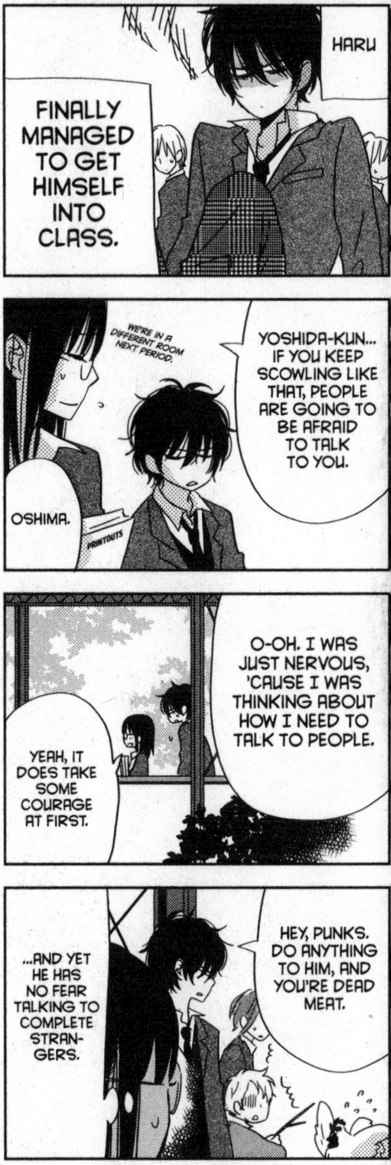
HARU
FINALLY MANAGED TO GET HIMSELF INTO CLASS.
YOSHIDA-KUN... IF YOU KEEP SCOWLING LIKE THAT, PEOPLE ARE GOING TO BE AFRAID TO TALK TO YOU.
WE'RE IN A DIFFERENT ROOM NEXT PERIOD.
OSHIMA.
PRINTOUTS
O-OH. I WAS JUST NERVOUS, 'CAUSE I WAS THINKING ABOUT HOW I NEED TO TALK TO PEOPLE.
YEAH, IT DOES TAKE SOME COURAGE AT FIRST.
HEY, PUNKS. DO ANYTHING TO HIM, AND YOU'RE DEAD MEAT.
...AND YET HE HAS NO FEAR TALKING TO COMPLETE STRANGERS.

I THOUGHT WE WERE FRIENDS

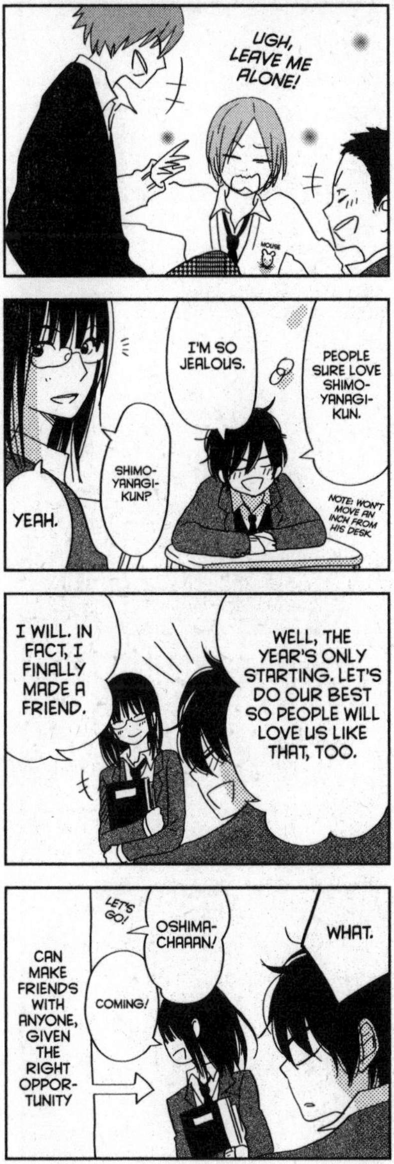
UGH, LEAVE ME ALONE!
MOUSE
PEOPLE SURE LOVE SHIMO-YANAGI-KUN.
I'M SO JEALOUS.
NOTE: WON'T MOVE AN INCH FROM HIS DESK.
SHIMO-YANAGI-KUN?
YEAH.
WELL, THE YEAR'S ONLY STARTING. LET'S DO OUR BEST SO PEOPLE WILL LOVE US LIKE THAT, TOO.
I WILL. IN FACT, I FINALLY MADE A FRIEND.
WHAT.
OSHIMA-CHAAAN!
LET'S GO!
COMING!
CAN MAKE FRIENDS WITH ANYONE, GIVEN THE RIGHT OPPORTUNITY

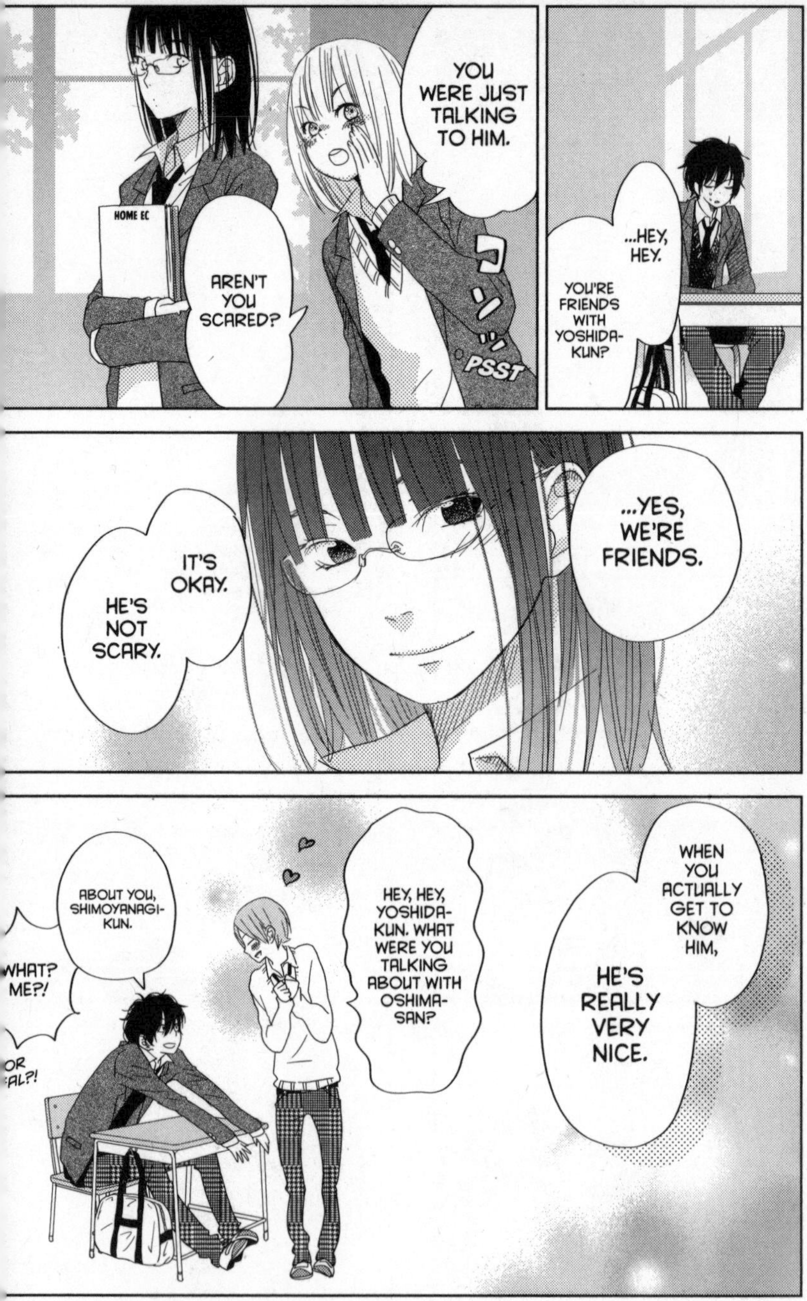
...HEY, HEY.
YOU'RE FRIENDS WITH YOSHIDA-KUN?
YOU WERE JUST TALKING TO HIM.
PSST
HOME EC
AREN'T YOU SCARED?
...YES, WE'RE FRIENDS.
IT'S OKAY.
HE'S NOT SCARY.
WHEN YOU ACTUALLY GET TO KNOW HIM,
HE'S REALLY VERY NICE.
HEY, HEY, YOSHIDA-KUN. WHAT WERE YOU TALKING ABOUT WITH OSHIMA-SAN?
ABOUT YOU, SHIMOYANAGI-KUN.
WHAT? ME?!

Robico

If you're interested in what I
do on my days off, I sleep, I
think about story, and I draw.
Sometimes I go out. It's
pretty much like that when I'm
working, too. This is volume
seven. I hope you enjoy it.

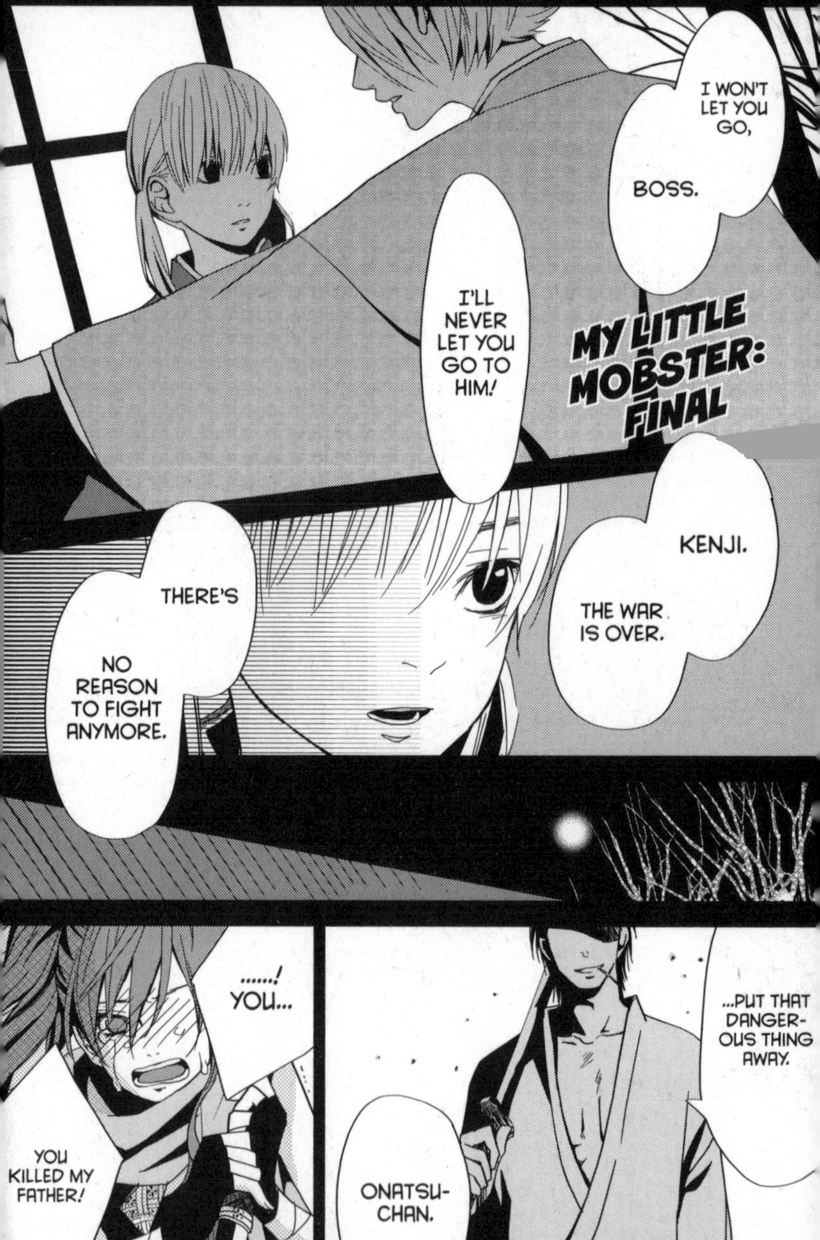
I WON'T LET YOU GO, BOSS.
I'LL NEVER LET YOU GO TO HIM!
MY LITTLE MOBSTER: FINAL
KENJI. THE WAR IS OVER.
THERE'S NO REASON TO FIGHT ANYMORE.
...PUT THAT DANGEROUS THING AWAY.
ONATSU-CHAN.
......! YOU...
YOU KILLED MY FATHER!

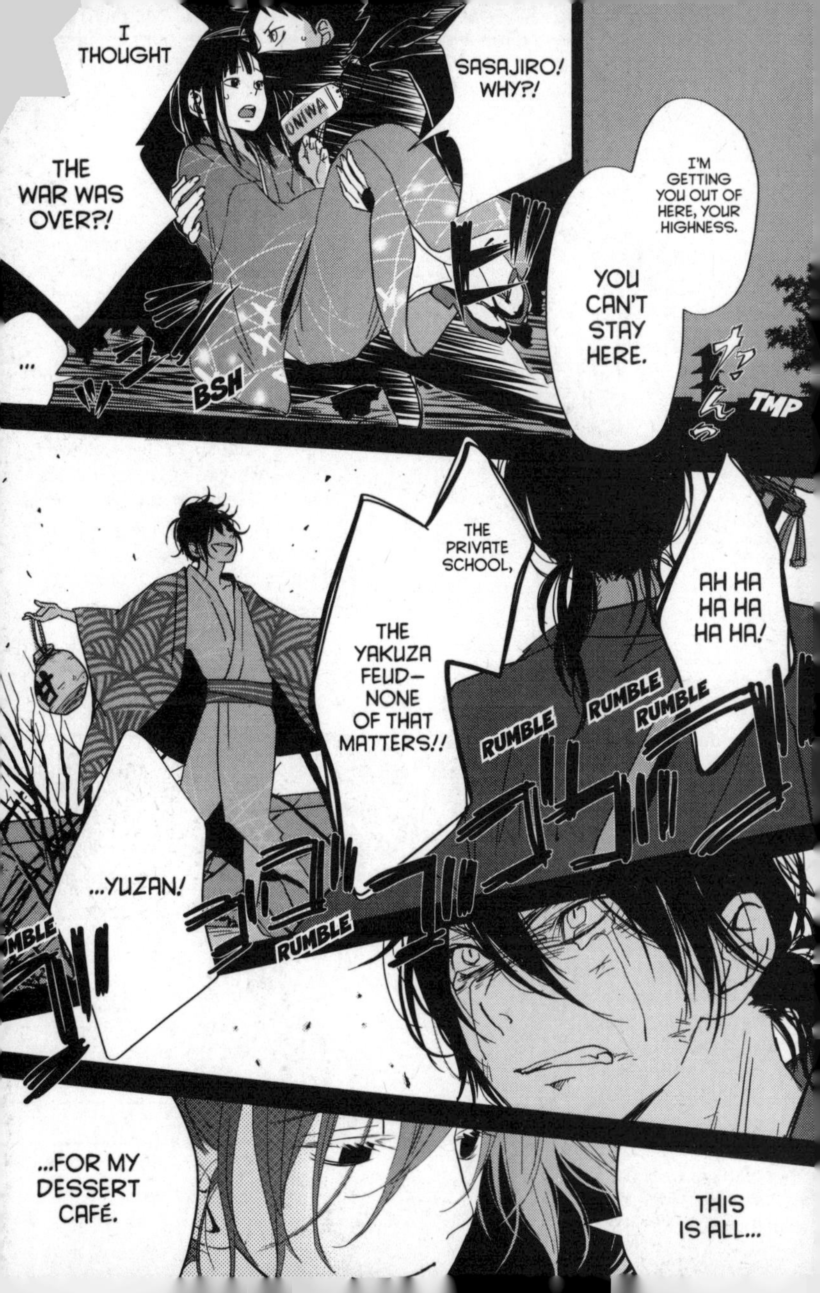
I'M GETTING YOU OUT OF HERE, YOUR HIGHNESS.
YOU CAN'T STAY HERE.
TMP
SASAJIRO! WHY?!
I THOUGHT
THE WAR WAS OVER?!
...
BSH
AH HA HA HA HA HA!
THE PRIVATE SCHOOL,
THE YAKUZA FEUD—NONE OF THAT MATTERS!!
RUMBLE
RUMBLE
RUMBLE
...YUZAN!
RUMBLE
THIS IS ALL...
...FOR MY DESSERT CAFÉ.

TRANSLATION NOTES

Japanese is a tricky language for most Westerners, and translation is often more art than science. For your edification and reading pleasure, here are notes on some of the places where we could have gone in a different direction in our translation of the work, or where a Japanese cultural reference is used.

IT'S LIKE DONBURI. YOU DON'T WANT A HALF UNI, HALF IKURA BOWL. YOU WANT A WHOLE BOWL OF EACH!
IF YOU WANT TO HAVE BOTH,
YOU JUST HAVE TO PUT IN TWICE THE EFFORT!!
BAM

Donburi, page 6
Literally meaning "bowl," donburi is basically a meal of meat and vegetables served over rice in a bowl. Because it's the bowl that makes donburi what it is, and not the contents of the bowl, there are many different kinds of donburi. Shizuku's mother's favorite kinds are apparently uni (sea urchin) and ikura (squid). While you can get a nishoku, or "two-colored," bowl with two different proteins, the sad result is that you get less of both. It's kind of like ordering a pizza that's half pepperoni and half Hawaiian, instead of ordering a whole pepperoni pizza and a whole Hawaiian pizza.

Chocolate de ring and devil French, page 37
Asako's favorite donut franchise is Master Donut, which is her world's version of Mister Donut. Mister Donut's menu includes the Pon de Ring style donut, which looks something like a giant pearl bracelet made of donut holes. The chocolate version is Pon de Chocolat, but at Master Donut, it is Chocolate de Ring. Mister Donut also offers an "angel French," which is a French cruller half-dipped in chocolate. Master Donut appears to prefer the dark side of things.

LET'S SEE...
THREE CHOCOLATE DE RINGS,
TWO DEVIL FRENCHES...
I HAVE DONUTS FOR MITTY, DONUTS FOR HARU-KUN...
AND...
NEW!
BITTERSWEET
A MORE MATURE TASTE

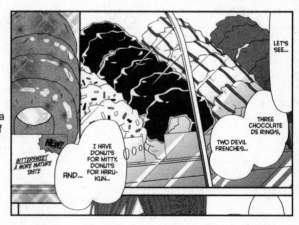

Heartbreak, page 61

The Japanese word for heartbreak, shitsuren, literally means "lost love." So a more literal translation of Shizuku's thoughts would be, "If you don't seek after something, then you never actually lose it," meaning if she doesn't to get love, then she'll never feel the pain of having lost it. The translators altered it slightly to keep the connection with the concept more familiar in an English-speaking setting, a broken heart.

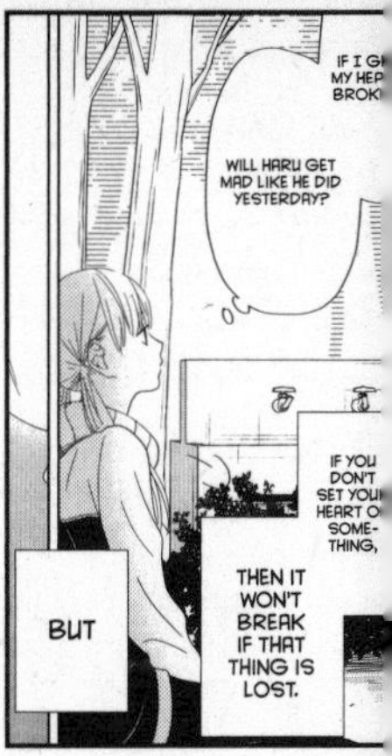
WILL HARU GET MAD LIKE HE DID YESTERDAY?
THEN IT WON'T BREAK IF THAT THING IS LOST.
BUT

Xavier-san, page 63

This is a reference to Francis Xavier. He was a Jesuit missionary who brought Christianity to Japan in the sixteenth century. Based on Shizuku's reaction to Asako's comment, Shizuku must have been discussing some other part of history when she interrupted Asako's thoughts.

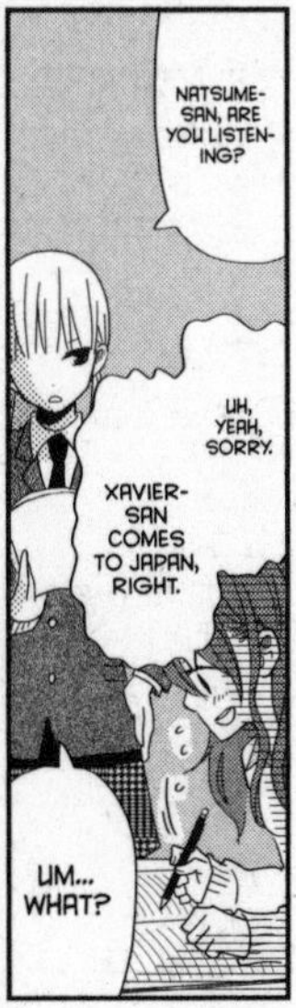
NATSUME-SAN, ARE YOU LISTEN-ING?
UH, YEAH, SORRY.
XAVIER-SAN COMES TO JAPAN, RIGHT.
UM... WHAT?

Bald spot like a monk's, page 86

This is a reference to the tonsure, or round shaved head of some Catholic monks. The reference made in the original Japanese was to the supernatural creature known as the kappa, which has a similar bald spot on the top of its head. It may or may not be interesting to note that in Japanese, kappa can also refer to a bob cut.

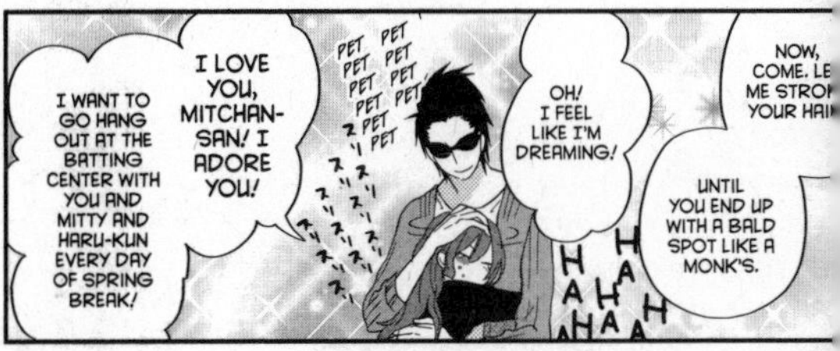
UNTIL YOU END UP WITH A BALD SPOT LIKE A MONK'S.
HAHAHAHA
OH! I FEEL LIKE I'M DREAMING!
PET PET PET PET PET PET PET PET PET PET
I LOVE YOU, MITCHAN-SAN! I ADORE YOU!
I WANT TO GO HANG OUT AT THE BATTING CENTER WITH YOU AND MITTY AND HARU-KUN EVERY DAY OF SPRING BREAK!

Taking a Spring Break, page 88

The Japanese title of this chapter is a pun. Literally, it means "spring break," and the word for "spring" is haru, so it's also a Haru break, in accordance with Shizuku's observation that she hasn't spoken to him all vacation. The translators attempted to convey the meaning of "a break from Haru" by making the chapter title "taking a (spring) break," as in a couple who are "taking a break" from each other.

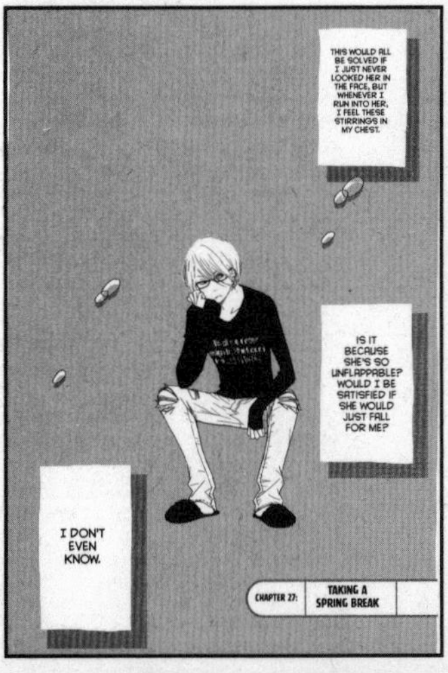
THIS WOULD ALL BE SOLVED IF I JUST NEVER LOOKED HER IN THE FACE, BUT WHENEVER I RUN INTO HER, I FEEL THESE STIRRINGS IN MY CHEST.
IS IT BECAUSE SHE'S SO UNFLAPPABLE? WOULD I BE SATISFIED IF SHE WOULD JUST FALL FOR ME?
I DON'T EVEN KNOW.
CHAPTER 27: TAKING A SPRING BREAK

Center Test questions, page 90
The National Center Test for University Admissions is a Japanese standardized test much like the SATs. After the tests are administered (in mid-January), questions and answers are published in newspapers so students like Shizuku and Yamaken can try the test for themselves and get an idea of what to expect when they take it.

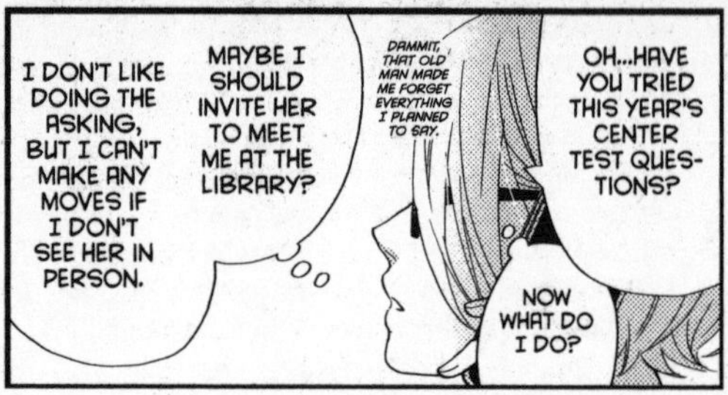
OH...HAVE YOU TRIED THIS YEAR'S CENTER TEST QUESTIONS?
NOW WHAT DO I DO?
DAMMIT, THAT OLD MAN MADE ME FORGET EVERYTHING I PLANNED TO SAY.
MAYBE I SHOULD INVITE HER TO MEET ME AT THE LIBRARY?
I DON'T LIKE DOING THE ASKING, BUT I CAN'T MAKE ANY MOVES IF I DON'T SEE HER IN PERSON.

Hasami-yaki, page 95
Hasami-yaki is basically a fried sandwich. Hasami means "to put something [in this case, pork] between two things." Hasami-yaki is often made by putting the meat and other filling between two slices of lotus root and frying the whole sandwich.

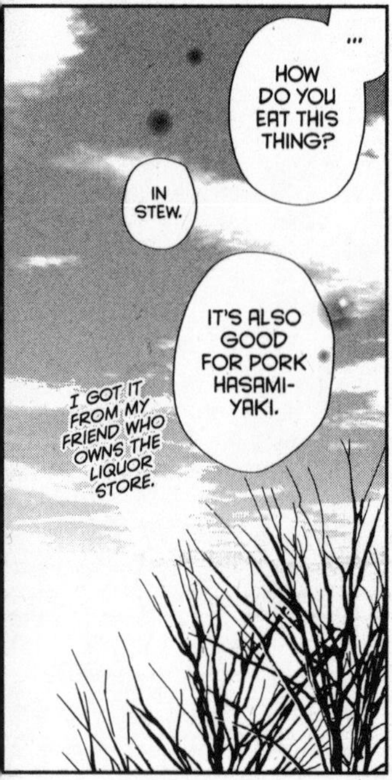
...
HOW DO YOU EAT THIS THING?
IN STEW.
IT'S ALSO GOOD FOR PORK HASAMI-YAKI.
I GOT IT FROM MY FRIEND WHO OWNS THE LIQUOR STORE.

Manju, page 114
Manju are a kind Japanese dumpling, with a sweet red bean filling. In this case, Haru bought onsen manju (hot spring manju), which means it was made with wheat flour and brown sugar, and was most likely bought at a hot spring resort.

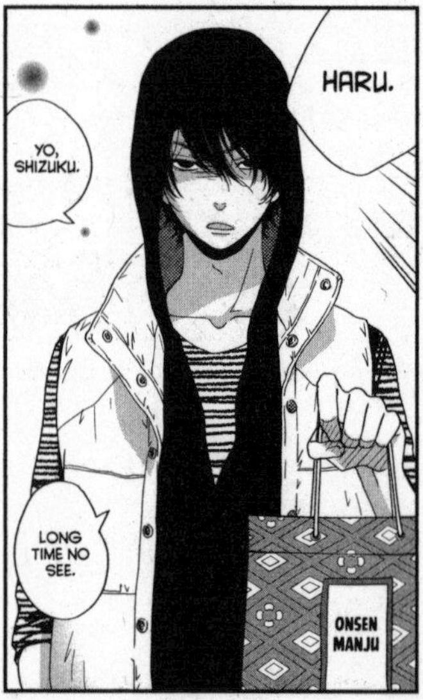
HARU.
YO, SHIZUKU.
LONG TIME NO SEE.
ONSEN MANJU

Kinoko vs. takenoko, page 125

This is a reference to two popular snack foods in Japan, Kinoko no Yama (mushroom mountain) and Takenoko no Sato (home of the bamboo shoots). Kinoko no Yama are little mushroom-shaped cookies, with the stem made out of a breadstick dipped in a chocolate mushroom cap. Takenoko no Sato uses the same concept to make bamboo shoot cookies, but with a slightly different type of breadstick and a different ratio of chocolate to cookie. As Asako's text suggests, everyone has their own preference. But both snacks are made by the same company, so whichever side of the debate you're on, Meiji wins.

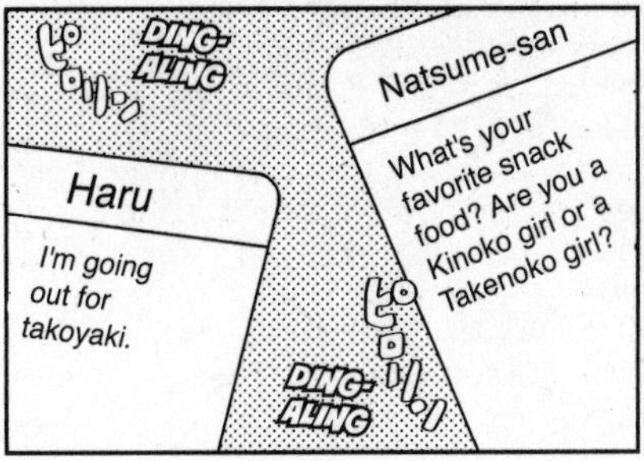
DING-ALING
Natsume-san
What's your favorite snack food? Are you a Kinoko girl or a Takenoko girl?
Haru
I'm going out for takoyaki.
DING-ALING

Sly old tanuki, page 131

While Ando's face my remind Haru a little of the stoneware statue that he brought as a gift, Haru is not referring to his looks. In Japanese folklore, tanuki are known for tricking people. Hence, the word "tanuki" is used to describe someone who pretends to be nice and friendly—sometimes naive or foolish—to hide their true, crafty nature.

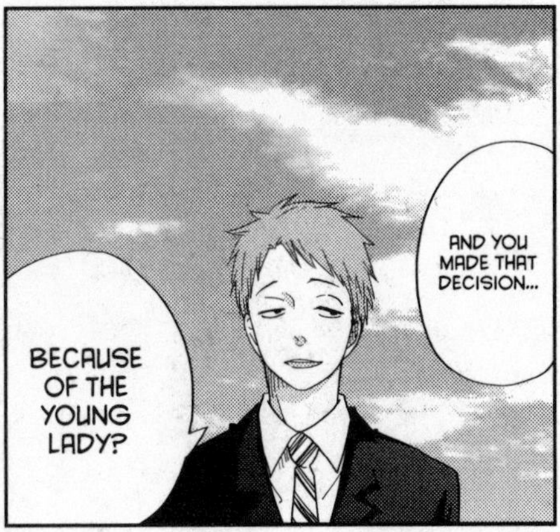
AND YOU MADE THAT DECISION...
BECAUSE OF THE YOUNG LADY?

Praise for the anime:

"The show provides a pleasant window on the highs and lows of young love with two young people who are first timers at the real thing."

-The Fandom Post

"Always it is smarter, more poetic, more touching, just plain better than you think it is going to be."

-Anime News Network

SAY I LOVE YOU.

Mei Tachibana has no friends — and says she doesn't need them!

But everything changes when she accidentally roundhouse kicks the most popular boy in school! However, Yamato Kurosawa isn't angry in the slightest—in fact, he thinks his ordinary life could use an unusual girl like Mei. But winning Mei's trust will be a tough task. How long will she refuse to say, "I love you"?

SANKAREA

undying love

"I ONLY LIKE ZOMBIE GIRLS."

Chihiro has an unusual connection to zombie movies. He doesn't feel bad for the survivors – he wants to comfort the undead girls they slaughter! When his pet passes away, he brews a resurrection potion. He's discovered by local heiress Sanka Rea, and she serves as his first test subject!

A Kodansha Comics Trade Paperback Original.

My Little Monster volume 7 copyright © 2011 Robico
English translation copyright © 2015 Robico

All rights reserved.

Published in the United States by Kodansha Comics, an imprint of Kodansha USA Publishing, LLC, New York.

Publication rights for this English edition arranged through Kodansha Ltd., Tokyo.

First published in Japan in 2011 by Kodansha Ltd., Tokyo as *Tonari no Kaibutsu-kun*, volume 7.

ISBN 978-1-61262-991-9

Printed in the United States of America.

www.kodanshacomics.com

9 8 7 6 5 4 3 2 1

Translator: Alethea Nibley & Athena Nibley
Lettering: Kiyoko Shiromasa